ENGLAND IN THE NEW MILLENNIUM
ARE WE PREPARED TO SAVE OUR COUNTRYSIDE?

John F. Barker

First published 2000

Published by Gaia Watch
Charity number 1060769

Printed by
ALD Design & Print
Sheffield

ISBN   0 9533532 1 4

GAIA WATCH
33, Bingham Park Crescent,
Sheffield S11 7BH

Spring

Oh, spring is good for leaves in the spinney, good to forests,
In spring the swelling earth aches for the seed of new life.
Then the omnipotent Father of air in fruitful showers
Comes down to his happy consort
And greatly breeds upon her great body manifold fruit.
Then are the trackless copses alive with the trilling of birds,
And the beasts look for love, their hour come round again:
Lovely the earth in labour, under a tremulous west wind
The fields unbosom, a mild moisture is everywhere.
Confident grows the grass, for the young sun will not harm it;
The shoots of the vine are not scared of a southerly gale arising
Or the sleety rain that slants from heaven beneath a north wind, -
No, bravely now they bud and all their leaves display.
So it was, I believe, when the world first began,
Such the illustrious dawning and tenor of their days.
It was springtime then, great spring
Enhanced the earth and spared it the bitter breath of an east wind -
A time when the first cattle lapped up the light, and men
Children of earth themselves arose from the raw champaign,
And wild things issued forth in the wood, and stars in the sky.

Virgil

Pied Beauty

GLORY be to God for dappled things -
    For skies of couple-colour as a brinded cow;
        For rose-moles all in stipple upon trout that swim;
Fresh-firecoal chestnut-falls; finches' wings;
    Landscape plotted and pieced-fold, fallow, and plough;
        And áll trá111es, their gear and tackle and trim.

All things counter, original, spare, strange;
    Whatever is fickle, freckled (who knows how?)
        With swift, slow; sweet, sour; adazzle, dim;
He fathers-forth whose beauty is past change:
          Praise him

Gerard Manley Hopkins

To Autumn

SEASON of mists and mellow fruitfulness!
    Close bosom-friend of the maturing sun;
Conspiring with him how to load and bless
        With fruit the vines that round the thatch eaves run;
To bend with apples the mossed cottage-trees,
    And fill all fruit with ripeness to the core;
        To swell the gourd, and plump the hazel shells
With a sweet kernel; to set budding more,
    And still more, later flowers for the bees,
    Until they think warm days will never cease,
        For Summer has o'erbrimmed their clammy cells.

John Keats (verse one)

Contents

PART TWO   THE STRATEGY

Photographs, cover, diagram and map design, by the author.

Acknowledgements

The author gratefully acknowledges various permissions to quote:

HMSO in connection with various Government publications of GAD, HO and ONS (acknowledged individually in the text).

HarperCollins for a figure in Sherlock (1991).

WWF International for figures from the WWF "Living Planet Report 2000".

UNEP for a quotation from "Global Environment Outlook 2000".

Prof. A.J. Oswald for graphs from his "The housing market and Europe's unemployment: a non-technical paper".

Random House UK Ltd. for a section from C. Day Lewis's translation of the Georgics of Virgil (originally published by Jonathan Cape).

Jack Parsons for quotations from his books

Oxford University Press for a dictionary definition.

The author would like to thank the many people who gave of their time to discuss particular aspects of the environmental situation and related matters and sometimes provided the author with written information.

Chris Thomson taught the author some basic computer technique. It was his computing skill that transformed my drawings for the book cover, map and diagrams into a fit state for publication. He also formatted the book for printing.

Two people made generous contributions towards the cost of producing this book. For their support I am very grateful.

I thank my wife for tolerating my neglect of house duties, which made writing this book possible.

Above all I stand in awe of the beauty of the natural world and of all living creatures, and acknowledge the pain I feel over mankind's destructive activities.

Abbreviations

a) Organisations

ADAS	Agricultural Development and Advisory Service
BLI	Birdlife International
BTCV	British Trust for Conservation Volunteers
CAS	Centre for Agricultural Strategy, Reading University
CC	Countryside Commission
CPRE	Council for the Protection of Rural England
DETR	Department of the Environment, Transport and the Regions
DH	Department of Health
DID	Department of International Development
DoE	Department of the Environment
DT	Department of Transport
EC	European Commission
ECL	Environmental Council
EEC	European Economic Community
EFSG	Environment Forum Steering Group (in Sheffield)
EMGS	Ethnic Minority Sector Group
EN	English Nature
ETSU	Energy Technology Support Unit
EU	European Union
FAO	United Nations Food and Agriculture Organisation
FC	Forestry Commission
FRCA	Farm and Rural Conservation Agency
FoE	Friends of the Earth
GA	The Green Alliance
GAD	Government Actuary's Department
GP	Green Peace
GSS	Government Statistical Service
HMSO	Her Majesty's Stationery Office
HO	Home Office
HoL	House of Lords
IEEP	Institute for European Environmental Policy, London
IIASA	International Institute for Applied Systems Analysis
IIED	International Institute for Environment and Development
JNCC	Joint Nature Conservation Committee.
JRF	Joseph Rowntree Foundation
LAs	Local (government) Authorities
LEAF	Linking Environment and farming
LPAs	Local Planning Authorities
MAFF	Ministry of Agriculture, Fisheries and Food
NAS	National Academy of Sciences
NAVF	Norwegian Research Council for Science and the Humanities
NFU	National Farmers Union
NGO	Non-governmental organisation
NPA	National Park Authority
NRCSH	Norwegian Research Council for Science and the Humanities
OF	Open Forum (in Sheffield)
ONS	Office for National Statistics
OPCS	Office of Population Census and Survey
OUP	Oxford University Press
PPJPB	Peak Park Joint Planning Board
PDNPA	Peak District National Park Authority
RA	Ramblers Association
RAYH	Regional Assembly for Yorkshire and Humberside
RCEP	Royal Commission on Environmental Pollution
RDC	Rural Development Commission
RIIA	Royal Institute of International Affairs
RS	Royal Society

RSC	Royal Society of Chemistry
RSPB	Royal Society for the Protection of Birds
SAFE	The Sustainable Agriculture Food and Environment Alliance
SAUS	School for Advanced Urban Studies
SCAM	Sheffield Campaign for Access to the Moorlands
SCC	Sheffield City Council
SEF	Sheffield Environment Forum
SEFSG	Sheffield Environment Forum Steering Group
SEP	Sheffield Environment Partnership
SEW	Sheffield Environment Watch
SHLS	Sheffield Housing Land Survey
SI	Swedish Institute
SO	The Stationery Office
SSE	Secretary of State for the Environment
SWCG	Sheffield Wildlife Conservation Group
SWGMT	Steering and Working Group of the Ministry of Transport
SWT	Sheffield Wildlife Trust
TCPA	Town and Country Planning Association
TLIO	This Land Is Ours
UDP	Unitary Development Plan
UKBSG	UK Biodiversity Steering Group
UKG	UK Government
UKRTSD	UK Round Table on Sustainable Development
UN	United Nations
UNEP	United Nations Environment Programme
UNPD	United Nations Population Division
UNPF	United Nations Population Fund
WCL	Wildlife and Countryside Link
WWF	Worldwide Fund for Nature

b) Other abbreviations

AAPS	Arable Area Payment Scheme
AONB	Area of Outstanding Natural Beauty
ARA	Accessible Rural Area
ASS	Arable Stewardship Scheme
CAP	Common Agricultural Policy
CAS	Countryside Access Scheme
CC	Carrying Capacity
EA	Environmental Appraisal / Assessment
EF	Ecological footprint
ESA	Environmentally Sensitive Area
CSS	Countryside Stewardship Scheme
FCGS	Farm and Conservation Grant Scheme
FWPS	Farm Woodland Premium Scheme
HLCA	Hill Livestock Compensatory Allowance Scheme
HS	Habitat Scheme
ICM	Integrated Crop Management
LCGS	Land Conservation Grant Scheme
MS	Moorland Scheme
NNR	National Nature Reserve
NSA	Nitrate Sensitive Area
NVZ	Nitrate Vulnerable Zone
OAS	Organic Aid Scheme
OFS	Organic Farming Scheme
PDO	Potentially Damaging Operation
PGS	Project Grant Scheme
PPG	Planning Policy Guidance Note
RES	Reserve Enhancement Scheme
RRA	Remote Rural Area
RS	Ramsar Site

SAC	Special Area of Conservation
SAPS	Sheep Annual Premium Scheme
SCPS	Suckler Cow Premium Scheme
SD	Sustainable Development
SEA	Strategic Environmental Assessment
SLR	Standardised Land Requirement
SMEs	Small and Medium Size Enterprises
SPA	Special Protection Area
SSSI	Site of Special Scientific Interest
TFR	Total Fertility Rate
VOC	Volatile organic compound
WES	Wildlife Enhancement Scheme
WGS	Woodland Grant Scheme

ERRATA

Page 14. Paragraph starting "I said earlier..." second sentence which begins "It is interesting then most environmentalists...". Insert "that" before "most". Same sentence, change "... altered deliberately;" to "... altered directly."

Page 22. Paragraph beginning "The answer depends...". Insert the sentence "And immigrants, heavily concentrated at younger ages, will increase the number of women at childbearing ages." after "...fall in the number of births".

Page 180. Second paragraph, first line. Insert "some" between "tendency for" and "freedoms".

Page 181. Second paragraph, first line. Remove "probably".

Page 184. Paragraph beginning "In Chapter 2, I showed...". Change "Section B" to "Section D".

Page 259. First paragraph, second line. Change "Fist, global warming" to "First, global warming".

Introduction

The general environmental situation in the world at large seems almost daily to get more and more serious. We hear of floods and famines, conflict and coups, the possibility that the tiger may become extinct and the knowledge that many other wildlife species become extinct each year. Unlike a few years ago, it is now generally accepted that global warming is taking place with potentially disastrous consequences, but world leaders seem unable to secure adequate measures to ameliorate the situation.

If we narrow our field of view to our own land, we have no cause for complacency. Crime rates seem to be up; conflict over asylum seekers has increased. Our roads become more and more clogged with traffic, and the pollution from that traffic increases disease incidence for those who live nearby. The divide between an impoverished North and an affluent South seems to show no sign of lessening. The increase in the number of households leads inexorably to more countryside disappearing under new housing. Farming other than that controlled by the big agri-businesses, is in crisis so that the number of farmers going bankrupt or committing suicide has risen greatly.

The countryside used to be a peaceful place of flowery meadows bordered by hedgerows and stonewalls, full of wild places - marshes, heaths and broad -leaved woodlands. There were many birds everywhere. Now there are far more roads and much more traffic so that most countryside areas have lost their tranquillity. Flowery meadows are uncommon, in some areas most of the hedgerows and in other areas many of the walls have been removed, and many well known marshes, wetlands and broad leaved woodlands have disappeared or been very much reduced in size, and heath lands have become covered in conifer forest. Many birds that were very common in those days are much less common now. In fact, most farmland is now only a desert as far as wildlife is concerned.

It is when you take a long-term view of the situation that one realises the real magnitude of the environmental problem. The attention of most people is however firmly focused within a short time span, during which environmental changes are small and so have little impact on the imagination. People are primarily concerned about present conditions, and perhaps secondarily about how things will be when their children grow up. Rarely do they think about the environment of later generations. For most people, the only occasions when they seriously look ahead is when they are dealing with a mortgage for a house or planning old age insurance. So long-term changes are not matters that engage their attention and cause them concern. Politicians too, working to a five-year election horizon, tend to focus their attention on the short or at best medium term.

Now it was sensible for neolithic man to concentrate his attention on the present. His concerns were justifiably immediate - that another person might knock him on the head or wolves devour his child. But it is not a sensible attitude now, and has not been so for generations. For in Neolithic times, the population was very small, and grew so slowly, and the environment seemed limitless. There was no need to be concerned about the environment beyond the horizon - there was so much of it, no need to think of the environment in the future. Now the population is very much greater, is growing much faster, and is spread over practically all the world except arctic and some other desert regions, and world wide environmental degradation has accelerated to the point where if we go on as we are doing, the environment will not be worth living in shortly. Yet man's attitude has not changed. Mankind is short sighted.

Living in the present with no clear picture of the past and no vision for the future can reduce people's perception of the extent of environmental deterioration, and repress any sense of urgency to do something about it. People can become inured to severe deprivation. As Day (1992) puts it "the fluid nature of human values is a major threat to any effort to block progressive deterioration of environmental quality. It underwrites the ever-present tendency to adjust to debasement of the environment by lowering our standards; by, that is, being willing to settle for less".
Day gives an illustration close to the central concern of this book - the loss of green land. He quotes the American demographer Cole to the effect that many younger people see nothing wrong with many of the changes that older citizens decry. Cole himself felt deprived by the disappearance of open land round Princeton, but comments that his own children never miss it.

Any attempt to develop a long-term strategy must be based on an analysis of the present situation, and those forces that have been operative in bringing that situation about. Now it would be nice if it were possible to make an objective analysis. Unfortunately, it would be naive to imagine this was possible, particularly as the environmental situation is so complicated. Any analysis must to some extent bear the imprint of the point of view of the investigator. Consequently I give my analysis of the situation in <u>Part One of this book</u>, before developing a strategy for the future. This analysis is not a comprehensive survey of all environmental problems. Thus for example, energy conservation is only briefly considered;

the state of England's marine fishing industry is only alluded to.

The analysis focuses on the countryside - the loss of green land to development, deterioration of landscape, loss of wildlife, the breakdown of rural community life. The countryside cannot however, be considered in isolation from urban areas, because developments in the latter influence developments in the former. For example, housing policy in urban areas affects the extent that green countryside land is lost to development. So the analysis extends to aspects of urban development. Underlying changes in town and country are population factors – the growth of the human population and its changing distribution between urban and rural areas. The manifold relationships between population and the state of the countryside are therefore explored.

The book focuses on the situation in England. Consequently some issues, like free trade, which would have to be considered in any full global analysis, are omitted. However, the situation in England cannot be considered in isolation from the situation in the rest of the UK, Europe, and indeed the whole world. So the analysis begins with a brief consideration of the global scene, and at various later stages the wider European and global contexts are taken into account.

Part Two of the book is concerned with developing a strategy for the future.
Just as it is only when we take a long term view that we fully realise the magnitude of environmental deterioration, so, in the writer's opinion, it will only be possible to devise an adequate strategy for the future if we take a long term view and base our strategy on a vision of what we would like our country to be like many decades hence. And I will argue that at the heart of this strategy will be policy on human population size and distribution.

In the writer's view, human population growth itself is one of the major, arguably the major cause of the world's environmental problems. The depletion of non-renewable resources, the accumulation of solid waste and the release of toxic chemicals into the environment and the production of greenhouse gases leading to climate change, are all matters exacerbated by continued population growth. The need to increase food production to feed the growing population, with concomitant deterioration of the soil and depletion of water aquifers on land, and depletion of fish stocks in the oceans, increases the prospects of non-sustainable food production. The loss of greenland to housing and other development worldwide, reduces the area of the globe which through the various natural cycles control climate. It also leads to loss of valuable wild life habitat. As population density increases, so does the risk of the massive spread of communicable diseases. Increase of population density also increases the potential for strife within and between nations, which in turn makes it more difficult for them to develop their economies, sustain their food production, and enter into effective programmes of collaboration to deal with environmental problems.

It is the writer's hope that the analysis made, and the strategy developed, might focus readers' attention on the long-term future, the environment of our descendants. Readers may accept or reject the strategy, in whole or in part. But if they reject it, it is the writer's hope that they will themselves try to work out alternative elements of the strategy. Hopefully too, this book will stimulate more people to become actively involved in trying to influence Government and Local Government policy.

The environmental situation is so serious that many environmentalists feel we only have at most a couple of decades to make drastic changes if we are to avoid irreversible environmental decline. It is vital then to develop without delay, a comprehensive strategy to deal with the environmental situation. For decades, policies adopted locally and globally have failed to deal adequately with the environmental situation. This suggests that only much more radical policies will now be adequate.

A word about terminology. Some discussion involving the differences between wealthy countries like Britain, and poor countries like many in Africa, is included. So there is need for terminology to distinguish these two different groups of countries. Various pairs of terms are used in the literature. These include "north v. south"; "industrialized countries v. non-industrialized countries"; "first world v. third world"; "developed world v. developing world". None of these terminologies is perfect. I will use the last mentioned pair. There are numerous organisations which work on environmental issues. Some are concerned with all aspects of the environment; others are involved principally with some particular aspect. Many of these are non-governmental organisations, which will be referred to by the standard abbreviation, NGO.

Finally, this book attempts to take things forward as far as early autumn of 2000, when major revision of the book ceased so that the book could be prepared for publication. A brief postscript deals with major developments since then.

Chapter 1

The Global Context

1972 saw the publication of the book "The limits to Growth" by Meadows and colleagues. The authors had used a computer model to study five global trends:

      1) accelerating industrialization;
      2) rapid population growth;
      3) widespread malnutrition;
      4) depletion of non renewable resources;
      5) deteriorating environment.

They concluded that if the then existing trends continued, the planet would reach the 'limits to growth' within the next hundred years, with the likely result that there would be a rather sudden and uncontrollable decline in both the size of the human population and in industrial capacity. This publication re-ignited the controversy about the extent that the world will be able to support the rapidly growing human population. This controversy can be traced back to the essay by Malthus at the end of the 18th Century, in which he predicted that human population growth would inevitably outstrip food supply leading to starvation and misery.

In the intervening years since the publication of the Meadows' paper many other persons and organisations have issued warnings that we cannot continue to go on as we have been doing in recent decades, drawing attention to the implications of the massive projected growth in the human population. Thus for example, the Royal Society (of the UK) and National Academy of Sciences (USA), in 1992, expressed doubt about the ability of the world to provide a reasonable standard of living for the ever increasing population while avoiding an irreversible degradation of the environment (RS & NAS, 1992).

While controversy continues to this day about whether or not will be able to feed the much bigger human population that is projected to exist in future decades, what cannot be denied is that since Malthus, the human population has grown exponentially. It is equally certain that global environmental deterioration has continued since the time of Malthus, and has accelerated since the Second World War. This deteriorating world environment has serious implications not only for food production, but also for other aspects of human health and the survival of other species. We now examine the two issues of human population growth and environmental degradation.

A. Population growth

Although the world population growth rate has fallen in the last 40 years, during this same period the total world population has doubled. How is the world population likely to increase in the future?

The United Nations periodically prepares a set of projection scenarios for future world populations. These scenarios differ from each other in the fertility assumptions underlying them. The medium fertility scenario assumes that the total fertility rate will stabilize at replacement level (2.05-2.09 children per woman) around the year 2050. The high-fertility scenario assumes fertility rates will stabilize at about half a child higher (2.5-2.6 children per woman). The low-fertility scenario assumes fertility rates will stabilise at about half a child less than the medium scenario (1.5-1.6 children per woman). The total world population will have changed, by 2150, from its present level of about 6 billion, according to these scenarios, as follows:

      Low fertility   3.2 billion
      Medium fertility 9.7 billion
      High fertility   24.8 billion

The medium scenario is usually thought of as the most likely outcome. This would have the population growing by nearly 60% by 2150. The projections for these scenarios and other scenarios are shown in Fig.1 (UN, 2000).

These most recent projections replace those published in 1998, which had the medium scenario population reaching 10.8 billion by 2150. This difference between projections results from decline in fertility in many nations (many countries now have populations where fertility has been below replacement level for some time). And this has led to a difference in assumptions between the new projections and the previous ones. The previous projections assumed total fertility rates would ultimately stabilise by the year 2055 at replacement levels. The new projections assume that fertility rates in

England in the New Millennium

World population according to five projection scenarios, 1950-2150

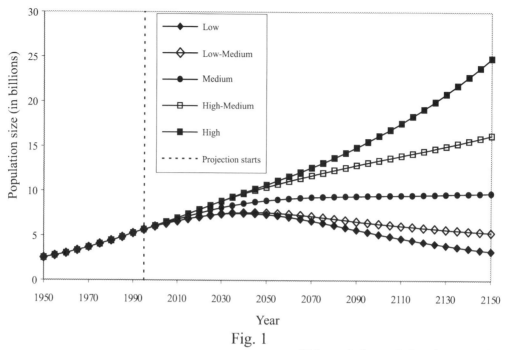

Fig. 1

UN permission verbal; written permission pending

countries where the rate is at present below replacement level will remain below replacement level until at least 2050 and then rise slowly to replacement level.

It must be born in mind that a major part of this future population growth (perhaps as much as half) is, short of genocide or serious pandemic, unavoidable, because it has an inbuilt momentum. This arises primarily from past high fertility causing ever increasing numbers of young women to enter the reproductive period of life; and all the women who will be mothers during the next twenty years have already been born. The expected further mortality decline among adults will also contribute to this population momentum.

It is indeed difficult to comprehend the implications of such an enormous population increase. It means for example that we would need to provide living accommodation for nearly 4 billion more people. Think of the miserable conditions of millions in present developing world cities. Now it has been argued that many of the problems associated with such cities are caused by rapid city growth rather than city size per se, and that there need be no limit to the size that a viable city may attain (Lowry, 1991). However, rapid city growth is widespread in developing countries - countries that will be unlikely to secure the financial capital to set up anything approaching the ideal city.

97% of future population growth will occur in developing countries, indeed the largest increases will occur in regions where poverty and unemployment are endemic (references in Raleigh, 1999). This raises the fears of what is called "demographic entrapment" –the situation where, without indefinite food aid, the future is one of starvation and slaughter. And some workers think that some countries are already demographically entrapped (McMichael and Powles, 1999).

Policy makers nevertheless hope to alleviate the population problem by slowing down population growth. United Nations policy, re-iterated at the 1994 Cairo conference on Population and Development, has as a starting point the principle that individuals have the fundamental human right to determine the number and spacing of their children. One may question the propriety of UN policy makers coming out so strongly in support of this principle, when one member country, China, with one quarter of the worlds population (and a seat on the Security Council), has a population policy directly opposed to such a principle. Be that as it may, starting from acceptance of this principle, the UN considers that the aim should therefore be to create the conditions where parents will wish to reduce the number of children they have to replacement level. Most policy makers are agreed about the measures needed to produce this effect. On a worldwide basis poverty must be eliminated, primary health care, basic education, contraceptive advice and devices (some would add abortion facilities) made available, and the status of women improved. A useful discussion of measures is provided by Bongaarts (1994). Few would dispute that all these measures are good ones. However, they have all been promoted for decades. And while progress has been made in most parts of the world, many doubt that world population growth will be substantially reduced below the United Nations medium projection.

B. Environmental deterioration

Except where otherwise specifically indicated, what follows is based on the yearly publications of the World Watch Institute in Washington USA (Brown et al 1999a and b and earlier), together with the UNEPs 1999 Global environment outlook 2000. In this section we will look at just three aspects of environmental deterioration; but we will return to the subject later on.

(i) Loss of greenland to housing and other developments, and through global warming.

'Greenland', including natural and semi-natural areas like rainforests, agricultural land, even small patches of green land within urban areas, together with the oceans seas and lakes, maintain life on earth. Plant photosynthesis provides the atmospheric oxygen we breathe. Plants and animals provide us with the food we eat. Fungi and bacteria, mainly in the soil, enable the decay of living things, which maintains the cycle of renewal of all living organisms. Together with the waters of oceans and seas, and the atmosphere itself, greenland and its organisms are involved in the great cycles of oxygen, carbon dioxide, nitrogen and water which together maintain the equitable climatic conditions by which our planet is distinguished from all the other planets in our solar system. For example, consider carbon. Plants, like animals, liberate carbon dioxide into the atmosphere in respiration, but extract it from the atmosphere in photosynthesis - a cyclic effect. The carbon cycle also involves the constant exchange of carbon dioxide between the atmosphere and the oceans. The carbon cycle is actually more extensive than just described, involving also ocean sediments, peat, coal and other rocks. But sufficient for present purposes to say that the exchanges between land, water and the atmosphere, maintain the atmospheric level of carbon dioxide within limits which help to prevent our planet from becoming too hot or cold, levels which are now being altered by mans activities (global warming through what is termed the greenhouse effect).

However, we value greenland for more than food and an equitable climate. Greenland provides us with landscape, the fascinating diversity of living things, and the chance to get away from the constricting circumstances of city life into areas of comparative tranquillity. So the conservation of the size and quality of greenland - one of the main themes of this book, should be a matter of overriding concern to all of us. That is why we should be exerting maximum effort to protect our countryside.

The massive increase of housing and facilities worldwide entails a large loss of greenland. One can focus ones imagination by taking an example of the sort of thing involved. Thus it has been estimated that in the thirty years between 1950 and 1980, it is probable that the total area of land lost in the European Economic Community (EEC) to urban use was greater than the total surface area of Belgium (Clout, 1984). And in 1995 it was estimated that in the previous three decades, roughly 15 million hectares of arable land worldwide were converted to other uses - equivalent to the total crop land of France and Italy combined.

The world's population is expected to become increasingly urbanised. So cities will be under increasing pressure to use green land for housing and industry etc. Unfortunately, cities have historically been close to rich agricultural areas, so urban expansion often takes away really good agricultural land. City expansion and the development of new cities is particularly marked in developing countries where there is considerable population growth combined with massive urbanisation. Bangkok will serve as an example. Its built-up area rose from 67 km^2 in 1953 to 426 km^2 in 1990. In China, over 200 new cities have arisen in recent times. In the past decade, by 1996, China had already paved over 435,000 hectares of cropland - enough land to feed 10 million Chinese. However, the rate of loss of arable land to cities and other developments is now estimated to have reached 200,000 hectares a year. A 1990 World Bank study of Indonesia reported that some 10,000 hectares of agricultural land is needed each year just for housing. According to one estimate, urban expansion in Asia could engulf the equivalent of the continents remaining uncultivated but cropable land twice over.

Mankind is like a vast brooding parasite, spreading over the face of the earth.

To this loss of green land through the growth of settlements must be added the loss of greenland through rising sea levels caused by global warming ('greenhouse effect'). Average sea level is projected to rise by 15 to 95 cm during the present century, most likely around 50 cm. Furthermore, there is such an inertia in the whole climate system, that even if greenhouse gas concentrations in the atmosphere could quickly be stabilized, warming would continue for several decades, and sea levels could continue to rise for centuries. Now the chief significance of this is that much of the most fertile land in the world is found round river deltas, and this too is where many cities and towns have developed - in Bangladesh, China, Egypt, Nigeria, and elsewhere. It is thought for example, that nearly half the world's coastal population (nearly 500 million people) are now housed in urban conglomerations along Asian shores.

Even a 50 cm rise in sea levels would lead to the displacement of millions of people in low-lying delta areas, the loss of vast areas of agriculturally productive land, and the wiping out of some small island states. Now take this line of thought further. Displacing millions of people has serious economic and social consequences, which, since much of the damage will be in developing countries, may well stretch financial and health service provision way beyond the limit. And these displaced people will have to be housed somewhere, leading to large areas of green land being lost to urban development simply to accommodate such refugees. And it sea levels rose even further in the future, things will of course be much worse. A one-metre rise would for example flood most of New York City. Future possible scenarios, including the effects of accelerated ice cap melting are very frightening. Warnings about such scenarios have been made for a long time, for example, by Milne (1998). Not only is the total area of greenland decreasing, but also, in many areas, the quality of remaining green land is deteriorating, with erosion and loss of subsoil, pollution etc. See section D below

(ii) Deforestation.

We all know that different parts of the countryside both in England and throughout the world, hold different collections of plants and animals, for example, in our own country, deciduous woodland and heather moorland, or on a global level, the arctic tundra or the Amazonian rainforest. These different collections are referred to as communities. Of course, there are also aquatic communities. Now these communities, together with the habitats they inhabit and which support them, are referred to as ecosystems.

In a full study of the global environment it would be necessary to consider all ecosystems in turn. For our present purposes this is unnecessary, and I will just consider one small group of ecosystems - forests. I say group, because clearly the word forest is a blanket term covering a variety of ecosystems - consider for example a sub-alpine conifer dominated forest and a tropical rain forest. Yet at the same time the word forest clearly distinguishes a major part of the world from all other ecosystems. For readers interested in non- forest ecosystems, examination of the references given earlier in Section B will demonstrate how deterioration, far from being confined to forests, has been widespread in global ecosystems.

I chose forests for the following reasons. First, forests cover a large part of the globe, occurring in all regions apart from deserts and the polar regions. Second, forests play a vital part in the carbon cycle briefly described earlier. Much concern has been expressed in relation to global warming, about the extent that forests can absorb (the usual term is 'sequester') carbon dioxide, and thus help to buffer the atmosphere from changing carbon dioxide concentrations. Third, the greater part of the total biodiversity of our planet is contained within tropical forests, and there is considerable concern about decrease in biodiversity.

80% of the forests that originally covered the earth have been cleared, or at least fragmented and otherwise degraded, and this deforestation has accelerated since the Second World War. During just the 1980s, the Latin American region lost 62 million hectares (6%) of its natural forest, the largest loss in the world during those years, with a further 5.8 million hectares a year lost during 1990-95. Africa lost 39 million ha of tropical forest and 10 million ha in the first half of the 1990s (UNEP, 1999). In 1994 it was estimated that considering all tropical moist forests, they were being destroyed at a rate of roughly 150,000 square kilometres (15 million ha) per year (Myers, 1994). Another estimate of forest loss is that total world forest cover, excluding plantations, decreased by 13% between 1960 and 1990. This is equivalent to an annual loss of about $160,000km^2$ – an area half the size of Norway – or 0.5% a year (WWF, 1998 LPI).

In addition to the 'normal' deforestation through small scale slash and burn, logging etc. there have been in very recent years some massive fires that have swept through vast forested regions, partly at least related to drought caused by the El Nino effect and changing global weather patterns related to global warming. The forest fires in Southeast Asia in 1997 were the worst for 15 years, with at least 4.5 million ha burnt of which about one million ha were in Indonesia, and smoke and haze adversely affected 70 million people.

In tropical forests in high rainfall areas like those in the Amazon valley, the trees break the fall of the torrential rain. When forest cover is removed, the rain impacts directly on the ground leading to soil erosion. Soil fertility is anyway often poor, so agricultural use, cattle ranching or crop production is not very productive, and crop yields tend to rapidly fall off.

Forest clearance can have major economic impacts a long distance away from where the deforestation actually takes place, by causing or increasing flooding. The main catchment area of the Ganges river is in the Himalayas. Monsoon rains lead to elevated river water levels. In the past this has been buffered by the water holding capacity of forests in the Himalayas. However, deforestation, principally in Nepal, has led to severe and widespread flooding in downstream communities of India and Bangladesh, regularly causing damage to crops, livestock death and property destruction or damage worth $1 billion a year, which has contributed to deteriorating relations of the three governments (Myers, 1993a).

(iii) Environmental deterioration and political stability

When the environment of a region or country deteriorates, this can then, lead to conflict between the peoples living there. This is discussed at length by Myers (ibid). He points out that environmental problems are rarely exclusive causes. Many other variables are also involved – inefficient economies, unjust social systems, repressive Governments – all factors that can predispose a region or country to instability. Nevertheless, Myers believes that environmental problems can be a major cause of conflict. He cites numerous examples, which he considers, support his thesis. He argues the case that environmental deterioration in Africa and elsewhere has often led to rising food prices, sometimes real food shortages; these in turn have triggered civil disorders, food riots, occasionally the overthrow of governments. And later in this chapter (Section F) I will return to this theme. Myers goes on to discuss how human population growth often drives the environmental deterioration that leads to such political instability.

C. Biodiversity

The decline of natural areas in the world, together with the intensification of agricultural practice has led to great loss of biodiversity. No one knows how many species there are in total in the world. The greater part of this diversity consists of species that have never even been described (many not even seen). Thus about 1.7 million species have been seen, but estimates of the number of existing species vary from 10 to 100 million! Tropical moist forests are thought to have half or more than half of the total worlds species, yet this is where habitat depletion is occurring most rapidly. Now extinction of species is a natural part of evolution - perhaps of the order of 1-10 species a year. But now, through mans activities, extinction has accelerated to at least 1,000 species per year. And one estimate is of an annual loss of 60,000 to 90,000 species from tropical forests alone each year! One 1997 analysis considers that one out of eight plant species surveyed is potentially at risk of extinction. There are probably about 100,000 tree species worldwide. A 1998 survey of around 10,000 tree species found that 6,000 were under some threat of survival, of which 976 were 'critically endangered'. Raven (1999) considers that a third of the estimated 300,000 species of vascular plant (plants excluding algae, mosses and liverworts) may be extinct or close to extinction by the middle of this century. Many in fact think that we are in the opening phase of a global mass extinction of species which will rival the known mass extinctions of past geological times (various authors referred to in Myers, 1994).

While some species are under direct threat from hunting and poaching, the biggest threat generally comes from environmental degradation and changes in land use - for example tropical forest removal, cash crop growing in vast areas of savanna, reclamation of wetlands, pesticide and other forms of pollution. And the problem is not just the loss of individual species - entire communities and ecosystems of plants face extinction, for example, the Andean laurel and oak forests of Colombia.

Biodiversity is also lost by the widespread accidental or purposeful introduction of plant and animal species to areas outside their natural ranges. In such situations, native species have never been exposed through competition, to these species, and some have their ranges reduced or their numbers decimated, and some have become extinct. This danger is particularly pronounced in closed systems. One of the best examples concerns Lake Victoria in central Africa. This has been known to zoologists as a paradise for a group of fishes called the cichlids, which had diversified into a large array of species in the lake. Now at least 60% are estimated as having been exterminated through the introduction of the predatory Nile perch.

A measure of the health of ecosystems and biodiversity worldwide is provided by the living planet index (LPI) (WWF, 2000). This is obtained by combining together three indices – the forest index, the freshwater index, and the marine index. Each of these indices is based on available data about changes over time in populations of a large number of animal species. Basicly this is changes in population size, either estimated directly or by proxy measures such as the number of nesting sites. The Living Planet index fell by 33% between 1970 and 1999. Fig. 2 shows the Living Planet Index together with the World Ecological Footprint, which will be discussed in Section F.

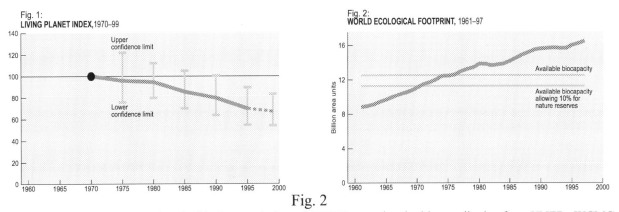

Fig. 2
Reproduced with the permission of WWF International with contribution from UNEP - WCMC.

Biological capacity as used in Fig. 2 is defined by the WWF as being the total biological production capacity per year of a biologically productive space, for example inside a country. It can be expressed in "area units", i.e. the equivalent area of space with world-average productivity.

D. Will we be able to feed the growing population of the future, and will we be able to achieve sustainable development?

These are questions on which opinion is divided.

Some scientists believe we will be able to feed the human population even when it has increased to the point where it stabilises. They point to the dramatic increases in food production this century, made possible by mans technological achievements, and consider that it will be possible to go on increasing world food production. The focus here at the moment is on Genetically Modified Organisms. These will allow the mass production of crops where pest control - in the past one of the main problems in increasing food production - will be a much easier matter. Combined with conventional plant and animal breeding methods, further increases in yield are to be expected.

Improved agricultural regimes will also play a major part. Instead of monoculture crop production in the context of the developing world rural community setting, mixed cropping regimes like permaculture will increase overall food productivity as well as more sustainable methods of energy production. One farming method which has recently shown its potential for increasing food production is marine fish farming (aquaculture), a technique based on the traditional Asian practice of raising fish in ponds. Aquaculture output has grown dramatically in recent years.

Other scientists however, remain worried over the prospects of increasing world food production. They point out that much of the rapid increase in production since the Second World War has been based on increasing use of fertilizers. In many areas, the limit of possible yield increase through fertilizer use has been reached, and the intensive use of such fertilizers has already given rise to serious pollution problems -in other words, much current fertilizer use goes against the principle of sustainable development. And GMOs, in which some place so much faith for future food production, are themselves possibly a serious cause of decline of wild plant populations.

Now grain of one type or another is the staple diet of the greater part of the total world human population, and more people are involved in grain production than in any other economic activity. Not surprisingly then, grain production is often used as an indicator of the ability of the world to feed the human population. Now it is true that total world grain production has trebled since 1950, and continues to rise. However, Grain production per head of population reached a peak in 1985 and has since declined. The reason for this lies in the decline in the annual percentage rate of increase of the global grain yield. In 1985 it fell below the rate of increase of the human population. Now it has been estimated that a minimum of 200 kg of grain per person annually is needed for survival, and the grain production per capita could fall for some years and still be sufficient (provided it was distributed properly across the globe). However, the now tiny rate of increase in yields suggests that the limit of further increase may not be far away, which is serious since demand is likely to nearly double through rising population size (Brown et al 1999b, King, 1999a). Furthermore, this whole problem must be seen in the light of increasing deterioration of farmland in many part of the world.

Now seeds, like all other parts of a plant are produced through the capture of the suns energy in the process of photosynthesis. Increase of grain yield brought about by plant breeding has been essentially through increasing the share of photosynthate (the product of photosynthesis) that goes into seed production. Until modern times, domesticated wheats converted about 20% of photosynthate to seeds, the remainder being used for sustaining leaves, stems and roots. Increase in yield in modern times has led to more than 50% of photosynthate going into seed. But there is not much chance of any big advance on this – scientists estimate that the upper limit is 62%. Anything beyond that would be to deprive the rest of the plant of the energy needed to function, thus ending with a reduction of yield (Brown in Brown 1999a).

Furthermore, much grain production is not sustainable. This particularly applies where production has been extended to areas that are not really well suited for grain production. An extreme case is Kazakhstan. Large areas of fragile pastureland were converted to grain production in the 1950s, resulting in severe erosion, such that half the area has been abandoned since 1980 - a drop in area from a little over 25 million hectares to about twelve million hectares (Halweil in Brown et al 1999b). Much grain and other crop production depends on water abstraction from the ground. Now in many parts of the world, water tables are falling caused by excessive water abstraction, partly for agriculture. This topic will be returned to in Section G below.

Soil degradation which is widespread, is induced by poor land management, including forest clearance, the clearance of other marginal land for cultivation, overgrazing, over-use of fertilizers and pesticides, poor managements of watersheds (e.g. deforestation leading to rapid soil erosion and floods), uncontrolled dumping of wastes, and the deposition of pollutants from the air. In 1991 it was estimated that some 1,900 million ha worldwide exhibited soil degradation. The largest area affected is in Asia and the Pacific - about 550 million ha. It has been estimated that in Africa 500 million ha have been affected by soil degradation since about 1950. And in China alone, between 1957 and 1990, the area of arable cropland was reduced by an area equal to all the cropland in Denmark, France, Germany and the Netherlands combined, mainly because of land degradation (UNEP 1999).

One aspect of soil degradation is actual loss of topsoil. For example, in tropical and semi-tropical areas of savanna, overgrazing by cattle leads to soil exposure and eventual soil run off. On a worldwide basis, it was estimated in 1990 that farmers were suffering a net soil loss (loss of existing soil minus new soil formation) of about 24 billion tons per year from cropland (Brown in Brown 1990).

When soil is degraded, crop yields fall. In Africa crop yields could be halved within 40 years if degradation of cultivated land continues at present rates. Some areas, which were once important crop growing areas, have been so degraded that crop production has already been abandoned.

Marine fisheries make a very important contribution to food supply. And in the last half-century the total oceanic fish catch has increased nearly five times (McGinn in Brown et al 1999a). Now there is a limit to the amount of fish that can be taken per year without causing depletion of stocks. However, in recent years most oceanic fisheries have been fished at or beyond their capacity (Brown 1995). Top predators - sharks, tuna and swordfish are being depleted, and in the course of this over-exploitation, fishermen are taking smaller fish which tend to reproduce at a younger age, and are generally less valuable commercially. The total fish catch in Africa and the Indian Ocean islands grew by more than 50% during 1975-1990, but has been falling since. In Southern Africa, a yearly catch of about 3 million tonnes in the 1950s was reduced to only 1.25 million tonnes in 1995 (McGinn, ibid). As fish stocks in European waters decline, more European trawlers are fishing off the West African coast, depleting the fish stocks there. Now between 1970 and 1990, the United Nations Food and Agriculture organisation (FAO) recorded a doubling in the world fishing fleet. And now most big fishery nations have got fishing fleets bigger than is required to land current catches. On a worldwide basis, the fishing industry has about twice the capacity needed to land the annual catch (Brown, 1998). Scientists consider that the stocks of most commercially exploited fish in the North Sea are in a seriously depleted condition, and the North Sea fishing fleet needs to be reduced by 40% to match fish resources.

In the present writer's view, calculations about the ability of mankind to feed itself in the future seem to be often conducted as if the world was like a field experiment, subject to careful control, in which the only significant variables were population size and food supply. Unfortunately, the situation in the real world is very different. In the first place, even if it becomes possible to continue at a significant rate, to increase food yield per hectare, this is most unlikely to remove the pressure to continue to convert the remaining areas of the world, which are not yet used for agriculture, to food production. We are likely to see much of the remaining forests, and most other wild and semi wild areas disappear. We could end up in a world, which consisted of cropland and cities. The first point to note here is that almost all the land that is really suitable for food production is already being used for that purpose. Other land areas, which could in theory be brought into agricultural production are those of low fertility and often very liable to soil erosion. Agricultural production, at any really useful level, would probably rapidly diminish, and the problems caused world wide by land degradation - dams filling up with top soil, flooding caused by loss of water retentive ecosystems, etc - would be enhanced.

Then again, not only as natural areas diminish, but as extensive agricultural methods continued, species diversity would suffer further devastating decline (the causal relationship between intensive agricultural practice and species decline will be discussed in Chapter 5). And the beauty of the world, depending as it does on its varied landscape, and the existence of wilderness areas, so important for mans spiritual existence, would be largely destroyed. And this destruction would be forever. Of course we cannot return to Arcadia. But we would not even be able to bring the world back to its already severely damaged present state.

This discussion of food supply adequacy leads us on first, to a consideration of the question of the role of population growth in causing the environmental situation, and second, to some other concepts which are much used in discussions about that situation.

E. Is population growth the main problem?

At the risk of some over-simplification, environmentalists can be divided into two groups.

The first (the great majority) see an interacting group of causes of the global environmental problem. Population growth itself is at best, just one of several causes. The extreme position within this group – held however by perhaps the majority of the members - is that poverty is the fundamental cause of the environmental dilemma, of which population growth is a symptom not a cause (see Section G of Chapter 10).

The second, very much a minority group, which includes the present writer, sees population growth as the fundamental engine of the world's environmental problems, although acknowledging that it is not the only serious cause.

Both groups are agreed that it is eminently desirable that population growth should cease, that human population numbers should stabilize, as quickly as possible. However, the two groups differ in that the first group think that all we need to do is to assist population stabilization by promoting contraception and other ways already discussed in our section on population growth. On the other, the second group consider that such measures are insufficient. We need not just population stabilization, but massive population reduction. Both for stabilisation and reduction we must take direct action aimed at halting population growth as quickly as possible and then bring about a massive population reduction. This requires Government intervention by a system of sticks and carrots; it may involve coercive measures.

We will consider each point of view in turn.

(i) The view that population growth is not the main, or even a major cause of our environmental dilemma

Human population growth is not by any means the only cause of world wide environmental degradation. Consider for example, the ever-continuing loss of tropical rainforests in the Amazon basin and elsewhere. As much as three-fifths of the deforestation is probably caused by landless peasants using a slash and burn technique. But these peasants are often forced to this activity in the forests because of inequitable land distribution elsewhere. Contributory factors are lack of property rights and tenure, low-level agricultural technology, deficient rural infrastructure and insufficient policy support for subsistence farming (Myers, 1994). And Monbiot (1997) concludes that all over the tropics, as traditional landowners (often peasants holding land in common) are dispossessed, and large proprietors and private business take over ('land alienation'), people's natural habitats are destroyed: the people had looked after the land, but when their commons were privatised, the priority of the people who took over was to make money, leading to excessive exploitation of forest resources, and the destruction of a wide variety of diverse natural ecosystems to provide land for the production of the most profitable product, for example wheat monoculture in East Africa replacing woodlands and savanna.

Countries with tropical rainforests often have large debts to the developed world; they are inclined therefore to over-exploit their forest resources so as to raise the desperately needed foreign exchange. Such debts also mean there are fewer financial resources to tackle problems like peasant poverty (Myers, ibid; see also Huckle, 1988). The excessive high standard of living, the wasteful lifestyle, of the developed world, is also a major cause of deforestation - causing excessive timber extraction, forest removal to establish beef farming, etc. This wasteful lifestyle shows itself in other ways. For example, the USA is said to be consuming up to 40% of the world's energy requirements, while constituting only 6% of the world's population (Milne, 1988). Such a lifestyle is not necessary to secure a reasonable standard of living. Further, at a time when developed world countries are encouraging developing world countries to conserve their resources such as forests, the latter countries very reasonably reply that the developed world should set a better example.

Considering arguments such as these has led many people to conclude that population growth per se is not the main, or even a major, cause of our present environmental predicament. One variant of this argument was developed a long time ago by the American economist Henry George.

At the end of the 19th century, Henry George put forwards his revolutionary taxation proposals (George, 1879). We will return to his taxation ideas again later in the book. It is sufficient here to note just the following points:

> 1) He rejected the Malthusian idea that it was population growth pressing against the finite available resources, which led to poverty, social inequality and misery. Rather, he saw these problems as arising from the injustices of land ownership.

> 2) He maintained that the only legitimate right of ownership concerns those things that a man's exertions have produced (for example, a house). Land in his view is one of the 'gratuitous offerings of nature' - it exists independently of mans exertions.

> 3) Observing that what a person required of the land was not land ownership per se, rather it was the security of knowing that 'improvements' he has made, such as building a house on the land, will remain his own, he went on to elaborate a novel taxation system. The then existing taxation system would be abolished and replaced by taxation on the value of land.

According to George, under this system, no one would care to hold on to land unless to actually use it, and land then withheld from use would be everywhere made available to others and thrown open to improvement. The then existing taxation system, he argued, hampered the efficient development of industry on which prosperity depended. In his view, it was this change in taxation method, which was the means to solve the problems that others attributed to population growth. And there has been a coterie of people right up to the present day who accept and promote the basic taxation idea of George.

Many who consider population growth is not the main problem, are equally convinced that mankind will be able to cope with future population growth. They hold to what McMichael et al, 1999) described as the first of "two wisdoms":

"The first wisdom denies that population increase is a cause for alarm. This view is common on the neoliberal right: complacent, consumerist, and laissez faire. Although population has been increasing a little faster than globally averaged grain yields per person since the mid-1980s, this wisdom expects that technical advance will 'fix it'. Education, particularly female education, combined with economic development will bring fertility down to replacement levels fast enough. Increasing agricultural productivity, boosted by genetically modified foods, provides the surest route to reducing rural poverty and malnutrition. The increasing global inequality will right itself, in a world that will collectively reach the consumption levels of California. Global warming, if confirmed, can be adapted too. Regional crises of demographic entrapment are not anticipated, Malthus has been proved wrong, the human rights edifice remains unflawed and paramount, and China's one-child families are an unjustifiable aberration. Humanity is safe in the hands of the United Nations".

(ii) The view that population growth is the fundamental cause or at least a major cause of our environmental predicament

Returning for a moment to the coterie of people in the Henry George taxation camp, we find that some members of this group, such as Harrison (1991), still believe that the basic threat to the global environment comes from inequitable distribution of land rights, not from population growth. But there are other advocates of land value taxation, such as Andelson (1991) who believe we need both land taxation of the Georgian type and population control.

Andelson points out that George lived before the massive increase in population during the last century. George might have been right in his time in identifying land monopoly as the fundamental social maladjustment responsible for poverty, discounting the spectre of overpopulation. But impoverishment need not be narrowly economic in the sense of insufficient food, clothing, shelter, or access to medical care and education. To be bereft of the chance to breathe clean air, or drink pure water, or eat uncontaminated food, is also to be impoverished. To be crowded in on all sides by human masses in a setting of asphalt and concrete, brick and glass, is also to be impoverished. Never to see unspoiled forests or animals in the wild; never to wade in a stream free of sewage or swim in a lake not choked with trash, is also to be impoverished. No doubt, with proper land ownership and taxation arrangements, and the application of advanced technology, the earth could support, after a fashion, vastly greater population into the distant future.

But, Andelson argues, we also need population control. Consider the classic example of environmental damage already mentioned - the destruction of the Amazon rain forest in Brazil. It might be possible to stop peasants removing forest to grow crops, by equitable land distribution. But as population continues to increase, sooner or later peasants would have to revert to cutting down the forest to grow more food crops. Andelson sums up by saying:

"The fact is that land monopoly engenders artificial overpopulation, whereas overpopulation exacerbates the ills of land monopoly. The population problem and the land problem are both serious and real; neither should be used as an excuse to avoid recognition of the other".

The argument that human population growth is the single biggest cause of global environmental decline can be briefly stated. The more people there are, the more non-renewable resources are used, depleting the stocks and causing environmental damage in the process of extraction (removal of vegetation to get at mineral sources, damage to landscape through quarrying, etc). The more people there are, especially in the developing world, which is more dependent on wood for fuel than the developed world, the more forests are cleared. The more people there are, the more food is needed. The increased need for food has partly been met by improved strains of crops and livestock animals, and by improved agricultural technology, which have increased yield per area. But this intensification of agriculture has brought with it problems such as increased soil erosion mentioned earlier. The increased need for food has also been met by the expansion of agricultural area at the expense of habitat for wild life. Then again, the more people there are, the more waste products are produced, and hence the greater the pollution of soil, water and atmosphere, increasing health hazard, bringing about global warming. And the more people there are, especially as resources are reduced, the greater the risk of conflict over scare resources. For further discussion of the relationships between human population growth and environmental degradation see Preston (1994).

In terms of the "two wisdoms" mentioned earlier, the second wisdom is stated as follows:

"The second wisdom is not confident of science's ability to double global grain production sustainably. It suspects that large parts of sub-Saharan Africa (where population is set to more than triple) and South Asia (set to almost double) may already be demographically trapped. It also suspects that the human psyche cannot accept constraining reproduction and, indeed, imposes taboos on attempts to do so. This second viewpoint identifies population growth as the unrecognised multiplier of most major world problems: the persistence of inequality, poverty, and malnutrition; resource shortages; ecological disruption and environmental pollution; the loss of biodiversity and wildlife habitats; and conflict and violence. Even natural disasters like floods are made worse because population pressure forces more people to live in vulnerable locations – such as areas prone to periodic inundation" (McMichael et al, ibid).

F. Carrying capacity, Ecological Footprints and Environmental Impact

Carrying capacity may be defined as:

The population of a given species that can be supported indefinitely without permanently damaging the ecosystem on which it is dependent.

Clearly in determining the world's carrying capacity for man, we need to consider other factors besides food supply. For example, besides food, we need forests, not only to supply wood products, but also to absorb sufficient carbon dioxide emissions to alleviate global warming. Then again, if we are to gradually change energy supply from non-renewable resources (coal, oil) to renewable resources (biomass, wind), we need land to provide these energy sources.

What is also clear is that in trying to determine the carrying capacity of the world or a nation, we must specify the lifestyles of the peoples. If everyone were to have the lavish lifestyle of North America, the world could support far fewer people than if everyone had the modest lifestyle of the average citizen of India. One estimate is that with the North American lifestyle the world could support only 1 billion people, whereas with the Indian lifestyle it could support 11 billion (Ferguson, 1998a).

Another way of putting it would be to say that some nations use more than their fair share of the world's resources; and at the same time they contribute disproportionately to the burden of waste matter and polluting emissions, which the world and the world atmosphere must absorb. This leads us to the second concept - *ecological footprints*- a concept developed and explored by Wackernagel and colleagues (Wackernagel and Rees, 1996), and more recently by Andrew Ferguson of the Optimum Population Trust. Ecological footprint may be defined:

The resource consumption and waste assimilation requirements of a defined human population or economy in terms of a corresponding productive land area.

This term perhaps can most readily be understood if you consider the footprint of a city – which is what the term is most used for. If we think just of resource consumption, and within that just food consumption, it is clear that a city does not grow all its own food within its own boundaries. Vast areas of land outside the city in fact supply most of the food consumed, and this is part of the 'productive land' area mentioned. Then again, if we think of waste and just one component of waste - CO_2 - the city will need an area of vegetation (especially forest) to absorb excess CO_2 and avoid contributing to global warming. This vegetation will cover an area of productive land.

One can go on from here to specify some particular footprint and ask what would be the carrying capacity of a given area using such a footprint. Bearing in mind that people in the developing world would like to raise their living standards towards the standards of the developed world, but at the same time that we need to reduce global CO_2 emissions, on can define a 'modest footprint' as:

The size of the ecological footprint which is broadly related to a European lifestyle, except that the use of fossil energy is reduced to about two-fifths of present consumption – to an emission of 4 metric tons of carbon dioxide per capita per year. For specific nations this energy allowance is halved (these latter are nations which are currently emitting less than 2 tons/capita) (Ferguson, ibid).

Using this definition one can attempt to estimate the carrying capacity of a nation or group of nations, as Ferguson does using spreadsheets provided by Wackernagel (Ferguson, 1998b). The calculations involved are based on world productivity. They use the areas of land that would be needed at worldwide productivity, each type of land (arable, pasture, forest, built-over land and energy land – the latter needed either to assimilate CO_2 released by burning fossil fuels or to produce energy from renewable resources - being considered separately. Countries differ in the size of each component of land, and also in the productivity of that land. So for each category of land, the area of that land in a country is taken and multiplied by a yield factor to take into account its productivity. For example, if the productivity of arable land of a country was twice the average world arable land productivity, its arable area would be multiplied up by a factor of 2.

Ferguson takes European Countries together with 11 other countries for which adequate statistics are available, making a total of 30 nations. The countries were:

a) Western Europe: Austria, Belgium, Czechoslovakia, Denmark, Finland, France, Germany, Greece, Hungary, Ireland, Italy, Netherlands, Norway, Poland, Portugal, Spain, Sweden, Switzerland, UK.
b) The Russian Federation, Australia, Bangladesh, Canada, China, Egypt, India, Indonesia, Mexico, Pakistan and the USA.

Population figures used were for 1993. Together, the populations of these countries comprised the larger part of the whole world population. The carrying capacity works out as 1,784 million. The actual population was 3,583 million, suggesting that in this 'world' there is over-population to the tune of 1,799 million (Ferguson uses the term 'excessive population').

Population in millions

	'World'		Western Europe	
Actual population	3,583		445	
	Current Situation	Modest Footprint	Current Situation	Modest Footprint
Carrying Capacity	1,784	1,325	247	300
Excessive Population	1,800	2,259	199	145

Population minus carrying capacity equals excessive population. Slight inequalities here due to rounding off errors.

Ferguson comments that the increase of the excessive population for the 'world' when one moves to a modest footprint should come as no surprise. The great majority of people are living so far below the standard of a modest footprint, that an increase to that level of consumption would swamp the counter effect that would result from Western nations decreasing their own footprints to a modest size. This seems to present writer a very important point. People tend to forget, when considering balancing the needs of the developed and developing world, that the latter is far, far more populous than the former. Any per capita change over the developing world will make a far greater difference than in the developed world. Ecological footprints then, like carrying capacity, must be specified in relation to some specific lifestyle. And this leads us to the last concept in this section (We shall come back to the ecological footprint concept in Chapter 10).

Environmental impact.

The impact (I) of a human population on the environment depends on three factors: First, the size of the population (P), second, affluence (A) - the average persons consumption of resources, and thirdly, the harmful effect of the technology that provides the affluence (T). This impact is often expressed as the sustainability equation:

$$I = PAT.$$

Sometimes per-capita energy use is used as a surrogate for AT. An often used alternative formulation of the sustainability equation is I=PCT where C stands for consumption. David Willey of the Optimum Population Trust notes that consumption is influence by lifestyle and organisation (improved organisation in rich countries could lead to reduced per capita consumption, but in many poor countries better organisation might lead to a huge increase in consumption). He prefers the formulation I=PLOT (population, lifestyle, organisation, technology)

Thinking in terms of this equation we can see that the contributions of the factors will vary from one country to another. Most importantly, we can see that the factors have different relative values in developed world countries compared with developing world countries. In the former, A will make a greater contribution to I than in the latter. The opposite may often be true for T, although the situation here is rather more ambiguous. Thus environmental standards are often less stringent in a developing than in a developed country, for example, over polluting emissions from factories. On the other hand, a

developing country might have much less industry anyway.

Clearly then, if environmental impact is to be reduced, it can be done by reducing one or more of these factors. The logical thing to do would be to reduce all three, which in my view we should do. Indeed, it has been argued for a long time by P. Ehrlich that it is imperative to do just this (for example, Ehrlich and Ehrlich, 1990). However, it is sometimes argued that the emphasis should be different between the developed and the undeveloped world. In the developed world, population growth has slowed down considerably, but affluence is very high. In contrast, population growth is still considerable in the developing world but affluence is low. So it is argued, it would be fair if the developed world concentrated more on reducing affluence, and the developing world in reducing population through lowering birth rate. However, as we will see later, there is still a need to reduce the population size in developed countries.

I said earlier that it would be logical to reduce all three of the contributory categories of Impact. It is interesting then most environmentalists and environmental NGOs seem to assume that P, population, is a given, that cannot or should not be altered deliberately; This seems to me to be irrational. FoE, judging by its publication "Tomorow's World" (McLaren et al. 1997) seems to adopt this attitude. And as Val Stevens points out in her critique of the book, while advocating that the developed world should reduce consumption, the book does not speak of the corresponding duty of the developing world to stabilise its populations. She notes the emphasis placed by FoE of improving technology. However, she comments that while a bad technology can be shut down overnight and a better technology installed over a period of 5 to 20 years, each year there are about 80 million extra people, and we can't shut them down. She also notes the view of N. Myers that with the best of intentions, technical solutions have often gone wrong and thrown up more problems than they solve (Stevens, 1999). I shall return to the approach of FoE and other NGOs in the opening Section of Chapter 9 and Section G of Chapter 10.

G. What are the most serious environmental problems facing the world at the beginning of this new millennium?

Opinions differ on what are the most serious environmental problems globally. Here is my choice. Most environmentalists would I think include the first two and possibly the third on their short lists. But the fourth one is frequently ignored, and I think it could eventually be the most important of all.

(i) Shortage of fresh water

Water is essential for all life. It is the biggest constituent by volume of our bodies and most other living things. It is essential for agriculture. As a major component of the atmosphere it is an important part of the whole climate regulatory system.

Now global freshwater consumption rose six fold between 1900 and 1995 - at more than twice the rate of population growth. And already water shortages occur in various parts of the world. For example, 108 cities in northern China report water shortages. Where there are shortages of good clean water, people have to make do with whatever they can get. And it is estimated that about 20% of the global population currently lacks access to safe drinking water (and a much larger percentage, probably around 50%, lack access to safe sanitation which often reflects water shortage). Looking to the future, it is estimated that by AD 2025 more than a billion people will be living in countries facing absolute water scarcity.

Worldwide, agriculture accounts for more than 70% of freshwater consumption, mainly from the irrigation of agricultural crops. 40% of world food production comes in fact from irrigated land (including roughly 70% of the grain harvest in China). And irrigation is credited with more than half the growth in agricultural output between the mid 1960s and the mid 1980s. Now much of the water used in irrigation is groundwater. Several major agricultural regions of the world pump groundwater faster than it is recharged by rainfall, an unsustainable practice leading to a fall in water tables (the level of water in ground reserves). This will curtail output once aquifers are depleted or become too expensive to pump. Excessive withdrawal of groundwater, in quantities greater than the ability of nature to renew the aquifers, is now widespread in parts of the Arabian peninsula, China, India, Mexico, the former Soviet Union and the southern Great Plains of the USA. In fact the water table has dropped by tens of metres in many places where there is intensive groundwater use. A survey covering 1991 to 1996 indicates that the water table under the north China plain is dropping an average of roughly 1.5 metres a year. And since this area accounts for nearly 40% of China's grain harvest, this is a matter of serious concern. In parts of India over-pumping from aquifers is causing water tables to fall 1-3 metres a year. If this continues, India's grain harvest could fall by as much as 25% (Brown, in Brown et al 1999a).

But ground water is not just used for agriculture, it is also used by industry and for people, and these other uses of groundwater are contributing to falling water tables and aquifer depletion. In fact, groundwater supplies all the water needs of about one third of the world's population. So growing demands for water by people and industry is increasingly limiting the availability of water for irrigation. For example, aquifer depletion is already forcing farmers in parts of the USA to change to dry land farming, with concomitant reduction of yield, and in parts of arid Arizona diversion of water to rapidly expanding cities has led to large areas of productive farmland reverting to desert. In general, there are now fears that the world's fresh water supply will not be able to sustain the present or bigger levels of agricultural production, and therefore it will be inadequate to sustain the increasing human population.

An estimated 65% of public water supplies in Europe come from ground water sources, and groundwater withdrawal in the European Union rose by 35% between 1970 and 1985. And more than half the large cities in Europe are over-exploiting their groundwater resources (UNEP, 1999).

Over - extraction of water from rivers can lead to them running dry before they reach the sea. A spectacular example comes from China. For the first time in China's 3,000-year history, the Yellow River - that cradle of Chinese civilisation, failed to reach the sea for 15 days in 1972. Over the next dozen years it ran dry intermittently, but since 1985 it has run dry for part of each year. In 1997 it failed to reach the sea for seven months. Another example comes from Central Asia - the Amu Darya, one of the two rivers feeding the Aral sea is drained dry by Uzbek and Turkmem cotton farmers; as a result the Aral sea is shrinking and may eventually disappear (Brown, ibid, Brown in Brown,1997)).

The problem with ground water is not just that of decrease in quantity, it is also decrease in quality. In many areas of the world ground water has become salinized, and most crop plants will not grow in a saline medium. Salinization is often accompanied by waterlogging, preventing plant root gaseous exchange ('breathing'). The mechanism of salinization and waterlogging is complicated. But essentially, water used for irrigation contains minute amounts of salt. Now much of the water used is either lost to the atmosphere by evaporation from the soil, or lost by plants by their transpiration of water to the atmosphere through their leaves. The salt is left behind and gradually accumulates. Some of the irrigation water however may penetrate deeper into the soil, leading to the water table rising and eventually causing waterlogging.

Salinization can take place both in coastal areas and elsewhere. Over-abstraction in coastal areas can lead to seawater intrusion along shorelines. As a result, some arable land, such as on the Batinah coastal plain of Oman, has been completely lost. It is estimated that the saline interface between the sea and groundwater advances at an annual rate of 75-130 metres in Bahrain. In Madras, India, salt - water intrusion has moved 10 km inland, rendering many irrigation wells useless. Salt - water intrusion is of particular concern in small island states, where the limited groundwater supply is surrounded by salt water 9 (UNEP,ibid).

But salinization is not confined to areas close to the sea. It can occur remote from seas and oceans, principally in the hotter and drier parts of the globe. Already by 1994 it was estimated that between 20 and 30 million hectares - 8-12 % of world irrigated area - was suffering from serious salinization, with an additional 60-80 million ha believed to be moderately affected. The World Bank found that salinization affected 28% of the USA irrigated area, the corresponding figures for Mexico, China, Pakistan and India being 10, 23, 21 and 11%. Such salinization seriously reduces crop yields in the countries concerned. For example, it was estimated in 1987 that in Pakistan that salt build up in the soil reduced crop yields by 30%.

Salinization is not the only way in which water is polluted. For example, sewage pollution of ground water is common in many developing countries. And intensive use of pesticides and fertilizers has led to chemicals being leached into freshwater supplies in many places. Nitrate pollution from excess fertilizer use is now one of the most serious water quality problems. Maximum allowable levels of nitrates in drinking water are exceeded in some places in every country in Europe and in many countries in other regions. Industrial wastes are significant sources of water pollution - contamination with lead, mercury, arsenic and cadmium. In Japan, a study of 15 cities showed that 30% of all groundwater supplies are contaminated by chlorinated solvents from industry. It is estimated that polluted water affects the health of about 1,200 million people and contributes to the death of about 15 million children under five every year (UNEP, ibid).

Myers (1993), whose work I referred to earlier, wrote extensively about the potential of water shortage, or fear of water shortage, for causing conflict between nations, especially as world population grows. Of more than 200 major river systems, around 150 are shared by two nations, and more than 50 by 3-10 nations. These river systems supply nearly 40% of the world's population for all uses. In recent times there have already been water disputes between India and Pakistan (because of water diversion from the Indus), and between India and Bangladesh over the Ganges river for much the same reason.

Myers writes about the situation in the Middle East. Israel at the time Myers wrote was getting about 60% of its water from the Jordan River, but only 3% of the Jordan river basin lies within the pre-1967 Israeli border. Jordan on the other hand was taking about three-quarters of its water from its tributaries. However, it wants to take much more: the country imports a lot of its food, which costs the country a lot of money; and its population growth rate is one of the fastest in the world. Consequently it needs to greatly increase its own food production, and this would be almost entirely through increase in irrigation (unlike Israel, only a small part of its land was irrigated in 1993). King Hussein of Jordan has asserted that water shortages are the only reason his country should go to war with Israel. And Myers stated he met General Moshe Dyan who told him that Israel unleashed its planes and tanks in the war of 1967 as soon as it learned that Syria an Jordan were moving to cut off water flows from rivers that originated outside Israel's borders.

(ii) Global warming

It is now generally accepted that global warming is man-induced. The surface temperature of the globe has been rising irregularly during recent decades, reaching a new record of 14.57^0C. in 1998. El Nino contributed to this, but was probably not the only cause; anyway, this particular El Nino was a particularly severe one and the severity might be itself at least partly caused by global warming. The rapid warming of the last 25 years is greater than in any similar length period since temperature measurements began (Flavin, in Brown et al 1999b).

Global warming is caused by the increase of certain gases in the atmosphere, most noticeably carbon dioxide (CO_2). The sharp jump in surface temperature in 1998 was accompanied by the biggest increase in atmospheric carbon dioxide concentration since data was first collected, in part caused by the extensive burning of tropical forests, which accompanied the El Nino. Be that as it may, in the late 1990s CO_2 annual emissions were almost four times the 1950 level, and atmospheric concentrations reached their highest levels in 160,000 years.

Global warming leads to rising sea levels, with corresponding inundation of low-lying coastal areas, as mentioned earlier. The rising of sea levels depends on the expansion of oceanic water as it gets warmer, and the addition of water from melting land based ice. Global warming is likely to alter several atmospheric parameters, including precipitation, wind velocity, and increase the incidence of extreme weather events - storms, deluges, cyclones and drought. Such extreme events have colossal economic consequences.

The surface waters of oceans will become warmer and more temperature stratified. Now these surface waters are the home of the minute plants which make up the phytoplankton, the fundamental basis for the whole marine food chain. This increased warming and stratification may reduce phytoplankton productivity, and in turn the productivity of all other ocean creatures, including fish stocks. This reduced phytoplankton productivity may be enhanced by a combination of increased acidity caused by increase of CO_2 concentrations and ultra-violet light penetration. The oceans of the world, together with the forests, remove vast quantities of CO_2 from the atmosphere - being described as 'sinks'. Rising surface temperatures over oceans and land may greatly diminish this CO_2 absorbing capacity with obvious implications for further global warming.

Global warming will alter climate patterns all over the world. Some areas will become drier, some wetter; while many will become hotter, some may become cooler. These changes will have far reaching disruptive effects on agricultural production. They will also have serious consequences for wild life. Many species of plants and animals, indeed whole ecosystems, will need to move, usually further away from the equator, to survive. Since many habitats have a very disjointed distribution, it will be difficult, sometimes impossible, for species with poor dispersal mechanisms to make the required movement in space in the required time.

Studies of the history of climate change show that changes in temperature have not always been gradual. There seems to have been threshold temperatures which when passed led to abrupt changes in temperature - rapid shifts from one equilibrium state to another. If such an abrupt shift were to occur in the near future, it would cause devastating disruption both of the natural world and economic activity.

Many will have heard of the system by which cold denser water in the north Atlantic sinks beneath the warmer less dense water of the northwards moving ocean currents of the north Atlantic drift - the fanning out of the Gulf Stream. This is part of vast water 'conveyor belt': the water that sinks downwards then flows southwards. Further south in the tropics, water rises and moves north in the Gulf Stream. It is this northern drift of warmer water that maintains the mild climate of coastal Western Europe. Any massive addition of freshwater (from melting polar icecaps) in the north Atlantic could reduce the surface ocean salinity and turn off the conveyor belt, very rapidly plunging western Europe into arctic conditions with disastrous effects on agricultural production and much else besides. This may only be a remote possibility, but it is a very real one. To such a possibility it is well worth adding the comment made by the authors of the UNEP (1999) book referred to at the beginning of this chapter. There may be other, unforeseen events, related to mans' alteration of the environment, which could turn out to be the key environmental events of the 21st century.

A word needs to be said here about something that is potentially more serious than all that has been discussed above. This arises from what are called positive feedback mechanisms. An example is the wage-price spiral. Wages increase, causing prices to increase, leading to demand for higher wages, leading to ... in other words a 'vicious circle'. With global warming, warming of seas and oceans can lead to an increased rate of water evaporation, increasing atmospheric humidity. Water vapour is a greenhouse gas, so the effect would be to reinforce the greenhouse effect. This in turn would increase surface water temperatures ... the possibility then is climate change spiralling out of control.

Finally, what eventually happens depends on whether man is able to reduce greenhouse gas emissions sufficiently, and sufficiently rapidly. Now through the United Nations Framework Convention on Climate Change and the Kyoto Protocol, efforts are being made to reduce greenhouse gas emissions. However, greenhouse gases are still being emitted at levels above the stabilization target, and the Kyoto targets alone, would not sufficiently reduce emissions to produce stabilisation. It is important, too, to realise that there is a great inertia in the climate system. Climate change occurs slowly, and once a significant change occurs, it is not going to disappear quickly through mans counter-measures. So even if greenhouse gas emissions were stabilised, global warming would continue for several decades, and sea levels could continue to rise for centuries. It helps to visualize the seriousness of the situation when one realises what climate models tell us about required emission reductions. Stabilizing atmospheric CO_2 concentrations at safe levels would require a 60-80% reduction of carbon emissions from present levels! Immediate stabilization of the atmospheric CO_2 concentration at its present level, about 360 parts per million (which is far too high), is of course not possible. But lets assume it was. To achieve this one would have to immediately reduce emissions by 50 - 70 % with further reductions later (UNEP, 1999).

(iii) Depletion of oil stocks and its economic and political consequences

This sub-section is based mainly on Willey (1999a and b).

Oil plays an almost all pervading role in world economy. Almost all the world's aircraft, and 700 million motor vehicles run on some form or derivative of oil. Many power stations use it. But the role of oil in the world economy is more pervasive than merely providing the energy for cars and power stations. Many of the products in daily use are made from or partly made from petroleum derivatives - plastics, fertilisers, textiles and pharmaceuticals. Maintaining a supply of oil is then critical for the world economy.

The rate of oil consumption is increasing every year, caused by increased use per person and increase in human population size. Yet world oil production is likely to peak during the first decade of this 21st century, and thereafter decline (oil production per capita is thought to have peaked in 1979, since when it has declined by 0.08% per year).

It is true that more sources of oil may be discovered. But global discovery peaked in the 1960s and has been falling ever since. And it has been estimated that oil is being depleted four times more quickly than it is being discovered. It is also true that improvements in technology will make it possible to extract more oil from less productive sources such as tar sands, and this will help in making the transition from oil to other sources of energy. But there will nevertheless be a shortfall in supply and prices will increase. Now some increase of price will of course make it more profitable to try to extract oil from less productive sources. But the damage to the environment might be considerable. Furthermore, in terms of the overall costs of production, it is not the dollar cost of oil extraction itself, which will be the crucial factor. As oil extraction becomes more difficult, more energy will be used in its extraction. The net energy produced may not equal the energy used in producing it. It is the energy cost of energy that is the crucial thing.

Willey reports on a future scenario which Colin Campbell, a petroleum consultant thinks is likely, and described in a talk in the House of Commons in July 1999:

It seems increasingly likely that oil price will rise steeply and in the near future. This will arise out of the balance of power between the major oil producing countries and the rest of the world. Of the approximately one trillion barrels of oil left to produce, about half lies in five Middle East Countries. In 2001, it is likely that Middle East producers will achieve what may be called the "swing share" of production i.e. the share required to control oil price. They will then have the confidence to impose much higher prices. This price shock may come as early as 2001, and will probably trigger a stock market crash. There will be increasing political and economic tension as Europe, America and Japan compete for access to Middle East oil. And the developing world will be badly harmed since it will be unable to afford to import much oil. By 2008 the "swing countries" will be approaching their own depletion midpoint. Production there will then start its inevitable long-term decline at about 3% a year. There will be increasing shortages and the global market will eventually come to an end because of high transport costs. In the view of Walter Youngquist, reaching and passing the oil production peak will be the most important thing to happen in human history, affecting more people in more ways than any other event. This will happen during the lives of most people living at the present time.

(iv) Population competition

We have seen various ways in which population growth is having effects on the environmental situation - for example, the need for intensification of agriculture with its various adverse consequences such as fresh water depletion, global warming, etc. But the growth of the human population also affects the environmental situation indirectly through its sociological effects. Many people have drawn attention to the widening gap between the wealthy (the 'haves') and the poverty stricken (the 'have nots'). And in a United Nations Press Release of 11th May 1993 Jacques Cousteau of the Cousteau Society warned that if the global population did ever reach the then forecasted 11 billion, this population would be composed of 1.5 billion rich people who were getting richer, and 9.5 billion people living in misery. He warned that in such a situation, jealousy and famine produce anger, then violence, and then an unimaginable genocide.

To a considerable extent, we can consider the sociological implications of population growth, through what is termed 'population competition'. As population density increases, competition for resources increases, leading to social tensions and internecine strife. This may take the simple form of squabbling over resources (this is my bit of land, not yours) but it also impedes any attempts to implement any rational environmental policy.

Population competition has however, another dimension, namely its effect on the interactions between ethnic groups. A minority ethnic group in a society may feel threatened by the numerical superiority of the dominant ethnic group. This might lead to the group being unwilling to adopt birth control practices (because it fears these practices are being introduced to keep its numbers down) or even to actively attempt to produce greater numbers of babies to redress the numerical imbalance. The result might be accelerated population growth and thus increased pressures on natural resources. Whether or not increased population growth does in fact result, the majority ethnic group might feel threatened by the numbers and / or economic success of the minority ethnic group, and might actively try to increase its own numbers or its proportion of the total population, supported by the ruling government. Once again, whether or not accelerated population growth does or does not ensue, racial tension is likely to rise between the ethnic groups concerned, and this in extreme cases may lead to genocide and ethnic cleansing. This whole complex subject of human population competition is discussed at great length by Parsons (1998).

Events in recent times appear to provide examples. I consider here the recent conflicts in the Great Lakes region of Central Africa, involving the Hutu and Tutsi tribes. The account that follows is based primarily on Willey (1997) who in turn based his account on a report of an interview given by the historian Carlo Carbone, but also on Stanton (1996).

The Hutu, who are mainly farmers have lived in the great lakes region since 1,000BC. The Tutsi, who are pastoralists, arrived in the region in the 13th or 14th century AD, possibly from the Nile region. For hundreds of years after the arrival of the Tutsi, there was some strife but basically the two groups co-operated peacefully - their different approaches to agriculture complemented each other so both groups benefited. Population densities were low.

Then the colonial period began in the closing years of the last century. The Germans were the first Europeans to arrive. They found the Tutsi in dominant positions and incorporated them into the colonial administrative system. The result was that the Tutsi ended up with absolute political power in Rwanda, and near-absolute power in Burundi. Nevertheless, the system of managing land and resources worked reasonably well while the population density was low. But the colonially imposed peace, and health care led to a rapid build up of population, until in 1994 Rwanda's population density of 296 people per km^2 was the highest in Africa. The population of Rwanda eventually grew from 1.5 million to 9 million, Burundi from 1.3 million to 6 million. Violent conflict erupted, exacerbated by international attempts to re-insert into Rwanda, Tutsis who had fled the country.

There were probably several contributory causes to the genocide, including the effects of modernisation and urbanisation. But it was not primarily driven by some ferocious, ancestral, primitive instincts, rather it was driven by competition for limited resources, particularly land. The genocide in Rwanda then, cannot be explained without taking the factor of over-population into account.

Recent events in former Yugoslavia are only a continuation of a long-standing situation. As Parson (ibid) observes, former Yugoslavia was the most heterogeneous country in Europe, with five official nationalities, 12 ethnic minorities, and three major religions. Population competition and competitive breeding were, in his view, well launched before the series of civil wars erupted and Yugoslavia broke up. The rivalries between Serbs, Croats and Muslims were exacerbated by the great differences in birth rates and population growth rates. In 1989 the ethnic Albanians of Kosovo had the high fertility rate of 4.12. According to Stanton (1999) Kosovo's total population in 1953 was 0.8 million, roughly half and half Serb and Albanian. By 1991 there were 1.6 million Albanians and 0.2 million Serbs. Now the population is, he claims, 90% Albanian. Stanton's view is that for 50 years the Albanians had been quietly engaged in what he terms 'demographic colonization' of Kosovo (and Macedonia) and now their victims were fighting back.

Some discussion of the conflicts in Northern Ireland is very apposite here. And it is interesting to note that Coleman and Salt preface their quite extended discussion of Northern Ireland fertility rates with the comment that the picture one gets of 'assimilation and convergence' (a nice piece of euphemism!) between the two religious groups in Northern Ireland is perhaps the sharpest 'demographic contrast' between any two neighbouring communities in Europe outside Kosovo.

Roman Catholics are a substantial minority population, but their proportion of the population increased from 34% in 1926 to about 40% in 1981. The fertility difference between Protestants and Roman Catholics was noted in the 1911 census, had become substantial by the 1930s and has widened considerably since the 1960s. In the 1983 fertility survey average family size was Roman Catholic: Protestant, 3.3:2.3. Coleman and Salt (1992).

Because Roman Catholic natural increase was three times that of Protestant in 1971, there has been speculation that Roman Catholics will 'out-breed' Protestants and eventually form the majority (Kennedy, reported in Coleman and Salt, ibid). If most Roman Catholics remained republican in sympathy, a democratic vote could then go in favour of union with the Republic, against the wishes of most of the Protestants.

Now where minorities feel threatened by absorption or assimilation, a 'minority effect' may make the acceptance of family planning difficult and retard fertility convergence. This may, say Coleman and Salt, operate among Northern Irish Roman Catholics. In 1971, Roman Catholic fertility in Northern Ireland was slightly higher than in the Republic, part of which may be explained as such a minority effect (Coward, reported in Coleman and Salt, ibid).

What stands out perhaps most to the present writer in all this is the following. The Northern Ireland conflict has been for a few years one of the main recurring items on the BBC, as I personally witness because I regularly listen to the news bulletins on Radio 4 and nearly every day to a major part of the "Today" programme. Yet the demographic differences between the two communities are rarely if ever mentioned, and likewise rarely if ever mentioned as one possible cause of all the conflict. I say rarely if ever – it is possible there may have been a whole programme on this that I missed, but no one can deny that in the vast majority of discussions, which frequently include aspects of causal mechanisms, the fertility differences are not even mentioned. This is a good example of how demographic aspects of ethnic issues are, in the writer's opinion, rarely openly discussed. It seems likely to me that one day the whole situation may explode in our faces.

Stanton, partly through considering situations like the conflicts in the Balkans, has developed a useful concept that I will now describe.

Malthus Cutoff Level (MCL).

Stanton defines this as the highest level of population that a nation or other geographic entity afflicted by chronic internecine strife can reach (Stanton 1996). When a population rises above this level, it is liable to be cut back by strife. This population level will normally be lower than the carrying capacity of the geographic area concerned. And this serves to reinforce my doubts about the usefulness of carrying capacity estimates that would assure us that the world will be able to feed the projected future larger population.

Stanton gives examples, which he considers illustrate the MCL concept. Not being a historian, I cannot personally comment on their validity. He says that through Roman pacification following their annexation of the country, the population of England rose to about five million. During the years following the Roman withdrawal, tribal strife reduced that population to about 1.5 Million. The analysis of the situation in Central Africa given earlier is in Stanton's view an illustration of his concept. In only three months in Rwanda 1994, about one million people were massacred and another roughly million people fled the country. Of course we must be careful in situations like this last one not to assume that the higher population level was close to a genuine carrying capacity - the population might have been using resources in a way which was not sustainable in the long term and therefore was above the carrying capacity quite apart from the conflict which ensued.

Stanton also argues that nations may be able, perhaps for a considerable period, to avoid Malthusian cutback through powerful militarily backed restraint. He is pessimistic about the future of the middle-east region. He claims that massive American subsidies give Israel the strength to hold Arab neighbours at bay. Annual population growth rates in the region are high; he gives the figures 2.7%, 2.3%, 4.6%, 3.4%, 3.3%, 2% and 3.5% for Israel, Egypt, Gaza, West bank, Jordan, Lebanon and Syria respectively. He considers that the combination of growing land hunger with violent ethnic and religious hatred must soon end in what he calls a 'Malthusian showdown'.

H. A theorem concerning necessary action.

As world wide environmental deterioration accelerates, the possible solutions to the world's problems narrow to very radical solutions.

If the world wide environmental situation were not so bad as it is, non-radical solutions would have sufficed to deal with the world's problems. It would have been possible to produce sufficient food without recourse to excessive intensification of agricultural production and considerable conversion of non-agricultural land to food production; better management, including greater use of mixed farming, permaculture, etc. would have sufficed. To bring about a stabilisation of the human population level below the existing level, the spread of contraceptives, education for all, and the empowerment of women, if really effectively carried out, may have led to a tailing off of population growth to an acceptable population level, without recourse to any restrictive policies such as the one child per woman policy. If levels of consumption in the developed world had not risen as high as they have in recent decades, it would have been possible, with the resources available, to bring the standard of living in developing countries up to the level of developed world countries. Such solutions have now all become problematical. It is doubtful if we can provide sufficient food for the future world population by any means; but if we are to do so, it will be necessary to retain a high level of intensification and take more land into agricultural production. To slow population growth and then to reduce the population to a sustainable level will demand positive action, even coercive policies. To raise the standard of living of people in developing countries appreciably in a sustainable way will not be possible without a drastic lowering of consumption in the developed world. So radical policies will become increasingly necessary, and increasingly radical, as the environmental situation gets worse.

I give the last word on the global situation to the United Nations (UNEP,1999), which on page 362 draws the following conclusion:

"There used to be a long time horizon for undertaking major environmental policy initiatives. Now time for a rational, well-planned transition to a sustainable system is running out fast. In some areas, it has already run out..."

Text from united Nations Environment Programme's (UNEP's) "Global Environment Outlook 2000" with UNEP permission.

Chapter 2

Population growth and migration

A. Introduction

Starting in the eighteenth century, the population both in England and in Western Europe as a whole grew rapidly, but this growth is now tailing off. What has taken place in that time period is a transition from a long continued agrarian society, via the industrial revolution, to the modern industrial society.

The increase in population in the UK as a whole and in England in recent decades is as follows:

Population numbers (thousands) at mid-year

Year	UK	England
1971	55,928	46,412
1976	56,216	46,660
1981	56,357	46,821
1986	56,859	47,342
1991	57,814	48,208
1996	58,807	49,089
1998	59,237	49,495

Source: ONS 2000. © Crown copyright 2000. Data reproduced by permission of ONS.

There is a common misconception that the population of the United Kingdom and England in particular, is currently on the decrease. In fact, the population is still increasing. Further, there is considerable uncertainty about the long-term future. The main but not the only reason for this uncertainty lies in uncertainty about the extent of future inward migration.

Increase in population, its rate and duration, is vitally important to the whole debate on the loss of green land for housing. For if population increases this will tend to lead eventually to an increase in the number of households; this in turn leads to more house building which increases the pressure to release green countryside land for housing. So the likely growth of the population is a vital element in any assessment of the state of the countryside. Unfortunately, in all the discussions on loss of size and quality of the countryside, the whole question of population size and growth, and its influence on the countryside seems to be 'played down' or even ignored by environmental campaigners.

It is not just the total population size that has a bearing on the loss of green land to development, but where this population lives. The movement of many people away from densely populated cities (counter-urbanisation) s also therefore a matter that needs to be considered.

The ethnic composition of our population has and is changing. Ethnic groups differ in the youthfulness of their populations, their fertility rates and their distribution in the country. These differences are important for understanding population growth and movement in the UK, and have implications for racial harmony, which any consideration of the impact of the future population of the UK must consider.

This chapter gives some basic population facts and projections for the future, and explores some related issues.

B. Our population is still increasing

The populations both of the UK as a whole and of England, have been rising in recent decades, as we saw above, although at a decreasing rate. Contrary to what many people apparently think, these populations are projected to continue to grow slowly during the next three decades. Between 1998 and 2021 the population of the UK is projected to rise by 4.4 million, that of England alone by 4.2 million (this topic will be taken up again later in section G).

Since people are on average now living longer, the population as a whole has been ageing. And it is thought that this process will continue so that the mean (average) age will rise from 38.6 years in 1998 to 41.9 years by 2021. This ageing of the population is of concern because it means that more resources have to be channelled to the care of the aged. On the other hand, there seems to be a growing acceptance of the fact that older people have the potential to give a lot to the country in terms of experience and available time.

What are the causes of this population increase? First, natural increase (more births than deaths), second, migration into the United Kingdom/England. We will explore these factors further.

(i) Natural increase

Natural increase (excess of births over deaths), will contribute just under half the population growth to 2021. It may at first sight seem surprising that there is still a natural increase, bearing in mind, as will be discussed later, that the fertility rate of women is below the replacement level and has been so for about two decades. How then can there be more births than deaths in any given year?

The answer depends, first, on the fact that in the absence of migration, and with constant mortality, the rate of population change does not depend solely on fertility rate, but also on the historic age distribution in the population. Imagine two populations with no migration and the same fertility and mortality rates, but the proportion of persons in the 15-45 age groups (child-bearing age groups) was 60% in the one, and only 40% in the other. Clearly the former population will produce more babies than the latter population. Now people born in the second post war baby boom (mid 1950s to late 1960s), still now in the child-bearing age groups, have been and still are, helping to slow down the fall in the number of births. The answer depends, second, on the fact that the mortality rate is not constant over time. Expectation of life at birth keeps increasing - i.e. the death rate goes down, altering the ratio of births to deaths.

(ii) Net inward migration

There is both migration into the UK (inward migration) and out from the UK (outward migration). Since the early 1980s, the former has exceeded the latter - i.e. there has been a net inward migration. The actual level of net inward migration varied considerably from year to year, the lowest was in 1988 when it was 18,000. Between 1986 and 1995, the highest levels were recorded for 1994 and 1995 - nearly 109,000 each year. The 1996 and 1997 levels were 93,000 and 92,000 (ONS, 1999a). It is England that has received the majority of the net international migration.

Most recently, it has been concluded that... "the underlying trend for the UK as a whole has clearly been upward, with annual net migration in the four years leading to mid-1998 averaging over 100 thousand persons per year. Indeed, it is estimated that in the calendar year 1998, net inward migration to the United Kingdom rose sharply to 178 thousand, the highest figure on record" (ONS 2000).

How important is international migration compared with natural increase in causing the rise in the total population size in England? According to Champion et al (1998), during the 1990s it was responsible on average for over one-third of the country's population growth, and in the mid-1990s it was contributing more than natural increase. As far as the immediate future is concerned (to 2021), just under half the projected population growth is attributable to natural increase, *just over half to immigration* (Section G below)

So contrary to what many people think, in-migration will be a major cause of future population growth in England. **It is important to realise that this in-migration will therefore be a major cause of the loss of countryside to house building (the relationship between immigration and greenland loss to housing is clearly set out in Fig. 11 page 194).**

And finally, the extent of immigration has been under-estimated in recent times and this led to an underestimation of population growth. Thus Bramley (1996) comments that the rise in population in England in the 1980s was bigger than expected and concludes this was caused by two factors: (i) greater than expected longevity of the population; (ii) "more positive international migration flows".

C. Immigrant groups

(i) Composition and distribution

The following are some of the facts about the net immigrant populations of the last ten years (ONS, ibid, Champion et al. ibid).

(a) In terms of age structure, most of the immigrants belong to the 15 - 44 age groups. For example, for the period

1996-98, out of a net immigration of 83 thousand, 70 thousand were in the 15-44 age groups.

(b) Occupation categories. IPS studies for England and Wales showed that with both inward and outward migration, about 55% were employed people. Students and professional/managerial people both made much bigger contributions to the net inward migration than did the other categories (manual/clerical; housewives; other adults; children).

(c) Citizenship. The last ten years has seen a net loss of British Citizens, and a net gain of non- British citizens. For example, in 1995, it is estimated that the net loss of British passport holders was 27,000, while the net gain of non-British citizens was 136,000.

(d) Ethnicity. During the last ten years, the biggest contributions to net immigration for the UK as a whole have been the New Commonwealth Countries followed by the European Union. For England as a whole, the contribution from 'Other Foreign Countries' comes up roughly to the same level as EU (in official publications, immigrant citizenship and origins are often divided into the following categories: European Union (EU), Old Commonwealth (OC), New Commonwealth (NC) and Other Foreign Countries OFC). The Old Commonwealth consists of Australia, Canada, New Zealand, and the Republic of South Africa. The New Commonwealth includes all the other Commonwealth Countries and British overseas territories. "Other foreign" now includes Hong Kong).

(e) Geographical distribution of immigrants. In terms of the Regions of England, migrants have concentrated in London and the South East.

(ii) Growth and distribution since the Second World War of the ethnic minority populations

There have been considerable flows of ethnic minority groups into Great Britain since the Second World War. The countries of origin of these migration flows have changed over the years. The earliest major immigration came from the West Indies and Africa. Later, the major inflow was from India, followed later still by inflows from Pakistan and Bangladesh.

Continued immigration and high fertility has meant that there has been a massive almost continuous growth both of total ethnic minority numbers and the percentage of the total British population comprising ethnic minority groups. The approximate total size of the ethnic minority populations changed from 886,000 to 2.1 million from 1966 to 1980, and now stands at a over 3 million. The 'New Commonwealth' minority populations have increased rapidly from negligible numbers in 1945 to about 2.5 million in 1987; from 1971 to 1987 the population doubled (Coleman and Salt, 1992; Owen, 1996). It is thought that the ethnic minority/White mix in England will change from 5.55%/94.5% in the mid-1990s to 15%/85% at mid 21st Century (reported in Champion et al 1998).

In terms of the geographical distribution of ethnic groups immigrants since the Second World, these have tended to concentrate in the conurbations, and especially in the inner cities, partly because this is the only place that cheap housing is available, partly because members of ethnic groups like usually to remain in close contact with people of the same group. This leads to the next point.

(iii) The situation in London

At present, the total ethnic minority population of London is already very high – 24%, that is roughly one person in every four comes from an ethnic minority group (reported by Lett and Brangwyn, in Bate et al, 2000). We will see in the next section that emigration from London has been to a large extent balanced by international immigration. At the same time we saw above that the ethnic minority groups are a very large component of the net immigration stream. Further, the higher than average fertility of some major ethnic minority groups means that natural increase from the total ethnic minority population in London is higher than from the white group. The consequence of these facts is that the total ethnic minority share of the London population is projected to increase. We will return to the London situation in the next section.

D. Migration within England

(i) Movement away from cities

Throughout the world for a very long time people have been moving from rural areas into cities - the process of 'urbanisation'. The rapid growth of the world population in recent decades has accelerated this process. We now have numerous cities world wide that are so large that they are termed 'mega-cities' (defined by the United nations as cities with at least eight million inhabitants).

The more developed parts of the world show a high degree of urbanisation - In 1994, more than 75% of the population of Northern Europe, Western Europe, North America, Japan and Australia-New Zealand were urban dwellers. Within Europe, more than 85% of the population were living in cities in the Netherlands, the UK, Denmark and Germany. Southern Europe has a lower level of urbanisation (UN 1995b).

If we consider the UK and the period since 1950, the total number of people living in rural areas has actually declined, while the total number of people in urban areas has increased. So the proportion of the UK population living in urban areas has increased (UN, ibid):

% of population residing in urban areas

Date	1950	1955	1960	1965	1970	1975	1980	1985	1990	1995
%	84.2	84.9	85.7	87.1	88.5	88.7	88.8	88.8	89.1	89.5

However, in recent decades, there has been considerable migration in the opposite direction   - people moving from large cities to small urban areas, and from both of these to rural areas - the process of counter-urbanisation. This was particularly marked in the 1970s and 1980s. So that although throughout the period from 1950 to the present, the percent of the total UK population residing in urban areas as a whole has increased, several cities, including Birmingham, Leeds, London and Manchester, showed negative growth between 1970 and 1985, and barely grew between 1985 and 1995. London especially, experienced a negative rate of over 1%, losing 1,259,000 people between 1970, and 1985 (UN, ibid).

The inner cities in Britain have in general been losing population through counter-urbanisation for decades, and evidence from the 1991 census showed this process was still continuing. This is interesting in the light of the fact that successive governments since the mid 1970s have been trying to regenerate inner cities. We will return to this matter in a later chapter.

Counter-urbanisation was defined above as movement from large cities to small urban areas, and from both these to rural areas. So it is not just a question of movement from town to country. We can think of a hierarchy of areas with different degrees of 'urbanness', from inner parts of cities, to outer parts of cities and to small towns and so on down to remote rural areas. This process of counter-urbanisation then can be likened to a cascade from the most to the least urban areas, so marked that it is more like a downpour than a trickle. Furthermore, the process was consistent across Britain (Champion, 1997; see also DoE, 1996).

This hierarchy of urbanness in relation to counter-urbanisation is well illustrated by looking at the percentage change of population size (positive or negative) in relation to population size. This is done for the period 1981-1991 in the form of a histogram by Breheny and Rookwood (1993). The smallest population size category 'remote, mainly rural areas' had the biggest positive change in population. At the other extreme the largest population category is 'metropolitan, principal cities', with the biggest negative change in population. Intermediate categories such as 'resort, port and retirement districts' and small cities show a gradual progression from one extreme to the other. The situation was broadly similar in 1990-1991.

However, the situation is more complicated than the above analysis based on net migration implies. First, the degree of counter-urbanisation, and in terms of rural areas, the degree of rural in- and out-migration varies between age groups. Now for some time there has been a national pattern of a general ageing of the population structure, which of course has taken place in rural as well as urban areas. But the increase of the older age groups in many rural areas has been increased by the in-migration of retired, or about to retire people, drawn by the peacefulness and beauty of the countryside. At the same time opportunities for education and employment in towns has led to young people moving from rural to urban areas. In fact considering all age groups, the 16-19 and 20-24 age groups show a net movement up the urban hierarchy towards more urban places, the only age groups to do so. Second, at a local scale, there is a great variety of patterns of population movement. For example, within larger rural areas where the population has been growing, partly through in-migration, there may be many parishes which show overall population loss (Rogers 1993).

Net-inward migration is a major source of population growth for England outside the more urban counties; the population of less urban counties has also been growing through natural increase. This is because earlier in-migration has produced a large second-generation population entering family -building age. This however, has not happened in some counties, especially those where retirement inward migration has taken place along the South Coast, and their populations are only maintained by fairly high levels of inward migration (Champion et al 1998).

Counter-urbanisation in the SE Region, and especially London has been partly offset by inward migration, not only from other regions, but also more particularly by international migration. During 1987 -1994, while London lost 55,000 people a year through migration with the rest of England, it gained around 2,000 a year from the rest of the UK and over 37,000 a year through net immigration from overseas, including the Irish Republic; this meant that the overall migration deficit was just under 18,000 a year. It is thought that the high level of out-migration is either caused by or at least facilitated by the large net immigration gains. The biggest contribution to the international immigration to London came from the New Commonwealth countries. The counter-urbanisation involving London shows variation between ethnic groups. The Outer London Boroughs are experiencing substantial losses of Whites, while other ethnic groups such as Bangladeshis show net inflows to Outer London from Inner London (Champion et al ibid).

Now the movement out of London and other cities is dominated by wealthy people (T. Champion, in Bate et al 2000); on the other hand, while immigration to London includes many well to do people from other parts of Britain, it is dominated by international migration, of which a substantial part consists of relatively poor people. **So it is not surprising that a recent seminar organised by JRF concluded that migration is currently worsening the polarisation of society into the rich and the poor** (Bate et al, 2000).

A basic cause of counter -urbanisation is the attraction of living in a rural environment. FoE (1994) mentions a 1992 study by R. Mintel, which found that when people were questioned about this matter, ten percent said that they planned to move from an urban to a rural area in the next five years, and 45% gave their main reason for wanting to make such a move, the appeal of open space in rural areas. And a survey by the CC in1997 showed for city dwellers 51% of inner city residents and 43 % suburban residents would like to live in a village or the countryside, and across England as a whole, 54% would like to do this - well over twice the proportion that do so now (Champion et al, ibid).

Counter-urbanisation and its causes will be taken up again later. But this counter-urbanisation stream predominantly involves the better- off White families headed by 25-44 year olds who can afford to buy their own homes; low-paid workers and members of ethnic minority have been little involved, except for the sort of inner to outer city movement described above for London.

(ii) Movement between and within the Regions of England

Population re-distribution within England during the 1990s has been dominated by the counter-urbanisation cascade, in comparison with which inter-regional shifts of population have been subdued. However, the general North to South shift has continued (except for a brief period around the beginning of the 1990s). All four northern regions (North West, North, Yorkshire and Humberside, West Midlands) experienced net loss of population. The South, the South West, East Anglia and East Midlands regions experiencing net gains. In contrast, the South East has averaged out-migration to the rest of England. In terms of counties, it is the less heavily populated counties in the South West, East Anglia and the Midlands which have experienced the fastest relative rates of population increase through internal migration; but in most years it is the shire counties around the edge of the 'Greater' South east which have experienced the highest absolute migration gains (Champion et al, ibid).

London has played a very important role in the picture of migration within England. We have already seen that it is the major destination for international migrants. It also received migrants from other urban areas in England. But in turn, London is often the main supplier of immigrants to other regions.

Finally, although attention is often, and rightly focused on movement between regions, it must be remembered that the majority of internal migration moves are over short distances. More than half the moves probably were within districts. And about a quarter of moves took place between districts but within regions (Champion et al, ibid).

E. The causes of migration within England

It is difficult to determine the relative importance of possible causes of migration within England. In the first place, many different factors are involved, and they interact in various ways. In the second place, even if survey indicated an association between two variables, this would not prove that one caused the other. For example if there were a correlation between strength of a migration stream and the supply of new housing, this would not prove that housing supply stimulated migration, or the opposite possibility. In other words, correlation does not prove causation. The situation is further complicated by the fact that any given person may have two or more reasons for making a move. Further, a particular migration stream will usually contain people with varied motivation. Nevertheless, there seems to be general agreement on the range of factors that to different extents determine migration within England, and some agreement on their relative importance.

One classification of determinants of migration is given by Champion et al (ibid). I give one example of each determinant:

      (i) Demographic factors. Locations where higher education places and jobs are available will attract young adults.

(ii) Social and cultural attributes. If one speaks of an 'occupational hierarchy' (managers and administrators at the top and manual workers at the bottom), it seems the higher up this hierarchy a person is, the further that person is likely to have to move to find a suitable job.

(iii) Labour market factors. People move from where the right job is not available, to where it is available.

(iv) Housing factors. Council tenants are less likely to migrate inter-regionally than owner-occupiers.

(v) Environmental factors. The physical attractiveness of the countryside is one factor drawing in certain categories of people such as those who are retiring.

(vi) Public policy factors. People may move between boroughs because one borough may have lower taxes than another borough.

In view of the fact that a central concern of this book is the loss of green land to housing, we need to think which of the migration flows are particularly relevant to this topic. Probably the two most important are first, the counter-urbanisation - putting pressure on green land around all urban areas; second, the north to south movement which puts undue pressure to provide housing in one Region while leaving behind vacant properties in other regions. We now explore these flows.

(i) Causes of counter-urbanisation

As far as counter-urbanisation is concerned Champion et al (ibid) identify the main reason for leaving cities as being that they fall short in social and environmental terms (a 'push' factor), and at the same time, and perhaps more importantly, people are questing for the 'rural idyll' (the 'pull' factor). These factors are combined with an overall preference for lower density living, which means that rural areas are preferred to towns. The 'rural idyll' however, has two components. First, rural areas offer a physically more pleasant environment (quieter, attractive landscape, etc). Second there is the perception that communities in rural areas are closer to an ideal than city communities - they are more compact, more sharing, they have a 'traditional' set of social activities. To the present writer it is ironic that the very people who have moved into rural areas in search of this idyll are often the very people who are destroying it.

The underlying reason for preference for the rural scene seems to be that there is a strong predilection to live in the countryside -there is a force deep in the English psyche, which is driving people to aspire to a rural lifestyle. There seems to be some difference here between England and continental countries where more people seem to prize urban living.

Employment factors are also involved in counter-urbanisation. The general de-centralisation of business means that there are more opportunities for non-agricultural employment in rural areas now than there were a few decades ago. Furthermore, the migration into rural areas of retiring people and families leads to increased needs for services, which attracts labour. Too much should not however be placed on this factor in view of the fact that many villages have seen a decline in their services.

Finally, as Champion el al (ibid) observe, underlying the whole movement out of cities, there is, arguably, an element of 'one-upmanship' - the move into the countryside being the pinnacle of social achievement. To put it another way, there is a 'social cachet' conferred on people who are able to afford to move into the countryside. The result of this is that "the countryside has become increasingly 'middle-class' and remains almost exclusively 'white' ".

(ii) Causes of movement from the north to the south

The interaction between the various possible causes of inter-regional migration are so complex, that it is difficult to make any generalisation about any one factor without qualifying it with so many 'ifs' and 'buts' that the generalisation itself ceases to have much value.
And most of the generalisations that can be made are so obvious anyway, that one scarcely needs lots of painstaking data collection and statistical analysis to reach them. Further, the whole situation is complicated by the fact that migration flows change with changes in the overall economic circumstances and business cycle.

If we consider the classification of circumstances at origin and destination, it seems safe to conclude the following factors influence the amount of migration flow between regions:

(i) Labour market factors: The extent of job redundancies at origin, and job vacancies at destination, together with the earnings offered with new jobs.

(ii) Housing Factors: 1. The availability of vacancies in the different housing tenures (public sector housing; privately rented housing; owner-occupied housing). 2. Variations in house prices and rents, in terms of national averages, and more particularly, variation between regions.

(iii) Environmental factors: Much the same factors are operating here as were considered in relation to counter-urbanisation above. So there will be an element of counter-urbanisation in the movement both of people from the north to the south, and vice versa, although this is unlikely to be a prime cause of movement. It seems likely to the present writer however that there may be a difference in the balance of 'push' and 'pull' factors. In all regions, many people will find that city congestion, pollution, high crime rates etc. act as push factors. But in as far as people may judge that the general urban environmental situation is not so bad in the south as it is in the north, that might be an additional factor spurring migration towards the south.

(iv) Public policy factors: 1. The provision of higher education places, which is associated with yearly migration of students. 2. People may move from one borough to another because boroughs have different tax levels. 3. The amount of land allocated by Local Authorities for housing.

The relative importance of these various factors vary with the age and employment status of individuals. Labour market factors are more important for the 25-59 year age groups than they are for retired people. And house price factors seem less important for those in work than those not in work, like retired people.

It seems to be generally agreed that housing factors are a critical factor underlying migration patterns in the UK (Champion et al, ibid). Here there is a strong interaction between the extent of migration and type of housing tenure. In terms of housing availability at destination, of the three types of housing tenure - public sector housing, privately owned housing, and privately rented housing, in the UK it seems to be the last category which most facilitates migration. And it is very relevant here that Britain has a relatively small percentage of its total housing in the privately rented sector compared with the USA and most European countries.

A useful insight into the relationship between housing tenure and migration comes from a study of housing tenure and employment across Europe. Two of the conclusions of the study were 1) countries with a high percentage of home ownership tend to have more unemployment than countries with a low percentage of home ownership; 2) using male employment as an index of employment level, the employment level is highest in countries with the largest percentage of housing in the private rented sector (Fig.3) (Oswald, 1999).

The hypothesis advanced to explain these correlations is as follows; it centres on the need for labour mobility in the modern industrialised world. In the first place, selling and buying a home is expensive, making home-owners less mobile than renters. Second, young people often lack capital, so they are at a disadvantage in a situation where ownership is the dominant tenure. Third. In an economy where people are immobile, workers will tend to do jobs for which they are not ideally suited; this inefficiency harms the economy, destroying jobs. Fourth, areas where there is a high home ownership level may act to deter entrepreneurs from setting up new operations. And lastly, home owners commute much more than renters and over longer distances, leading to transport congestion, making it more costly for everyone to get to work; a basic reason is that home owners who lose their job are willing to commute long distances to find work. If getting to work is more expensive, then there is a greater incentive not to work. Such considerations could lead to a "rekindling of the private- rented housing sector" (Oswald, ibid).

The hypothesis is not without its critics. They point out that at the present, Britain has a high level of home-ownership but a low level of unemployment. Nevertheless, most commentators do consider that providing more rented accommodation in an area might alter migration flows.

Perhaps one way then to help stimulate the regeneration of northern areas would be for the Government to intervene by introducing measures to ensure that more rented accommodation is made available in the north. A deliberate attempt to increase the rented sector might also reduce commuting, with obvious benefits of reducing traffic congestion and pollution.

Finally, the importance of government planning must be recognised as a major determinant of migration. Since the Second World War, Planning has developed to a) limit conurbation expansion through the development of Green Belts; b) direct growth outside of green belts to particular settlements, most importantly, the New Towns like Milton Keynes.

The amount of land allocated by Local Authorities for new housing will have an effect on migration flows. Now the situation in the past has been that sufficient land should be made available to ensure housing for the projected number of households in the sub-national projections. The problem with this is that these sub-national projections are based on past trends, and therefore will tend to be self-fulfilling - one assumes there is need in a given area for x new houses, so these

Unemployment Rates and Owner-Occupation Rates Today: The Main European Nations in the 1990s

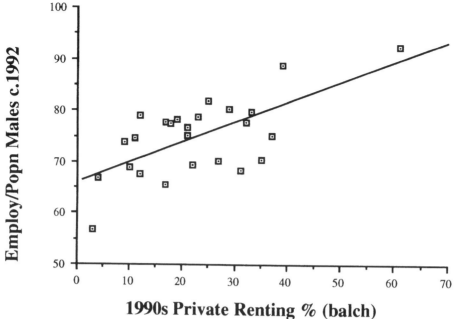

1990s Private Renting % (balch)

Each dot is a country. The observations are Austria (h=54%, u=5%), Belgium (65, 12), UK (65, 6), Denmark (55, 6), France (56, 11), W. Germany (42, 7), Italy (68, 12), Netherlands (45, 4), Spain (80, 18), Sweden (56, 6), Switzerland (28, 3), Ireland (76, 10), Finland (78, 13). Data for transition nations are not reliable and are omitted.

The unemployment data are the latest OECD numbers, and the owner-occupation rates are as recent as possible and are taken from UN census or similar sources.

The Relationship Between Countries' Employment Rates and the Size of their Privated Rented Housing Markets: 25 Industrial Nations in the 1990s

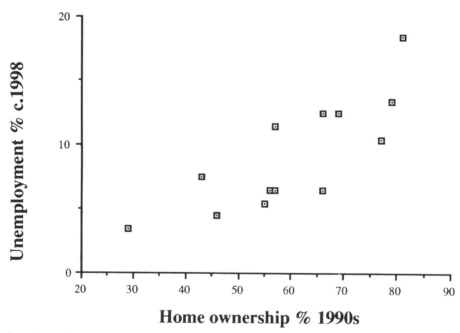

Home ownership % 1990s

The vertical axis is the male employment rate, expressed as a proportion of population. This is for men of ages 15-65. These data are for circa 1992 and come mostly from the OECD Employment Outlook, July 1995, Table A, 1992 column, p.204. For the Czech Republic, Hungary and Poland, the data are for 1993, and come from Table B, p.164, of OECD Employment Outlook July 1997. The horizontal axis is the proportion of people who rent. The data on housing are principally from Table 1.12, page 11, of Housing Policy in Europe, edited by Paul Balchin, Routledge, London and New York, 1996. For the Czech Republic, Hungary and Poland, the data come from the later pages of Balchin, including p.286. For New Zealand and Australia, the data are taken from p.184 of From Public Housing to the Social Market, edited by J. Kemeny, Routledge, London and New York, 1995. Marion Steele of the University of Guelph provided helpful information about Canada. Japanese and US data were imputed by making a small adjustment to (1 - home ownership rate), calculated from UN census data. The countries are Canada (renting % = 34, Employ/pop % = 69.5), Switzerland (60, 91.4), Japan (38, 87.8), Sweden (16, 76.7), Norway (18, 77.3), France (21, 68.5), Australia (20, 75.7), USA (32, 78.8), Netherlands (17, 76.5), UK (10, 73.6), W Germany (36, 74), Austria (22, 77.8), Belgium (30, 67.3), Denmark (24, 80.7), Finland (11, 66.6), Luxembourg (31, 76.8), New Zealand (20, 74), Ireland (9,67.8), Italy (8, 72.9), Spain (16,64.6), Greece (26, 69.1), Czec Rep (11, 78.1), Hungary (2, 55.6), Portugal (28, 79.4), Poland (3,65.9).

Fig. 3

Reproduced with the permission of Professor A. J. Oswald

are provided and this acts as a magnet to draw people into the area.

F. Uncertainties about future population size

In Section B above we saw how the populations of the UK and England are projected to continue to grow slowly for a few decades. It is generally thought however that around mid-century, population growth will cease, and population decline begin. But there are considerable uncertainties about these long-term projections, and there is the very real possibility that total population will continue to increase beyond mid-century. Before we explore these ideas further, a word about the population projections. These projections are made at least every two years. They are based on assumptions about birth rates, mortality rates, and fertility rates which seem most appropriate from the statistical evidence available at the time, although as far as migration is concerned, there has been a large subjective element in determining the migration assumptions (Shaw 1994). Sections (i) to (iv) and (vi) in the following account are partly taken from Barker (1998).

(i) General uncertainties about projections

There is a general uncertainty about long term projection as shown by Keyfitz (1981).
He examined a large number of past projections and compared them with what actually did eventually happen. He established that the interval of time over which a projection is made seems to have no effect on the accuracy. So the situation is that if we place confidence limits on a projection, these must fan out over time. Keyfitz concluded that relatively short - term forecasts, say up to 10 or 20 years, do tell us something, but beyond a quarter century, in his view we simply do not know what the population will do.

As far as England is concerned, uncertainty associated with projections is reflected by the fact that during the last two decades, population projections have under-estimated the actual rise in population (SSE, 1996; Bramley, 1996; Shaw, 1994; DETR, 1999a).

We now look at possible changes in fertility rate and net migration rate.

(ii) Total Fertility Rate

One measure of fertility used by demographers is Total Fertility Rate (TFR). Without going into its precise meaning, and how it is calculated, it can be regarded as a measure of the average number of children a woman would be expected to have during her reproductive life. Offspring are male and female, roughly in the proportion 1:1. Therefore one would expect the TFR corresponding to a stationary population (one neither increasing or decreasing) would be approximately two, which it is. However it is not exactly two. For the sex ratio at birth is not exactly 1:1 - there is a slightly lower proportion of females than males. Further, allowance has to be made for the small proportion of women who will die before the end of their reproductive life. So the TFR corresponding to a stationary population in Western Europe is about 2.1 rather than 2 (Brass, 1989).

Since the 1960s, TFR has fallen in western Europe as a whole, and it recent times has been under the replacement level (the Republic of Ireland is the most noticeable exception) (Lutz, 1994). In the United Kingdom TFR was fairly steady around 1.8 from 1981 to 1992, but fell to a low level of 1.7 in the mid 1990s. It is projected to rise to about 1.8 soon (ONS 1999).

The changes in fertility rate in recent decades in industrialised countries had taken place during a period of great sociological change. We may note first major changes in marriage and non-marital unions (Lutz, ibid):

   a) Divorce rates have increased in all industrialized countries.

   b) In many industrialized countries, including Britain, the proportion of the adult population that is married has decreased; at the same time there has been an increase in non-marital unions.

   c) There has been a trend to get married at an older age than in earlier decades.

Second, concomitant with these specific changes there has been a general sociological change, characterised by some as a change from a 'community' structure to a 'society' structure. Whereas in the 'community' structure, there are strong family ties and inter-dependence of people, in the 'society' structure family ties are loosened and people are more independent of each other (Lutz, ibid). These changes in turn have taken place against an economic background of changes in income, material standard of living, unemployment rate, etc.

What then of the future? Various factors could lead to either a decrease or an increase in fertility rate as discussed by

Day (1992), Sporton (1993), and authors in Lutz ed (1994); see also UN (1992b). These factors will be discussed in the following sections. Sufficient here to sound a word of caution: demographers have been proved wrong in the past as Brass (1989) explains. He points out that a fall in total fertility in most of Western Europe led to many demographers in the early 1930s to expect a major population decline in the then near future, and indeed this was the major theme of the second General Conference of the International Union for the Scientific Study of Population held in London in 1931. But a few demographers were not convinced, seeing the existing trend as a temporary fluctuation: the minority view was expressed that there was a real possibility of a restoration of the birth rate under certain possible cultural circumstances. And one worker reprimanded those who seem to regard human vital statistics, represented by curves in plotted charts, as inevitably destined to continue in the directions they had already taken, as if they were comparable to the curves of the heavenly bodies in space! In the event, these sceptics proved correct. Brass comments that demographers have no claim to be prophets, and urges them not to repeat the mistake of the 1930s. He argues that significant and unanticipated changes can take place from the interaction of external events and social responses.

Another example comes from a later decade. Projections made shortly after the Second World War failed to anticipate the baby boom of the 1960 (Shaw1994).

(iii) Decreased Fertility

Various considerations lead to the conclusion that fertility could decline further, or at least stay at its present level.

First, it is argued that the sociological changes discussed above in terms of a change from a 'community' structure to a 'society' structure, will maintain fertility below replacement level. Continued high divorce rates and low marriage rates might hold fertility down. For responsible people, the trend towards individualism and the desire not to limit future choice may mean that people are reluctant to commit themselves to have children with the future responsibilities that this entails. Further, knowledge of the existing high rate of parental separation, and that there is evidence that parental separation may do great harm to existing children, may lead to the avoidance of having children.

Second, there are likely to be further improvements of contraceptive technology. This will tend to reduce the number of unwanted births, as could extension of the practice of abortion.

Third, recent years have seen the development of increasing economic independence of women as more women enter the labour force. If this trend continues it may result in a more general postponement of marriage, which will tend to reduce total fertility.

Fourth, many hold that one cause of the recent decline in fertility has been the increasing hold of materialistic 'consumerism' on society. The idea is that people would supposedly rather invest in pleasure for themselves than in children; they would rather buy a new car than have another child; they would rather spend their time watching TY than changing babies diapers. Underlying this view is the notion that having children is work and not fun (Lutz, ibid).

(iv) Increased fertility

It is argued that there could be a return to an emphasis upon family and parenthood. Day (ibid) has pointed out that in the past, divorce has tended to reduce fertility levels, but he considers that this tendency might have reversed at least in the USA. He argues that divorced people, who, if they had remained in their first union might have only had one or two children and then ceased reproduction, might, on the formation of a subsequent union have desired more children because a) this could strengthen the new union, b) creation of further children would be a tangible expression of success following the failure of the earlier union. On the other hand there is evidence that fertility of cohabiting couples is lower than of their married counterparts, and if cohabitation increasingly became an alternative to, rather than a precursor of marriage, this might reduce fertility. If people find they receive insufficient emotional or psychic support from their jobs, religion, kin or neighbourhood, greater emotional value may be attached to children. The same thing could happen if society changes so that people perceive that their own control over their destinies is eroded, leading to further withdrawal into the support of a nuclear family.

Women's involvement in the labour force, which has increased in recent decades, could decrease, in favour of a return to the traditional mother and homemaker role. Various perceptions could lead to this change, for example, the perception that there are fewer opportunities for promotion for women than for men. Employment creates problems like the need for commuting and the lack of time for oneself or to be with ones children, and this could also encourage a reversal of role.

Changes in social policy and the economic situation could significantly reduce the need for an income, allowing more women to cease to be part of the labour force:

a) Some services or experiences may become available at a lower or even zero cost - e.g. aspects of entertainment and home maintenance.

b) The rate at which wants are created and maintained depends on various factors, but prominent amongst these is the advertising campaign. Change of government attitude, say to the environment, could lead to further limitations on advertising thus reducing the pressure to buy.

c) Certain goods, readily available now may become less available in future, reducing the need to produce an income: (i) goods that cease to become available because of increasing controls aimed at environmental quality; (ii) with continued decrease of available 'green land' and increasing pressure to prevent its loss the possibility to build vacation houses or buy a larger plot of land might disappear; (iii) certain "sights and experiences" such as those provided by areas of tourist appeal may be ruined or destroyed by overuse or over-development, leading, presumably, to reduced desire to spend money getting to or travelling in these areas.

d) Among the factors that encourage women to join the labour force, is the desire to have money not just for the bare essentials of life, but all the things that are considered desirable over and above the bare essentials. It is not impossible that a state of satiety may be reached.

Finally the conflict between a desire to be employed and a desire to bear and look after children and look after the home might be ameliorated. Participation in the labour force might become less demanding (as for example through the increasing development of home and computer based methods of earning an income, or though child care services being extended), allowing what have in the past been conflicting roles to be reconciled.

(v) Fertility in ethnic minority populations

So far we have treated the population of England as if it was a homogeneous group. However, there is a significantly sized ethnic minority group sector (EMGS) in the total population and this has been increasing faster than the population as a whole as we saw earlier. The fertility of this group then may have a significant effect on future total fertility rate. So we now briefly look at EMGS fertility rates. It must be born in mind that data from which to fully assess EMGS fertility rates is very incomplete, partly because of under-enumeration and refusal to answer survey questions, partly because surveys were not designed primarily for fertility studies (Coleman and Salt, 1992).

In the past the general picture is that with any particular ethnic group, the immigrant population had a higher fertility than the national fertility rate on arrival, but over a period of years in Britain, the fertility rate of that group gradually declined towards the national average (Haskey, 1992; Coleman and Salt, ibid). As mentioned in an earlier section, and thinking of mass flows post World War Two, the earliest to arrive were the Blacks (West Indians and Africans), followed by the Indians and later by people from Pakistan and Bangladesh (Haskey ibid). Now the fertility of the West Indian group has declined to a little above the White rate, the Indian group has declined a little, but not so much. With the Pakistani and Bangladesh groups, although fertility has declined, it is still high. Only Chinese and Arabs have probably a lower fertility than the Whites.

The age structure of present day EMGS populations gives a clue to the contribution of these populations to total future population size in England. It is worthwhile here to illustrate two main types of population structure. Fig. 4a shows the age structure of a slowly growing population -what we might call an 'old' population. Figure 4b shows the age structure of what we may term a 'young' population -the shape is pyramidal. So in contrast to the population of 4a, there are a greater proportion of young people and people at peak reproductive age. Consequently, a population like 4b is likely to have a higher birth rate than a population like 4a.

The majority White population group has an age structure similar to 4a. If we take the EMGS as a whole, it has a structure approximating to that of 4b. However, this overall EMGS structure masks considerable differences between different ethnic minority groups, and these differences partly at least are what you would expect from what has just been said about time of arrival and fertility rate decline. The Pakistani, Bangladeshi and 'Black Other' (i.e. Blacks not included in West Indian and African groups) have structures broadly similar to 4b, while the Indian, West Indian and African groups have age structures intermediate between the 4a and 4b types (Owen, 1996).

We can see that the Pakistani, Bangladeshi and Black Other groups are extremely youthful, so have the potential to continued rapid increase in the medium term (Owen, ibid).

How will the fertility of the EMGS groups change in the future? While there may continue to be convergence to the While fertility rate, there are considerations which make this uncertain, at least in terms of the speed of this convergence.

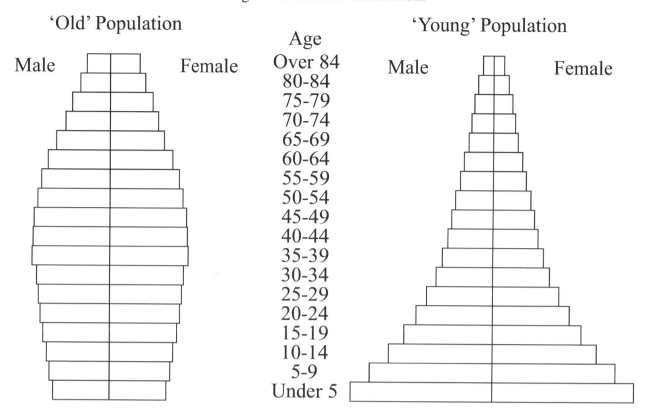

Numbers of people in different age groups
Fig 4

In the first place, there are features of society in the countries of origin which, carried over into England, may at least slow convergence in particular groups. For example, Pakistani and Bangladeshi groups are predominantly Muslim. The limited role outside the home, which is associated with Islam, may keep the fertility of these groups above the average. Second, Asians tend more than West Indians to have extended families, and there is with them a high occurrence of family enterprises. These differences may make high fertility seem less disadvantageous with Asians than with West Indians, as already mentioned (Coleman and Salt, ibid).

But there is another factor to be taken into consideration when considering possible future ethnic minority fertility rate, that is population competition. This was discussed in Chapter 1 Section G; it was pointed out there that one form of such competition is where a minority group feels threatened by 'absorption' into the majority group, making acceptance of family planning by that minority group more difficult (Coleman and Salt ibid). A minority group may even consciously adopt a policy of having large families to swell the ranks of its group.

(vi) Migration

At the outset it should be noted that the impact of migration on a community partly depends on the fertility rate. If the native population is growing through high fertility rate then migration will tend to have a smaller impact than if fertility is at low levels and remains like this for a long time. In the past, as far as Britain is concerned, there have been periodic migration flows in and out of the country but the effect on population growth in the longer run has been small (Brass, 1989). Now, if overall fertility continues at a little below replacement level, migration has the potential eventually to have a bigger effect.

On a world basis, just as there is great uncertainty about future fertility rates, there is great uncertainty about migration rates. In the first place, statistical information is often very limited, especially in developing countries. Statistics on legal immigration are fragmentary, but to this must be added sparseness of information on illegal immigration. Second, where statistical information is available, there is variation from country to country in what exactly is measured - on the indicators that can be used to assess migration (the United Kingdom has a relatively good system for this purpose, based on survey of travellers entering and leaving the UK by the principal air and sea routes, although this does not cover all immigration). Third, governments may be reluctant to give information for political reasons, including sensitivity to ethnic considerations. In fact countries are often guilty of "benign neglect", preferring to ignore the magnitude of flows rather than measure them adequately. Despite these uncertainties, it is concluded that international migration (between major world regions) has increased in recent years (Zlotnik, 1994).

What of the future for Europe and the UK? An important consideration here is the difference between an elderly, wealthy population in the developed world, and a young and poor population in the developing world, creating a potential for migration from the latter to the former. The wealth of the developed world is then a 'pull' factor. Another 'pull' factor in recent decades has been the recruitment of labour in Europe from the developing world. 'Push' factors in the developing world are starvation, persecution and wars (Oberg, 1994). An interesting 'pull' factor was mentioned by M. Gibney of Oxford University in a BBC current affairs discussion on immigration into England 16-12-99 (I shall refer to this programme again in Chapter 10), although I don't think he used the term 'pull factor'. He noted that migration connections establish themselves over time and so what starts off as a relative trickle of people migrating from one country to another, can emerge into a greater movement once migrant communities become settled within a particular country.

Clearly the immigration policies of countries are important in determining the extent of immigration. And Europe in general has very restrictive policies towards migration from other continents. But a restrictive policy is one thing, controlling illegal immigration quite another. As world population grows, so might illegal immigration. Any future major environmental catastrophe in the developing world could cause large migration flows. The predicted rise in sea levels through global warming will cause floods and loss of land in already overcrowded areas. The cities in these areas are usually already grossly overcrowded, so where can the people living in rural areas go? . Further, if ozone levels continue to be depleted, some areas of the globe may become uninhabitable. Loss of low-lying agricultural land through flooding and possibly ozone depletion will make it even more difficult to feed everybody. It seems then inevitable that an ever-increasing number of people will seek to enter countries in the developed world. We may note here the general conclusion that international migration is expected to show greater "volatility" in the future (Oberg, ibid).

Finally, if we think in terms of the determinants of future population size – fertility, mortality and migration, demographers seem to be agreed that the greatest uncertainty lies with migration. And ONS (1999b) points out that it is virtually impossible to predict changes in migration patterns beyond a few years into the future. This must be borne in mind when we come to look at actual population projections later.

(vii) Net Immigration into England

A note first on sources of information on immigration. It would be nice to have a single set of statistics that gave us reliable information on all aspects of migration to and from our country, and migration within the country. Such a set is not available. Where then does immigration information come from? For international migration, the most important source of information is the record of travellers entering and leaving the UK by the principal sea and air routes - the International Passenger survey (IPS). In general, this does not cover asylum seekers; it also does not include what are known as 'visitor switches' - people who enter the country as short term visitors, and would not therefore be classed as 'migrants' by the IPS. The Home Office supplies information on these categories of people. Finally, the IPS does not cover migration with the Irish Republic, which however is covered by the Labour Force Survey (LFS). Another important source of information on international migration is the Census, which is also important for within - country migration. However, the main source for monitoring migration within the UK is the National Health Service Register, which also provides some information on in-migration to the country. Additional sources of migration information are electoral registers and the Inland Revenue.

It is important to realise that none of these sources is perfect; they all have their drawbacks (Champion et all, 1998). For example, the IPS is based on interviews with a small fraction of the total number of people entering or leaving by air or sea; it is a voluntary survey (as is the LFS), not a random survey; and it is difficult to assess its accuracy because there is no other comparable survey. With the census, it is known that there is under-enumeration. It is thought, for example, that the 1991 Census might well have been about 2% short of the real figure for the total population of Great Britain. This is serious because it is thought that the missing people were mainly 20-29 year olds - the most migratory of the age groups. Coleman and Salt (1992) refer to what they call the classic problem in the enumeration of poor immigrants or minority populations from the Third World, for various reasons including deliberate evasion.

This leads on to the question of illegal immigration. While some vague estimates of the extent of this can be attempted, it is impossible to form a really adequate picture. One gets hints from various sources suggesting that such immigration might well be a flow of some size. For example, the National Criminal Intelligence Service this year reported on organised immigration crime (Internet link from BBC News 2nd Aug 2000), noting that the UK is currently one of the main destinations for nationals from various source countries, including the former Yugoslavia, Romania, China, Congo, Angola, Colombia and Ecuador. The report also refers to many illegal immigrants obtaining entry into the UK by assuming false identities. And by far the most common method of clandestine entry in 1998 was in heavy goods vehicles. Readers will recall the incident of the 58 illegal immigrants who died in the back of a lorry at Dover in June of this year.

Then there have been various reports of illegal immigrants working on farms and in factories supplying supermarket chains and in hotels and restaurants in London and elsewhere (for example, the BBC Panorama programme and subsequent correspondence - see BBC News 19th and 22nd June this year). However, some illegal immigrants are detected: in the twelve months up to June 1999, there were 16,400 recorded illegal entrants. This was about 1,400 more than in the previous twelve months (Jackson and Chilton, ibid).

Uncertainty about immigration statistics is encapsulated by Salt (1996) when he writes that one of the few things that migrant and ethnic minority groups have in common is that they are "generally poorly captured" in the official statistics. These uncertainties add to the difficulty of making long term projections of future migration patterns.

How accurate have projections turned out to be? In recent decades, the extent of future net immigration has been repeatedly underestimated, as was pointed out earlier. This fact is reflected in the migration assumptions underlying projections made at different times, assumptions that are based on analysis of average net inflows, especially data from the IPS surveys. For the UK as a whole, in the 1994-based projections, as in previous projections, it had been assumed that there would be a net inflow in the immediate years following, of 50,000 persons a year. The 1996-based projections raise this to 65,000 per year. And the 1998-based projections increase the number to 95,000 per year for 2001-02 onwards (91,000 for England alone).

But there was another change of assumption between 1994-based and earlier projections on the one hand, and the later projections. In the former, it had been assumed that after about twenty years, net immigration would gradually decrease to zero. But ONS (1999b) reporting on the 1996 -based projections say that it is no longer possible to justify this assumption. So for the 1996-based projections, a net inflow of 65,000 persons is maintained up to the end of the whole projection period. And the 1998 based projections also take the same line – the 91,000 per year is again maintained for the whole projection series (Government's Actuary's Department web site www.gad.gov.uk).

It is worth noting the effect that immigration has on overall fertility rate, as described in the commentary on the 1998-based projections. In recent times, migrants have been heavily concentrated at younger ages (15-44 age group). Now the increase of women at childbearing ages means that the projected future number of births also increases. We can add to this however. For it is not just a question of the proportion of the population that consists of women of childbearing ages. It is also a question of the fertility rates of the immigrants. We saw in Section C that the biggest contribution to immigrant inflow came from New Commonwealth Countries. The Pakistani group - one of the biggest ethnic minority groups in Britain, is the one receiving the greatest net immigration, and the source populations have high fertility rates.

It therefore seems likely that ethnic minority groups as a whole are going to make a very significant contribution to future population growth. Now if immigration flows increase considerably in the future (as seems likely to the writer at the moment), this will cause the total population to grow faster than currently projected (the projections being based primarily on past events), and what is more, instead of the population levelling off mid-century, it could continue on its upward path.

(viii) Net immigration and asylum seekers

Now the total net immigration figures for the 1994,1996 and 1998 based projections break down into components as follows:

	1994-based projections	1996-based projections	1998-based projections
IPS	+25,000	+45,000	+65,000
Irish Republic	+5,000	0	-5,000
Asylum seekers	+5,000	+5,000	+20,000
Visitor switchers	+15,000	+15,000	+15,000
Total	+50,000	+65,000	+95,000

Sources: ONS 1999b; ONS 2000. © Crown Copyright 1999, 2000. Data reproduced by permission of ONS.

There is considerable uncertainty about the future numbers of asylum seekers. Applications for asylum have been increasing. Thus Coleman and Salt comment that one of the important trends in international migration during the 1980s was the growing numbers of those seeking asylum. Indeed almost all countries in Western Europe had experienced increased applications.

From 1982 to 1988, the annual number of applications varied around 4,000, but they rose up to 44,845 in 1991. Applications then fell in 1992 and 1993, following the introduction of measures to deter fraudulent applications, but the rose again. And these figures, as also the ones now given, exclude dependents.

1988	1989	1990	1991	1992	1993	1994	1995	1996	1997	1998
3998	11640	26205	44840	24605	22370	32830	43965	29640	32500	46015

Data in HO (1999). Crown copyright material is reproduced with the permission of the Controller of HMSO.

Now Jackson and Chilton (1999) record that the number of applications for asylum received in the UK in the twelve months ending 30 June 1999 was 57,800, which was 22,000 more than in the previous 12 months.

It is widely accepted that many persons who are not suffering persecution, try to get accepted as asylum seekers when they really are simply seeking a better way of life – that is they are really economic migrants. Now it is often very difficult to be sure that an applicant has really been fearing persecution and is therefore eligible for consideration for asylum. And there is evidence which suggests that sometimes, people might have be granted asylum who have not really been under threat of persecution. This matter was brought to the public attention on the 13th of January this year by an article in the Independent Newspaper and reporting on the BBC. Apparently some legal firms have been abusing the asylum procedures to get people in to the UK who have no legitimate claim to asylum on the basis of current law. This will be enlarged upon in Chapter 13 Section A.

If we leave on one side bogus asylum seekers, and think in terms only of people with a genuine fear of persecution, there were probably already around 15-20 million in the world in 1992 (Coleman and Salt,1992). If as seems likely to the present writer, strife and persecution become more widespread in the world, the number of people who are persecuted or who fear persecution may well rise considerably, leading to a massive increase in the number of people seeking asylum in the developed world.

G. Actual projections for the future

(i) Europe

Projections for future populations are based on assumptions about the three determinants of population trends – fertility, mortality and migration. Various scenarios are prepared differing from each other in these assumptions. According to the United Nations, the most likely outcome, with 'middle of the way' assumptions about the three variables, has the total population of the whole of Europe decreasing fairly rapidly (in millions): 1995: 728; 2000: 729; 2025: 702; 2050: 628 (UN, 2000); on the other hand Lutz and Scherbov (1999) have the population of the 15 member states of the European Union (EU) rising from the then level of 375 million to about 390 million in 2020, followed by a moderate decrease to 377 million by 2050 and they concluded that population decline in the medium term is not a likely prospect for the EU. Two things must be noted about these estimates. First the UN projections include the former communist East Block and these countries have a faster declining population than Western Europe. Second, assumptions and methodology differ between the two projections.

It is widely believed that the population of Europe will continue to age. Lutz and Scherbov (ibid conclude that the proportion of the EU population above age 60 will increase from 22% in 2000 to 34% in 2050. However, this process of ageing will not go on indefinitely. With constant fertility and mortality rates it will normally not take more than two or three generations to produce a stable age structure (Day, 1992, referring to the work of S.H. Preston and colleagues).

(ii) UK and England

We saw above that the UN prepares projections in relation to various scenarios which make different assumptions about fertility, mortality and migration. UK Government statisticians do likewise. The most likely outcome scenario (the Principal scenario) yields the following information (ONS 2000):

Principal Scenario projections

The population of the United Kingdom is expected to rise from 59,954 thousand in 2001 to 63,642 thousand by 2021. The corresponding figures for England are 50,187 and 53,715. It is projected that the UK and England populations will peak at nearly 65 million and 55 million respectively in 2036, and then gradually start to fall. So the population of England is projected to increase by roughly 5 million before it begins to decrease – a massive increase. Migration will cause a little over half the projected increase in population (ONS, 2000; data © Crown Copyright 2000, reproduced by permission of ONS).

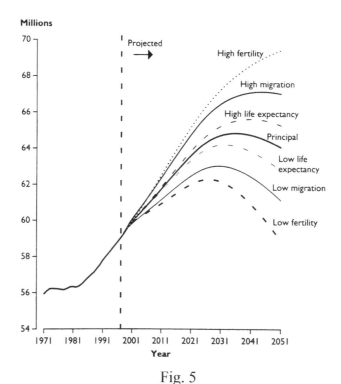

Actual and projected population according to principal and illustrative variant projections, United Kingdom, 1971-2051

Fig. 5

Source: ONS 2000. © Crown Copyright 2000. Graph reproduced by permission of ONS.

It is worth noting the very great differences between different scenarios (Fig. 5). In particular note how the high migration scenario would have the UK population rising to a much higher level than in the Principal scenario. Note also that these different scenarios are not meant to be upper and lower limits to what may occur, but only "plausible alternative scenarios" (ONS, ibid)

Earlier in this chapter I pointed out that in recent decades, population projections have underestimated the actual total rise in population. It is therefore interesting to compare two of the recent projections for England – the 1996 and 1998-based, the latter in italics.

Projected components of change, Annual averages in thousands

	1996-2001	2001-6	2006-11	2011-16	2016-21
Births	607	585	575	583	591
	605	*594*	*589*	*598*	*606*
Less Deaths	525	520	514	515	526
	521	*512*	*506*	*507*	*520*
Natural Increase	81	65	61	68	64
	81	*82*	*83*	*91*	*86*
Migration	75	66	66	66	66
	135	*91*	*91*	*91*	*91*
Total increase	156	131	127	134	130
	216	*173*	*174*	*182*	*177*

Sources. 1996-based: C. Shaw 1998, © Crown Copyright 1998, data reproduced by permission of ONS.
1998-based: GAD, 2000, data reproduced by permission of GAD.

Once again we see the later projection giving a higher population rise than the earlier projection.
And we see the importance of net immigration as a cause of the difference between the projections.

Finally, just one more word about the limitations of all long term projections, and therefore all long term forecasting. We have already referred to the failure of demographers to foresee fertility changes. This and other forecasting failures were taken up by Keyfitz (1996). He draws attention to the complexity of the issues involved with forecasting. There are a large number of causative factors at work, which interact in a complex way. Sometimes we are not even sure of the direction of causation. For example, what is the relationship between women going out to work and women having fewer children? Is the relationship that women have increasingly gone out to work and therefore have had fewer children? Or is the relationship rather that some other factor caused women to have fewer children, which together with more automated homes made housework less of a full time job, so that it was less necessary for households to have two co-operating adults, with the result that women could increasingly go out to work? Forecasting really can only be optimised through a close co-operation between specialists in various fields - demographers, economists, social scientists, etc. But the whole tendency in the development of science has been towards the development of more specialised disciplines, making it more difficult to adopt an inter-disciplinary approach. This is aggravated by the fact that the various disciplines start from such different assumptions that their results can become irreconcilable.

H. Growth in the number of households in England

Clearly, if total population rises, the number of dwellings needed will rise, and the more greenland will be lost to housing development. To explore this further we need household number statistics and projections.

(i) Projections

The 1996-based projections (DETR Oct 1999a) have the number of households in England increasing from 20.2 million in 1996 to 24.0 million by 2021 – an increase of 3.8 million (19% increase). This is clearly a massive increase, which will inevitably lead to increased pressure to release greenfield land for housing. However, when I had virtually finished writing this book, a report of the JRF was published (Bate et al, August 2000). This concludes that the increase in the number of households from 1996 to 2021 will be far greater than projected from the 1996-based projections – 4.3 million households instead of 3.8 million! The basic reason for this increase is that the 1998 population projections put the 2016 population of England 999,000 higher than the 1996-based projections. And the reasons for this increase in projected population are that a) male death rates are lower; b) the net rate of immigration from outside the UK is projected to be higher than in the earlier projections (as we saw earlier in this Chapter).

The DETR (ibid) publication just mentioned provides the latest full analysis of the situation, so the following notes are based on that report. Now in recent times household growth has been at a faster rate than population growth, because other factors besides population growth, such as increase in one-person households, contribute to the growth in household numbers. So to what extent is population growth responsible for household number growth?

Now it is possible to analyze the increase in the number of households into its component causes. These components are:
- C1.The projected growth in the total adult private household population.
- C2. The change in the age structure of the population;
- C3. Changes in the marital status of the population;
- C4. Changes in 'household representative rates'.

The last component requires some explanation. The 'household representative' in censuses is generally the oldest male in the household (but with female lone parent households it is female). Household representative rate is the proportion of a population group that are household representatives.

In the following table I have combined the last two components with the 'remainder' (figures from DETR, ibid).

Changes in number of households (thousands)

Component:	C1 adult Population		C2 age structure		C3 & 4 & remainder		TOTAL
	No.	%	No.	%	No.	%	
Period							
1971-1996	1,996	47	841	20	1398	33	4235
1996-2021	2,163	57	780	20	870	23	3814

Crown copyright is reproduced with the permission of the Controller of Her Majesty's Stationery Office.

From this table we can see that the growth of the adult population is the biggest contributor to the total household growth in terms of arithmetic percentage. Further, this percentage, 47% in the earlier 25-year period, is projected to rise by 10% to 57% for the current 25-year period. If we put together changes in the size of the adult population and its age structure, the figures are 67% and 77%.

The projected increase in households can also be analysed in terms of types of household which are:
Married couple household representatives;
cohabiting couple household representatives;
lone parent household representatives;
other multi-person household representatives;
one-person household representatives

Both in 1971-96, and in the projections for 1996-21, the reduction in married couple households is slightly more than offset by an increase in cohabiting couples. But the most noticeable fact from the analysis is that the one-person households make the biggest contribution to increase of total households in both periods.

(ii) Uncertainties about the household projections

It is important to remember that there is considerable uncertainty about the projections. They are based on a series of separate assumptions, which may be grouped into three categories:
Assumptions about population – birth, death and migration rates;
Assumptions about marital status and cohabitation;
Changes in household representative rates.

In view of the facts that this book places special emphasis on population factors, and that the adult population growth accounts for over half the projected increase in households, we deal here just with the population aspects.

Of the three components of population change – births, deaths and migration, the latter is officially regarded as the most uncertain, as was discussed earlier. Now the population projections give, besides the 'central' or most likely scenario projection, variant projections that assume higher or lower values for the three components, based on reasonable upper or lower limits for these components. Now the high/low migration projections assume a net immigration of 40,000/year plus/minus the values for the central projection. Translated into number of households this gives +/- nearly half a million households by 2021 (plus 450,000, minus 410,000).

(iii) Regional distribution

In view of the movements of population within England discussed in an earlier section, it should come as no surprise that the increase of households during the projection period is spread unevenly over the country. The largest increases in households are projected to occur in southern regions, the lowest increase in the North-east Region. Within the south, London is projected to have the highest growth of the four southern regions. There are significant differences between the pattern of changes that took place in the 1971-96 period and the pattern projected for 1996-2011. Thus 42% of the increases in the former period were in the midlands and north, in contrast to only 34% of the increases projected for 1996-2021. London experienced 7% of the net increase 1971-96, but is projected to receive 17% in the present projection period (DETR, ibid).

The later JRF report referred to earlier (Bate et al, ibid) emphasises the pressure that will be put on the South East Region. This regions population is expected to rise by 50,000 people a year.

This increase comes from a) natural increases (more births than deaths), b) the net migration out of London to the rest of the South, c) the net inward migration from outside the UK. It is concluded that even if the hoped for urban renaissance in the North and the Midlands materialises, there will still be large increases in population in the South.

I. Loss of greenland to housing and other development

Green land is lost because of a variety of types of development – mineral extraction, the building of reservoirs to increase water supply, industrial development, road building and housing. The last three categories collectively account for continued urbanisation (although of course, road building is not confined to towns), and it is urbanisation that causes most of the loss of green land. Since housing accounts for about seven tenths of land in urban uses, house building can be regarded as the driving force behind green land loss (SSE, 1996). It is important to note that new house building has environmental effects over and above the loss of green land for houses and related facilities (roads, etc). Thus in 1998 CPRE estimated that on the basis of then current household projections, new housing development could generate demands for over 80 new quarries, as well as requiring extra water resources equivalent to 20 million baths a day and disposal sites for rubbish equivalent to 180,000 dumper loads per year (CPRE, 1998).

How much land will be lost to continued urbanisation in the future?

A fundamental problem here is how to define urban land. It is generally agreed that by urban land one does not just mean the area of cities; 'urban' also includes built up areas in the countryside (small towns and villages). But how does one classify an area such as a city recreation ground, which in any case may be partly green and partly concrete? As for predicting future changes, does one do this on the basis of recent conversion rates, or on current stated policy objectives, or on the projected number of future households, or what? Not surprisingly then, there is disagreement both about the area of land already urbanised and the rate of future (short and medium term) conversion of rural to urban land. We now examine two approaches used a few years ago, which led to different conclusions.

The first was that of the DoE (1996a) and Bibby and Shepherd (1997). They estimated the size of urban area directly from ordnance survey maps and statistics on land use change, as described by the latter authors. The method for projecting future conversion of rural to urban land is based on relating urban area to the level of housing output. Use is made of the standardized land requirement (SLR), which is a measure of the net change in the area of land in overall urban use associated with every 1,000 houses built (Bibby and Shepherd discuss the various factors that affect SLR - urban recycling is a very important factor: in urban areas SLR will tend to be low because much development can be accommodated in recycled land, without using new green land). The assumption underlying the projections for the future is that sufficient dwellings will be built to match projected changes in the number of households. In other words, the projections are based on the government's household projections.

The second approach was that of Sinclair (1992), who is critical of the reliability of the official statistics used by the DoE for its estimates of present urban area and future projections. His procedure is to divide England into four land use categories - managed land, rough grazing, woodland, and urban. The first three of these categories together make up rural land. Using various data sources available he develops what he calls 'consensus figures' for past and present areas of the three rural categories. Basically, the urban area is then determined as the difference between the total rural area and the total land area of England.

The estimates given in DoE, and Bibby and Shepherd are as follows. In 1991, about 10.5% of the total land area of England was in urban use. Since 1981 the average rate of loss of rural land to urban land was estimated to be 6,800 ha/year. By 2016, the urban area was projected to increase to 11.9%, the average rate of rural -urban conversion being similar to the present average, i.e. 6,800ha/year.

Sinclair estimates the land in urban use in 1991 to be much higher - about 14.9% of the England total land area. The current rate of rural -urban conversion was estimated at 11,000ha/year. If current rates of rural - urban conversion continue, the urban area would have increased to 17% by 2016, and 20% by the middle of this coming century! Further, Sinclair estimates that between 1945 and 1990 the total area of land changing from rural to urban use was greater than the combined areas of Greater London, Berkshire, Herefordshire and Oxfordshire.

Now I reported the above estimates on loss of land to urban development in my previous publication (Barker ,1998), concluding:

"Even if we suppose that the DOE figures are closer to the mark, the figures are deeply worrying, especially if we consider the long-term future. People alive in two centuries time will not so much be concerned with what has happened in just the next two or three decades, but rather what has happened in the whole two centuries. What is likely to happen in the future? Clearly the rate of rural-urban conversion will depend first on government policy - on the extent that the government is concerned to prevent further urban sprawl and the extent that its aims are put into practice"

However, new population projections and new household projections have become available since this publication, as we saw earlier. These suggest there will be far more households by 2016 than was previously thought to be the case.

In Section F (vii) I pointed out that net immigration is projected to increase the UK population by 95,000 every year, rather than 65,000 as earlier thought. Now that is equivalent to a town the size of Oxford every 18 months (Coleman, 2000a). But in section B I gave latest actual immigration figures, pointing out that the net immigration figure for 1998 was 178,000. If immigration in future were to be on this scale, the loss of green land to development would obviously be much worse. And it is interesting to note that no reason is given why the figure 95,000 is used for the projections in the face of the 1998 estimate of 178,000 (Coleman, ibid).

We can conclude, that the total greenland loss situation is likely to be much worse than calculated earlier. This makes it even more imperative to make every effort to stop population growth as soon as possible and as a component of this effort, to reduce or stop the flow of immigrants into our country (Chapter 10).

Chapter 3

Towards the ideal city

If we are to stop counter-urbanisation and its concomitant loss of green land to development, we must make cities attractive places in which to live. At the same time, cities have an adverse impact on the environment in the surrounding countryside (solid waste disposal, pollution and water levels in rivers, atmospheric pollution, the need for non-renewable countryside resources such as minerals, with consequent quarrying), an impact that must be reduced. So drastically improving city design and function is vital to any attempt to save our countryside. We need to work towards a vision of the Ideal City.

Probably people have developed a vision of the ideal city since the early days of civilisation. Components of the vision have varied through the ages, and would obviously reflect particular circumstances at the time. We at the present have to develop a vision in the face of the manifold failures of the past, and the severe environmental problems of the present.

The ideal city would be like a complex living organism - every aspect of its structure and organisation integrated to allow healthy functioning of the whole. It would also be like a distinct ecosystem in the wild - a collection of plant and animal species that have evolved a web of relationships with each other and the physical environment to create a stable sustainable whole. Let us explore these ideas further, bearing in mind that climatic and other conditions vary across the world, and out study focuses on England.

A. Elements of the Ideal City

(i) The Green City

The city viewed from the air, is a predominantly green place, in contrast with the present day city, which is dominated by grey concrete and dark slate. Closer inspection reveals that this overall greenness has a series of distinct components. 20th century green components like parks and roadside trees are prominent. But an even bigger component is rooftop gardens, which cover parts of public buildings, shops, and dwellings, the soil playing a vital part in building insulation The sides of buildings are partly covered with creepers, giving a restful appearance to the human eye and contributing together with the numerous city trees, to CO_2 emission absorption. Now concrete and other conventional building materials reflect solar heat, causing warming of the atmosphere above cities that contributes to atmospheric warming. The greening of the city reduces this harmful effect.

Rooftop gardens are primarily used for food production, as is much of the space around dwelling units, and allotments are a common city feature. Food production is focused on vegetables and fruit, so that the city is virtually self-sufficient for these items. Fowl are kept for eggs and meat.

This agricultural activity has done more than supply food. It has helped to redeveloped/strengthen the link between people and the natural world, the link that was the norm before the industrial revolution. This has increased peoples understanding of, and respect for, the 'natural' world, the green world on which we all ultimately depend. City food production provides employment for a not inconsiderable workforce. It helps people to achieve greater satisfaction with life through becoming more self-sufficient. It has been used to encourage cooperation and community development. The programme of urban food production has considerably reduced the 'ecological footprint' of the city (Chapter 1).

In 20th century cities, rain water, instead of being usefully absorbed into the ground, was wasted because it nearly all passed quickly into rivers and out to sea, contributing on the way to flooding in times of heavy rainfall, and occasionally causing sewage overflow into water channels which was damaging to wild life and a potential threat to human health. In the ideal city, these problems are largely eliminated. Roof top gardens slow water run-off, and the permeable surfaces of pedestrian ways and other hard covered areas allows water absorption into the ground. Rain water in certain areas, is used to refill aquifers and then recycled into urban use. Some water from sewage works, after primary treatment, is fed into forest areas during the summer months. This water contains excess nitrogen and toxic metals, which are damaging to human health. However, in the forest, the nitrogen is taken up into the foliage in summer. In winter, no more effluent is added to the forest system. Nitrogen from fallen leaves is gradually released, but at a rate that ensures ground water does not develop a high nitrogen concentration. And toxic metals become bound with soil particles in a surface soil layer and so immobilised.

Wildlife is encouraged within the city. For example, during the 20th century, building design changed in such a way that buildings became less suitable as refuges for birds like the swallow, and for bats. In the ideal city, buildings are designed to provide wild life refuges.

(ii) The energy city

All the city's energy needs are generated from renewable energy sources. Prominent here are energy crops, judiciously planted close by the city but interspersed with other vegetation, so that the general landscape of the countryside is little disturbed. Another major energy source is the slurry from the sewage system and from livestock production in the surrounding countryside. Solar, wind and water-power are also used, depending on the location.

Gas produced from landfill plays a very minor part since landfill has been drastically reduced. Heat energy is also taken from the ground beneath the city: many buildings had twin pipes penetrating into the ground to a depth of 35 metres, where the steady temperature is 12°C. These are heat exchangers, enabling the production of a steady 20°C in the buildings above. The system is rather like the reverse of the cooling system of a refrigerator. Sustainable local energy production, in addition to reducing the use of non-renewable resources, has other benefits. First, it is a major source of local employment. Second, city folk become much more involved with the whole strategy of energy production, strengthening the sense of community within the city.

In building design, the principle is adopted that the best way to save energy is to reduce the need to produce it in the first place. Considerable external input was needed in the past for heating and lighting. Improved design had greatly diminished these needs. The way to reduce heating energy need lies through good insulation; to reduce external lighting energy input, increased use is made of natural lighting. However, preventing heat loss through insulation can lead to unacceptable air temperatures in summer. And increasing light entry through larger external glass surfaces can aggravate the situation. Excess heat had in the past led to the need for air-conditioning systems, which also require energy.

Now, using insulating materials that have a high capacity to absorb heat, some daytime excess heat can be absorbed, and released again at night. And in wintertime, the heat of winter sunshine during the day can be stored overnight, thus reducing morning heating needs. Adjustable natural ventilation can allow heat to be better distributed within the building or escape. Light can also be controlled to maximise its availability in winter, while minimising its impact in summer. Useful here are deciduous trees, which through their leafiness can provide a light filter in summer, whereas in winter when the leaves are shed, they allow through the maximum amount of light. Control of day-to-day light fluctuations (cloudy or clear days) can be achieved by horizontal shutter bars, which can be controlled by people living and working in the buildings. Control of heat and light can be increased by having either a glass covered atrium with adjustable shutters and ventilation covering the space between two buildings or an equivalent structure atop a single building (Fig. 6)

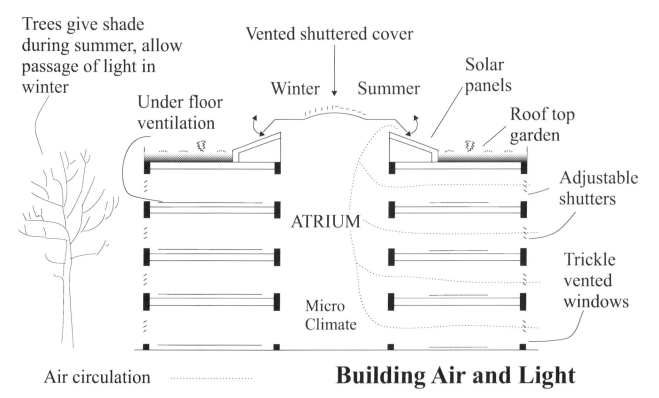

Fig. 6

(iii) The reduce – reuse – recycle city

The whole way that the city deals with the problem of waste is radically different from the late 20th Century in two respects.

First, waste management has changed from a linear model to a cyclic model. The traditional sequence of events had been: production - use - discard - store waste in landfill or burn - although there was already a limited amount of recycling. This changed to a predominantly cyclic sequence. In the ideal city there is more sorting of waste into categories, enhancing the possibilities of recycling, and the latter had become the norm, with drastic reduction in the amount of waste that could not be recycled. Landfill for waste disposal has been abandoned - large sums of money had been spent in researching the technologies to ensure that no waste has to be stored, for example, through changes in the materials used in the manufacturing process. Pre-existing landfills were been emptied as ways were found to remove, treat, and recycle materials. Maximising recycling of waste helps to minimise the input of energy and raw materials required by the city.

Second, there has been a return to older approaches to products:

a) During the earlier days of mass production, the culture of making things to last had been gradually eroded. Manufacturers had found they could increase their profits by manufacturing goods that would only last a short while, and by frequently bringing out new versions of products which advertising claimed were 'better'.

b) There used to be a culture of re-using containers. Those of us who can remember the days of the Second World war will recall how it was normal practice to do this wherever possible. Now towards the end of the 20th century, bottles and cans were increasingly deposited in superstore banks, then crushed and the material re-used (recycling). This increase in recycling was a useful development in terms of conserving raw materials and avoiding landfill, but a lot of this activity could have been avoided if bottles and cans were used again. Re-use in the ideal city is much commoner, facilitated as far as plastic containers are concerned, through changes in the type of plastics used.

These various changes, has led to a strategy that is sometimes summarised *Re-duce   Re-use   Re-cycle*: reduce the quantities of products that need re-cycling first. Then as much as possible, re-use products, and lastly, with products that cannot be re-used, recycle the material of which they are made.

This overall strategy has minimised the need to import energy and materials into the city. Combined with the green city strategy described earlier, the result is that the city has come to have a high degree of self - sufficiency.

(iv) City layout and function

The overall layout of the city incorporates various interesting features. From the air, it would appear that the city is a collection of large units surrounding a small central area. This central area has the larger public buildings, which are necessary for major cultural and leisure activities (for example, a concert hall). It also has the main rail station of the national rail system, linked with the local light rail or tram system, which operates within the city, and a bus station. There is very little car parking in this central area, for the majority of people access the area by public transport, bike or foot, so there are one or more cycle parks.

However, one would look in vain for the mass of roads that previously marked city centre areas and even major arteries in and out of the city. This mass had almost entirely disappeared. Traffic is almost entirely underground: the roads are underground; and every city has a well developed underground 'tube train' system extending out into all the suburbs. Unloading of goods, even heavy goods, is entirely by way of lifts or steep slope pulley systems, from underground service areas. All vehicle parking is underground; this applies not only to parking at businesses and transport terminals, but all residential parking as well. Removal of surface parking has freed up land for other uses including food production. One would look in vain for derelict land, or unused buildings.

The large city units are termed 'urban villages'. This term emphasises two essential features of the traditional rural village - plenty of green space interspersed with and around the buildings, and a strong community spirit. Each village is a semi-independent community of people who have all the basic facilities at hand within the village   - so the village contains food shops, stationers, post office, community health centre etc., together with a bus and/or tram terminus. All of these facilities are small scale. The village is a residential and employment unit. So the majority of the people who work in the village also live there - large housing estates, such an all-pervading feature of 20th century cities, had disappeared. Small work units are sometimes separate buildings within the village; sometimes they are incorporated in the same buildings as shops or dwellings.

The village is sufficiently small to ensure that everyone living there can easily walk to visit friends in other parts of the village, get to and from work, and make use of communal facilities. The network of underground roads facilitates buses travelling quickly around and between villages, and to the city centre. The village is also small enough for individuals to actually get to know a sizeable proportion of the whole village population. There are communal open spaces serving various functions – children's play areas, local sewage treatment areas, relatively wild areas serving partly as nature reserves and food production areas.

The main overall aim with housing had been to increase housing density well above the late 20th Century national average, thus eliminating the need to take up any more green land for urban development. It had at last been realised that it is perfectly possible to achieve such densification without decreasing quality of life in terms of essential elements (space to move around in, peace and quiet, privacy, green areas for leisure and gardening activities). Housing, in terms of height, is predominantly what is called 'medium rise' (mainly four storeys), and it consists entirely of flats. So semi-detached and detached houses are no longer found. Sometimes there is a moderately high-rise building somewhere in the village (it had been accepted that the social defects associated with post World War 2 high-rise buildings were not necessary consequences of high rise itself). Housing is entirely publicly owned, all dwellings are rented. Rent is not determined only by things like dwelling size and location. There are variable rent scales for all housing which take into account the behaviour of inmates in the broad sense of this term - to what extent the dwellers cooperate in community ventures such as food production, etc.

Densifying housing, and more generally creating compact cities, makes it easier to reduce total energy consumption. Less energy is used in transport. And having users concentrated in a small area make it easier to reduce energy consumption by schemes like combined heat and power.

The concept of the urban village is incomplete if only described in terms of finished structure and function. Essential to the concept is the way the village develops. Ideally the village is conceived and planned by the then local residents, so that it incorporates those features that they desire, consistent with the overall features of an urban village above described, and so the local people are involved with all stages of the development of the village.

It is clear that urban design along the lines described above will both reduce vehicle travel and accompanying energy use, and stimulate a healthy community spirit which will project the city from vandalism and ensure that people take a pride in becoming involved with maintaining the fabric of their city.

It would be a mistake to think of the ideal city as an entity designed apart from the countryside around it. Rather, it is developed within the context of its surroundings, or if you like, it is planned along with the planning of the structure and functions of the surrounding countryside. So the city and the countryside around it make up a 'city region' for planning purposes. The city cannot be made entirely self-sufficient in term of food production. Subject to the limitations of local climate, topography and soil, the countryside around the city supplies as great a part of the urban food requirement as possible, over and above the vegetable production of the city itself, both in terms of arable crop and meat production. In the countryside, villages remain, and their re-organisation is carried out in relation to the re-organisation of the city. 'Green Belts' are retained, but play an important role in food production for the city.

(v) City size

Cities conform to the concept of optimum city population size. Considerations taken into account here are:

> (a) The city should have a coherence of structure and function so that people within it feel that they belong to a unique community. If the city is beyond a certain size, people tend to lose the sense of overall community, and it becomes more and more difficult to maintain democratic control of city functioning.

> (b) The bigger the city, the more difficult it becomes to get away from it into the countryside. Since the development of the ideal city depends on getting people to live within the city rather than moving out into more rural surroundings (outer suburbs, village enlargement), it is important that the people can quickly get into the countryside, so reducing the desire to live there.

> (c) While most of the life of a citizen is spent in a particular urban village, people do need to get to the central area of the city quickly; there is also the need for movement between the different urban villages within one city (for trading purposes, visiting friends, etc). All these things are easier, and consume less energy, the smaller the city.

> (d) At the same time, the city needs to be big enough to enable people to experience all normal city functions. For example, make a city too small, and there will not be enough people to fill a concert hall or support an orchestra.

As a result of these considerations, it had been agreed that the optimum population size for a city is half a million. Larger cities had been reduced in extent to the size needed to accommodate this number - made possible by the reduction of total national population size.

(vi) A final word on social organisation (based on Gorz, 1985)

Part time working is universal. With continued advances in automation since the late 20th Century, the total workload of the nation had continued to decrease, making full-time employment an anachronism - in fact it is unknown. Society is organised through the application of two principles. First, people receive a guaranteed income for life, which represents their share of socially produced wealth, the income largely provided by the taxation of automated production. Second, every adult has the right and opportunity to work.

It had been calculated that the total workload of the country was such that, spread equally, it amounted to 20,000 hours per person per lifetime. For calculation purposes, the working life was taken to be 40 years. This would be equivalent then to each person working only 500 hours a year. Such part time work is so limited in extent that work has ceased to be a grinding obsessive obligation, but something that everyone welcomes as a change and a chance to meet other people and establish different routines. Even top professional persons work such a very limited part time schedule - gone was the need to work long hours to secure success through competition; and by thus working less, professional people have made it possible for many more people to enjoy specialised professional work than used to be possible. However, there is no compulsion about the time anybody spends working each year, and at the same time many people continue to work into their nineties.

Life for most people is centred in the 'urban village', and the co-operatives which have increasingly provided the goods and services the people require, and opportunities to work. There is much innovation: a small group of people, or a family, will often set themselves up to provide some specific goods or services for the community. Some urban villages had a union of co-operatives making money dealings of little importance. Members make goods or provide services for the community for which they clock up hour equivalents (for example, a decorator doing work in peoples homes). The union, in return provides vouchers for goods or services - even for holidays. Supermarkets had long ago disappeared; but the 'local shop' is once again prominent, often developed by and passed on within a family.

B. Moves in the direction of the ideal city

Policy on urban planning has been moving in the general direction of the Ideal City in recent decades. This can be seen by examining various government policy statements, and the publications of organisations which carry out research on urban development, work sometimes commissioned by the Government. I will not attempt to cover all aspects of the Ideal City – that would require a book of its own. Rather I concentrate on aspects most relevant to the central theme of this book – the size and quality of green land. So I focus on those aspects of urban planning which are central to any attempt to reduce green land loss, more especially, making cities attractive places to live in, and making the maximum use of existing urban areas to accommodate the growing human population. Only a brief discussion of documents is given here.

Before however, examining documents, it is useful to understand how housing provision has been managed in the planning process. The process in place until recently has been described as 'predict and provide' and it is described in the box on the following page.

We turn now to documents.

(i) Government publications

Planning policy guidance notes.

Within the framework of various Acts of Parliament, the Government gives guidance on planning in the Planning Policy Guidance Notes or PPGs for short. Probably the most important at the moment for our purposes is PPG3 Housing (DETR, 2000), which I now consider in some detail. We will also look at PPG13 (transport) and PPG12 (development plans).

PPG3 notes that the government's target is to provide, by 2008, 60% of additional housing on previously developed, land (para 22), and it promotes a package of policies which collectively will increase the extent that new housing provision can be accommodated, and local communities developed, within existing built up areas.

Observing that "land is a finite resource", the process of achieving the 60% target must involve local planning authorities (LPAs) in undertaking urban housing capacity studies (para 24), for which they should make use of the recently established

<u>Household projections and housing provision</u>

This provision of housing, including new house building, is based on the projected increase in the number of households, which in turn depends partly on projected increase in population. The calculations are based on past trends, including migration trends. Therefore the past trend of population towards the south of the country, for example, becomes incorporated into the projections. The process of preparing household projections can be summarized as follows.

The government produces Household Projections, which serve to show how population and number of households will increase nationally and regionally, if past trends are continued. The underlying basis for the preparation of the projections is the extrapolation of past demographic changes into the future. The projections are updated roughly every three years. The method of preparing the projections is discussed in Bramley and Watkins (1995). See also SSE (1996). The main features of projection preparation are:

(i)   Projections of future population growth are made at both the national (England) and area levels, breaking down the numbers by age and gender and marital status. This takes into account birth and death rates, population age structure changes, and migration. With the national projection, the migration considered is net international migration. With the area projections, it is local net migration.

(ii)   Household membership rates (called Headship rates until recently) are then calculated. By this is meant the proportion of each population sub-group (by age, sex and marital status) which heads a separate household in the base year of the projection period. The rates are calculated separately for married couples, cohabiting couples, lone parent, one-person households, and other multi-person households who share common housekeeping or a living room. These rates are then extrapolated into the future on the basis of past rates.

(iii)   The membership rates are then applied to the population projections to produce the required household projections.

The final household projections are produced down to the level of Counties and what are termed unitary authorities (see below). It is important to emphasize what was said at the beginning of this section - these household projections are 'trend based' - they illustrate what would happen if past trends in household formation were to continue into the future. But they also illustrate what would happen if past migration trends continue.

A note here about administrative divisions in England. These have changed considerably in recent times, to produce a planning structural framework, which is extremely complicated! At present, Britain is divided into non-unitary authorities- the non metropolitan counties or shires, numbering 35 in 1998, and unitary authorities, which in England are: London Boroughs and the Corporation of London, and Metropolitan Districts (32 in number). Planning in the Counties is on a so-called two-tier structure. Counties prepare Structure plans, which set the general, strategic planning policy for the development and use of land, including land for housing. Counties are divided into districts, each of which produces a local plan. Local plans are produced within the framework governed by the structure plan, and provide the local detailed guidance on development, including housing. Then structure plan and local plans are combined to make a Development Plan. In Metropolitan Districts, the Corporation of London, London boroughs, and some other unitary authorities, the planning is 'one-tier', in that these authorities produce a single Unitary Development Plan which combines the functions of structure and local plans. Some unitary authorities however, prepare both structure and local plans.

In terms of housing provision, the Government is concerned that in the past, household projections have been used too rigidly to decide the amount and distribution of new housing (the 'P*redict and Provide*' approach). In the new Planning Policy Guidance Note no. 3 (housing), Government advocates the alternative '*Plan, Monitor and Manage*' approach, and gives general guidance to Regional planning bodies (see Chapter 11 Section A) and local planning authorities. The planned level of housing provision and its distribution should be based on a clear set of policy objectives, linked to measurable indicators of change. It is general Government policy to make maximum use of previously developed land for housing provision. Now in some Regions, such land is very unequally distributed between different planning authorities, so these authorities should co-operate together to focus new housing development to previously developed land.

National Land Use Database (para 27). The sequential approach to allocation of land to housing development (para21) should be adopted. Here the presumption is that previously developed sites should be used before Greenfield sites (para 32). And in identifying sites to be allocated for housing, there should be a search sequence, starting with previously developed land and buildings within urban areas, then urban extensions, and finally new development around nodes in good public transport corridors (para 30).

The PPG advocates a certain degree of densification of housing. Thus in carrying out the urban capacity studies, LPAs should consider "various options in relation to density of development" (para 24). Densification is appropriate where there is good public transport accessibility – around existing centres and public transport nodes (paras 11 and 58). The PPG observes that new housing development is currently using an average density of 25 dw/ha, but more than half of all new housing development is at under 20 dw/ha. This level of land use cannot be sustained. And policies which place "unduly restrictive ceilings" on the amount of housing that can be accommodated on a site should be avoided. The PPG suggests the aim of between 30 and 50 dw/ha. However, the proposal to set minimum density standards for new development, on previously developed sites or greenfield sites, put forwards in the draft PPG, seems to have been dropped.

Much land is currently used for car parking, which reduces overall density of development. The PPG observes that car-parking standards for housing have become increasingly demanding, applied too rigidly, and often set minimum provision standards (para 60). Car parking standards have often resulted in more than 1.5 off-street car parking spaces per dwelling and this is unlikely to be consistent with the Government's emphasis on securing "sustainable residential environments". In contrast, LAs should introduce "greater flexibility" in the application of parking standards (para 11). They should not adopt minimum standards in their parking policies (para 60) and should revise their standards to allow for "significantly lower levels" of off-street parking particularly with developments a) in locations readily accessible without a car, b) with housing for the elderly, students and single people where parking demand will be less than for family housing; c) in converting existing buildings when it might be difficult to design parking into the scheme (para 61).

The PPG promotes mixed housing development and creation of local communities, although it avoids the use of the term 'urban village'. LPAs should 'provide wider housing opportunity and choice' by providing a better mix of housing in terms of size, type, and location than is currently available, and seek by this means to create mixed communities (para 2). Paragraphs 10 and 11 expand on this theme. The aim is to create mixed and inclusive communities, which offer a choice of lifestyle. Mixed development includes houses of different affordability with a mix of tenure types, and offering choice of lifestyle, adding that the government does not accept that different types of housing and tenures 'make bad neighbours'.

The PPG advocates greening the environment (para 46). It comments that 'greening initiatives' can improve environmental quality, for example, improving surface permeability to rain water, reducing storm drainage and improving biodiversity. Well-designed developments can also bring greater energy efficiency to new housing (para 52). Existing open spaces and playing fields should be protected, and adequate new provision provided close to new housing (para 53).

If we think in terms of the Ideal City, I think that the following criticisms can be made of this revised PPG.

a) Housing density. On the issue of the need to maximise density to reduce the loss of green land to development, we have seen that the PPG does advocate some densification of housing. But it does not come out in favour of any policy of general densification. Further, it does not mention how adopting middle-rise housing development can increase density, and so does not advocate adopting such a building mode.

b) Achieving a mix of housing types and tenures. While the PPG is in favour of such development, its treatment of affordable housing seems to lead to the same failure to achieve mixed development, as we will see in the following chapter at Whirlow in Sheffield. Para 16 says..."the objective should be to ensure that the affordable housing secured will contribute to satisfying local housing needs…". Since there is not a 'need' in affluent suburbs for affordable housing (since poor people don't live there), the guidance does not encourage mixed development including affordable housing in such areas. So the fundamental division between wealthy and poorer housing areas is not really lessened by the affordable housing policy.

c) Greening the environment. This PPG is about housing, not general urban development, nevertheless it does take up the idea of greening the city, and so we are entitled to ask whether what it proposes is adequate. The greening advocated in the PPG simply lists a few particular advantages of a greening policy. Much is left out. Mention is made of improving biodiversity; but nothing is said about the need to achieve a network of green spaces within the city and linking to the countryside, to achieve an improvement of diversity. Nothing is said about the use of green land for urban food production and how this can give employment, bring people to have a better understanding of environmental problems, and help to create community spirit. Above all, there is no fundamental vision of the overall significance of greening for urban communities, and therefore for housing planning.

Several policies advocated by PPG3 are now part of what one might call the accepted wisdom about urban development – trying to accommodate as much housing development on brownfield land, a limited densification in housing schemes and promoting the idea of the urban neighbourhood. And these ideas are picked up in other PPGs, for example PPG13, 1994 (transport) which I now briefly consider (this PPG is currently being revised).

PPG13 says that planning should enable people to reach their destinations with less need to travel, and should promote less use of the car, more use of public transport, and foot and cycle travel (paras 1.5, 4.12-4.19). It notes that car-parking provision might be more important than levels of public transport in determining means of transport. LAs should integrate their transport planning with housing development planning, for example by concentrating higher-density residential development near public transport centres or alongside corridors well served by public transport (para 3.3). Car parking takes up a large amount of space and reduces density of development (para. 4.4). So LAs should ensure that parking requirements are in general kept to "the operational minimum" (Para 4.5).

The Government later published PPG13. A guide to better practice. Reducing the need to travel through land use and transport planning. This book expands on the meaning of PPG13 and provides examples of good practice. It has a location of development section corresponding to that section in the PPG. In the sub-section on housing, it describes with obvious approval, conclusions of the Joseph Rowntree Foundation (JRF), including the recommendation that plans should impose minimum housing density standards and relax maximum standards.

Sustainable development.

The development of the future city needs to be considered within the framework of the concept of *sustainable development*,
which basically means carrying out development in an environmentally responsible manner (we return to the concept in Chapter 9).

Sustainable development. A better quality of life. A strategy for sustainable development for the UK (DETR, 1999b).

The document is not primarily about cities, but does have some things to say about city structure and function, advocating the concentration of new development within existing urban areas (para. 7.56). The document also advocates mixed-use development, integrating housing (including affordable housing) with shops, and employment opportunities (para 7.58). It notes the importance of land use planning to improve the links between homes, jobs and facilities by promoting walking, cycling and public transport. While it advocates the location of high-density developments near existing transport corridors and town centres (para. 7.58), it does not promote densification as such. The document also recognises the importance of involving local communities in the planning process (paras. 7.87 to 7.97).

PPG 12. Development Plans (January, 2000).

The key chapter as far as sustainable development is concerned, is Chapter 4. This notes that Development Plans should be drawn up in such a way that environmental considerations are comprehensively and consistently taken into account (para 4.4), indeed LAs are expected to carry out a full '*environmental appraisal*' of their development plans – para 4.16 (environmental appraisal will be discussed in the following Chapter). The chapter also specifically speaks of bringing Agenda 21 into the Planning process (para 4.30.

One key element in sustainable development is *development density*. For example, if we wish to be environmentally responsible, we will want to minimise green land loss to housing, which will be helped by increasing the density of new housing development.

Documents concerning density in planning, and related matters.
.
 Advice on the use of density in planning comes in various publications.

The use of density in urban planning (DETR,1998a). This lists the advantages of densification of housing, for example, reducing the need to travel, making it more possible to provide a range of local services, improving overall energy efficiency.

The document *Sustainable residential quality*. Exploring the housing potential of large sites (Llewelyn-Davies, 2000), commissioned by the DETR and others, considers the question of density in relation to urban design. Its main importance, I think, is that it knocks on the head the widespread belief that increasing density leads to loss of environmental quality (see also Llewelyn-Davies, 1997).

Planning for sustainable development. Towards better practice (DETR, 1998c). This is the document that adopts the most radical approach to housing densification. It comes out unambiguously in favour of densification, because that can

improve urban design (para 2.4.1):
- it will reduce the amount of land used for development;
- it makes possible a fuller exploitation of locations with high public transport accessibility;
- it increases the range of local services that can be supported;
- it improves the potential viability of public transport and freight services by providing more patronage;
- it increases the opportunity to provide a range of housing types, including affordable housing;
- it makes it easier to improve development;
- it makes it possible to design for energy supply and use more efficiently;
- it provides opportunity for design enhancement of town centre and local centre character;
- it provides the opportunity for more pedestrian-friendly environments.

The densification idea is applied principally to town and suburban centres (para 2.1.12), but also seems to suggest that densification may be applied more generally (para. 2.1.12 and 2.1.13).

The document discusses how the basic principles of sustainable development can be integrated into the process of preparing development plans through environmental appraisal (briefly described later in Chapter 4 Section H). In terms of visions of the future, this document is also interesting in suggesting that urban planning should relate to a vision of what things could be like in about 25 years time (para. 2.1.4). Many of the ideas in this document are endorsed by the recent PPG 12 that was mentioned earlier.

Two important documents on planning strategy.

Increasingly concern has been expressed that the 'predict and provide' approach described earlier, has led to housing provision in different parts of the country at variance with other government policy on development, indeed many have claimed that the household projections were self-fulfilling prophesies. The Government has now recognised that the system has been a contributory factor in perpetuating urban sprawl and discouraging investment in urban areas and the next document describes the present Government's response to these problems.

Planning for the Communities of the Future (DETR, 1998b)

The document states that the Government wishes to break away from the predict and provide approach and bring greater local flexibility rather than imposing rigid figures from Whitehall. The Government wishes to give more responsibility to the Regional Planning Conferences (regional groupings of LAs that have been in existence for some time and which produce Regional Planning Guidance). Paragraph 27 of the paper says that when the Government published future household projections it "would make it clear that the figures were for guidance rather than, in effect, prescriptive" (para 27) (however the same paragraph went on to qualify this statement by saying that if regions wished to depart from the projections they would need to produce good reasons for doing so in the draft RPG and be prepared to defend their proposed departures publicly). The Regional Planning Conferences would be expected to monitor development using a series of indicators such as house and land prices, housing standards and local housing needs. This new approach to planning is known as 'plan, monitor and manage'. Regional Planning will be discussed further in Chapter 11.

To take forwards the whole question of urban development and urban renewal, the Government appointed an Urban Task Force. This task force was headed by the architect Lord Rogers. Its beautifully produced report is usually known as the Lord Rogers Report.

Towards an Urban Renaissance (Urban Task Force, 1999)

The mission statement of the task force was:
        "The urban task force will identify causes of urban decline in England and recommend practical solutions to bring back people into our cities, towns and urban neighbourhoods. It will establish a new vision for urban regeneration founded on the principles of design excellence, social well-being and environmental responsibility within a viable economic and legislative framework".

This massive and clearly argued report, brings together all the ideas developed in the documents discussed above, making use of excellent diagrams to illustrate critical points. It adds to these ideas the concept of the 'spatial masterplan': in the past, planning has used two-dimensional zoning plans, which have simply defined areas of use, density standards, and access arrangements. In contrast, the spatial masterplan is three dimensional, allowing us to see how streets, squares and open spaces of a neighbourhood are to be connected, and defining the heights, massing and bulk of the buildings in a sophisticated 'visual' model. The task force visited various European cities during their work, and noted that successful urban projects (such as in Barcelona and Rotterdam) have been based on implementing spatial masterplans. The task force observes that such a plan:

- makes it possible to understand what the public spaces between the buildings will be like before they are built;
- shows how the open spaces, squares and streets of a neighbourhood are to be connected;
- defines the heights and masses of the buildings;
- controls the relationships between public spaces and buildings;
- determines the distribution of uses (shops etc);
- determines the network of peoples movement patterns (by foot, bike, public transport and car);
- identifies the location of landscaping, lighting etc.;
- makes it possible to understand how a new urban neighbourhood can be integrated with the surroundings.

Figure 2.6 of the report illustrates the advantages of this approach. It depicts three ways of utilising an area with the same dwelling density –75 units/ha – high-rise, medium-rise and low rise, demonstrating that middle rise has the greater potential for community benefit than the other types, and at the same time showing that density per se is not an indicator of urban quality. This provides an answer to critics of the use of higher densities, which is very relevant to the strategy I develop in Chapter 11.

The report argues that if urban regeneration is to succeed, it must be design led. Good design can lead to beautiful cities and people respond to that beauty. The term 'urban neighbourhood' is central to the report. This has some of the essential features of the urban village as described earlier, such as integrating transport provision with housing planning and encouraging ordinary people to participate in the design and development of the neighbourhoods. But it fails to really bring out what one might call the 'green elements' of the urban village. Thus the importance of promoting urban food production and environmental industries is omitted.

This document will be referred to again in Part 2 of the present book.

(ii) Non-governmental publications advocating aspects of the ideal city

So far we have just looked at publications of the Government and publications commissioned by the Government. But during recent decades there have been many publications by independent authors and NGOs that have advocated various facets of the ideal city, although they may disagree with each other on certain aspects of urban development. Here are just a few examples of publications from the beginning of the last decade. My purpose in including these documents is 1) to show that there was already a good understanding of the ideal city concept a decade ago (and readers of these documents will find references which show that the strands of the ideal city concept were already being developed decades earlier still), and consequently, 2) Government and LA planners have had no excuse at all for neglecting Ideal City components.

Canfield, C. ed. (1990). *Ecocity Conference 1990.*
Readers of this document, especially the presentation by P. Horsbrugh, will recognise how it provided some of the inspiration for the opening green city section in my account of the ideal city.

Gordon, D (1990). *Green cities. Ecologically sound approaches to urban space.*
This develops the concept of the self-reliant city: our current cities work according to the import-export paradigm, importing vast quantities of food water and energy and dumping vast quantities of waste outside. Rather we should miniaturise the economy, reducing transport costs and related energy use, and bringing with this the psychological and social benefits of local self-reliance. The self-reliant city concept is also taken up in Cadman and Payne (1990) *The living city: towards a sustainable future.*

Sherlock (1991). *Cities are good for us.*
This book develops the idea of the city as consisting of closely-knit communities. Selective densification is necessary to re-establish the high concentration of local facilities without which these communities cannot develop. Sherlock sees streets transformed so that they are once again safe for children to play in. He discusses conversion of existing buildings and design of new housing that would enable such communities to develop. He puts forwards a new high –density street housing scheme we will refer to in Chapter 11. He discusses possible conversion of traditional city Georgian houses.

Elkin et al (1991). *Reviving the city. Towards sustainable urban development.*
This FoE publication is the pièce de résistance of my little collection. When I came to browse through this again today, years after I first read it, but now looking at it after reading the Lord Roger's report and various other recent Government publications, I was immediately struck by the fact that most of the ideal city elements were already here, at least in embryo, and frequently well developed (spatial master-planning being one noticeable exception). Yet we have to wait nearly a decade for the Rogers report!   So we have community involvement in planning, the main principles of urban design such as densification, reducing energy use, integrating land use and transport development, and improved building design for greater energy efficiency. We should work with the processes of nature in urban green space (e.g. composting

and recycling), and encourage food production thus re-establishing a connection between people and nature.

There are many problems in trying to attain to the vision of the ideal city. And a Joseph Rowntree Foundation publication, although not written for this purpose, provides illustrations of some of the difficulties.

Darley et al (1991). *Tomorrows new communities.*

This concerns a competition to produce development designs for different types of urban development. However, the various papers in the publication give insight into the problems of creating new communities. G. Darley notes that potential residents for a new development would opt for high quality architecture and environment, but not necessarily for those communal and social features that are essential ingredients of a real community. Further, in the past, communities fired by idealism have tended to find it difficult to strike the right balance between the needs and wishes of the individual and that of the group. D. Lock in his paper takes up these problems in discussing the necessity of cultivating the 'social dimension'. This requires 'unashamed social engineering'. It requires deliberately inducing the networks and social institutions that in the past have often taken generations to develop. And P. Hall in his paper raises the question of whether it is still possible to create a new community in the world of multiple car ownership and two-earner households that characterise the late 20th Century. However, Darley, assuming it is possible, lists the principles that history shows must be adopted if we are to create new communities.

Since the beginning of the last decade, there have of course been many more publications with a bearing on the ideal city concept. Here is a sample of publications that might interest readers:

Joseph Rowntree (1944a); Llewelyn Davies (1994); Haughton and Hunter (1994); Barton (1995); Taylor (1995); Llewelyn-Davies (1997); TCPA (1997c); Carley-Kirk (1998); Smith et al (1998).

C. Conclusions

It must be very obvious to readers that English cities are far from becoming like the Ideal City described at the beginning of this chapter. This remains true even if it is accepted that not all features of the Ideal City described earlier are judged to be essential elements. Government policy has only slowly been moving in the direction of the ideal city, in particular, towards the idea of a city as consisting of an interconnected set of urban villages embodying high density living.

Non-governmental publications show that local government city planners have for a long time had all they need to develop a vision, but our cities show that either they have not tried, or have been unable to translate the vision into practice.

Now city development is controlled in the short term by existing plans, especially Unitary Development Plans (UDPs) discussed in the following chapter. These in turn are developed under the constraint of existing law and government policy. But there is nothing to prevent planners stating a vision in the plans they develop, and trying to edge things in the direction of the ideal city. Have they done this? In the next chapter we examine what has been going on in one City – Sheffield, and what we see suggests that planners have had no radical vision at all.

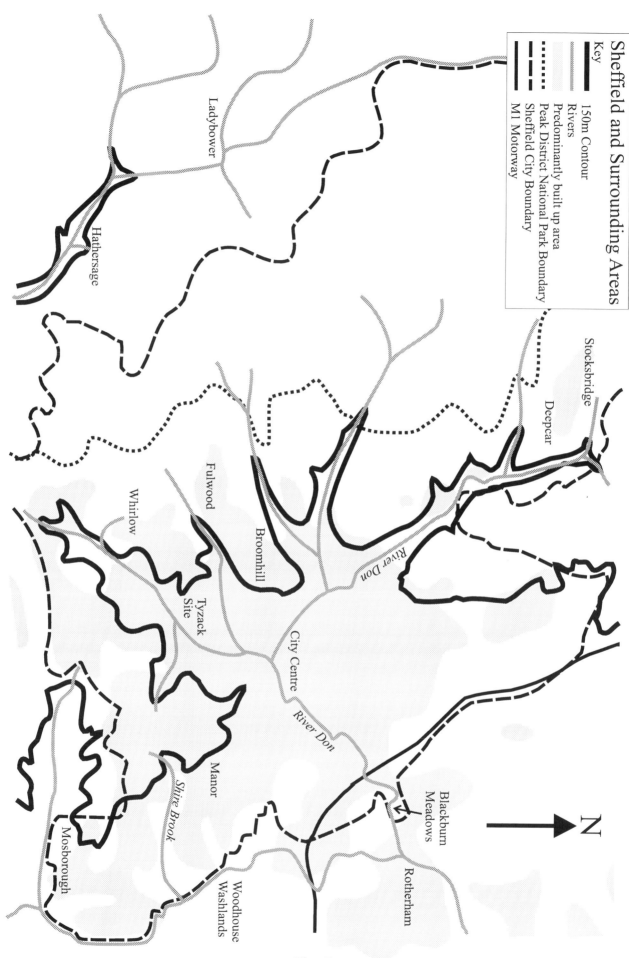

Fig. 7

Sheffield and Surrounding Areas

Key

150m Contour
Rivers
Predominantly built up area
Peak District National Park Boundary
Sheffield City Boundary
M1 Motorway

Ladybower

Hathersage

Stocksbridge

Deepcar

Whirlow

Fulwood

Broomhill

River Don

Tyzack Site

City Centre

River Don

Manor

Shire Brook

Mosborough

Woodhouse Washlands

Blackburn Meadows

Rotherham

N

Chapter 4

Case Study 1. Sheffield – not an ideal city

The Sheffield local authority area is situated on the eastern lower slopes of the southern Pennines. It has a total area of 36,397 ha. Of this 12,953 ha are in the Peak District National Park on the western side of Sheffield. Of the remaining 23,444 ha, half is Green Belt (South Yorkshire Forum, 2000) – see Fig. 7

A. Sheffield in the past

Sheffield is similar to other cities in England in some basic features. It has a city centre, where most of the big general-purpose shops are, together with major law firms and other businesses. It has large homogeneous housing estates, a few of which have become very run down and have many vacant dwellings. Terrace housing is common in the inner and middle suburbs, although the characteristic housing type in the middle suburbs is the semi-detached. Outer suburbs are predominantly semi-detached and detached houses.

The features of Sheffield, which distinguish it to a varying extent from other cities, relate to its physical geography and its industrial past. Sheffield lies on the lower eastern flank of the southern Pennines. Several small rivers drain down from the Peak District in fairly wide valleys and converge on the river Don that exits the city to the east. The waters of these rivers, trapped in mill dams, were used to drive the water wheels that provided the power for early industry - cutlery, agricultural equipment, etc. With the advent of steam power, industry became less dependent on waterpower, and the need to be near main roads and the coalfields led to the numerous small industries run by the 'little masters' developing more inside the city, manufacturing cutlery, surgical instruments, machine tools, silver plate. In the 19th century the need for large scale steel production (for railways, steel framed buildings, armour plate for warships, etc.) led to the establishment of the large steel factories on the flatter land of the Don river valley on the north-east side of Sheffield. Factories poured forth their fumes, and the open coal fire heated houses their smoke, until the decline of heavy industry and the passing of the Clean Air Acts post World War 2.

In the 18th Century, the houses where the rich townsmen lived were in the streets of the city centre. However, this was close to the noise and smell of industry. The predominant wind direction is from the southwest, blowing all the smoke away towards the northeast. This together with the attractive countryside to the west of the city, arising primarily from the topography, meant that in the 19th Century, affluent people tended to move out from the city centre to the area immediately to the west (although another affluent suburb developed on roads leading to the attractive private park of the Duke of Norfolk on the low hills in the south east part of the city centre). From the 1830s onwards, housing for more affluent people developed further out to the west and southwest, principally on the south-facing slopes of Broomhill, Broomhall, Ranmoor, Fulwood, Ecclesall, Nether Edge and Abbeydale. Most commonly houses were large or fairly large, detached or semi-detached, with ample gardens. These western suburbs have continued to attract the affluent up to the present day, although these suburbs have been expanded to include more conventional housing estates (see photo page 142).

The Second World War left a legacy of many derelict-bombed sites. Some of these remained for decades. One got the impression that those who ran the city had no vision, and a complete inability to use the opportunity to transform our city, as numerous German towns were in fact transformed after the same war. Then the decline of heavy industry brought with it unemployment, and Sheffield has never fully recovered. Thus the men who worked in the steel works lived on housing estates such as the Manor Estate (which will be discussed later), and this unemployment was one factor that led to the deterioration of such estates. The Objective 1 document (South Yorkshire Forum, ibid) puts this decline in the regional context:

> "South Yorkshire's economic decline between 1979 and 1995 was both steep and relentless. Its severity was unique in comparison to any similar area of the European Union. Whilst other parts of the UK – Glasgow, Leeds – also suffered problems of recession in the 70s and early 80s, these areas have now tackled many of the key constraints and have made significant progress in re-orientating the city–region. For South Yorkshire, the experience is recent and raw. Communities are still feeling (and still, in many cases, mourning) the loss of the traditional industries upon which the sub-region was dependent".

Sheffield is fortunate in that it has numerous parks and other open green spaces. Between 1833 and 1848 two important parks were opened to the public in Sheffield - the Botanical Gardens and Norfolk Park owned by the Duke of Norfolk. However, by the 1870s Sheffield's total open space within the built up area was small, and the Council moved to acquire land for parks and recreation. During the rest of the 19th century and during the 20th Century, many more parks were opened, some on land donated by wealthy benefactors. The Council's Leisure Services (now the Development, Environment and Leisure Services Directorate) currently manages 4,522 acres of parks and other public open space, and 3,460 acres of woodland. Sheffield also has a large Green Belt, secured in part by the Sheffield and Peak District branch of the Council for the Protection of Rural England (CPRE), which helped to persuade the Council to adopt a Green Belt policy.

B. Population, households and housing provision

(i) Growth of the population and the number of households; dwelling provision

Sheffield provides examples of post World War Two national trends. First, with housing tenure, there has been a massive increase in owner-occupied housing. Second, there has been a decrease of average household size. One-person households increased from 9.5% to 24.8% of all households between 1951 and 1981. Over the same period, 3-5 person households decreased from 56% to 39.5% (A.D.H. Crook, in Binfield et al, 1993).

In 1987 the City Council prepared new population and housing projections. At that time the population of Sheffield had been falling because of out-migration resulting from unemployment. These projections were needed for planning purposes – the City was about to embark on preparing its Unitary Development Plan (UDP), which will be discussed later, and needed to know how much land to earmark for housing. The projections were the usual trend based type i.e. based on past trends and not taking into account possible policy changes that could affect migration etc. The conclusions were as follows:

- Sheffield's population is likely to continue to decline by 7,000 every five years, mainly due to out-migration;
- however households in Sheffield will increase until the early 1990s. After this the number will decline;
- between 1986 and 1996 Sheffield would need an extra 3,500 dwellings to accommodate these households (not allowing for replacement of housing stock).

These projections for population and households have proved to be very wide of the mark as later (1996 based) figures show. The population has continued to increase, as has the number of households. Currently the population is a little over 531,000, i.e. a little over half a million, and is expected to reach 539,100 by 2021. The main reason why the population has continued to increase is an unexpected rise in the number of students coming into Sheffield to study at its two universities and other institutions, and for the future, *a major cause of the projected increase is refugees*. The number of households is now projected to probably go on increasing until about 2016 then start to flatten out.

From the 1987 projections one would expect that the number of extra dwellings needed would decline to very low levels, but later projections altered this expectation. The UDP (1998) in its Housing Policy no.1 estimated that between 1991 and 2001, 10,700 new dwellings would still be needed. Price and Greig (1998) said that during the then next 25 years, we might need to build up to 40,000 new homes. And the 1999 Housing Land Survey to be discussed in the following section calculated that during the next five years (1999 to 2004), 4990 new dwellings will be required. The City Council, like all housing authorities, has to plan ahead to ensure it will have the required dwelling accommodation for the projected numbers of households. The assumption is always made that more land will have to be set aside for new dwellings. The government provides the guidance that local authorities should maintain a five-year supply of housing land at all times (PPG3). The housing land survey estimated that between 1999 and 2004, 5484 dwellings will be built – a margin (excess) of about 500 dwellings over the projected requirement.

Estimates of past, and projections of future population and households

Year	Population		Households		Dwellings
	87 based	96 based	87 based	96 based	87 based
1971	578,800				
1976	561,800				
1981	547,600		211,717		215,511
1986	534,324		212,128		218,242
1991	525,577	529,300	214,151		220,343
1996	519,982	530,400	215,478	226,737	221,722
2001	514,658	531,400	214,853	230,090	221,073
2006		532,500		234,050	
2011		535,000		239,196	
2016		536,800		244,215	
2021		539,100		248,229	

1987 data from SCC (1987). 1996 based data supplied to author by City Council.

(ii) House building, housing density and some notes on house prices

Information on these matters is provided by The Sheffield Housing Land Survey (SHLS) (Sheffield City Council, 1999a). The document explains that it is the latest record of land in Sheffield on which housing *could* be built (my italics). So what categories of land does the survey cover? First, sites which have already got planning permission for housing development; second, sites allocated specifically for housing in the City's development plan (the UDP); third, land in other areas where the development plan says it would be acceptable to build houses.

The survey says that 249 hectares of land are thus identified for house building. An assessment of the capacity of each site was made using known densities (see below). This gave a total capacity of 6,173 dwellings on a total of 363 sites. What is the distribution of this land across the city? The biggest amounts of land are found at Mosborough (on the south-east outskirts of Sheffield (29% of dwelling units – an area of land ear-marked for urban expansion in the UDP) and the Inner City (36%). **It is significant that existing suburbs are only projected to provide for 21% of new dwellings.** Finally, in terms of site size, 85% will be on large sites (defined as 0.4 hectares or larger).

The survey investigated past house building in terms of what is termed the 'market sector' – that is, the classification of housing based on prices and size. For this purpose the category of sectors used by the House Builders Federation was adopted:

Low up to £60,000 dwellings, such as starter homes, terraced, small semis suitable for first time buyers, small families and single people.

Medium £60-125,000 dwellings such as large semis, detached family houses, bungalows, high quality flats.

High £125,000 and upwards, large houses, luxury flats, bungalows and houses of individual design.

The survey comments that there has been a noticeable recent trend towards building almost exclusively for the medium sector, typically large 3 or 4 bedroom detached houses, even on sites originally categorized as suitable only for low market sector housing. While purely high market sector sites only account for 2%, the survey did not include small sites, and many high market sector houses are built on small sites, particularly in the southwest area of the city.

What we see here, I conclude, is the result of house-builders preference to build big expensive houses, and the inability or lack of will of the Council to control housing size. It is very ironic that we have this trend towards bigger/more expensive houses at a time when household size has been decreasing, and so many young people wish to find solo accommodation. The trend panders to those affluent people who want large houses although they do not really need them in terms of their household sizes

Housing density is studied in relation to market sector. The range is from 14 dwellings per hectare (dw/ha) in the high market sector to 37 dw/ha in the low market sector. Appendix 2 of the survey gives various details for sites over 0.4 ha:

Sector	Average Densities (dw/ha)	Number of Dwellings
Low	37	861
Low/Medium	27	1960
Medium	23	1431
Medium/high	20	363
High	14	59

The mean densities for all sites < 0.4 ha and all sites >0.4 ha were: 61 and 27. The mean density, all sites, was 29 dw/ha.

Once again we see the influence of affluence. Poor people have to accept high densities, while wealthy people can spread themselves out (and take more than their fair share of land).

It is worthwhile at this point to say something about the attitude of Council planners to housing density. In 1997 a paper appeared in the Town and Country Planning journal headed " Local Authorities and residential densities – an attitude problem?" (Breheny, 1997). This paper points out that recent Government policy statements were urging planners to maintain or increase densities. Yet, the paper argued, the planning profession has not taken density planning seriously for many years. The paper then goes on to make extensive use of research carried on at the university of Reading in which a questionnaire had been sent out to local authorities enquiring how they dealt with the density issue. Authorities varied in their attitude to density, in the extent they tried to achieve certain density levels. The issue resolves around what are called 'density standards'. Such standards refer to a prescribed density level that planners attempt to achieve. Standards can be expressed numerically or non-numerically. Numerical standards can be expressed in dwellings per hectare, habitable rooms per hectare, or bed spaces per hectare. An example of a non–numerical standard would be a level of housing density "consistent with surrounding residential development". One would expect that authorities, which take the density issue seriously, would adopt plan-based numerical standards. The Reading survey showed however, that only a little over 30% of authorities had such numerical standards. And about 20% of Authorities did not reply to the questionnaire, at least in time for the research to be completed.

So I thought I would ask in the Planning Department what was the situation in Sheffield – although from what I had read in the UDP and elsewhere, it did not look as if Sheffield had adopted numerical standards. The person I spoke to was not certain that the Sheffield City Council had even responded, although thinking it probably had, adding that "the Council receives very many requests each year, some have to be dealt with in our lunch breaks, and I would have to go back through all our correspondence to find out"! The person confirmed that the Council had not adopted numerical based standards.

We saw above that many high market sector houses are built on small sites, particularly in the southwest area of the city. I now explore the implications of this.

Right on the southwest fringe of Sheffield is the leafy Whirlow district.

What then is the situation at Whirlow? The SHLS survey (ibid) gives details of six current and planned developments there.

Site no.	2251	2392	60	368	691	571
Average Density dw/ha	20	17	9	9	14	15
Total capacity (no. dw)	1	1	23	12	21	6
Site area, ha	0.05	0.06	2.64	1.27	1.5	0.4

So where the most of these dwellings will be built the density will be 9 or 14/ha!

Now the City Council wants to get rid of the affluent- poor area divide in the city. And the Council's own guidance on affordable housing in its Supplementary Planning Guidance policy guidance G1 states that the application of this guidance together with the main guidance in the UDP Housing Policy Four (H4) reflects the City Councils desire to improve the spread of different housing types and tenures *across the city as a whole* (my italics) The supplementary guidance gives a map showing those parts of Sheffield where affordable housing may be sought. This amounts to almost all of Sheffield apart from a fairly large area in the central, east–central part of the city. The whole of the southwest built up area is included in the area where affordable housing may be sought, including the Whirlow district.

So I have recently been out to look at development in this Whirlow district. What I see is several small developments, all of which are exclusively for luxury houses, in various stages of completion. There are no cheap houses in these developments. The photographs on page 59 show the at-site advertisements of three of the developments that are in the early stage; They give a very clear message about exclusivity. Where the developments have reached an advanced stage or are recently completed, you can see just how big the houses are (photos page 60). They are detached, very often with double garages. One set of houses has mock ancient Greek style columned porticos! As you might expect, the prices are way beyond what the average household could afford. For example, the Bloor Homes site at Whirlow Green has eleven houses, all described as 'executive houses'. Eight are 5-bedroomed homes with prices varying from £370,000 to £415,000. Two are six-bedroomed homes, at £317,500. One is a 7-bedroom executive home for nearly £563,000. It's also worth pointing out that while most of these developments lie close to a major bus route, most are not within easy walking distance of any shops. The developers know, and the City Council knows, that the house owners are not going to use public transport for shopping and getting to work – they are going to use their cars!

As you approach Whirlow and Sheffield on the main road from the Peak District via the Fox House pub (the A625) there is now what looks like an official City of Sheffield Notice saying Welcome to Whirlow (photo page 60). The notice is crowned by the Sheffield coat of arms. But it bears the name of one of these housing developers at Whirlow. I wonder how much money the Council received for allowing this advertisement to be included? Surely the Council should not be singling out any particular developer in this way. And I do not think that any of these housing developers are a fitting symbol of Sheffield.

Creating a whole area of exclusive very expensive houses at Whirlow hardly fits with stated Council policy on the affluent- poor divide. When I pointed this out to one planner in the Forward Planning section, his reply was to the effect that the Council wished to encourage business to locate in Sheffield. This means that the Council must see that the sort of housing, and the sort of location for that housing wanted by top business executives, is made available, otherwise the businesses would locate elsewhere! This comes to the heart of the problem. Encouraging business as a top priority, divorced from other considerations, can lead to development which prevents broad strategic objectives being met.

While the Council wants to overcome the rich-poor locational divide, some sections of Council policy militate against achieving such a result. For qualifications are added to policies H4 and G1. Thus while H4 says that the development of affordable housing for people on relatively low incomes will be promoted, it goes on to say: "Where a need is identified, the provision of affordable housing will be encouraged as a proportion of large housing schemes..." (my italics). And G1 says that the provision of affordable housing will be negotiated where it is needed to offset shortages of a particular type of housing for those whose needs cannot be met by the existing housing stock in the area round the site. Well obviously there is no need for affordable housing in the Whirlow area – poor people do not live in such opulent surroundings! Indeed poor people rarely live in any rich suburb.

Then again, developers seem to like small sites for we saw the housing land survey commented that much high market housing development goes on in small sites. Not surprisingly, Small sites are exempt from any requirement to provide cheaper housing (buffering the rich inhabitants from too much contact with the hoi polloi!):
The Council's Supplementary Planning Guidance policy G2 states that in the areas where affordable housing may be sought (discussed above), there is a size limit – only above this limit will affordable housing provision be sought from developers. The limit is stated as sites of more than 1.5 ha or having a capacity for over 40 dwellings.

Now from the table given earlier we can see that most of the Whirlow sites are small. But one is well over the area limit (2.64 ha). Added together the total area of all the sites is about 6ha - a large area, and the total number of dwellings is well over 40. If the Whirlow area had been taken as a single planning unit, it would have had even more than 6 hectares because there is other greenfield land and existing housing.

The Whirlow area is big enough to have made it possible to turn it into an urban village, perhaps with its main employment focus on horticulture since there is plenty of green land around. But that would have required the Council and the planners to have just a tiny modicum of imagination and pioneering spirit, and to stand up to developers.

The developments at Whirlow illustrate other aspects of Council policy. The Council has the right to ask developers to make a contribution to the Council arising out of the fact that granting permission for housing development pushes up the value of the land and the Council should share in this profit (called 'planning gain'). The Council has a policy of providing open space for the residents in new housing developments, and asking developers to contribute towards developing this open space. Now a report to the development committee dated 19th April this year had a table headed "Schemes where monies have yet to be received from developers". This covered various parts of Sheffield including five sites the South West Region (among which were two of the Whirlow housing sites). The table lists the position on open space provision for each site –e.g. "minor improvements to open space", or "construction of pocket parks by the developer". For each of the South West Region sites however the table says "surveys to be undertaken and views of panel(s) sort". So the Council had not decided in advance of development taking place, just what they wished to achieve. When I asked a planner about this I was told that if they had sought the views of the local people in advance it would have been a long process, which would have held up development! Surely however, the Council should have a spatial plan for the area in place before any development permission was given, let alone any development begun!

Now the report table I just mentioned has a column giving the monetary value to the Council of developers' contributions (which can take the form of money paid to the Council or work done on site). I asked about the general situation on this planning gain in Sheffield – how much did it amount to overall? I was told that the Council had not calculated that. Yet the sums involved are not trivial. Just for the South West Region sites in the report, the total value approaches £100,000.

A further word about luxury houses in peripheral areas. Whirlow is not some exceptional case in Sheffield. Go to Mosborough – an area designated by the Council to make a major contribution towards meeting Sheffield's housing need. Here, housing has been and is still going up as I write this chapter. Overall there is a mix of housing types; so there are some small semi-detached, and a few short terraces. But the preponderant housing in some developments is in the 'medium' sector. One of these little estates for example has a few semi-detached houses and terraces of three houses; but most of the houses are detached 3 and 4 bedroomed houses with garage.

Go to Deepcar on the west side of Sheffield adjacent to the large village of Strocksbridge and the main A616 road which links Sheffield to the A628 and hence the Manchester area. It is a few miles away from the main built up area of Sheffield. Here you will see a fairly large new housing development consisting of luxury houses. Apart from a few bungalows, all the houses are semi-detached or detached houses (predominantly the latter). They have three or four bedrooms; all the houses have garages .As with much of the housing as Mosborough, the houses are of standard 'picture book' type - typical 'nice', 'respectable', sloping tiled roofed housing of the affluent. There is no 'affordable' housing, no shops. Now planning permissions for this development were being given half way through the process of the preparation of Sheffield's Unitary Development Plan, and before the Supplementary Guidance on the provision of affordable housing was produced, policies which <u>could</u> have led to a mix of housing prices and tenures and inclusion of shops in the development. But a recent letter to me on the subject from a Council planner says: "However, even if the policy or guidance (on affordable housing) had been available, it is unlikely that we would have asked the developer to provide affordable housing there. Adequate housing is available in that area for rent and cheap housing is available to purchase in that part of the city". In terms then of housing need arising from the number of households to be accommodated in this area, this housing was not needed.

Now Whirlow, Deepcar and Mossborogh have regular bus service connections with central Sheffield. I doubt very much, however, if most of the residents use the bus rather than the car.

(iii) Vacant land and premises

For a few years now it has been generally accepted that maximum use must be made of brownfield land for housing. And the Government has set the national target of building 60% of new housing on brownfield land, leaving 40% to be built on green land. However, the availability of brownfield land varies across the country - large former industrial cities in the north of England have more brownfield land available than say East Anglia. So Government expects the target for brownfield development to vary from area to area. And the SHLS concludes that in Sheffield, 71.5% of the capacity for housebuilding is on brownfield land.

One component of brownfield land is Derelict land, and a survey carried out in the early 1990s showed Sheffield had 395 hectares of such land. In industrial cities like Sheffield, derelict land is often contaminated, so before it can be considered for housing development, the extent of contamination has to be determined. Council policy on this matter is contained in UDP policy GE25 which says that where there are reasonable grounds to suspect contamination may exist, developers and landowners will be required to produce a land contamination survey before planning permission is granted. So the onus for carrying out contamination surveys is passed by the Council to the developer. While such survey work is expensive, it could be argued that if the Council were really serious about making maximum use of vacant land for development, it would have itself carried out a contamination survey of all derelict land.

If use of green land for housing is to be minimised, not only is it essential to make maximum use of brownfield land for new building, but in addition, maximum effort must be made to make use of existing but vacant dwellings. Therefore you would think that a top priority would be given by the Council to keeping an up-to-date record of vacancies. Recently I asked a planner what was the vacancy rate at the present? I was told that this was not known and that the most recent

Housebuilders
advertising boards.
"prestigious..."
"luxury..."
"exclusive..." Not
exactly the way to
achieve the aim of
mixed and inclusive
communities though
'mixed development'
(houses of different
affordability and type
of tenure).

Luxury housing. We
have to provide this,
otherwise business
people will go
elsewhere and stop
Sheffield from being
'First'!

Sign on the A625
entrance road to
Sheffield, at Whirlow.
A succinct statement of
City Council values?

information on the number of vacant dwellings came from the 1991 census! The figure then was 9,043 – that is a lot of dwellings.

Furthermore, if the need for house building is to be minimised, not only must maximum use be made of vacant dwellings to house people, but a determined effort must be made to make use of vacant space in other buildings. This space can be either used directly for accommodation, or used for other purposes such as offices and in this way make space available elsewhere for accommodation. Now a feature of the central shopping area of Sheffield close to the Town Hall is rows of buildings with ground floors in use for shops or other purposes and most of the rooms on upper floors vacant (see photo page 65). While the Council is currently trying to do something about the situation, this has been a very noticeable feature of Sheffield for a long time. It seems strange then that the Council has a whole collection of its offices in a new building on Carbrook Hall Road, a mile or more away from the city centre, down towards the southeast of Sheffield and the Meadow Hall shopping area (there are other Council offices elsewhere). This means that the two major groups of Council officials (the other one being in the Town Hall) are a long way apart. I suspect too that the central shopping area is probably nearer to the residential areas in which most Council officials live than the Carbrook area is. So for officials based at Carbrook, there is probably a lot of quite unnecessary commuting between work places and between work place and homes. Why has not the Council made the strategic decision to house Council officials in rooms on upper floors of the central shopping area, within five minutes walk or less of the Town Hall? It could possibly also have bought sites of derelict buildings near the city centre (discussed later) and built offices there.

Finally, discussions about brownfield land and vacant dwellings in connection with accommodation are part of more general 'urban capacity studies'– investigations of the extent that existing urban areas can accommodate future development. Now in the case of Sheffield and other authorities in the Yorkshire and Humber Region, a study was commissioned on this matter. But the report was only finally published in 1998 (Baker et al 1998).

(iv) Rich and poor – the divided city; further information

Recently the City Council set up a series of Area Panels for consultation with local groups. For this purpose Sheffield is divided into 13 areas. The South West Area here includes the whole South West part of the City plus most of the urban area west of the city centre and so it includes the districts of Dore, Ecclesall and Hallam. A July 2000 publication of the South West Area Panel (SCC, 2000a) provides documentation about the affluence divide in Sheffield, from which I extract the following information.

	South West	All Sheffield
Population (1996)	58,200	530,400
% employed people in higher occupation grades*	73.4	33.1
% households receiving income support	5.1	20.1

* professional plus managerial and technical

Housing type	% SW Area	All Sheffield
Owner occupied	88	56
Private rent	4	6
Council	5	33
Housing Association	2	3
Other	1	1

Average House prices, 1998 (increase since 1997); cars per head of population, 1991

Dore	£93,000 (10.9%)	0.44
Ecclesall	£74,000 (2.8%)	0.47
Hallam	£83,600 (11.8%)	0.45
Sheffield	£56,700 (1.8%)	0.30

(In this table Dore includes two areas not in the South West Area Panel).

I would suggest that the house price increases give good indication of the continued desirability of the South West Region as a place to live for the wealthy.

Finally, the Panel publication gives statistics on crime in various parts of the city, concluding that the South West Area has lower rates of (reported) crime than other parts of the city.

Various other publications show how the quality of physical life is considerably better in south-western districts than in inner city areas, as shown by health indicators like mortality ratios, infant mortality rates and percentage of low birth weights. In the last 15 years the mortality ratio for some of the poorer wards in the city has increased significantly, while in wealthier areas it has fallen. Long-term unemployment is higher and school performance tends to be lower amongst the peoples of inner city areas compared with the south-western parts of the city (see the series of "Sheffield Trends" documents published by the City Council and the "Sheffield First" document – the latter to be discussed in a later section).

(v) Conclusions

Sheffield illustrates some general features of city development in England in recent decades. Housing continues to be built on peripheral greenfield land, and this, through the inadequate control of developers, has contributed to the continued segregation of affluent from poorer people in terms of dwelling district location, a segregation which mirrors differences in quality of physical life.

C. Some changes in the Physical environment since the Second World War

Sheffield provides examples that illustrate national trends.

(i) State of the parks

Mention was made earlier about the large area of parkland within the city boundary. Unfortunately, the amount of money that the Council has spent on the parks has declined in recent decades and park keepers were made redundant; so now there is visible park deterioration. Sheffield is not of course the only authority to find it difficult to maintain its parks. Indeed, the House of Commons Environment, Transport and Regional Affairs Committee reported in 1999 about Parks in general:

"We are shocked at the weight of evidence, far beyond our expectations, about the extent of the problems parks have faced in the last 30 years. It is clear that if nothing is done many of them will become albatrosses around the necks of local authorities".

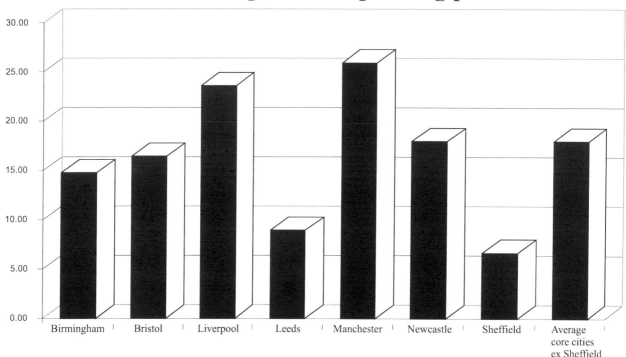

Fig. 8

By kind permission of K. Crawshaw

All that being said, Sheffield does not compare favourably with other major cities (Fig 8). Thus Birmingham, Bristol, Liverpool, Leeds, Manchester and Newcastle all spend more on parks per head of population, than Sheffield does - in fact all except Leeds spend more than twice as much!

Now the Government does not believe in government intervention to earmark government money to local authorities for parks, so it is up to the local authorities to decide how much money they allocate to parks maintenance. The Council maintains that it just has not had the money to maintain parks adequately, and hopes to draw in external grants and establish partnerships with private businesses and local community organisations to improve the situation. But the question remains, should not the Sheffield City Council really spend a greater percentage of its budget on the parks, which do give so much of value to the citizens of Sheffield?

(ii) Deterioration of habitats and wildlife

There has been loss of moorland, ancient grasslands (e.g. in the Moss valley) and low-lying heaths within the Sheffield area, and there has been neglect of some of the remaining ancient grasslands as well as of ancient woodland. For example, in the last twenty years, the number of wildlife-rich unimproved grassland fields in the area has fallen by 88%. There has been development on greenfield sites, sometimes for housing, and against the wishes of local residents, with damage to woodland and woodland species. In the Ewden valley wildflower meadows were destroyed as part of water supply developments. Much tipping of household waste, and waste from industrial and extractive industries, into disused quarries, and onto pasture and moorland has taken place. Much paper waste has been spread in the Rivelin-Loxley valley areas, ostensibly for agricultural improvement, but several feet thick paper is surely tipping and of no benefit to the land

A report prepared on tipping, landfill and pollution in the Sheffield area, and submitted to the Environment Forum (now the Sheffield Environment Partnership –see later) by environmental campaigner Les Harris, gives disturbing details. His map of the Bradfield area shows almost a patchwork quilt of damaged sites.

There has been considerable loss of watercourse habitat. Many riverbanks have been replaced by concrete. Sections of many rivers and streams have been put into underground culverts resulting in streamside habitat loss. The modification of drainage systems associated with development, is probably responsible for some urban streams either drying up or having very reduced flows in summertime, and some rivers became heavily polluted (although some have been recently improved). There is a continued threat of untreated sewage and agricultural run-off into waterways; and of course, Sheffield has an extensive legacy of post-industrial contamination (mine-water discharges, etc).

Not surprisingly, there has been a considerable decline of wildlife, with some species becoming locally extinct. For example, with plants, the cowslip, primrose, wild daffodil, sundew, ragged robin, butterwort and chickweed wintergreen have become very rare. With birds, there has been a massive decline of the barn owl, nightjar, black grouse and nightingale. Much of this decline mirrors national decline. At the same time there has been spread of invasive, sometimes non-native species, including bracken, rhododendron, sycamore, Himalayan balsam and Japanese knotweed. Grey squirrels have replaced the red squirrel (Rotherham, 1995).

(iii) Vacant and derelict buildings

Like numerous other cities, Sheffield has housing estates where some houses are empty and boarded up, graffiti is scrawled on walls, and litter accumulates in odd corners. Dereliction is not however limited to housing estates. A short walk round the central parts of Sheffield is to some extent a depressing experience. I could take you to places within five minutes walk of the Town Hall where there are derelict buildings (see photos page 65). You also find various car parks, which are simply the remains of derelict sites (photo page 90). They are bordered by partly demolished walls with protruding remnants of wall and floor, with willow herb and other weeds flourishing in odd corners. There is absolutely no sense of civic pride! I wonder to what extent this is made possible by temporary planning permissions on derelict land. Extend your walk from the Town Hall for twenty minutes or half an hour and you would find plenty more derelict buildings. Now developments are afoot to make use of some of this derelict land for housing and other purposes, but why has so little been done in the past?

(iv) Pollution and traffic congestion

Gross air pollution was greatly reduced following the passing of the Clean Air Acts, and the decline of heavy industry, but traffic caused pollution has increased greatly. This is principally due to increased car commuting to the city from residential suburbs. In north-eastern parts of the city (Tinsley etc) the development of motorways has also greatly increased pollution as well as noise. By 1998, private car commuting in and out of the city had increased by about 17%

since 1985. But the number of people travelling by car only increased by 15%, which means that cars were carrying fewer passengers than in 1985. Buses and coaches travelling in and out of the city had increased by 16% since 1985; but the total number of passengers decreased by about 39% during the same period (Price and Greig eds.1998). As far as the city centre is concerned, there has been some limited success in changing transport use patterns. The rate of car traffic growth in the City Centre reached a peak in 1996 but has decreased by about 2.5% since. In terms of structural developments, over half the major developments in Sheffield approved during the period 1997-1999 were in supertram corridors, and supertram use increased 2.5 times since its first year of operation. Over 45 kilometres of new cycle/footpaths were designated between 1994 and 1999 (Sheffield City Council UDP monitoring report, SCC, 2000b).

Despite these improvements, Traffic congestion on major arterial roads is currently very serious. Dedicated traffic lanes for buses (an incomplete network) has speeded up bus travel at rush hours, but buses, like other traffic, are greatly impeded at round-abouts and other junctions. If I travel out by bus from the city centre at the evening rush hour, I note that half the time for the whole couple of miles run is taken up at two round-abouts. And if I am waiting at the bus stop in the morning to get into town (the stop is at a junction between one major and one minor arterial road) I note the widely known phenomenon – the majority of vehicles are cars, and the majority of these carry no passengers. At the same time, I may see no or only a couple of cyclists traversing the route while I wait.

D. Environmental organisations

There are of the order of 50 groups in Sheffield involved in conservation in some form or another. Some of these are branches of national groups: Friends of the Earth, Ramblers Association, Green Peace, Royal Society for the Protection of Birds, the Council for the Protection of Rural England (CPRE) and Sheffield Wildlife Trust (SWT). All these local branches of national organisations cooperate to varying degrees with local environmental/neighbourhood groups. I have already mentioned CPRE's role in securing a Green Belt for Sheffield. It engages with the City Council and with the National Parks Authority as they develop policy plans (Sheffield's UDP –see later, and the Structure and Local Plan of the National Parks authority). It also keeps a watching brief on planning applications.

SWT is playing an increasingly important role. It was set up in 1985 with three aims:

> (i) to promote conservation and improvement of Sheffield's physical environment;

> (ii) to advance education in environmental matters;

> (iii) to provide facilities for recreation based on wildlife and the environment as a way of improving the quality of   life in the city.

SWT has been and is presently, involved in a lot of habitat survey work, for example, its survey of the Manor castle area (this area is discussed in a later section). The Trust has a large and varied education programme. For example, it is running a Green Youth Action Network Programme, working with young people to raise their awareness of environmental issues and give them the chance to get physically involved in conservation work. It organises a varied calendar of educational activities in schools. And it has a long history of working with schools planting trees. SWT supports and facilitates a certain amount of restoration and other improvements in City Parks. For example, it assisted the City Council in mounting a successful bid for Heritage Lottery Funds for the regeneration of Norfolk Park.

Like the CPRE, SWT monitors and comments on Planning Applications submitted to the City Council and also like CPRE, it has the possibility of influencing planning policy by virtue of membership of bodies such as the South Yorkshire Objective 1 Environmental Priority Group. Finally, the Trust produces its own magazine – the Kingfisher.

Most groups concerned with conservation are local groups concerned primarily with their immediate neighbourhoods. They vary in the emphasis that is given to conservation as distinct from other community activities. Considering together local branches of national groups and local groups, membership size varies from under twenty to several hundred. However, the percentage of the memberships that are active members and fairly regularly turn up on 'action days', as distinct from people who just pay a membership fee and may or may not occasionally go to a talk, is usually small. As a couple of group leaders have said to me, many people consider that they have done their bit for the environment when they have paid a subscription to the local group. Membership is also generally age-skewed, with older people making up the majority. The most active members often belong to more than one group.

I estimate that the total number of members in Sheffield is of the order of 6,000. And although it is difficult to define what one means exactly by active membership, I would estimate that as being less than 20% of membership (almost certainly far less). But suppose we take the figure of 20% that would give a total of 1,200 people. Now the total population of Sheffield is over half a million. So the proportion of the population belonging to, and actively involved in groups would

Vacant floors in city centre buildings. So why allow dwellings and offices to be built elsewhere?

A derelict building - back and front - within 5 minutes walk of the Town Hall. Why has this 'space' not been utilised?

be of the order of 1% and O.2% respectively. This suggests that most people are not very concerned about the natural environment. And many people don't act very responsibly in public green spaces.

This is confirmed for me by what I see in parks my own area. The Council has gone to the trouble to put up big clear notices stating quite unambiguously that dogs must be on a lead, and no cycling (see photo page 90). The vast majority of people completely ignore these signs. If you speak to someone, they are likely to say they have not seen the sign or they thought the sigh did not apply to that particular bit of path they are on! Sometimes they are abusive and even threatening. I have never seen a Council official walking around since I returned to live in Sheffield in 1993. I know that a few years ago, three Park Rangers were allocated to work primarily to our valley. I never saw them around in my neck of the woods except, at the edge of my particular area on a rare 'action day' by a local group. Recently I saw a couple of young mothers walking the left of one path, with one toddler walking free on the path side of one mother. A cyclist goes hurtling past without warning. Nothing happens. But supposing the toddler had faltered to the right. There would have been disaster. Some dog owners regularly throw large sticks into the brook for their dogs to retrieve, causing bank erosion and making it impossible for plant life to regenerate. It is so unnecessary and disturbing for any birds that may be associated with the river (like grey wagtails). In the next park up the valley there is also the problem of soil erosion in an old oak wood occupying a steep slope. This is caused by people and dogs walking/running up and down the slope. There is an asphalted path below the slope, and a good horizontal footpath above. So there is no need for vertical movement. At the entrance to the Park is a notice that dogs must be on a lead. Again, most people take no notice. Dogs are encouraged to run up and down by their owners; children play on the slopes – periodically rope swings have appeared and the ground beneath badly eroded, and periodically these swings have been removed.

 In my view the main thing the Council has been concerned about is to protect itself legally. But the Council must be well aware that it is utterly useless putting up prohibition notices unless it polices its land. So for example, if a person was injured by a cyclist, the Council would not have a leg to stand on despite all its notices, because many could testify that the Council makes no real effort at enforcement, and the Council cannot be ignorant of the fact that these notices are ignored. While we are on the subject of dogs, you will often find notices on streets requesting dog owners to scoop up dog faeces. There is one such notice on the lamppost outside my house, although I never asked for such notices to be put up. Dog owners simply ignore these notices. Dog shit is liable to be deposited anywhere. And I have never seen someone scooping it up. **The vast majority of people just do not care about the environment beyond their own property**.

While the Council will not find money for policing, it has been very active in sending people round parks cutting off branches of trees, even cutting trees off halfway up, to avoid the rare possibility of a rotten branch falling on someone. There is one piece of woodland a long way out from the City on what is known as Blackamoor. There is a sunken track. In one area it has become overgrown with brambles. So people walk along the top of the bank, causing soil erosion over tree roots. A hundred yards or so higher up the track, there is a group of old trees including a massive beech with widely spreading low branches – it was a real beauty. If the Council people had any nous, they would clear the brambles off the track. This they don't do, but they lop off a large branch of the beech, destroying the magic of its beauty. When I mentioned this to a senior staff member at Sheffield Wildlife trust he commented – "perhaps the Council tree people got a grant for cutting branches"! One used to assume that if you went through a wood, you accepted the possible consequences. Surely this cutting activity should be stopped. Once again I think the motive for the policy is simply a legal one.

To come back to local groups. Despite their small active membership, local groups do sometimes significantly contribute to the conservation of the environment, and occasionally are able to secure funds for major renovation - for example the Botanical Gardens, currently being restored. Even such successes, however, have a negative side. The conservation and restoration of environment is really the responsibility of the City Council, which likes to speak of the efforts of local groups in terms of 'partnership with the Council', claiming the Council has neither the money nor the manpower to deal with the local environment adequately. By doing the Council's work, local groups let the Council off the hook, and so do not encourage the Council to adopt a more responsible approach to the environment.

There are associations that enable environmental groups to meet together and exchange views. Sheffield Wildlife Conservation Group (SWCG) is a long-standing association, chaired by an official from the Museum (now a Council official), which meets in the Town Hall. As a means of heightening awareness of environmental problems, the group serves a very useful function. For a couple of years I attended the meetings fairly regularly. My predominant memory of the meetings was that they were often like a litany of complaint about the City Council – the Council was doing this harmful thing, or not doing this useful thing, the Council did not genuinely listen to local opinion, Council officials did not keep their word, etc. This mirrored my experiences in one local group, which I had helped to set up.

Then in 1995 members of local groups felt that a crisis was looming. The City Council put forwards proposals to modify the deposit version of the UDP (see later) to allow limited infill on green land, on 47 developed sites within Sheffield's Green Belt, something that many people opposed. Also, the City Council owned about 8,000 acres of land on the western fringe of the city – farmland, moorland and woodland. The council was planning to sell off some of this land (especially farms which were managed by tenant farmers). People were very concerned that once the Council lost control of the land, it would be easier for developers to move in. This would especially apply if the tenants, now owners, subsequently sold on their farms. This might for example allow further spreading of paper waste (which was already in some areas destroying habitat and damaging landscape) and prevent the Council opening up more footpaths for the public (a matter of considerable concern in Sheffield). Lastly, there was the perception that the Council was not doing enough to utilise derelict land for development rather than using green land.

I wanted SWCG to pass a resolution objecting to the proposed UDP related changes, and that would have been supported by most people in SWCG. But we were informed from the chair that it was not possible for the group to pass resolutions. I thought that was very odd, and suspected that the chairperson, being employed by the museum which needed to retain Council support, was unwilling to damage her own prospects by allowing anti-Council resolutions; and indeed I was told by one Council official later that it was nonsense that the Group could not pass resolutions. Be that as it may, we were unable to take action. My feelings were that we needed to form a new umbrella group that was completely independent of the City Council, which could pass resolutions!

So two other environmental campaigners and I decided to try to set up an independent umbrella organisation and we succeeded. Eventually it was called Sheffield Environment Watch. The group was democratically organised – the organisation of the meetings – chairman, secretary, choice of venue passed from one group to another, sharing out the responsibility and cost. The early meetings were well attended by representatives of local groups. As far as sales of land was concerned we felt strongly that the City Council owned this green land on our (the publics) behalf – the land was our land, and the Council did not have the right to sell it. We passed resolutions, wrote letters, issued press releases etc. At the same time many people in Sheffield, both private individuals, and people writing on behalf of local groups were, independently of SEW, campaigning about these various issues. Prominent here were the Shirebrook Conservation Group, the Rivelin Conservation Group, the Ramblers Association (RA) and the Sheffield Campaign for Access to the Moorland (SCAM) - all of which were represented at SEW. It so turned out that it was only shortly after SEW was formed that the Council, bowing to the considerable pressure from the public, withdrew its proposals for the 47 sites, but SEW continued to campaign on the other issues. The Council did not abandon its plans to sell farms. But the Campaigning, principally by RA and SCAM, but also by SEW, led to concessions being obtained from the Council. In particular the Council agreed to dedicate new footpaths before sales of farms took place. And we were assured that covenants on sales would have built in provision to protect the environment.

So on the development of the 47 sites and on the sale of rural land fronts, a sense of achievement was felt by local groups: serious threats to green land had been combated with some apparently real success. However, attendance at SEW gradually declined, and at the present time SEW is moribund. Perhaps the sense of threats averted led some people to consider attendance at SEW was no longer a priority. However, I think there were two other reasons why membership declined. First, I had wanted SEW to do a lot more than react against potential harmful developments. My vision was of a group which worked out for itself, quite independently of the Council, an environmental strategy for Sheffield and then use all available means to get the strategy adopted by the Council. In other words, I hoped we would become a pro-active rather than a re-active group. However, only a very few other people apparently shared the view that this was both necessary and feasible. I think this is to some extent an example of the NIMBY phenomenon (a development is not my concern provided it is not in my backyard), (Barker, 1998). But in addition, in Sheffield, as I suspect elsewhere, it is really only a handful of people who do most of the work. The most active environmental campaigners are often members of two, three or more groups. They accept an almost intolerable burden of responsibility (indeed I would say that in recent years, most of the positive developments on the environmental front which have resulted from campaigning, have been primarily the work of not more than a dozen individuals – what one can call the key players). Taking an active part in SEW was, they found, a burden too many, once the reasons for the groups initial founding apparently strongly diminished. However, if such activists had really felt the strategic approach was vital, and feasible, they would I think have dropped some other responsibilities and kept on with SEW. I believe it is a great pity that SEW is moribund. As one member of the Ramblers Association put it in a recent meeting – the Council does not worry about isolated groups making a noise; divided we fall.

Another liaison group is the Sheffield Environment Forum (SEF):

"SEF was established in 1990 as a partnership of organisations, groups and individuals committed to the conservation of Sheffield's environment and to the solving of local, national and global environmental problems" (Council leaflet). It is composed of the Open Forum (OF) and the Environmental Forum Steering Group (EPSG). OF consists of occasional public meetings organised by the EFSG at which particular issues are addressed, one or more guest speakers being invited to introduce the topics chosen, the wider general public being invited, and the Forum Annual General Meeting is held. The body is not really independent of the Council, and until recently a Council official acted as secretary.

The EFSG consists of elected members of the OF, who collectively represent a variety of organisations. It organises the Open Forum meetings; on behalf of the forum it discusses environmental problems, develops recommendations for action and policy statements, and passes on its findings to Sheffield Environment Partnership (SEP), (described later) through its membership of that organisation.

The question must however be asked, has the Forum had much effect on Council policy, and is it likely to have much effect in future? This might occur in two ways:

    (i) the Open Forum meetings might galvanise people to actively campaign on a shared vision and encourage local group cooperation;
    (ii) the Forum might have a more direct effect on Council environmental policy through the Steering Group's membership of SEP.

It is not possible to fully evaluate these possibilities. All I can do, as a member of the Forum and the Steering group since early 1997, is to draw some tentative conclusions of my own. As far as the Open Forum meetings are concerned, attendance has been very variable. At a couple of meetings since I joined, there has been a good attendance. More commonly attendance has been moderate or poor, consisting largely of members of local groups –i.e. those already converted to the environmental cause. Probably the value of the OF meetings has been similar to that of SWCG. I don't think the open meetings have galvanised people to concerted environmental campaigning.

With the Steering Group, attendance has also been variable. Ten people are the most we have had at a meeting, and latterly it has usually been far fewer. We have formulated proposals and criticisms of Council strategy and presented these at SEP meetings. In the period that I have known it, we have never managed to get properly organised. I do not think the City Council takes the Steering group seriously - we hear that some Council officials say that we are not truly representative of environmental groups in Sheffield, and I think they have a valid point here.

We have in fact found it very difficult to recruit any new members to the Steering group. At our recent Annual General Meeting (6th July) there was only a moderate attendance. Despite exhortations from both Co-Chair persons, only one member of the meeting volunteered to join the Steering Group. Present Steering group members were re-elected on the nod. I personally do not think we have had any significant effect on Council attitudes, although I am aware of a couple of colleagues who take a more sanguine view.

Sheffield Environment Partnership(SEP) is an official City Council Committee with representatives from the voluntary and business sectors of the City and chaired by a member of the City Council. It meets several times a year and discusses a whole range of environmental matters and relevant Council policies. Formerly called the Sheffield City Council Environment Working Party, its name was changed to SEW after the change in political leadership of the Council, which took place in May 1999.

SEP considers reports from various bodies, for example the Council's Countryside Strategy Working Group and its own sub-group on waste management. Since the change of political leadership the meetings have in my view, become more structured and therefore potentially more effective. We now have the situation where each meeting focuses on a particular issue (while at the same time allowing reporting on and discussion of, other issues). Speakers both from the City Council offices and outside bodies (e.g. Sheffield University), are invited to address the meetings on the issues chosen, and it is possible to question and criticise speakers. While these changes have been taking place, we in the EFSG have adopted a similar timetabling approach, and in addition attempted to coordinate our approach to the Council's by for example having an open meeting on an issue around the same time as the Partnership meeting on the same issue, and having our own meeting on an issue in advance of SEP considering that issue, so that we can constructively contribute at the forthcoming SEP meeting. Meetings are usually only poorly attended by representatives of the business community. It is too early to evaluate the significance of SEP in determining Council policy.

E. The development of environmental policy in Sheffield in recent times

For many years conservation organisations and individual environmental activists have campaigned for the Council to take more seriously environmental issues. An important new stimulus for change came from the Heads of Government 'Earth Summit' in Rio de Janeiro, Brazil, in 1992. This adopted the Agenda 21 for sustainable development (the 21 means the 21st century). From this summit arose national and local commitment to produce agenda 21 action plans. In Sheffield the City Council brought together a group of people with interests in the environmental, health and social fields to discuss how to respond to the Agenda 21. The result was the document "Our city – our future" (Price and Greig, ibid). It noted that the four key aims of sustainable development were environmental protection, reproducing social inequalities, sustainable economic development, and participation (by everyone, in the Agenda 21 process). And it points out we need to recognise the connections between social, economic and environmental issues, finding 'common areas of action' and 'joined up' solutions instead of pursuing the 'fragmented approaches' of the past. The Council also appointed a person specifically to take forward Agenda 21.

Since the above document was published, there has been a lot of talk, lots of correspondence, lots of pretty diagrams produced by Council officials, and meetings. Two years on, you would have thought that by now a detailed strategy would have already been drawn up, put into practice, and a first monitoring report produced. Not so. At the recent meeting of Sheffield Environment Partnership (17th July 2000) we were told about a new document "Sustainable Development Strategy 1999/2000". This is full of all the usual rhetoric, repeating what was said in the earlier document. But it says that as part of the Council's commitment to Local Agenda 21, "we will begin a programme of action planning with city wide and area based partnerships. The first Local Agenda 21 action programme for Sheffield will be published in Autumn 2000".

One stimulus to the City Council to secure sustainable development, which also arose from the Rio meeting, comes from the Government's eco-management and audit scheme for UK local authorities (EMAS). This is designed to assist local authorities to improve their environmental performance. The Council has set the target of developing an EMAS scheme and getting it accepted ('accredited') by government, by 2003. The Council will establish environmental auditing procedures. All Committee reports will have to deal with environmental implications. To assist managers an explanatory document has been circulated which includes a 40-question checklist of environmental matters that should be considered. More recently it has issued what it calls an "environmental identifications matrix sheet" which lists all the various possible environmental effects of departmental proposals. The Council says it is committed to assessing in advance the environmental effects of all new policies and activities, ensuring that where there is any doubt about environmental consequences, the precautionary principle should be applied. It certainly sounds very good.

However, when the whole question of EMAS came up for discussion at the 8th May 2000 meeting of Sheffield Environment Partnerships there was some scepticism. Three concerns were:

> (i) It is all very well briefing major planning managers. But the actual key people are the asset managers. If policy directives fail to trickle down to them (as has tended to happen in the past), EMAS will have little effect.

> (ii) Much of Council work is done by contractors. In the past they have often ignored their responsibilities. Unless the Council holds contractors to their statutory responsibilities, EMAS will achieve very little.

> (iii) Other organisations besides the City Council and its contractors are involved with development. Managers require training in EMAS. A Council spokesman said that it would take until 2003 to train just its own managers, without taking on any other organisations. I wonder why it should take three years to train the Council senior staff!

One Rio Earth Summit commitment consequence was that 150 countries, including the UK, signed the Biodiversity Convention. Following on from this, the UK Government in 1994 produced "Biodiversity: The UK Action Plan" which amongst other things, promoted the development of local action plans. An Action Plan for Sheffield was launched in March 2000. This built on an audit of national priority habitats and species, carried out through the cooperation of various parties including the City Council's Ecology Unit, the City Museum's Biological Records Centre, the local natural history society (the Sorby) and the Sheffield Bird Study Group. This plan lists key habitats and species in need of protection. The plan itself is a component of the Council's "Sheffield Countryside Strategy", launched in March 1999.

It was in the context of the developing local action plan that Sheffield Wildlife Trust initiated its green corridors and biodiversity project. This project starts with the acceptance of the hypothesis that establishing connections between isolated habitat 'islands' (which is what many of Sheffield's green spots are), benefits the wildlife populations of these islands. The project also accepts that corridors are a useful tool in landscape planning. The project seeks to combine wildlife surveying with practical conservation work and promoting wider public participation. The project is part funded by the Government's Environment Action Fund.

It was recognised that most people in Sheffield have little awareness of biodiversity. So during the project development several approaches were taken to raise public awareness. Members of he general public were encouraged to take part in simple wildlife surveys of selected species. Various practical conservation activities were undertaken.

Mention should be made of Council's environmental priorities, drawn up for consideration by the Environment Agency for the latter's developing Local Environment Action Plan. This states as a basic Council 'philosophy' that the Council will give priority to environmental improvements which:

- are in or close to areas of poverty;

- bring about change where the environment is poorest;
- are where the problem is greatest;
- will contribute positively to economic regeneration.

Some of the priorities are cross-referenced with the Unitary Development Plan (considered later).

The "Sheffield's Countryside Strategy" mentioned above, reports on recent developments that affect the countryside and green spaces within the city. As is usual in documents of this type it sets forth a long list of general aspirations, aims and priorities. To me it seems to have some aims that are irreconcilable bearing in mind how many people live in the City of Sheffield. It wants to conserve biodiversity, and part of its vision is of countryside that is a source of peace and spiritual well being. On the other hand it wants to improve countryside access for everyone, apparently in almost all habitats, including river corridors, around reservoirs, woodland and farmland. And its countryside vision includes, ominously I think, "a place to participate in stimulating and challenging pursuits".

F. Positive developments.

There have been some good developments in Sheffield in recent times in addition to the ones mentioned so far.

(i) Urban food production and recycling

Own food production has a long history in Sheffield.

There were, in the early decades of this century, several blocks of allotments in Sheffield. In some of these blocks, paths between the rows of allotments were bordered by quite high hawthorn and privet hedges, in which blackbirds and song thrushes nested in spring. By the end of the Second World War, most of the allotment holders were elderly, and as they died off, this left vacant allotments. In recent decades, the whole work ethos has changed. The entertainment industry has expanded; the lure of television, and for younger people, visits to pubs and clubbing at weekend, have all taken their toll. Now many allotments are overgrown.

In some parts of the city vandalism has wrecked allotment huts, greenhouses, and plants, for example, at the large allotment site on the Manor estate, which lies adjacent to the large City Cemetery. The cemetery had been repeatedly vandalised, and the police took action to control this. But one result was that vandalism spilt over in to the neighbouring allotments- the burning of sheds, and the destruction of plants. It is now important in some areas of the city, to provide security fencing around allotments. But some other allotment sites have not been vandalised, and a hawthorn hedge and gates seem to be quite adequate for protection (as is the case with one allotment block very close to where I live).

Some allotment blocks have remained active, like the one I have just mentioned. In Sheffield as a whole, the allotment holders are a cross section of the population from university lecturers and dentists to working class people. All age groups are involved. And the allotment holders are not only from white Sheffield families but Jamaicans and Pakistanis. The allotments provide food for many households. And in recent times there has been an increase in allotment use - more people taking up plots, indeed waiting lists have in some places been increasing.

However, the allotments are not making anything like the maximum contribution to food production that they could make. According to one observer, one-third of all allotments are not used or are underused, and yet there is a waiting list for allotments! Part of the problem is tenants who hang on to allotments that they are not using because they think they may retrieve the land later- say when a son grows up and take a hand in the work. Allotment holders are required in theory to keep plots weed free, keep the land in 'good heart'. The Council has powers to issue notice to quit. But then a person can appeal to a local ombudsman, and the whole process is time and money consuming.

The majority of allotment blocks are City Council owned - 74 sites with from two or three to over 100 plots each. There are a total of 3,350 plots, covering a total of over nearly 290 ha. The biggest one, in the Meersbrook/Heeley area has over 400 sites. In addition there are a small number of privately owned allotment blocks. There are several allotment societies where tenants can get advice. The City Council is actively promoting allotment uptake, and has produced leaflets to advertise allotments, promote their uptake, and provide advice on how to get started in crop production. However, the Council Officer in Charge has no assistants, other than one part time secretarial helper, and explained to me that this is insufficient to really police, monitor and promote allotments.

The allotments now have statutory recognition so that the Council cannot get rid of a site without the support of the Allotment Federation. In the past there have been pressures from housing developers who wished to use allotment land for housing. They cannot however now take over allotment sites if the tenants do not wish to move. There was a struggle over allotments at Soaphouse Lane, Woodhouse district, S13. Housing development was on both sides of the site, and a developer wanted to take over the allotment sites. The tenants however, refused to move, and eventually the tenants achieved the retention of the allotments, and the developer agreed to provide security fencing. In general, if a developer wishes to use an allotment site, he can do so provided he can provide a site elsewhere which is convenient to present tenants, and the tenants agree to the move; then the developer has to pay for security fences, sheds and greenhouses at the new site. This is taking place at one site at Darnall. Also, the Council is bound to provide new allotments, which are accessible, if six or more people request this.

There are organisations that are promoting own food production, and especially production on organic agricultural lines. Sheffield Organic Food Initiative, a Charity started in 1999, is concerned with providing horticultural education, and through food production improving the health and well being of people, and at the same time alleviating poverty by the re-distribution of resources. They give advice to local groups, and offer short education courses – indoors in winter, but involving practical work outside in summer.

Heeley City Farm – part of a nation-wide network of city farms - is a registered charity and company limited by guarantee. Financially partly self-supporting, it also receives European and DETR funds. Situated in the inner suburbs at Richards Road, close to one of the cities main arterial roads, and not far from the Tyzack site which will be mentioned in the next sub-section, it carries out both livestock and horticultural farming (fruit and vegetables). It too offers courses on food production and related topics and helps prepare students for NVQ qualifications in horticulture and agriculture. While not strictly organic in its practices in the past, work is currently underway to redevelop the fruit and vegetable gardens using organic farming methods. There is a café (offering vegetarian courses and breads etc., using organic produce where possible and its food is GMO free) and small children's play area, so parents and teachers can bring children and school parties and 'make a day of it'. A small garden centre sells the farms own produce – plants and compost.

The Farm is now heavily involved in recycling, and invites visitors to bring their newspaper, glass, plastics, textiles, aluminium cans and foil. But it also welcomes organic and vegetable waste. And this links to an important project – the Community Composting Project. They have succeeded in involving 130 local householders in donating their kitchen waste, either through a weekly kerbside collection or by bringing it to the farm. The farm has also accepted loads of leaves collected by the City Council. Combining this material with green waste from the farm and animal manure, the farm produces compost - they are now selling about £5,000 worth of compost a year. In cooperation with Sheffield Organic Food initiative, the farm has also delivered loads of leaves to different groups of allotments.

Not only is this project doing useful recycling work, but it also shows how developing organic waste composting has the potential to make a major contribution to help the City Council in two respects. First, the more household organic waste is recycled, the smaller the need for landfill. Currently in the European Union, landfill produces about one third of the greenhouse gas methane. Secondly, garden waste dumped in householders wheelie bins is causing considerable problems at the city's incinerator – the high water content of organic waste makes it difficult to burn, and also causes problems for the air scrubbers (which remove harmful emissions).
However, the Community Composting Project is the only one of its type in the city. One might ask, why has the City Council not itself taken composting more seriously? Why are not householders provided with the means to put out for collection their organic waste separately from other waste, as happens in some European Cities?

The next example concerns the recycling of plastics, metal cans and textiles. In 1989 the British Plastics Federation opened their first household plastics reclamation plant in the UK, in a Sheffield City Council shed in the district of Attercliffe. The manager was given free rein to appoint a workforce. He chose to take on adults with severe learning difficulties. The project grew. After three years the Federation believed it had demonstrated what could be done, but that it was time now for others to take up the challenge. The result was that the manager of the business and his 17 strong workforce took over the business, setting up a limited company, Reclaim. The company, borrowing a collection vehicle, sorting and baling equipment, and with a cheque from Dow Chemicals, has now grown until it employs 70 adults with learning disabilities, collects industrial and household plastics, cans and textiles from across Yorkshire and the Humber, and the East Midlands, occupies 40,000ft. of rented factory space in the district of Owlerton, and turned over £ 0.75 million pounds in 1999. Reclaim handles ever-increasing volumes of waste materials, and provides fully accredited training for its workforce. To cater for people with learning disabilities who want to work in other settings, Reclaim has set up an employment agency, and has been instrumental in setting up an umbrella organisation concerned with the training and employment of adults with learning difficulties.

This example shows not only an aspect of what can be achieved in waste management, but it has also demonstrated how such an environmentally friendly operation can give positive social value by providing employment, and in so doing, help people who are usually considered unemployable by other agencies to live fulfilled lives. Reclaim then combines environmental and social goals, and what is more, it is a system that is replicable. We will return to Reclaim later. Another recycling organisation, started in 1998, is the RECYC Shop. This collects and accepts donations of a wide variety of materials and has been involved in some major litter collecting projects. It recognises that while paper and glass recycling may be a relatively simple affair, many products include a variety of materials so recycling is complicated. Therefore it is sometimes best to take such products, clean and refurbish them and pass on to new users, which is one activity that RRCYC has taken on board.

(ii) Creation of wildlife areas from marginal 'waste land' and derelict green space

The decline of heavy industry left behind areas of waste land, sometimes interspersed with remnant pockets of countryside, especially along the river systems to the east of the city. Various projects have reclaimed parts of this wasteland. Three cooperative ventures on the eastern side of Sheffield illustrate how proper management of unused wasteland can bring environmental benefit. These are the Shirebrook Valley project, Woodhouse Washlands Nature Reserve and the Blackburn Meadows Nature Reserve. In addition to major industrial wastelands, there are numerous small pockets of green land within the city, which are not actively managed, and often strewn with litter or building rubble. If properly managed, these could make a valuable contribution to city environment. A well-known example of where this has happened is the Ponderosa Project, which I will also describe.

In the south–east region of Sheffield, in the wide <u>Shirebrook valley</u>, which included a large area of derelict land formerly occupied by a sewage works and an old colliery. Fly tipping and motor biking contributed to damage the area. In 1982, Sheffield City Council decided to establish a Countryside Management Project for the Shire Valley. The Council bought the closed sewage works from Yorkshire Water for a nominal sum and assembled the remaining land mainly through Compulsory Purchase orders. Through its Countryside Management Service (CMS) it entered into consultations which local volunteers, which led to the establishment of Shirebrook Conservation Group being formed. This group and the CMS developed a Management Plan for the valley. The plan fits into the wider context of Sheffield's Green belt and its Nature Conservation Strategy. Proposals from the Management Plan were also included in the Unitary Development Plan (dealt with later). The Council has a project Officer who throughout the whole development process has acted to initiate and enable many tasks.

Contact with local schools led to their involvement like establishing tree nurseries for the site in school grounds. By 1996, many children and schools had become involved in some way or other with the development of the site. Volunteers had given over a thousand days of work.

Waste material and structures on the site were recycled, for example, old concrete tanks were ground up and the materials used for making footpaths. Over a hundred tons of rubbish had been removed. Over a thousand metres of mixed native hedge and 1,500 native trees were planted, 18 hectares of wildflower meadows created and managed, and a new a new Countryside Stewardship scheme approved. The area has now achieved the designation of a Local Nature Reserve (personal communication, Sally Pereira, CMS, and DETR, 1996 - which also gives details of the regeneration of the Hillsborough Park walled garden area following the Hillsborough football disaster).

Immediately east of the Shire Brook site the <u>Woodhouse Washlands</u> lie on the floodplain of the River Rother on the extreme eastern outskirts of Sheffield. Bordered by industrial sites on one side, this area has been subjected to periodic flooding over the years. Local people had known for a long time that there was lots of wildlife there. For generations, local kids had played, and sometimes boated, in 'the swamps' and known it to be 'full of snakes and newts'.

The River Rother Wildlife Strategy Group (consisting of local authority, government agencies and wildlife trusts representatives) wished to see the site properly managed for wildlife and local communities, and when Sheffield was drawing up its Nature Conservation Strategy, this site was designated as a Site of Scientific Interest. The development of management plans was a cooperative venture involving the local people, the Environment Agency, South Yorkshire Forest Partnership, the Countryside Commission and the Yorkshire Wildlife trust. The land is owned by the Environment Agency, but it has now been leased for management as a nature reserve to Yorkshire Wildlife Trust. Funds came initially from the South Yorkshire Forest Partnership, now they mainly come from the Countryside Stewardship scheme, with some income coming from grazing (land let for farming).

Now this is a regularly monitored site with action programmes to improve wildlife diversity. For example, parts of the area had been overgrazed. A more wildlife sympathetic grazing regime was introduced through the Countryside Stewardship Scheme. A judicious division of the area into open access and closed parts enables both local people to benefit from the environmental value of the site while wildlife is protected and enhanced. As a result, the washlands are now one of the top sites in the whole region for a number of uncommon species - dragonflies and damselflies, great crested newt, Snipe, Jacksnipe, Redshank and Lapwing, Sand Martin, Harvest Mouse and Water Vole (paper by C. Handley and Ian Rotherham at the South Yorkshire Biodiversity Conference March 2000).

<u>Blackburn Meadows</u> also lies on the eastern side of Sheffield, but nearer the centre of Sheffield than the Woodhouse

Washlands. It lies between the river Don to the south the tow path of a canal to the north, immediately east of the City's main sewage works. The oldest map of the area shows a small patchwork of fields, and later a farmhouse was built on part of the land. As part of the floodplain of the river Don, the area must often have been waterlogged. Early this century the meadows were developed as a sewage farm. The deposition of sludge led to the site becoming a raised platform, so that apart from rainwater it received no water except by the sewage route. Not surprisingly, the area is classed as a 'heavily polluted landfill'. Managed by Yorkshire water, the site became largely non-operational except during emergencies (floods), although some tipping of sewage cake still takes place.

It was really through the tenacious efforts of two local bird specialists, who realised the wildlife potential of the site, that eventually the Blackburn Meadows Trust was established to promote the reclamation of this site for wildlife. The Trust, which is now a registered charity, has four trustees together with representatives of local authorities, the Countryside Commission, South Yorkshire Forest, Yorkshire Wildlife Trust and local natural history societies. And the development of the site has come about through the cooperation of this Trust with Sheffield City Council, Rotherham Metropolitan Borough Council, Yorkshire Water and local wildlife groups. The site is now leased to the Sheffield City Council by Yorkshire Water, but management of visitors and the education service will shortly be transferred to Sheffield Wildlife Trust. The Centre for Environmental Conservation and Outdoor Leisure at Sheffield Hallam University provides advice on habitat management and education services.

Funds for the development came initially from two sources. First, a nearby area was to be developed for opencast mining. The Council secured planning gain from this development in the form of money to help pay for habitat restoration at Blackburn Meadows. Second, a Derelict Land Grant was secured which would pay for a full investigation of pollution at the site, and major physical development of the site. Later an Urban Programme grant (75% from government, 25% from the EU) was obtained.

One major problem that had to be dealt with was pollution from the sewage – heavy metals, and methane gas. The whole site was levelled, covered with an impermeable triple layered sheet, and then soil added on top. The twin objectives of installing the sheet were retaining water and preventing pollution from the layers beneath reaching the new soil layer. Much methane is produced by the landfill, so stone filled channels beneath the sheet and round the periphery allow the methane to escape. Besides rainwater, some water is also pumped into the site by a wind pump situated by the canal.

The site has been turned into a diversity of wetland habitats with pockets of urban prairie, surrounded by trees (see colour photo page 172). The public are encouraged to use the area. There is a car park, paths, a bird hide, a little pond where children can do pond dipping, even a poem board and sculptures in one of the wetlands. The towpath is a trail for all users, including horse riders. Some farm bird species, declining nationally, occur here as well as other bird species. Among residents and regular visitors are lapwing (breeding), little ringed plover, heron, whinchat, linnet, whitethroat and sedge warbler, red legged partridge, redshank, tufted duck, little grebe, and on the River Don alongside, the kingfisher. The site is also contributing to the general economic development of the region since industry and other businesses prefer to locate in pleasant surroundings. Blackburn meadows has been proposed as a Local Nature Reserve.

The development of Blackburn Meadows however, illustrates just how very expensive it is to clear up all the mess man has made in urban areas. The planning gain obtained for the site was about £60,000. A Derelict Land Grant and Urban Programme monies amounted to approximately £600,000. New funds (£36,000) have been secured from a new tourist development adjacent to the Meadows, in which a new Blackburn Meadows Education Centre will be developed (J.Cartwright and I.D. Rotherham, Sheffield Hallam University, personal communications).

There has also been a negative aspect to the whole development sequence. It is commonplace now to talk about the need to get local people involved right from the start of a project. Unfortunately, when this project was started (late 1980s), the City Council had a very patronising attitude to such developments. The plans were prepared and then shown to local people. In fact the locals regarded the site as just a rather nasty smelly site. And although a very few local people have come along to planning meetings, there is still no real local involvement in site management.

My wife and I visited Blackburn Meadows for the first time on a hot sunny Sunday this June. Apart from a few people sitting just inside the entrance when we arrived (who had departed when we left) we did not see a single soul in the reserve the whole hour we were there. We experienced a totally peaceful rural scene. In contrast, there were several people around the canal tow path when we arrived and when we departed, partly interested in the passage of a barge through the locks, but more so on a youth who, with a three-wheeled wide-tyred bike, was racing up and down the tow path making clouds of dust. This does not create the impression either that local people are the slightest bit interested in the reserve, or that all the educational efforts of the City Council and others have had any effect. On the other hand, I am told by one person heavily involved with the meadows, that locals are increasingly using the site for recreation (dog-walking etc) and local wardens have been appointed.

In addition to industrial wasteland there are other pockets of green land within the city which are often not managed in any way, and frequently strewn with litter or building rubble. In recent years one of these has come under positive management, as I now describe.

<u>The ponderosa project</u>

A gully between housing estates just north east of the main buildings of Sheffield University is an open space that deteriorated over the years. It became just wasteland where parents felt it was not safe for children to go, so residents largely did not use the area. Through the activity of the Sheffield Wildlife Trust and using European funding, a management scheme was developed. Paths and lighting have improved safety. The appearance and biological value of the site has been improved by planting 850 trees as a frame for the exposed lower half of the site without breaking up the dramatic view across the gully. Children from a nearby school helped to plant several thousand daffodil bulbs, and other local people made bird boxes. A man-made climbing boulder has proved a considerable attraction. So now the area is once again used, an its value for wildlife probably at least marginally improved.

(iii) Manor regeneration

One of the most deprived areas of Sheffield in recent times has been the Manor estate. It is situated east of the railway station, on the upper slopes of a hillside overlooking the Don valley. The estate formely provided part of the work force for the steel industry. The collapse of that industry led to unemployment, and many families moved out of the area, so that many properties became untenanted, and much of the property is now considered to be not worth renovating. The area became known for its high unemployment, its population experiencing bad health, low education level, and high crime rate (vandalism rife, car stealing a sort of 'rite of passage' for teenagers). The area has however a lot of open space - park land and derelict land arising through housing demolition.

A worker in the area explained to me: The people really have no connection with the open space - a huge dis-association from the land. A tree is just something a thief or mugger can hide behind. A bush is just a nuisance because litter collects around it. Otherwise the people don't seem to notice the open space, except to regard it as a dangerous place where perverts lurk, so children are told they cannot play there. But truants from school gravitate to these areas. Now the open spaces, grass verges etc. have not been properly looked after. The City Council has contracted out the maintenance work, but does not carry out an effective monitoring of the work done. And the City Council's idea seems to be that the best thing is to get rid of the open space by building on it, whereas it could be greened and play a vital part in the regeneration of the area.

However, new players have come into this dismal scene. One is Manor Rebuild Ltd, a non-profit making organisation that is providing new housing in the area. 80% of the people involved in the work of the trust are local people- they are involved both on the actual building side and also in the management of the work; some of these people have trained at Manor Rebuild. They plan for a thousand homes, some privately owned, and the Housing Association is involved with the designing of homes. Shops will also be built.

This is not to say that the whole of what we might call the Manor Rebuild project is perfect.
Thus, I first heard about it at a meeting where someone extolled the development as an example of local people being empowered to take an active part in the design and development of their own area. So it was with some keen anticipation that I went to meet an official of Manor Rebuild. He explained that it was not like that really in that there had been very little involvement of local people at the planning stage of the whole development -the local people were shown what had already been planned.

Also, if we reflect for a moment on the type of housing we need in the regeneration of cities, we might have expected that a determined effort would be made to persuade people to accept middle rise terrace/flat housing. However, the actual housing design has been based on what the people want, and they don't want flats. So we are likely to get the semi-detached houses.

A more recent development has been the formation of the Manor Castle Development Trust. This has developed a strategy for development, which comes close to the green city concept. The Trust has a Steering Group made up of business and local people. Sheffield Wildlife Trust has seconded a staff member to help the Trust, and at an early stage was involved in making a survey of the area. The area covers about ten different communities, and several local groups are getting involved. A determined effort is being made to secure maximum involvement from the local people - they are trying to contact everyone in the area. The Trust has projects in the schools. In one area, Farleigh, there used to be a shopping centre with several small shops, but most shops have closed down. The remaining shopkeepers have formed a development company to re-generate the shopping centre. The Trust has already secured some funds from various sources, and staff are confident they will be able to raise remaining monies. The big need is for capital investment, and the trust is preparing an investment portfolio. It is also hoped that the Trust will generate some income from the ground rent of new housing.

The environment is regarded as the 'key dynamic factor'. The Trust wants to promote farming in the widest sense. They would like to see all the 'green space' regenerated within 18 months. This space is extensive. It partly arises from the removal of derelict housing. Then there are five derelict allotment sites; and many of the houses have quite large 'back gardens'. The objective is to promote farming in the widest sense, and at the same time increase biodiversity. Various proposals are being considered. The Trusts favour cooperative ventures. Thus people should be encouraged to produce food in their back gardens but also cooperate to plant fruit trees on neighbouring land ('edible landscape') where people could pick fruit free of charge. Allotments would be fully restored. An Asian community is planning a market garden, making use of polytunnels. On some open areas, meat production from goats might be developed. Green industries would be promoted - growing bio fuel, composting, wind farm to provide energy for the settlements. In some areas, topsoil was previously removed, leaving a rather barren landscape, but these areas would be good places to establish wild flowers, which usually do best on a nutrient poor substrate (Sue France, Manor Castle Development Trust, personal communications).

(iv) Devonshire Quarter

This area of the city lies in the southwest quadrant of the city centre. The area contained until recently quite a lot of derelict property, as well as a large area of green open space. In the last few years various developments have been taking place. Now, to take the whole development of the area forwards, a team of Council planners have produced, over the last 18 months, a Devonshire Quarter Action Plan which I learnt about as I completed writing this book (early September, 2000, at which time I was told the Plan would be formally considered in the Planning Department the following month). The purpose of the plan is to try to integrate the various strands of Council policy and create a mixed-use region, which incorporates the principles of sustainable development and provides relatively high-density housing. The Council wishes to promote:
- energy efficiency and insulation;
- reduction of car use;
- cycling and walking;
- recycling of waste;
- water efficiency;
- re-use of existing buildings.

A community association has developed, which represents residents, voluntary organisations and commerce, and this has been involved in the production of the Action Plan; the Council hopes that more people will become involved as the development proceeds.

Already, many people of different ethnic groups live there – retired people, families with children and students. It has a school, churches, medical centre, community centre and some food shops within easy walking distance. There is good access by foot and bike. As far as car parking is concerned, some of this is basement parking. There is provision for limited visitor parking. Parking provision for residents varies, with a reduction of the usual car parking to only half a space per flat in a few areas, and a small amount of car free residential development (apart from parking for the disabled). Housing is of various types, including flats over shops, family housing and student flats. An example of proposed development is on Fitzwilliam Street, which will have family housing, local supermarket and shopping courtyard, student flats and basement car parking. It is hoped that provision of student accommodation here and elsewhere will free up some existing terrace housing in the area, which can then be renovated for other residents. The Devonshire quarter is well situated for student accommodation – the two universities in Sheffield are within fairly easy walking distance of the quarter. An example of the use of derelict areas comes at the former Trafalgar and Kangaroo works. It is hoped to develop this for business peoples' housing (for sale or shared ownership), craft workshops and studios (home working). The former Central Fire Station, a listed building, is being converted to a bar with flats above. New blocks of student flats are to be developed.

We have then here a move in the direction of an urban village. There is one important element which is however absent, and speaking to a planner I was told they had not even thought about it – the idea of own food production. And none of the housing, planned or already developed incorporates roof top gardens (in two developments, a landscape deck tops the building, but this is not conceived for food production). Further, although the idea is to provide high density housing, when I asked what the overall density would be, a planner could not say, pointing out that the Council does not have any density control policy. Despite these aspects, this Action Plan does seem to be moving an area in the direction of an urban village.

G. Negative developments

(i) An example which encapsulates much that is good and bad about the situation:
Reclaim

I mentioned the recycling organisation Reclaim in the previous Section. Clearly this organisation has successfully expanded since it started, and makes a very positive contribution to the life of the city. So far, so good. But there is another side to this story. At a presentation given to the Sheffield Environment Partnership on 10th Jan 2000, the Head of Reclaim stated that the history of Reclaim is:

> "a sad example of wasted opportunity".

Every day since it began, most of Reclaim's energy has been spent in the struggle to survive. They failed to get much support from the City Council. And ... " the task of getting different local authority departments to join up their thinking, and to work constructively with each other, as well as with the private and voluntary sectors, is beset with parochial and cultural difficulties". In the early days of Reclaim, although Sheffield Cleansing Services gave their initiative their support, Sheffield Social Services, Sheffield Health, the Employment Service, etc. gave nothing. Providing day-care for adults with learning disabilities is an expensive business -£5,000 a year per day centre place is an average figure across the country. Reclaim receives a token grant from Social Services of about £1,000 per head per year, even though it is working with, and employing, a high number of adults with challenging behaviour problems, many of whom have been excluded from other services. Reclaim has been unable to persuade the City Council to set up proper kerb side collections for plastics and textiles.

There are great possibilities arising out of the work of Reclaim. Insulating material could be created from waste textiles, - adding another employment component to the work. It would be possible to develop an education centre about waste management; a new business sector could flourish.

(ii) Council energy policy

If we look at the Energy policy of the Council we see here that although there has been considerable progress in the sphere of building energy efficiency, there have been missed opportunities, and there has been a lack of vision. An important element of energy policy nationwide is the attempt to develop renewable sources of energy so as to minimise depletion of non-renewable resources.

Now through a European Union Energy Directorate contract, a renewable energy planning study was carried out for Lancashire and Yorkshire EC (EC Commission energy contract, undated). This study aimed to:

(i) identify renewable energy resources in the region and evaluate the opportunities for their deployment;

(ii) promote a local-level development plan policy framework for the utilisation of renewable energy sources, which is fully integrated with established land use and economic development strategies in the region.

The availability of the following resources was investigated:

Landfill gas	Municipal and industrial waste
Animal slurry	Biomass
Straw	Active solar
Passive solar design	Photovoltaics
Hydro	Wind.

The final detailed and comprehensive report was published in July 1997 am submitted to local authorities. Incidentally, in a closing chapter, the report noted that while Sheffield's deposit version of the UDP had an energy policy on the design, orientation and layout of buildings, location of development, and improvements to the transport network, Sheffield had no energy policy on energy from waste, landfill gas, solar energy, sewage or biomass.

A planning officer of the Council sent the report to the Environmental Policy Co-ordinator, with the comment:
> "I feel it is important to draw the results of the survey to the attention of as many people as possible who may be in a position to make use of them, and to take whatever opportunities arise to promote renewable energy developments".

You would think that the City Council would have seized upon this document and made every effort to make use of it.

Not a bit of it. It has lain there ever since (as I write 29th February 2000). It has not been used by the Council to develop energy policy. When in early February 2000 I made enquiries in the Planning Department I was told that the reason nothing had been done was that it was for private investors to take up. When I raised the issue of inaction on this report at the meeting of Sheffield Environment Partnership 28th Feb 2000, a Council planner replied that it might be considered that renewable energy policy really fell outside the remit of a local planning authority! And yet the purpose of UDPs is to provide a framework for development and safeguarding the environment. And Sheffield's UDP states it promotes a better environment and development, which is environmentally sustainable. So is renewable energy policy outside the remit of the City Council?! And the report itself, noting that renewable energy development requires planning permission from local planning authorites, says:

"If the potential of renewable energy is to be properly realised, there is thus a need to ensure that development plans take account of the availability of renewable resources and contain policies which will assist, rather than frustrate, the implementation of local projects".

This EC contract must have cost a lot of money, and it seems this money was completely wasted as far as Sheffield is concerned!

Now it is true that by the time this report was published, the preparation of Sheffield's UDP was in an advanced stage (see the section on the UDP). Nevertheless, the final UDP was not 'adopted' until March 1998. And forward planning in the Council does not just stop once the UDP has been adopted.

A meeting of the Council's Energy Working Party was held on 14th Jan 2000, the minutes of which make interesting reading. To this meeting a report was submitted summarising the current position with respect to the Council's energy policy, adopted in May 1990, which highlighted a number of developments, with the aim of updating the policy. This energy report made no mention of the Lancashire and Yorkshire study, or indeed renewable energy. But this Energy Working Party report does say in relation to another aspect of energy policy:

"The Council's approach to energy efficiency is for the most part relatively uncoordinated and its application patchy". And more generally: "On some issues, transport for example, there is no clear policy which deals with the energy and environment issues".

(iii) Car Brook Ravine

Here is an example which in my view epitomises the attitude of the majority of Council officials and of City Councils of the past (it is too early to say if the new Council will change things): it shows total lack of vision, lack of any genuine concern for the natural environment, the 'take the easiest way approach', avoiding at all costs any confrontation with powerful business interests.

The Car Brook ravine is situated on the east side of Sheffield between housing estates, with open country to the east. It is a wild place – woodland, a stream with marshy land and grassland. But it has not been looked after properly. When I went round it with a local activist in October 1999, I saw lots of tipping round the edge, and inside abandoned supermarket trolleys, a burnt out car, etc. The City Council certainly had not shown any loving care for this beautiful spot (see photo page 90). Now the City Council itself put in a proposal for a storm water storage dam in the Ravine, which would have badly damaged the habitat, and of course bring all sorts of pollutants into the area. This was apparently in response to the need to deal with surface run off and flooding problems that would arise from the new Manor housing development that was mentioned earlier.

Sheffield Wildlife Trust (SWT) strongly opposed the proposal:
"The Sheffield Wildlife Trust could hardly be more strongly opposed to any planning application than we are to this one. It is the wrong scheme, in the wrong place, planned and designed in the wrong way" (letter from SWT's Head of Conservation and Education to the Development Control Planning Officer dated 30-7-99).

This is what the Wildlife Trust's magazine Kingfisher said about the matter (Kingfisher issue 39, spring, 1999):

"Sheffield City Council has submitted an application for the development of a storm water storage facility in the Car Brook Ravine. The area is protected under numerous council policies, forms a part of a Site of Scientific Interest and is set to become one of Sheffield's first Local Nature Reserves. Despite all this, Sheffield City Council is proposing that one of Sheffield's most valuable ecological and historical sites should be used as a storage lagoon to bear the brunt of heavy rains on the new Manor housing development. The threatened area has a rich variety of plants – including marsh, acidic grassland and an area of wet willow carr woodland. These provide an important habitat for many species, including the Large Skipper Butterfly and a rare type of hoverfly (*Neoascia meticulosa*).

Although the council has a strong commitment to nature conservation on paper, these concerns sometimes appear to take a back seat in proposed developments, and the decision making process.

The trust understands the need to solve flooding problems and deal with surface water run off from the new Manor housing development. However, the Trust has submitted a strong objection to the developer's current solution. The Trust believes that alternative suggestions should have been investigated, and a comprehensive Environmental Impact Assessment of the proposed development carried out. The water storage facility forms an important part of regenerating the Manor and Castle area and the Trust still hopes that a more sustainable approach can be adopted".

The Gleadless Valley Wildlife Group also objected strongly in their submission to the Council's Department of Planning, Transport and Highways. They pointed out that the Council's Unitary Development Plan's (UDP) policy GE12 identified the Car Brook ravine as part of a proposed Local Nature Reserve – Bowden Housteads Wood (the UDP is dealt with later). Species uncommon in Sheffield and rare in the Manor and castle area are present. These include Betony, Devils-bit Scabious, Knapweed and Heath grass in the unimproved grassland, and Ragged Robin, Common Spotted orchid, large Bittercress, Lesser Spearwort and Hoary Ragwort in the marsh. I might add that another very relevant UDP policy is GE17, which says ... "all rivers and streams will be protected and enhanced for the benefit of wildlife…requiring that any development involving alterations to the channels of rivers and streams be designed in a way which is sympathetic to nature conservation…".

The City Council had received a consultancy report to Yorkshire Water Services. Forwarded to SWT, it evoked the response that the report side-stepped many of the most difficult issues and placed a misleading interpretation on the ecological data. SWT also made the general comment that all too often consultants favour their clients' interests. The Gleadless Valley Wildlife Group carried its own detailed survey of the site, and their careful analysis, SWT claimed, seemed to contradict many of the consultancy reports recommendations. And the group also pointed out that an alternative proposal would have put the storm water storage on open grassland to one side of the Ravine that lay outside the proposed local nature reserve.

Proposals had been put forward to mitigate the damage caused by the proposed development, but SWT questioned their adequacy. One measure suggested was translocating vegetation to another site. SWT pointed out that it is effectively impossible to re-create some natural habitats, and others would take years to develop. Further, there is a large body of evidence to support the view that translocation of habitats is almost always experimental, with no guarantee of success. Finally, SWT also pointed out another disturbing feature of the Car Brook business: The Council is always talking about involving and consulting local people. But, concluded SWT, there had been a failure to appropriately involve the non-government sector and the local people in determining an acceptable solution to the storm water problem (letter from SWT's campaign and Media Officer).

Since the Council seemed determined to go ahead with the development, SWT and the Gleadless Group looked at ways to mitigate the effects by altering contours etc. and these ideas have been accepted. The result is that the development will now cause less damage than the original proposal, including safeguarding more of the wetland area. However, the damage will still be considerable.

(v) Paper pulp spreading and landfill

Damage to the environment through these activities is a nation-wide problem, but the seriousness of the situation varies considerably from one area to another. To put Sheffield in a regional context, 90% of South Yorkshire's waste goes to landfill, the 4th highest position in the country and unsustainable in the long term. A regional waste management strategy, which includes the provision of waste management infrastructure, needs to be produced as a priority, covering industrial and domestic aspects (South Yorkshire Forum, 2000).

As far as Sheffield is concerned, a fellow environmental activist of mine, Les Harris prepared a report on the situation based to a large extent on his own work. He presented his report to the Environment Working Party on behalf of the Environment forum in January 1998. I base what follows on this report, although I have been out myself to look at some of the sites. Sheffield not only has general solid waste problems, but in addition the problem of spreading paper waste on agricultural land. This is a permitted activity for 'agricultural improvement'. Many fields have been covered deep in paper pulp (chemicalised paper waste), which according to Harris comes from the Jamont plant at Stocksbridge in the north-west part of Sheffield (over the 'phone Harris tells me he thinks the person doing the spreading gets £25 a ton for dealing with this paper waste and the amount of waste run into thousands of tons). Sometimes this has altered the whole contours of an area, including skyline. One field I myself visited had originally sloped down steeply on its western side to a gully. Now the field falls away abruptly on this side – the level of the field here has been raised by several metres. Not only are contours modified, but also in the process of bringing the material and spreading it, walls and trees are sometimes removed. Furthermore, much of this 'agricultural improvement' – if indeed it does make the soil more fertile- is exactly what we do not want. We will see later in this book how unimproved grassland, a valuable habitat for wild life, has been lost to the nation through intensification of farming practice. The chief culprit in all this business, is one developer who seems to go round buying farms for the purpose of spreading paper waste.

The chief areas of concern lie on the north-west fringe of Sheffield, partly within the boundary of the Peak District National Park. The whole situation typifies in my view, the whole of the urban –rural planning scene in England. I now give a few illustrations from Harris's report, about paper waste and other landfill/tipping scenarios.

> (1) paper pulp spreading. The report has a map showing the extent of this operation. This shows several areas as big as medium sized housing estates that have been subject to paper pup spreading, some inside the Green Belt. The worst area is west of Oughtibridge.

> (2) The Old Lawns Farm rubbish tip was re-activated to take spoil from the excavation for the foundations for the water treatment works, at Rivelin (Yorkshire Water). The material to be added was to have been 25,000 tons; but tippers carried on importing 100,000 tons of rubbish of all kinds from the 'supertram' contracts (in Recent years Sheffield has begun to redevelop the tram system which was taken away some time after the second world war). As a result the landscape and view has been drastically altered.

> (3) Tipping adjacent to Dyson's works, Stopes Road, Stannington. Permission for tipping was granted by the former Wortley Rural District Council in 1966, but unfortunately no time limit was placed on the permission. Initially permission for tipping was given in association with a proposal to develop a sports pitch and a fishing lake, which did not take place. Tipping was allowed to take place over the decades, resulting in:
> a) the stream had to be culveted in a drain, which is inadequate to accommodate storm water which consequently overflows onto badger setts which have been also submerged by tipping;
> b) a beautiful valley has been submerged to provide a cheap landfill site to a depth of about 50 metres.

Harris's report highlights two general problems. First, the law is inadequate to control paper waste spreading and tipping. Second, even when the law could in theory exercise some control, the law is not enforced.

Law inadequacy is illustrated by tipping near High Bradfield (near Cliff House farm and Kirk Edge). A letter from the National Park Authority to another environmental activist colleague of mine – Terry Howard of the Ramblers Association - stated:
> "I share your concerns over the nature and scale of the operations …The work which has been carried out on the land is typical of that undertaken on many sites in the High Bradfield area in recent years on the basis of agricultural improvement. Unfortunately, the Town and Country Planning General Permitted Development Order 1995 allows material to be brought onto the land for the purposes of agricultural improvement. Whilst the agricultural benefit of some of the material which has been deposited may be debatable this is a *loophole which has been exploited in the High Bradfield area*" (my italics).

Tipping is sometimes done on sites where planning officials do not visit. Harris mentions one site where tipping should have ended in 1994, but it was still going on. Harris claims that the Planning Department had not visited the site and attempted any kind of supervision on regulatory control. Which illustrates the second problem. Lack of enforcement is normally put down by the authorities to their inability to provide sufficient manpower for the task. This is one reason why many people were concerned when the City Council announced that it was proposing to sell off farms. Harris points out that written statements from Council planners claimed that safeguards were built into the sale agreements, is of little value when "there is not the legal organisation, staff and finance to enable the law to be enforced and seen to be carried out".

(v) The Tyzack site problems

Sheffield planners and public relations people talk a lot about the 'gateways' to Sheffield and their significance for giving a good impression of the city to visitors and newcomers. You would think then that it would be a high priority to devise strategies for development in all these gateways and ensure that all development conformed to the strategy. Recent events concerning the Tyzak site tell a rather different story.

The Tyzack Engineering Company formerly operated at Heeley bottom over quite a large area of land, which lies between two of Sheffield's main arterial roads (A621 and A61) shortly before they join to enter the inner city. Proposals to develop this site have angered local residents. This led to the formation of the Tyzack Site Action Group, which includes local residents, councillors, business and political parties in the Heeley, Nether Edge and Sharrow areas. Originally Morrison's wanted to use the site for a supermarket complex. This was strongly opposed and was withdrawn for the time being. We do not need another supermarket, and one on this site would have damaged the trade of small shops in the area. Later another proposal was put forward (planning application 99/0822P) for a mixed-use development. This is also opposed. It is not that mixed development per se is opposed, rather the particular mix and land allocation in the present proposal. The Action Group has submitted a detailed objection to the proposal from which the following brief notes are taken.

This proposal is for a leisure unit, retail units, pub/restaurant, play-barn and drive –through diner. It is expected that the development will be used chiefly by people arriving by car throughout the day. The overall effect of this type of development is a disbenefit to the local community, in terms of increased congestion, noise and pollution, and decreased safety and amenity of public space.

The group does not agree that Broadfield Road is an acceptable site for the leisure unit which would have 350 car parking places. The number of car parking places seems far more than would be acceptable under government guidance given in the draft PPG13.

The group questions the applicant's implicit assumption that the site is accessible to non-car customers, arguing that the proposed development makes barriers to those requiring access by foot, cycle or through public transport, contrary to PPG13.

Planning brief (Middlewood Hospital; Wadsley Park Village)

The brief describes the site: it is situated on a partly wooded north-east facing hillside overlooking the upper Don Valley, some 3.5 miles north-west of the City Centre. It is an area of 45 ha adjacent to and south west of a main arterial road (616). This is the site of the Victorian Asylum hospital – the Middlewood Hospital. Three of the asylum buildings are listed as Grade II. The remaining hospital buildings and grounds are described in the brief as representing a fine example of a purpose-built Victorian Asylum in a mature woodland and parkland setting adjacent to the Green Belt. One area where fossil tree stumps were discovered is now scheduled as a Site of Special Interest (SSI). Areas of woodland in the south-east and north-west parts are relics of ancient Wadsley Park woodland with areas of moderately rich ground flora and are now scheduled as SSI. The site is near to bus services. The brief gives five maps of the area showing various features and general planning considerations. It also lists all the numerous Unitary Development Plan policies (see later section) which are relevant to the development.

The brief gives a description of surface geology and mining history, so it explains, the possibility of mining seams beneath the site cannot be excluded. Details of the drainage requirements of the site are given. And it makes clear the Council's general strategy:

"In view of the importance of the site it is essential that development does not take place in an uncoordinated piecemeal manner. The City Council will therefore require a comprehensive approach to the site as a whole..." (para 1.8)   and

"In view of the scale of proposed development and the possibility of development being undertaken by more than one agency, the City Council will expect a high degree of design co-operation and respect between the possible various agencies..." (para 4.2.12).

The brief says that the natural environment must be protected and enhanced; developments damaging SSIs and areas of Natural History interest will not be permitted. The hospital buildings should play an important part in development.

It will be necessary for a Traffic Impact Analysis to be carried out at the planning application stage in consultation with the relevant authorities. Developers will be required to formulate a comprehensive footpath/cycle route for the whole site as an integral part of the development scheme. The development is to be served by an internal distribution road system (shown on one of the maps). An estimate of likely parking requirement including cycle parking, will be needed to assess and ensure adequate parking facilities. There are several housing areas scattered over the site (net area of 21 ha); developers will be expected to draw on the best of cottage estate and village design to arrive at suitable contemporary design solutions. Housing development should be maximised in proximity to transport routes.

The Council wants retention of existing, and provision of new appropriate community facilities. Community facilities particularly relevant to the site include religious/meeting places, health and child care facilities, educational/training facilities; recreation, play and natural history interpretation facilities.

The Group believes that the impact of the additional traffic will fall heavily on the local community. The transport impact analysis provided in the proposal considers only whether the highway can cope with the extra traffic generated at peak times. It fails to take account of the spreading of the peak load implied by the proposed uses, which means that the proposal would add substantially to the congestion and pollution already suffered in this part of the city. The proposed increased traffic flows contradicts the Council's stated aim in the Local Transport Plan to hold car traffic at 1999 levels or below, and no attempt is made within the assessment to address this issue.

Another issue is open space. The development would substantially decrease the quality of public open space on Broadfield Road. Contrary to the applicant's claims, the proposed substitute open space will fail to address this issue.

Finally, the Group objects to the development because it wastes a substantial resource. The Group argues that the site should either be used for industrial and business development as it was designated in the UDP, or it should be used for a revised mixed scheme, possibly including residential development. Either option should be planned to take an approach that takes full account of the needs of the local community.

As I write, we await the meeting where this planning application will be considered. Now all this trouble could have been avoided. The City Council has the authority to prepare Planning Briefs for new developments, which set out not only the conditions which must be observed but also the Councils preferred options. The Council did not prepare a brief for this site. When I asked a senior planner at the Council about this, his reply was that they only have the manpower and time to prepare briefs for really large sites! – this was confirmed by a Council Planner at the meeting of Sheffield Environment Partnership on 8th of May 2000.

Just a couple of comments on the last paragraph. First, Planning briefs can be a very valuable tool to ensure that all the different objectives for the site are brought together into an integrated whole. The Council's recent planning brief for the Middlewood Hospital Wadsley Park Village may be taken as an illustration (see Box oppsite).

You can see from this brief overview of the planning brief that it is quite comprehensive. Such a brief would have been immensely valuable at the Tyzack site.

But, and here is my second comment, the Council did not have the manpower and time to prepare a planning brief. Now if you go into the Planning Department to the public counter, you are likely to find, that in one or more of the little interview partitioned areas, there is a planning officer talking to some member of the public. About what? Well it's usually some small development request (for example, someone wishing to build on a conservatory) or complaint (the garage being built down our road damages the view). Council planners spend many hours with such clients. Only the other day when I was being served at the counter, an old lady came in and asked to see "a planner" – she had apparently spoken to one earlier. The woman behind the counter asked if she could remember the name of the planner - we have so many of them she added! Surely planners time should be better allocated, and spent predominantly on planning! They should clarify the information they provide about planning applications and complaints, so that people will have less need to meet a planner; then perhaps say that interviews with members of the public will be strictly limited to 20 minutes on any one issue, and the times for interviews restricted say to two afternoons per week. And finally, they should make a charge for interviews.

(vi) Council priorities and unnecessary developments

We may question the priorities of the City Council for new developments. We used to have the Peace Gardens adjacent to the Town Hall. A much loved, quiet green place. Of course there were sometimes problems – drunks and beggars. But the Council could have dealt with these problems (just as it could enforce its own regulations in the parks but does not do so). Instead, the Council decided, as one of its priorities, to completely reorganise the Peace Garden and surrounding area. In 1998 the Peace Garden itself was dug up and trees felled. A new open space was created complete with a loud multiple fountain which attracts noisy young people. Despite the fact that the Council claims there were extensive prior consultations, the development took many people by complete surprise, and sparked off a lot of controversy in the press. Most of the money for the development came from outside – the EU and the Millennium Lottery Commission. But the changes at the Peace gardens were totally unnecessary. The Council should have been trying to secure funds for much more important things. If the Council had wanted to improve the Peace Gardens, it could have called in a local gardening or landscape firm and done the job for a tiny fraction of the money used in this development.

And then we have the National Centre for Popular Music. It is housed in a new and extremely ugly building, which is totally out of keeping with its surroundings (it was described as four giant steel drums in the Independent on 24th October 1999). This whole venture failed to attract enough users and visitors, and got into debt. Once again, we have a scheme that was backed by funds from outside (National Lottery). But the whole idea shows the Council has wrong priorities, when you consider how many important things are crying out to be done in our city and its surroundings.

(vii) Two Vignettes on developer impunity and impotence of the City Council and local   people

A few years ago, Nether Green, a western suburb. One morning when people went into town to work they noticed, to their dismay, that some beautiful mature trees lining the road had been cut down. A developer had bought the land and wanted to put up an old persons home. Planning permission had not yet been obtained. But the developer moved in very early in the morning and cut down the trees. Local people were united in thinking that the developer did this because if the cutting down had been left until later in the day people would have protested and there would have been trouble.

There was then a protest. People met outside the site. And a meeting was called in the local school, which was addressed by a senior Council official. But that could not bring the trees back. And the development went ahead.

This next one is all very recent, in fact the matter came to a head in late May and is still rumbling on. It concerns a local landmark at Crosspool, another suburb in western Sheffield, the Kings Head Pub adjacent to a main arterial road – the A57 to Manchester. Opened in 1829, it is now one of the oldest buildings in the area. A company bought the site and put in a planning application to the City Council to build a set of old peoples flats on the site. Local people wanted the building retained, and if it was not to be a pub restaurant, it should be used for some community facilities. The flat buildings would not in their view be in keeping with the surroundings (for example, the roof line would be higher than neighbouring buildings). It is worth noting here that the pub was not a listed building, and was not in a Conservation Area (although it lies very close to a Conservation Area and the Green Belt), and therefore does not require permission to actually demolish. However, the LA does have a statutory duty to ensure that all demolitions do not pose health and safety hazards. To comply with its duty, Sheffield City Council issues to all developers a 'DEM1' by which the developer has to satisfy the Council that there will be no threat to health and safety.

The company became impatient at the delay by the Council in considering its planning application and started demolishing the pub before returning the DEM1 to the Council. Protesters alerted the Council to the start of demolition and two senior Council officials went up to the site to see the demolition contractor and point out that demolition was in breach of Council regulations; and in fact, the site had not been properly secured, so slates etc. could fall on people passing by particularly in a near by alley. This secured a temporary halt to demolition. Once the site was properly secured, the Council could not stop demolition unless it could persuade English Nature to declare the building a listed building. EN officials examined the building; it did not meet ENs requirements for listing, despite the fact that local people wanted it saving. Demolition went ahead.

During this whole process local people moved onto the site and occupied the pub – for a week a few people slept inside the pub on makeshift beds. They set up a petition to save the pub and collected 1,500 signatures (including mine). A City Councillor went in to meet the protesters; demolition of the roof was continuing and bits of the roof fell down narrowly missing the Councillor, which made him very angry. The police were there but did not intervene (as one local campaigner sagely remarked – "you see John, this was a civil not a criminal business so the police cannot intervene"!!!). The Developer threatened to take the occupiers to court if they did not get out. The campaigners sought legal advice; they wondered if they could sue the developer, or sue the Council for not enforcing regulations and were told they could perhaps take action but if they failed, there would be an enormous bill; also there was a division of opinion amongst the protesters as to whether they would want to take action against the Council; so they could not go down that route.

The protesters evacuated the site, and the pub has been raised to the ground. The planning application still as I write (August) awaits a decision. During this whole business, many articles and letters in the local newspaper, and the local M.P. commissioning research in the House of Commons library on the rights and wrongs of such situations. Some important matters arise from this whole business. First, if the Council had taken action against the developer, the maximum fine that could have been secured would have been peanuts compare with the profit the developer would eventually make, so the fine is not a real deterrent. Second, this is a civil not a criminal matter. If successful legal action were taken against the developer, the latter would not then have a criminal record. Third, it seems as if the future of a building depends on English Heritage, not the local authority. A building may be precious to local people but not conform to the criteria of English Heritage, so be demolished. These various considerations mean that local people have very little power or influence in their own neighbourhood. The whole business also shows us defects of our legal system (see Barker, 1998).

(vii) Concluding comment

I have given just a few examples of developments that are matters of concern. I could have gone on to consider other examples such as the serious atmospheric pollution levels in north –east Sheffield at Tinsley by the MI motorway, and the antiquated sewage system in the city. But I think I have given enough evidence to show that all is not well in the state of Sheffield.

H. Documents that will probably shape Sheffield

How is Sheffield likely to change in the future? A lot will depend on existing policy documents. Now I had prepared a long report on documents, but for reasons of space I have condensed this to the following review. Earlier documents are listed in Appendix 3 to the Unitary Development Plan (considered later in this section). More recent ones fall into two categories – documents for the South Yorkshire Region and documents for Sheffield itself.

(i) Regional documents

Probably the most important is the Objective 1 document (South Yorkshire Forum, 2000). The EU made the decision to make special funds available for the most deprived areas in the European Union through its Objective 1 programme. One designated area for the period 2000-20006 was South Yorkshire, which of course includes Sheffield. A submission to the EU was prepared by the South Yorkshire Forum (representatives from local LAs, business, health, educational and voluntary organisation sectors, together with the Regional Development Agency and the Government Office for the Regions). The submission was finally approved in July of this year. The final document provides a full survey of the economic situation in Sheffield within the regional context, and the whole programme has a primarily economic objective.

Another document which will affect Sheffield is the Provisional Local Transport Plan for South Yorkshire (South Yorkshire Local Authorities, 2000) which has the stated vision of supporting sustainable economic development by promoting measures which offer travellers genuine choice, encouraging sustainable transport decisions, improving and protect the environment and alleviating economic social and physical disadvantages. Significantly the Plan does not propose to make use of congestion charging or road pricing, on the grounds that the economy is in such a weak position that such measures would inhibit improvement.

Transport issues are amongst the matters dealt with in the Draft Regional Planning Guidance for the Yorkshire and Humberside Regional Assembly (DRPG) RAYH, 1999. This recognises the problem of traffic congestion. It notes that we must rely less on increasing ease of travel and more on attaining accessibility through proximity; this will mean that more journeys can be accomplished by walking, cycling and local public transport, with consequent environmental and health benefits. The need for increased integration of bus and rail services is stressed, and road investment should be largely concentrated on traffic calming, cycling and pedestrianisation. Housing is another issue discussed in the DRPG, which stresses the importance of the sequential approach to housing provision, and says that within the context of improving urban quality of life, opportunities for providing additional housing within urban areas will be vigorously pursued.

In my view, the regional documents will provide a framework within which Sheffield can develop its own policies, but the Sheffield documents now to be considered will be the most important ones for shaping the future of the city.

(ii) Sheffield's Unitary Development plan (UDP)

As explained in Chapter 3, Metropolitan districts, of which Sheffield is one, have to produce a Unitary Development plan, which serves the function of both Structure Plan and Local Plans found in Counties. The government gave the Council the go-ahead to prepare the present Plan in November 1989. A draft UDP for public consultation was ready in 1991. This led to significant changes and the publication of the 'Deposit Version' of the plan in 1993. The Council produced and put on deposit its proposed changes to the Plan in Sept/Oct 1994. Further consultations were followed by more alterations and then by a Public Enquiry in 1995, and the Inspectors issued their report in 1997. The resultant plan was finally accepted as the official document (in planning jargon, the plan was 'adopted') in March 1998 - the best part of a decade since the whole UDP process started. When you consider the speed at which all sorts of changes are taking place in recent decades, this is a very long process.

The Plan explains its function: The UDP is about the environment, the development and use of land, the design of buildings, and transport. It provides the legal framework for all future planning decisions. It determines where and how all developments that may be proposed in other strategy documents may take place. So the UDP is the most important document to study if one wants to try to deduce how Sheffield is likely to develop in the future.

General Strategy is dealt with in an early section (The Strategy Policies, SP). This section notes that a balance must be struck between competing land uses, and between new development, conservation and transport. One aim is to create a more accessible city, meaning that facilities should be located where a majority of potential users can get to them most easily. The city centre should be promoted as a major commercial and cultural centre, while the lower Don valley will be developed for industry, business and other large scale uses.

The Built Environment section (BE policies) asserts that urban design should make streets convenient and safe for people with disabilities, elderly people, young people and people with young children; design should ensure that road layouts facilitate the efficient provision of public transport. The Transport section (T policies) promotes public transport, bus use, walking and cycling; a pedestrian friendly network of paths should be created throughout the city.

The Green Environment section (GE policies) provides qualified protection for the Green Belt (GE 1-6). GE12 concerns sites of special scientific interest and local nature reserves. It starts by stating bluntly and unequivocally that development, which would damage such sites, will not be permitted. It goes on to say that further Sites of Special Scientific Interest may be designated by English Nature during the period of the Plan (UDP). It is intended that these sites should also be given the same protection. The policy also states that one way it will put the policy into practice is by "applying Environmental Assessment legislation, as appropriate".

GE13 concerns areas of natural history interest and local nature sites. It begins "development which would damage Areas of Natural History Interest will normally not be permitted". It goes on to say that where development would decrease the nature conservation value of an Area of Natural History Interest or Local Nature Site, that decrease must be kept to a minimum and compensated for by the creation or enhancement of wildlife habitats elsewhere within the site or local area.

Now we have seen how the Council views these policies in practice. Their own proposal would have very seriously damaged the Car Brook ravine area. And we saw how proposed compensation for loss would have been quite inadequate. No proper environmental assessment was carried out by the Council before it submitted its proposal, despite the fact that both GE12 and GE13 specifically mention applying environmental assessment legislation so you would think they would have tried to carry out an assessment.

It is in the area of the urban village idea and the related need for densification, that the UDP shows how far away it is from the Ideal City concept. In the Housing Policies section (H policies) some support is given for the idea of mixed development. Thus H10 and 13 affirm that while housing is the preferred use of land in housing areas, small shops, community facilities and businesses for local employment may be incorporated. And a separate 'mixed use area' section (MU policies) gives further support to mixed development. There is just a possible hint of the form of an urban village (or am I reading this into what is said?) in the somewhat enigmatic statement in BE5 that "in all new developments, design should be on a human scale wherever possible, and, particularly in large-scale development, the materials should be varied and the overall mass of buildings broken down".

However, other policy statements would seem to limit the applicability of some of the above policies, even partly contradict them, and suggest that the urban village concept is far away from the thinking of the planners.

For while mixing housing with other developments is allowed, the old idea of having separate housing estates seems to be alive and well. Nor only is housing the preferred land use in housing areas (H10), but in listing permitted new development or change of use in housing areas, H14 says the development should occupy only a small area and not lead to a concentration of non-housing uses "which would threaten the residential character of the housing area". And later – "… conditions are needed to ensure that the benefits of local services, facilities and jobs do not detract from the residential character of Housing Areas or are not at the expense of people living nearby".

Housing density is not the subject of any policy in the UDP, and densification is not promoted (recall -Chapter 3 Section B - how the advantages of densification had been pointed out a long time ago). Indeed some policy statements could be used as an excuse for avoiding densification. Thus BE5 says that while original architecture will be encouraged, "new buildings should complement the scale, form and architectural style of surrounding buildings". And H14, in specifying conditions of development (new or change of use) in housing areas says that new buildings should be " in scale and character with neighbouring buildings". Further, "the site should not be overdeveloped or deprive residents of light, privacy or security, or cause serious loss of existing garden space which would harm the character of the neighbourhood". 'Overdeveloped' can be interpreted practically any way you like. And if you put up middle-rise perhaps short terrace buildings in the typical semi-detached neighbourhood, this could be interpreted as harming the character of the neighbourhood (certainly the typical middle-class resident would take this view) and not complement the scale and form of surrounding buildings. And although you could have middle rise buildings and have as big a total area of green space as in an existing semi-detached area, this would be at the expense of existing garden space.

It does seem curious that the 'urban village' concept – so important for the development of a city vision, is not used in the UDP, although the Council is aware of the concept. For a letter from Councillor Matthews to SEW says:

"In Attercliffe/Darnall the local community have made it clear that they wish to see significant new areas of housing introduced into the valley even if this causes a loss of recently greened areas. Even though this loss of greenery is in one sense regrettable, there is another strong argument in favour of dense 'urban village' development in which people are located close to work opportunities, rather than commuting to work from distant suburbs".

Having carefully studied the UDP, I conclude that there is no clear holistic vision. One finds some elements of the ideal city, yet nowhere are issues grouped together around basic concepts such as the urban neighbourhood. And certainly there is no sense at all of the overriding importance of the environment in the broad sense, and the understanding that the environment can and should form the focus for all planning. This is very disappointing when you realise, from the discussion of documents available when the UDP was being prepared (Chapter 3 Section B), that there was already a vision of the Ideal City. Now the UDP met all Government requirements (it would not have been passed by the Inspector otherwise). But there was nothing to stop the planners building in a vision of the ideal city into the document, even if they could not, under existing planning guidance, specify all the policies that would be needed to achieve the vision.

The UDP is currently under review. Part of this process is the carrying out of an Environmental Appraisal (EA). Briefly, this process is designed to ensure that the environmental situation is properly evaluated, that environmental considerations become part of the mechanism for determining policy development and that participation of local people in the whole planning process is secured. The environmental impacts of alternative ways of achieving stated policy objectives are assessed so as to determine a way forward which has the minimal impact; ways are then explored to mitigate specific impacts. An environmental baseline is established by which, using indicators, the implementation of policy can be assessed. During the appraisal, there is public consultation at various stages. EA is potentially a powerful tool to achieve sustainable development and facilitate the development of the Ideal City. For a discussion of the concept and the similar Strategic Environmental Assessment see Barker (1998, Chapter 6), EC (1995b) and DETR (1998c&d). EA has been advocated by Government for a long time (see PPG12 of 1992 and DoE 1993).

Now the City Council carried out an EA of the UDP. But they did not do it until November 1994 and then did not follow completely the process as advised by Government. Recall that the UDP went into the deposit stage in 1993, the main stage for consultation and making changes. So vital time was lost. Why then did the Council not expedite the EA earlier and expedite it more fully? A clue can be found in the EA report itself para 3.3: "Given the constraints on time and resources within which the City Council has had to operate, it has not proved possible to follow all the stages outlined in the DoE Good Practise Guide". In other words, insufficient manpower and money. This suggests to me that the Council was not taking environmental considerations seriously.

At the final stages of the UDP preparation, the Government Inspector did make reference to the EA carried out by the Council. He even recommended that the following paragraph be added to the UDP:
> "An initial environmental appraisal has been made of the Plan, in accordance with national advice, to assess the likely environmental costs and benefits of its Policies and proposals. This work will be carried forward and refined as part of the monitoring and review process, and interested organisations will be consulted on it and invited to contribute".

However, when you read the Inspectors report, it is clear that he did not consider the EA to be very important. It is mentioned in relation to SP1, but in the early chapter on how Council Strategy developed, it is not mentioned.

What has happened subsequently? Well in May of the current year, the Council produced its First Monitoring Report (FMR) of the UDP, which has an extensive series of Indicators for studying how the UDP objectives may have been met. However, the review does not make use of the above EA; I asked a planner why. I was told that there had not been the time and personnel to make use of the EA in the monitoring review!

As I said above, the UDP is now under review. As part of this process another (draft) EA has been prepared, although this is now called a 'sustainability appraisal', reflecting more recent Government advice on appraisal mechanisms. The City Council plans to have a draft (deposit version) UDP ready by the end of 2001, and hopes that the new UDP will finally be adopted in 2003.

The monitoring report notes some positive developments. Thus the yearly percentage of houses built on previously developed land has increased since 1994. There has been some success in stimulating inner city development, with 42% of all land granted development permission being in the inner city; 1,190 affordable housing units were provided from April 1997 to march 1999; supertram use has increase considerably and four of the six Local Nature reserves proposed in the UDP have now been designated.

On the other hand, the attraction of the salubrious western parts of the city for house builders is confirmed. Thus the largest number of planning applications granted permission were in the South West and the North West. "This is partly explained by a relatively large number of small housing developments on infill sites" (p.18). Despite progress in reclaiming derelict sites, 563 ha, spread over 120 sites still remain to be reclaimed. There has been a lack of progress in achieving development on most of the major industry and business sites specifically identified in the UDP. While recognising that mixed development is important for creating and sustaining communities, the report says there has been too little development to come to a view about the success or otherwise of Mixed Use Areas in promoting a variety if development. And despite national concern about edge of town developments, most applications for major out-of-centre retail and leisure developments have been allowed because they would not have been appropriate in town centre locations.

(iii) The Sheffield First document (SFD)

The SFD, produced by the then City Liaison Group, now 'Sheffield First', is probably the most important document for understanding Council strategy. Indeed the Council's Corporate Plan, considered later, specifically states that the SFD, will be the strategic plan for the city.

The Sheffield First group consists mainly of business executives, but has two senior City Council officials, the Vice-Chancellors of both universities, and a senior police official. Despite all the prevailing rhetoric about ensuring ordinary people are empowered to take part in the decision making process, there is not a single representative of any local group, and no environmental organisations are represented.

The document explains that the task of the group is three-fold:(i) to identify and address the key issues facing Sheffield; (ii) develop a widely supported vision for Sheffield and produce a strategy to deliver it; (iii) present a united view to Government (UK and European) in attracting the support and resources to do what needs to be done.

The main body of the document is divided into sections. First, EDUCATION. The focus is on raising educational attainment in Schools and improving the employability and access to jobs of the unemployed and those in work "but operating old equipment". Second, ENTERPRISE. This deals with stimulating the start up of "high-growth business"; developing key sectors such as strategic business services and stimulating new investment and jobs. Third, EQUITY. This advocates increasing the ability of local residents to participate in and influence planning and the delivery of public services; reducing health inequalities across the city and tackling crime. Fourth, EXCELLENCE. This deals with improving traffic movement, improving local neighbourhoods, partly by involving the local communities, and "sharpening up Sheffield's image". Sheffield's good points are undersold, a vision must be developed which is attractive to potential investors and visitors. The document ends with a summary of proposed actions (including targets) and a section on how the Council proposes to take matters forwards.

The document came in for a lot of criticism at meetings of the Environment Forum Steering Group and Sheffield Environment partnership. **In the present writer's opinion, this is a disgraceful document, for the following reason**s.

1) The group exhibits appalling complacency, clearly failing to realise how fundamental and all-embracing Sheffield's problems are. What is needed, the document says, is to concentrate on a relatively small number of areas where substantial change is required. This is a total misreading of the situation in that substantial change is required on all fronts. The caveat that follows - the actions proposed are not the only important things that need to happen, very many other organisations and individuals are bringing about significant improvements in the city - ignores the fact that there is a total lack of any overall strategy which could ensure these other organisations do more than patching up a few holes here and there.

2) This document could largely have been written twenty years ago. It says little that is new. Sheffield, along with other cities has been battling for decades with problems like social exclusion, pollution, unemployment, the difficulty of attracting investment, educating the poorer members of the society, etc., without much success. Surely one needs a radically different approach. This document does not provide it. The document stands in stark contrast to recent government policy statements such as the "Panning for Sustainable Development" DETR, 1998) that was discussed in the previous chapter.

3) Underlying its approach is the belief in the power of competition to solve the problems. The very title of the document, and of the organisation which produced it, speaks volumes – "Sheffield First" - the devil take other towns in the area (and remember the reason, mentioned above, of why they changed the name to Sheffield First). They want, they say, to develop Sheffield as the major city of the South Pennine Region. Why? Does it need to become 'the major city' in order to become a sustainable one? The other side of this coin is that there is no recognition of Sheffield's responsibility to the rest of the region, the country and the world - thus the whole concept of ecological footprints does not get a look in.

4) All development in Sheffield is primarily determined by the constraints of the Unitary Development Plan (UDP). And Government has recently re-affirmed the central role of Development Plans in its Planning Concordat of February 1999. Now the document does say that developing a new vision for Sheffield would require revising the Unitary Development Plan. And it specifically states..."A review of the Unitary Development Plan to be announced in July and Completed by December...". But when in the autumn of 1999 I mentioned this to a senior Council planner he said that he had not heard of this; subsequently he told me it was not so –there were no plans to complete a UDP review by December, the

document was mistaken! And the document itself does not use the UDP as a point of departure, or cross-reference to it in the different sections.

5) There is no real appreciation of the all-pervading importance of the physical environment. It is true that the environment is mentioned. Early on, the document does acknowledge that the environmental impacts of new development are important. In the "key sectors" of the "Enterprise" section it does mention environmental industries - the provision of new techniques and technology to protect the environment. Reducing health inequalities across the city has a section of its own, but largely couched in terms of improving service delivery and making it easier for people to buy healthy food. And in the "Excellence" section, environmental improvements (removal of eyesores, enhanced lighting, design improvements), involving local communities in improving their immediate environment and environmental planting (presumably of trees) are mentioned. But the ideas are not developed.

However the environment is a fragmented concept in the document; there is no vision of the Green City, no sense that the environment provides the fundamental key to development. Consider healthy food. The document speaks of making it easier for people to buy healthy food. But there is no mention of the more important need to encourage people to grow their own healthy food, with all the additional advantages which impinge on all aspects of successful city regeneration - providing people with healthy exercise, the potential of food growing to encourage community action, encourage people to become involved in community life, to become involved with the development of their city, reducing the need for transport to carry food around, the potential for a major contribution to reducing unemployment by developing urban agriculture (you might have expected this theme to have been developed in the Employability subsection of the Education Section). No doubt members of Sheffield First would counter by saying there are existing organisations in the city, which are working on these topics. But their impact is very small at the moment and this is a key area that needs determined coordination and support at City level, which it is not getting. It is vitally important that an understanding of the environment and the ways that human activity threatens it is incorporated into all education programmes. Yet there is no mention of this in the Education section.

Pollution, energy conservation, recycling and waste disposal are not dealt with (you would have thought that pollution would be mentioned and given real prominence in the health section). Nationally, Councils are urged to build their strategies around the Agenda 21 concept, and local agenda 21 strategies. But Agenda 21 is not even mentioned in this document. Now the document was produced in July 1999. It was preceded by a draft discussion document of the same title issued in the autumn of 1998. And the final document discusses the response to the discussion document. It is ironic then that in some ways the finished document is even worse than the earlier discussion document. The latter did at least mention Agenda 21. And at the end it had a section on making the strategy sustainable, which says things like it is not impossible to reconcile job growth and development with environmental sustainability, and mentions green commuter plans. This section was dropped in producing the final document.

6) There is no holistic vision, not even an appreciation that such a vision is lacking in the city. So many important issues are either only just touched on, or else completely ignored, in the field of overall urban design. Mention is indeed made of the need to integrate transport modes to improve traffic movement, the need to invest in high quality transport corridors, of the need for railway (Midland Main Line) track improvements and introduction of traffic management measures (not specified) and encouraging long stay commuters to use public transport (but then also improving access by giving priority to shopper and visitor car parking). But there is nothing about specifically encouraging foot and bike access, or the need to integrate transport with housing provision. Housing is not dealt with except to say that poor housing is one cause of ill health. The need to increase housing density, the need for 'sequential development', the urgent need for urban capacity studies and making maximum use of brownfield land for development so as to reduce green land loss to development, mixed use development, the urban neighbourhood and urban village concepts, are all ignored.

Finally, it is a serious matter that the two universities, which have between them considerable expertise in all aspects of urban development and sustainable development, should have their bosses involved in producing and putting their names to such a document.

(iv) The Council's Corporate Plan document

This is a shorter document than the Sheffield First document. There is no publication date on it but I am told it was published July 1998. The document notes that the Council is a key member of The City Liaison Group, which, it says, is set to launch its strategic plan in the autumn (this is the Sheffield First Document discussed above).
The Council's vision is stated:

(i) to be among the best managed Councils, providing the best quality services, in the country;

(ii) to work in active partnership with the community to regenerate Sheffield, and improve the quality of life for all its residents.

I note the following key points in the document.

a) The Council is streamlining its decision-making, breaking down departmental and professional barriers. It plans a series of systematic reviews of service provision, etc.

b) Funding opportunities will be maximised by working to secure European funding and promoting a positive image of Sheffield.

c) The Council will get closer to the community by helping voluntary organisations to access funding and work together.

d) To make itself more sensitive to local circumstances, the Council is setting up Area Panels (referred to earlier in Section B) which will hold public meetings with local organisations and individuals in the different areas of the city.

e) The council intends to prevent class sizes increasing, provide more funds for school buildings and provide extra activities for young people in school holidays. While most service budgets are unlikely to be increased, the exception will be education.

f) A special team has been set up to take a tougher line on neighbourhood nuisance, and has prepared a crime audit of the city.

g) The Council will develop a more co-ordinated approach to the environment, which deals with things like litter and graffiti.

h) All services will improve as measured by national performance indicators. With the active involvement of our communities our parks will be a source of pride.

There are clearly some good moves and intentions here. The Council does indeed seem to be trying to streamline procedures, and the Area Panels have great potentiality for the development of urban neighbourhoods (discussed in the previous Chapter). However, I am left with a feeling of deja vu - most of what is said has been said before. And how is one going to achieve aims like making parks sources of pride (point h) unless service budgets are increases (point e).

Now the Corporate Plan document is not a one off statement of intent. Rather it is meant to be periodically revised or 'rolled forwards' as the jargon has it. Now the first revision has appeared. Once again there is no publication date, but it is signed by the Chief Executive with the date January 2000. Some progress is reported – improvement in senior management structures and the introduction of a Council wide system of employee appraisal. A three-year financial strategy has been drawn up and a new investment agency ("Sheffield First For Investment") has been set up.

I. Conclusions. Whither Sheffield?

How and to what extent will Sheffield change in the future? What are the chances of Sheffield becoming transformed in the short or medium term future to be a truly sustainable city, a city which at least approaches the 'ideal city' concept? In the writers view, it is unlikely that this will happen.

If we leave aside unforeseen global and national economic factors including changes brought about by global warming, the future of Sheffield will depend principally on the following factors –first, the present state of Sheffield; second, the extent that individuals, local groups and other non-governmental organisations exert pressure to change the developmental path of the city; third, changes in national law and planning guidance; fourth Council policies, and the attitude of the Council and the planning establishment of the City. We look briefly at each of these factors in turn.

Any future change in Sheffield has to start with what we have got at the moment – the city layout, existing buildings including housing, the present road network. No planning starts from scratch. Consider an extreme example. Suppose it was desired to change the Whirlow area into an urban village. Theoretically this is possible. But much of the building is recent or still being constructed, is presumably of solid workmanship and property is mainly privately and individually owned. The area is mainly residential. To create an urban village within the existing Whirlow built up area, with its variety of building heights and shapes, variety of house price, shops, community and employment opportunities, would at the very least require the most radical national policy. Even the more limited objective of an appreciable degree of densification would be only a little easier to achieve. Whirlow, an extreme case perhaps, but the same difficulties, although often to lesser degree, would apply in most parts of Sheffield. Further, building does not come in discrete stages. It is going on continuously. New planning applications, decisions on existing applications, site clearance for development, new building, are going on simultaneously all the time.

Local groups and NGOs could in theory exert a big influence on the future development of Sheffield. But as far as local groups are concerned, past experience suggests that while they may be successful in resisting some adverse developments (at least temporarily), or in facilitating some localised environmental improvements, they are unlikely to have any real impact on the development of the City Council's strategic policy. Bearing in mind however, the fact that the CPRE played a leading role in securing our Green Belt, we should not discount the possibility that some NGOs might be able to significantly alter the course of policy development.

The Lord Rogers task force and other bodies and individuals have suggested numerous ways to change planning law and guidance. But any attempt at radical change would probably receive strong opposition from present developers and from car and road freight organisations, who would do their best to impede change, ably and probably effectively backed by a legal system which is not fundamentally concerned about the environment anyway, but is expertly concerned with people making a profit irrespective of any damage to the community. Likewise, radical changes to the UDP will be opposed by the same parties.

We have seen how the Council has two main responses when it has failed to prevent environmental damage or to secure environmental improvement. The first response is to say that the Council is impotent to do anything because the law, in the widest sense of that word, is inadequate. The Council is undoubtedly correct – up to a point. But many people feel that they could have done more if they really wanted to.

The second response is to say that the Council does not have the personnel/ money/ time to cope with the situation. However, the Council to a considerable extent controls how it allocates its resources, and many people think that the Council should have concentrated more on environmental improvement. Sometimes the two responses are combined, as in the whole question of control of tipping and landfill.

Council policy is a very slowly changing organism. The basic planning document, the UDP, takes years to develop, and years to revise. And although changes to speed up the process have been proposed by Lord Rogers and others, it is likely to remain at least a fairly long drawn out process. The existing UDP could not deliver anything like an ideal city, however one might conceive that. Yet this UDP will still govern development for the next few years. The Council hopes to have a draft new UDP adopted in 2003, but that is still a long time away. However, I am told that provisions in PPG 3 (Housing) can be applied to the implementation of the existing UDP in the intervening time. It remains to be seen if the Council has the will to ensure developers comply with any changes resulting from the application of this PPG and other recent Government Guidance.

Most important of all, I think, is the attitude of the City Council, its planning fraternity in the Town Hall, and Sheffield's business leaders. The discussion of basic documents given earlier suggests that the Council may continue in its old ways, failing to take the natural environment seriously in its strategic planning, and being reactive rather than proactive on the environmental front. As far as actual environmental improvement itself is concerned, the Council has tended to leave this in the hands of others. Thus the numerous urban regeneration of waste land projects, some of which were detailed earlier in this chapter, have depended primarily on the enthusiasms of a small minority of private people and a few environmental organisations such as Sheffield Wildlife Trust, although the Council has cooperated and assisted in these ventures in various ways. However, the Council has failed to develop and implement an effective overall environmental strategy. Gradually changing Government policy will perhaps force the Council to a more active environmental role, and it is possible that the new political leadership of the Council may push things in the same direction; however, it is too soon to tell about the latter. And even if the Council itself wished to put the environment at the centre of development, they might well find themselves against the dead weight of its own planning department which will I think continue to do as little as possible consistent with existing law.

In the past, Council planners seem to have relied on observing the minimum requirements of national law and planning guidance on the particulars of development, and together with business leaders, have trusted that competition will revitalise the city's economy and bring about an urban renaissance, which so far has not occurred. Above all, there seems to be no strong all-embracing vision of how Sheffield might be transformed into an ideal city.

City centre car park. No sence of civic pride. Would this happen in Germany?

Prominent notice in Endcliffe Park. No one takes the slightest notice, but the City Council doesn't seem to care.

In the Carbrook Ravine. The City Council has not shown any loving care for this beautiful spot. But do most of the local residents care anyway?

Chapter 5

The Changing Countryside, part 1.
Population, Economy, Protected areas, Wildlife

A. Demographic aspects - urbanisation and counter-urbanisation

The processes of urbanisation and counter-urbanisation were dealt with in Chapter 2. We simply note here how they have impinged on the countryside. In the first place rural communities have altered – losing many of their young people, but gaining many well-off urban working people and people who are retiring. These changes in turn have contributed to the increasing commuting between countryside and town – working people living in the countryside but working in town; older people travelling to town for shopping. The influx of wealthy people has driven up house prices in rural areas, making it more difficult for young rural people to find accommodation.

The population of districts with a predominantly rural character grew faster than that of England as a whole (10.3% compared with 5.3%) between 1984 and 1998 (CA 2000). The main reason was that counter-urbanisation has been greater than urbanization in recent decades. This has pushed up the amount of house building in rural areas, and hence the loss of green land to development. The point to note here is that human population factors have been a major cause of countryside change. In view of this it is worth emphasizing again that a major cause of counter-urbanisation is the attraction of living in a rural environment. Thus FoE (1994) mentions a 1992 study by R.Mintel, which found that when people were questioned about this matter, ten percent said that they planned to move from an urban to a rural area in the next five years, and 45% gave their main reason for wanting to make such a move, the appeal of open space in rural areas. These various matters will be taken up again in following sections.

The general relationships of urbanisation and counter-urbanisation are summarised diagrammatically in Fig. 12 page 210.

B. Changes in farming - economic aspects

There has been a long-term decline in employment in agriculture from the mid 1940s when agriculture was the major employer of labour in rural areas (Baldock et al 1996). Between 1950 and 1994, the total farm labour force decreased from about one million to 431,000 (RDC, 1995). This decline has been a steady one over time, and continues (e.g. EC, 1997).

At the same time, there was a decrease in the number of farms and a general increase in farm size: the national average size by 1991 was nearly three times what it had been at the end of the second world war. These changes have taken place at a time of a big change in land tenure, partly caused by taxation policies. The traditional landlord and tenant system has largely broken down. In 1939, 65% of the land was held on a landlord and tenant system; this fell to 35% by 1990 (Soper and Carter, 1991). Many tenants bought farms or parts of farms, and big agri-businesses developed. The break up of estates led to increased opportunity for amalgamation of farms into larger units. This formation was also assisted by small farm business failure. Contract farming operated by specialist land management companies has become increasingly important. These companies will undertake to take over the management of a farm, paying the owner a fee and a share of the profits.

All these changes have been associated with, and as far as decline in farm labour force caused by, a fundamental change from a labour intensive, to a capital intensive industry. This has been made possible by increased mechanisation, and improved productivity per acre/animal through genetical improvement of strains, increased use of artificial fertilizer and increased use of pesticides in disease control. These factors have meant that productivity per man has risen dramatically. So the agricultural scene has become dominated by intensive farming, of which more will be said in another section. Farming has also become more specialised, with a decrease in mixed farming (Soper and Carter, ibid; Baldock et al, ibid).

Behind all these changes have been various financial pressures. In the first place, the change from landlord - tenant to owner-occupier system was often associated with tenants having to borrow money to buy their farms, thus saddling themselves with interest payments (Soper and Carter, ibid). Second, inflation led to very large increases in the costs of farm inputs – machinery, labour, fertilizer, chemicals, and, with tenant farmers, rent. But at the same time, prices of farm products did not generally keep pace with this inflation. Large farms could better cope with this disparity (economies of

Trends in Total Income from Farming and income per head in the UK (real terms, 1998 prices)

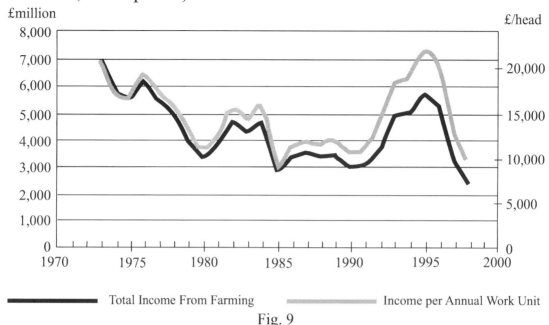

Fig. 9

From MAFF (1999a). Crown Copyright material is reproduced with the permision of the controller of Her Majesty's Stationery Office

scale). Also, standards of living have been rising, resulting in consumers spending a smaller share of their family budget on necessities like food. These factors have meant that agriculture's relative importance in the UK economy has been declining over the last twenty years, from 3% of GDP to 1% (MAFF, 1999). Total income from farming has declined considerably, although cyclic changes in market conditions and other factors (see below) meant that the decline was not a smooth one (Fig. 9).

Declining farm incomes and other financial pressures, especially in the late 1980s and early 1990s caused many farm families to look for alternative work to supplement their income – variously called pluri-activity, multiple job holding, and, especially when it involves alternative land use, farm diversification. At the beginning of the 1990s it was estimated that 40% of agricultural holdings in England undertook some form of non-farm business such as tourism or contracting (Tarling et al, 1993). The variety of activities undertaken is large –see Nix (1996).

The early 1990s saw a big, temporary upturn in farm incomes, partly caused by the devaluation of the pound, and much of the farming sector showed good profits - between 1991 and 1996 farm incomes rose by 65% in real terms (MAFF, 1997). However, since the mid 1990s there has been a sharp and severe downturn in farm incomes. There are various reasons for this, according to the NFU (1999):

    (i) the rise in the value of the pound has made UK exports less competitive;

    (ii) interest rates are much higher than on the continent so farmers borrow more money than their continental competitors;

    (iii) there is a higher level of regulation and 'red tape' compared to continental countries, much of which the NFU alleges, is the result of the UK governments interpretation of EU regulations (by inference, these regulations could have been interpreted in a more farmer friendly way);

    (iv) the UK has adopted particularly high environmental , employment and animal welfare standards, which raise the cost of farming. To this must be added increasing fuel costs;

    (v) a marked decrease in demand for agricultural products by Russia, Asian countries and Brazil.

To these reasons must be added the continued impact of the BSE crisis.

One final point about the declining total labour force. This decline hit components of the force to different extents. Thus between 1981 and 1991 the decreases were least for farmers, partners and directors (4.5%) and salaried managers (1%).

It was greatest for hired full and part time workers (31.5%). The decrease in seasonal and casual workers was much less (11%) showing the relative importance of this group had increased (Baldock et al, ibid, using figures of J.N. Pretty).

C. Business and the rural economy

In the following summary, "small businesses" or "small firms" will be repeatedly mentioned. The reader should bear in mind that such a category may be defined in different ways by different investigators. Some studies also concentrate on SMEs (small and medium sized businesses) in contrast to big businesses. Since the relationship of business to the changes in the rural economy relates to economic change in the country as a whole, some general features of UK economy will be considered first.

(i) Changes in the UK as a whole

Various factors have affected the changes in the rural economy. Some of these are changes in economic activity and employment in the UK as a whole, including the following (Tarling et al 1993; North and Smallbone 1993):

(a) In both the 1970s and the 1980s, total employment (including self-employment) increased by about 3%. However, employment fell in agriculture (by 13% in 1970s, 11% in 1980s) and in manufacturing (in the 1970s by over 20%, the 1980s, about 20%). The service sector as a whole showed increased employment.

(b) In recent decades there has been a trend to increasing proportion of white-collar occupations while craft, skilled manual, machine operatives, and many unskilled employment categories have shown a fall in employment.

(c) The proportion of small firms has increased in recent decades. In 1991, of the 1.54 million firms, 86% had a turnover of less than 0.5Million. Only 4% had a turnover of more than £2 million/year. At present, all sectors of the economy have large proportions of small firms. Again thinking in terms of firms with a turnover of under 0.5m a year, the proportion of such firms to total firms varied from 53% (energy) to 96% (catering); But in all sectors apart from energy and wholesaling, the proportion exceeded 70%.

(d) There has been a high rate of new business formation, but this has been accompanied by a high rate of business failures. The statistics used most widely for studying rates of birth and death of businesses are the VAT business registration statistics (although it must be remembered that not all de-registrations mean definite failure). The extent of this 'turbulence', and the balance of formation and failure can be gathered from the fact that between 1979 and 1990 there were 2.1m new business registrations, 1.7m de-registrations.

(e) In terms of number of businesses, most 'small firms' are very small. In fact, roughly 2/3rds of all small businesses consist of the owner alone; less than one in five small businesses have a workforce of five or more people. This situation is correlated to the fact that in the 1980s self-employment grew considerably - by 1.25m or 70%.

(f) In terms of sectors of employment, the number of businesses increased in all sectors except for agriculture and retailing. Financial and other 'services' grew faster than manufacturing and other production businesses.

(g) The increase in the number of businesses over the decade was however not uniform over businesses of all sizes. Amongst small businesses, it seems to be only the very small classes that have contributed considerably to new business formation. Slightly bigger businesses (20-49 employees) declined nationally. This suggests that new businesses are having problems in growing above a fairly small size.

(h) How then does increase of businesses relate to change in employment? It seems generally agreed that small firms created more new jobs than big firms, but opinions differ on how big the disparity has been. Perhaps even more controversial is the answer to the question - what proportion of small firms have really been involved in significant increase of employment - is it most, or only a few? North and Smallbone (ibid) incline to the view that it is a relatively small percent of the small firms that are particularly involved in job creation.

 As far as the manufacturing industries there is information available to compare small firms (here defined as 20-99 employees) with larger firms (100 or more employees) - data on very small firms (under 20 employees) - is unfortunately incomplete. Small firms, so defined, increased in the 1980s by 8%, and their employment by 7%. In contrast, large firms fell by 12% and their employment declined by 28%. This has obvious implications for rural areas where most manufacturing is done by small firms.

In the UK as in other major industrial economies, there has been a major re-organisation of production during the 1970s and 1980s - a shift from mass production systems to more fragmented production systems. Large firms have sought to shift some of their risks onto other firms, while at the same time retaining their overall control. This has been done in various ways such as worker buyouts of parts of large firms, licensing and subcontracting. This fragmentation has assisted the development of the small business sector of the economy.

(ii) Urban-rural differences

The economy showed strong growth in many rural areas in the 1980s. Employment grew at a faster rate than in towns (RDC, 1994, North and Smallbone, ibid), in other words, there is strong evidence for an urban to rural shift in employment in the 1980s (Tarling et al, ibid). Further support for this conclusion is provided by TCPA (1997b), which provides data on job changes 1981-1991 in terms of percentage increases/decreases in different types of area. Substantial decreases were recorded in Inner London, Outer London, and Metropolitan Districts. Substantial increases were recorded for 'Mixed and Accessible Urban/Rural' and 'Remote largely Rural' areas (as well as for New Towns). Dividing the country into metropolitan, urban, coalfield, accessible rural (ARA) and remote rural areas (RRA), metropolitan and coalfield areas showed a slight decline in employment. Employment in urban areas increased by 8%, but in both ARA and RRA it increased by 15%. In some ways RRA are at a disadvantage compared with ARR for obvious reasons. However, RRA did show similar employment growth to ARA primarily because employment increased rather more rapidly in them in the fields of some manufacturing, construction, transport, and public services areas (Tarling et al, ibid).

North and Smallbone (ibid) summarise studies by various workers, which show that rural areas fared better than urban areas in terms of number of new firms started. The situation is complicated by big variations in rate of new business formation in different parts of the country, the south showing more rural business formation than the north. But at the level of counties and conurbations, rural and semi-rural counties have generated more firms than urban-industrial counties and the conurbations (apart from Greater London).

As an overall generalization, rural areas have had a greater rate of formation of new firms, and employment there is particularly concentrated in small businesses and self-employment (RDC, ibid). In general, rural SMEs outperformed urban ones in terms of employment growth. But there was a difference between very small and medium sized businesses. One study reported on in North and Smallbone (ibid) showed that the rural -urban difference was largely due to the larger SMEs - firms in the 51-100 and 100+ employment categories.

Differences between ARA and RRA have been briefly touched on earlier, and this will now be enlarged upon. RRA tend to be more labour intensive than ARA. In general, ARA firms are technologically more advanced and innovative than RRA firms. Using a series of indicators of innovation, new products and technological expertise, firms in ARA were found to do better than those in RRA (or in urban areas). RRA firms tend to be imitators rather than innovators. ARA have a higher rate of successful introduction of new products and services, make better use of technology to develop their products, and are more inclined to make use of external business advice, and place more emphasis on marketing and management than RRA firms. These facts can be related to the following. First, RRA firms may experience less competition in local markets, which might have sheltered them from the need to be more competitive. Second, despite modern communications, RRA have been more isolated than ARA - firms have found it more difficult to recruit skilled labour, professional staff and managers; and they suffer because they are often further away from both their suppliers and their markets (North and Smallbone, ibid, reporting on the work of Keeble and others, Tarling et al, ibid).

(iii) Rural - urban convergence

In recent decades there has been a convergence between rural and urban areas in terms of the distribution of different sectors of industry and business, and the employment within these sectors. On the one hand there has been the decline of traditional rural industries. The total farm labour force declined from about one million in 1950 to 431,000 in 1994. Extractive industries (quarrying, coal mining, and china clay extraction in Cornwall) have also shown a big decline in their labour forces. Job losses in rural areas also come from the reduction of the armed forces and the USA military presence (RDC, 1995).

On the other hand the old concentrations of manufacturing industries in particular areas (especially urban), have been disappearing at the same time that new and growing industries have spread more evenly across rural and urban areas. Thus since the 1960s rural areas have shown a 20% growth in manufacturing employment compared with urban areas where declines in employment took place (ranging from 8% in small towns to 56% in conurbations). Ironically, some manufacturing which traditionally had a high presence in rural areas - e.g. animal feed manufacture, light engineering for maintenance and production of farm vehicles, now tend to be concentrated into larger producers which are often in urban centres. In terms of the percentage of employees in employment in each economic sector (agriculture, manufacturing, etc.) there is now little difference between rural and urban areas for manufacturing, distribution, hotels, and public services, which together account for 70% of economic activity in England (Tarling et al, ibid).

The regions of Britain vary in the extent that they are rural. Now in terms of occupational structure (professional occupations, clerical and secretarial, sales occupations, etc. etc.), employment seems to have become very similar between the regions, supporting the view that urban-rural differences have decreased (Tarling et al, ibid).

(iv) The relationship between rural business formation, and other factors, to the demographic process of counter-urbanisation

Several pertinent investigations are reported on by Tarling et al (ibid), and North and Smallbone (ibid). These show that in the majority of cases, at the time when businesses were set up in rural localities, the firm founders were people living in the same locality. In only about 15% of cases had firm owners moved their firm to the new rural location, three-quarters of these coming from urban areas.

However, when one studies those firms (the majority), which were set up by people living in the rural localities concerned, most firm founders were not born locally. These founders had moved into the rural area (usually migrating from an urban area) prior to setting up a new business. They had either moved into the rural area and later decided that they would set up business, or had made the move into the rural area with the specific intention of setting up a business. Taking all categories together, it is clear that business formation in rural areas is predominantly by founders who have moved from an urban locality to a rural locality. New firms in rural areas, while providing some employment to local people, will also act as a magnet drawing future employees from urban areas, particularly if necessary skills are not available locally, and so they contribute to the process of counter-urbanisation.

Various studies have shown that the beauty and other aspects of the rural environment have been the or at least one of the reasons for the counter-urbanisation of recent decades. And this applies to people setting up business in, or transferring business to, rural areas, as well as to people retiring or making a second home there. As far as the shift of business activity from urban to rural areas is concerned, other factors have played a part. These include good labour relations, low wage costs, cheaper land and low premise costs, in rural areas. Thus with the shift of manufacturing from urban to rural areas, the main reason has probably been the shortage of suitable space and premises in urban areas. But the problem of space is not a simple matter. For with firms in RRAs, once the existing site has been developed to the maximum, expansion has been difficult because larger premises were not available locally (North and Smallbone, ibid).

This movement of people and business from urban to rural areas, would have been much more difficult, and probably much less, were it not for changes in transport and technology. As Rogers (1993) wrote "the image of rural communities as desirable places in which to live may well have provided the motivation for change: developments in technology, and in particular the technology of transport, have essentially provided the means to make such wishes possible". The building of more roads, and the widening and straightening of existing ones, together with the great increase in the private ownership of motor cars, and the increasing use of large lorries, has made rural areas more accessible. This has not only helped in the development of rural business, but has created a vast commuting population of relatively well to do people who now live in rural areas and work in towns. The new communication technologies - computer, answer -phone, fax etc. have made physical distance much less important to trading, and are continually improving and the range of use extending - e.g. distance shopping, and so provide support for further development in rural areas.

(v) Social aspects - structure of rural communities

The traditional village remains a popular image of an ideal society for many. The village life was dominated by those people who were directly involved in agriculture and maintaining the agricultural landscape. It was a collection of people closely integrated as a group, and integrated with the environment in which they worked. The church and the pub were both centres of cohesion within that society. There was considerable respect for authority, and the local squire and the vicar played important roles in the life of the community. The community was a group of rather slowly moving, philosophical people, closely attuned to the vagaries of nature. There is no doubt much truth in this image, although it often tends to ignore another side of the picture - the poverty and sometimes poor living conditions, and long working hours, of the labouring class. And the integration was not always as harmonious as we might like to believe.

A thoughtful study of present rural society is given by Rogers (ibid), which forms the main basis for the following brief account. There is in fact not one type of rural society, not one type of village, rather a variety. And numerous researchers have attempted to classify these communities into a variety of categories. In the present context it is not necessary to go into that particular matter in detail. But the variety means that there are numerous exceptions to the following generalisations.

The traditional rural population could be divided into three groups. There was the primary, or agricultural population; then there was a secondary population, which provided the services for the primary group. The third group came from outside, and was rather accidental to rural life - i.e. it was an 'adventitious' population. Absent in many areas, it was considered to have little relevance to rural planning.

The ranking is today completely reversed. It is the 'adventitious' population that is central to the understanding of rural communities. It has dynamic young and middle-aged professional and managerial people, usually involved with business which is not intrinsically rural in character, such as most manufacturing SMEs and service industries. It has wealthy and influential retired people who were earlier in their lives not involved with rural life and the agricultural activity, which formed its backbone.

As Roger says of rural communities – "they are increasingly places where more and more of the population choose to live. Their social make-up is disproportionately biased towards those who, in terms of wealth, power and influence, are influential in deciding national policy and public opinion". To some there is still a significant class divide in rural society On the one hand there are these wealthier people with good housing and considerable political power (e.g. in policy matters like planning and education), and on the other hand, poorer people with little power, and who experience deprivation and poverty.

Rogers refers to Newby who visualised rural communities as having changed from 'occupational' communities based on agriculture, to small indigenous enclaves of farmers and farm workers that find themselves surrounded by newcomers with very different attitudes and ideologies. He also refers to Russell who sees the village as a group of increasingly separate interest groups, who differ in their views about what a village should be like and the future of the countryside.

Some observers place emphasis on a dilution of rural character, a loss of integration, of countryside communities. In villages, everyone used to know everyone else; now frequently people do not even know their neighbours. And the neighbours, raised under urban conditions, have a very different outlook on life, many still finding their emotional centre in the towns. On the other hand, CA (2000) draws attention to the fact that well to do people moving in from urban areas may become very active in local community activities as they attempt to 'belong' to their new surroundings.
.

There have been some interesting changes of attitudes amongst those who now live in these rural communities. For example, some farmers who until the difficult farming times of the 1980s were firmly anti-development, now see development as at least partly a good thing because it enables farm diversification to take place, and hence farmers to stay in business. Then there are many business people who when they arrived in the village as entrepreneurs, were in favour of development and growth in villages, but twenty years on, as retired people, they have discovered 'conservation' and are now firmly against further development as they want to protect their own 'private' environment. To the writer, this is a good example of the widespread NIMBY syndrome - development provided it is **N**ot **I**n **M**y own **B**ack **Y**ard.

The increased mobility given by motorcar ownership has contributed to the loss of rural character of country places, not only by allowing the development of the rural- urban commuter population. In the past, town people who wished to visit the countryside usually had to make the effort to get on a train or bus, or walk out into the countryside; now the countryside is clogged by people who either just sit in their cars reading the paper and listening to radios, or people who get out and walk a short way. Country pubs are no longer the place where one can retreat and be for a short while absorbed, however superficially, into a rural community, but are now sorry fakes of a way of life that has disappeared, so that in a pub one is surrounded by hosts of jostling town people who seem to prefer a noisy town -like atmosphere to peace and quiet.

(vi) Transport provision and housing

In recent times there has been a decline in public transport (road and rail), in rural areas. For example, between 1986/7 and 1990/1 spending on public transport in the ten most rural English counties declined by 24% (report by Transport Advisory Services, in Lowe and Murdoch,1993). As at 1994, 73% of parishes had no daily bus service (RDC, 1994).

Rural people are increasingly concerned about the financial pressures that prevent local authorities from doing more in the bus transport field. For example, there is concern about the cost of providing for statutory free school transport, for this determines the size of the bus fleet available to supply other bus services during the rest of the day, according to RDC (1996). Any reduction in this service would thus cause a reduction in rural public bus transport generally. At present, about 70% of rural parishes have no daily bus service. The reduction of public transport seems to be one cause of the massive increase of car ownership in rural areas. Many other facilities are frequently absent in rural areas. Only 60% of rural parishes have a post office, and also only about the same percentage have a permanent shop.

There is also a shortage of housing for people in low-paid employment - what is technically known as 'affordable housing' (where such housing is provided by non profit making groups like housing associations and local authorities, it is called 'social housing'). Various factors have contributed to this shortage. First, the in-migration of relatively wealthy people from towns has helped to push up house prices (RDC 1995). Second, during the 1980s there was a decline in

Council House building; by 1991 new council houses made up less than 7% of all new housing in the countryside (Lowe and Murdoch, ibid). Third, the sale of council houses as provided for in the 1980 Housing Act led to a substantial loss of council houses to the open housing market where their prices then rose. Fourth, Housing Associations are major providers of social housing. But reduction of Housing Corporation subsidies to Housing Associations caused rents to rise (RDC,1993a). Fifth (and linking with point three), there is the problem of keeping affordable housing affordable in perpetuity; if such housing is re-sold it is legally very difficult to ensure that it remains in the hands of the less well-off (JRF, 1994a). Finally it should be noted that the lack of affordable housing contributes to the dynamics of urban-rural migration; for lack of such housing in rural areas can be a factor causing people to move to urban areas.

(vii) And the future?

Counter-urbanisation is likely to continue, so that while the population of the UK as a whole will grow slowly, the growth is likely to be fastest in rural areas, through further in-migration. In other words, the likelihood is that the shift of population from urban to rural areas, especially more accessible rural areas, will continue. Indeed, on the basis of OPCS population estimates and projections, the RDC conclude that the urban-rural shift in population will not only continue, but intensify RDC, (1995).

For business, Tarling et al (1993) sums up the situation: "a major stimulus to the movement of founders (of businesses) into the countryside is the perceived environmental attractiveness of England's villages and rural areas as a place to live" and,
"the urban-rural shift is long established and the increasing awareness with environmental concern and quality of life issues in the population at large is likely to strengthen rather than weaken the attitudes which have resulted in the growth of manufacturing firms in the countryside".

At the same time, changes in agricultural policy are likely to lead to a continuation of the trend of job losses in this most traditional of rural activities. There will also be job losses in mining, which was often carried out in rural areas (RDC, 1994). These continuations of various existing trends in population movement, business and employment will bring about a further convergence of the economies of rural and urban areas (RDC, 1995). For the role of different sectors of business in future development in rural areas see Tarling et al (ibid).

Ironically, changes in transport policy, in themselves desirable, may further stimulate business development and population growth in rural areas. A policy which made travel by car more expensive and more restrictive in terms of say city parking, may, in combination with knowledge about pollution, and continued traffic congestion, lead to people developing a less car dependant mode of life, and a change of attitude towards commuting. Then, people who work in town but have moved to live in the countryside, might, if made redundant, prefer to look for work locally rather than in the urban areas. So there would be an increasing number of people looking for work in rural areas. (Lowe and Murdoch, ibid).

Now one implication of the trends discussed above is that there will be increasing pressure to release green land for development, which will be increasingly opposed by environmental organisations and rural residents. This will be discussed later.

D. Changes in farming - land use and agricultural methods

During and after the second world war the need to increase food production led to the taking over of much "marginal" land for food production -the draining of wetlands, the reduction of field margins and headlands etc. to increase the agricultural area. Hedgerows were also removed for the same purpose and also to make it easier to use the larger farm machines like combined harvesters. In lowland livestock farming hedges and banks have also been removed because with increasing herd sizes, soil structure in small fields can be damaged in wet weather by excessive treading, which can be reduced by increasing the field area. Also maintaining stone walls and banks in a stock proof condition is very costly since it is labour demanding, and labour is often not available; this provides farmers with additional encouragement to remove such features (Soper and Carter, 1991).

The need to increase food production led not only to extension of farming areas, but more particularly, to attempts - largely successful - to increase the yield per acre, whether this was the weight of grain in arable systems, or the density with which animals were kept in livestock systems, and in dairy farming the increase of milk production per cow.

This increase in production was made possible by various factors:

(i) plant and animal breeding producing higher yielding varieties (for example production of more prolific ewes by cross - breeding);

(ii) the use of large quantities of fertilizer (especially nitrogenous fertilizer) and pesticides (herbicides for weeds, insecticides for insects, etc);

(iii) improvements in farm technology (e.g. harvesting machinery);

(iv) various changes in farming practice - see later.

Generally this increased production per hectare is referred to as the intensification of production.

In recent decades, the total area in agricultural production has been decreasing. A continued advance in production of high yielding varieties has meant that production capacity has exceeded demand, with the result that some agricultural land has been becoming redundant. The total agricultural area in the UK in recent years has changed as follows (total area of agricultural holdings plus common rough grazing at June each year, millions of hectares): Average of 1988-1990: 18.932; 1995: 18.746; 1996: 18.750; 1997: 18.653; 1998: 18.599; 1999: 18.579 (MAFF, 1999b). This decrease in the area of land required for human food production is set to continue. In 1994 it was thought that a further 1.0 to 1.5 million hectares of land may become surplus to requirement for food production by the year 2000. By 2010 the figure could be 5.5 million hectare ETSU, 1994).

In basic terms there are three main types of farming system in Britain (Soper and Carter, ibid):

(i) all grass, livestock and milk production;

(ii) arable systems; traditionally a wide variety of crops were grown on a rotational basis;

(iii) mixed farming, with varying proportions of livestock and arable farming within the same farming enterprise.

In the past, the traditional farming method in Britain was mixed farming. There were of course, regional variations. Thus upland areas, and heavy land farming in the northwest tended to specialise in milk and beef production - i.e. grassland systems. In contrast, in some Eastern Counties some of the farms were pure arable farms. In recent decades, mixed farming has declined. This decrease was associated with the drive for intensification of production that has often involved specialising in either livestock or arable farming. There has been a big increase in arable farms. Especially noteworthy here is the development of specialised cereal farms, dispensing with crop rotation (or sometimes occasionally breaking the continuous cereal cropping by planting oilseed rape or a leguminous crop). And on remaining mixed farms, the proportion of cereals is often far higher than it used to be.

There are environmental advantages to mixed farming, especially when the crop and livestock sides of the enterprise are managed in an integrated way instead of being treated as two almost separate sections on the farm. Thus where land use is rotated, so that crops/livestock are not grown on the same piece of land in consecutive years, pest populations are less likely to build up, and livestock put back nutrients into the soil; so there is a reduced need for pesticides and fertilizers. Transport of materials and products may be reduced, which reduces costs and the harmful effects of transport on the environment. For example, slurry disposal is a major problem on livestock farms. Traditionally cows were housed in straw -bedded yards, where slurry was absorbed into the straw, which could then be carted and spread on the land in spring. With modern conventional livestock farming, either straw must be carted over a sometimes considerable distance from an arable farming neighbourhood, or slurry must be disposed in other ways. Then again, there would be less need to transport milk great distances (as happens now in arable dominated farming regions). Mixed farming generally creates a more interesting landscape, which often provides more varied habitats for wildlife; is also relatively labour intensive, a feature that could be advantageous for any attempt to increase rural employment.

In addition to these major changes of farming system, there have been other changes in farming practice that have an impact on wild life:

a)The intensification of grassland farming has generally involved increased use of fertilizer, especially nitrogenous fertilizer that stimulates a leafy crop, and the use of herbicides to remove weeds. Many pastures used to have quite a large variety of plant species. But by the early nineties over 50% of the pastures in Britain were intensively managed by growing high nutrient grasses - sometimes pure rye grass, and the wild plant species had largely disappeared (Baldock et al 1996, referring to the work of Barr and colleagues).

b) Harvesting and mowing techniques have changed through developments in farming technique and, so the whole process can be carried out much more rapidly.

c) Traditionally, upland areas have seen grass left until well into July and then cut for hay; by this time the grass was mainly fibre, and therefore not very nutritious. Cutting grass for silage was more a feature of lowland grassland systems. Now with the invention of the round baler machine, which can be hired by farmers, grass is cut much earlier in upland areas, while it is still green and highly nutritious, and put into silage - so one sees farms with stacks of large cylindrical plastic wrapped bales.

d) A traditional method of farming in arable areas was spring sowing of cereals. After the autumn harvest, the fields were left, the stubble remaining until the following spring. Now the system has changed with increase of autumn sowing, so stubble winter fields are a thing of the past.

During the last decade there has been a growing interest amongst farmers in a farming system known as Integrated Crop Management (ICM), promoted by the organisation LEAF (Linking Environment And Farming). This system shares several features with Organic Farming (discussed in the following chapter). It seeks to reduce the reliance on inputs of fertiliser and pesticides and fossil fuels, and minimise pollution of water, soil and air. It makes use of crop rotation, and biological control techniques to control pests, reducing the use of synthetic pesticides. To achieve this it aims to make full use of diagnostic and predictive techniques (time and likelihood of pest infestations etc) to ensure that unnecessary applications of pesticides are avoided. It aims to maintain landscape and wildlife habitats (LEAF, 1995; Baldock et al, 1996).

E. Changes in landscape in Britain

There have been massive landscape changes since the Second World War, largely as the result of changing agricultural practice that we dealt with in the previous section. These changes can be summarised as follows:

a) Woodland. The changes have been dominated by two tendencies - the reduction of broad-leaved woodland, and the increase of conifer woodland, although the total area of all woodland has increased over the period, particularly in the first two decades. The increase then, was largely due to conifer planting. By 1992 the total increase of woodland in England was about 180,000 ha, an increase of 20% (Sinclair, 1992). Considering the largely broad -leaved ancient woodlands, these had been reduced 30-50% by 1984 (FoE, 1991, using data from Nature Conservancy Council). Considering all broad -leaved woodlands in Britain, and just the period 1978 - 1984, 24,700 ha were cleared, over 60% of this area being converted to agricultural use (Baldock et al, ibid, referring to the work of C. Barr and Colleagues).

In recent years the overall increase in woodland is in line with the past trend, but a) there is a lower rate of conifer planting; b) broad leaved planting has increased from the mid 1980s onwards (HMSO, 1996). Ordinary people are making an important contribution here through non-governmental organisations (British Trust for Conservation Volunteers, Wildlife Trusts, Woodland Trust). Government schemes have also played a part (see section H below).

b) Rough Grazing. In England, the area fell progressively throughout the period, a total loss of 444,000ha, or 28%. The fall was mainly caused by afforestation and pasture 'improvement' (referred to in an earlier section) (Sinclair, ibid). For Great Britain as a whole, analyses by Adger et al reported by Whitby (1996) for the period 1947-1980 showed that the loss of rough grazing was predominantly to coniferous woodland.

c) Moorland. There has been a large decline in heather moorland in most upland areas. In the North Yorks Moors for example, over 30 square miles have gone in the last 40 years (undated leaflet of The Moorland Association). Moorland is being widely and seriously damaged by overgrazing (Baldock et al 1996, referring to work by Felton and Marsden; Harvey, 1997). The total area of moorland in Great Britain has decreased by about 20% since the 1940s (DoE, 1992b).

d) Heathland. This was mainly found in lowland England; it declined by 72% in Britain since 1830. The losses were caused by various factors - agricultural reclamation, afforestation, mineral workings, uncontrolled fires and recreation. Heathland does need management, and much of the remaining heathland is being lost as scrub invades it as part of the natural succession of vegetation types (RSPB, 1992).

e) Lowland wet grassland, marshes, fens. Lowland wet grassland declined in England by more than 40% since 1930. This was caused by drainage to grow cereals, intensive grassland management and water abstraction. East Anglian fens declined by 97% since 1650 and 40% since 1930. Grazing marshes of the Norfolk Broads declined by 37% between 1930 and 1984. Between the 1930s and 1982, 49% of the north Kent marshes, 70% of Romney marsh (south-east Kent), and 80% of east Essex coastal grasslands disappeared (RSPB, ibid). Remaining fens are becoming increasingly damaged by low water levels caused by abstraction (DoE, ibid).

f) Downland and meadows. In recent decades a large percent of meadows have been lost in many counties, for example, 33% in Worcestershire, 60% in Dorset, 90% in Derbyshire. Downland has been reduced by 71% in Berkshire and 66% in Hampshire (RSPB, ibid). Downland grassland has often been replaced with crops.

g) Hedgerows. There has been a massive removal of hedgerows in Britain since the Second World War. Between 1947 and 1985, 175,000 km were removed in England and Wales - the equivalent of a hedge stretching nearly four times round the world (Baldock et al, ibid, based on work of the Countryside Commission). This represents a loss of 22% of all hedgerows. DoE (1996c) estimated that the hedgerow stock decreased by an average of just under 22,000 km a year between 1984 and 1990. This fell to 18,000 a year between 1990 and 1993. Many of the remaining hedgerows are not looked after, and have become very gappy. Hedgerow planting schemes under agri-environment schemes (see following chapter) together with the new hedgerow regulations may possibly reduce net loss in the future. To quite a large extent, hedgerows as a means of enclosure have been replaced by the fence - often a few strands of barbed wire. Another traditional means of enclosure, stonewalls, have decreased in extent. Over 7,000km (4,500 miles) disappeared between 1947 and 1985. Many of the remaining walls are not stock proof and often are very broken down. Agricultural practice has again resulted in wall loss, but other causes are building developments and even people stealing stones for garden rockeries and decoration (CPRE, 1996c).

h) Orchards. Once a characteristic feature of the countryside, there has been a decline of over 50% by area of the UK orchards since 1970. Along with this has been a big reduction of the varieties of apple grown for mass production (WWF et al 1996).

i) Water features. Over the whole period 1880 to 1993, nearly one million ponds were lost (CPRE 1993, using data from Wildfowl and Wetlands Trust and Pond Action). Between 1945 and 1990, the number of lakes and ponds in Great Britain has decreased by 470,00 thousand to 330,000. Much of this recent loss is attributable to changing farm practice, making ponds redundant as watering points for livestock, and allowing infill to increase the area under cultivation. However, many new ponds are now being created. Thus in the period 1990 to 1996, in lowland Britain, it is estimated that 17,000 (+or- 3,900) ponds were lost, 15,000 (+or- 6,400) new ponds created (DETR, 1998e).

There has been a considerable fall in level and flow in many rivers in recent years. The National Rivers Authority in 1992 identified 40 rivers in England and Wales which, except after heavy rain, showed lowered flows, mostly as a result of water abstraction (WWF et al, ibid). There is also evidence of over abstraction of underground aquifers, particularly in the South East Region (Wade et al, 1999).

Increase in domestic water consumption is one cause of aquifer depletion and fall in river water levels, but there is another cause. Many valley features in the past have combined to form the equivalent of a sponge, which held a large store of water - unimproved meadows, woodlands, bogs and mires. Much of this 'sponge' has been removed, mainly through the intensification of agriculture; and soil structure and soil surface have been damaged (reduction in organic matter content etc.) by this same intensification, so that it is more difficult for water to penetrate, and less water is held in the soil.

The consequence is that rain water, instead of being retained in the soil, refilling underground aquifers and providing a steady flow of water into streams, simply runs off after heavy rain into streams and rivers, sometimes causing flooding, and is then lost to the sea.

F. Protected countryside areas

The environment in certain designated countryside areas is given special protection in one way or another. The purpose of the protection varies. With Areas of Outstanding Natural Beauty (AONB) and National Scenic Areas, protecting the landscape is the primary consideration. With National Nature Reserves it is the conservation and study of nature. With National Parks there are two primary objectives - protecting the outstanding countryside they contain and providing opportunities for access and outdoor recreation. With Environmentally Sensitive Areas (ESA) the purpose is to support environmentally friendly agriculture. And with Sites of Special Scientific Interest (SSSIs) the purpose is to safeguard special features - flora, fauna, geological or physiographical features. All types of area, not only the SSSIs, offer some protection to wildlife. The most relevant legislation, both National and European, governing the protection offered, is summarised in the government's Planning Policy Guidance note no.9 published by DoE in 1994. The Conservancy Councils are the bodies that advise government on nature conservation, establish reserves and monitor conservation. In Scotland the Council is Scottish Natural Heritage, in Wales the Countryside Council for Wales, and in England the Nature Conservancy Council for England (known usually as English Nature).

In terms of physical size (area covered, in sq. km), and considering England alone, the biggest categories are

	Area	% of total land area
National Parks	9,934	8
SSSIs	10,538	8
AONBs	20,393	16
ESAs	5,235	4

Area data Sources: CA, 2000 (National Parks and AONBs); EN Annual report 2000 (SSSIs); MAFF, personal communication (ESAs -uptake, not eligible area).

The legal powers to enforce protection are considerable. First there are the powers associated with general national law - pollution controls, planning controls, etc. Then there are the specific legal powers given to the authorities that control these areas. Third, these authorities are in many cases able to introduce byelaws to further strengthen aspects of the protection. For example, with Nature Reserves, where nature conservation is the objective, protection may be enhanced by passing byelaws excluding all visitors from the area. But byelaws cannot be used to overthrow vested rights of landowners. A common feature of these areas is the use of the management agreement between the landowner and the authority, which determines how the land is to be managed. Under such agreements the landowners agree to certain environmentally friendly practices. To a lesser extent, land has been bought by the public authorities for the purpose of protection (Reid, 1994).

Collectively all the protected areas were about 15-20% of the land area at the beginning of the last decade according to Potter (1991) who sees such areas as possibly forming the basis for a future Conservation Reserve. However, at present, the countryside in the protected areas is not inviolable. Developments of one sort or another are allowed, which may reduce the total area of green land or diminish the environmental quality of the area. In this connection we ill consider two types of protected area - the National Parks, and the SSSIs.

National Parks. It is first important to note that these are not just wild areas. They contain villages and towns, and limited house building is allowed. There is also industry (for example mineral extraction). National parks are best regarded as areas where stricter controls operate than in the countryside at large (although these controls largely do not cover agriculture and forestry within the parks). The park authorities have discretionary powers which make it possible to bring in byelaws to do things like restrict traffic on roads and ensure people do not unduly interfere with the enjoyment of other people.

As said earlier, the Parks have two objectives (1) the preservation of outstanding countryside; 2) the promotion of the enjoyment of the countryside by the public. These two objectives are not entirely compatible. Increased recreational use can damage land, e.g. walkers causing erosion, and increased recreational use is promoted by building facilities for visitors, which reduces the green area (car parks, cafes, accommodation and camping sites). Deleterious changes have taken place in farmland in National Parks. For example, the national trends in reduction of walls and hedgerows and loss of rough grazing, mainly through afforestation and conversion to "improved pasture", mentioned in an earlier section, have been matched by similar trends within national parks (Baldock et al 1996). Hedgerows and rough grazing are important habitats for wild life.

National parks are promoted as areas where people can go to get away from cities and enjoy the beauty of the landscape. At the same time the population of England has grown considerably since the Second World War, and car ownership has increased dramatically. Not surprisingly then, the Parks, especially in summer, have increasingly become crowded places where it is difficult to find real solitude. Chapter 7 deals fully with one National Park and explores the above issues.

SSSIs. These areas are very important to conservation strategy. There are slightly over 4,000 SSSIs in England. The idea of the SSSI scheme is to identify sites that are of especial biological or geological interest, and to secure management of these sites to maintain their biological and geological value.

Basically the SSSI scheme involves notifying owners and occupiers of the land of the SSSI designation, the notification containing a list of 'potentially damaging operations' (PDOs) such as quarrying, building development, and on agricultural land, changes to grazing regime, or application of fertilizers and pesticides which owners or occupiers should avoid. The aim then is to prevent such damaging operations being carried out and secure positive environmental management. The responsibility for notifying and overseeing the SSSIs belongs to the Conservancy Councils, so in England this is English Nature. Some SSSIs are nature reserves managed by the Conservancy Councils' or voluntary conservation bodies, but for the majority of sites, the success of the scheme depends on the co-operation of the landowners and occupiers. Some owners have already adopted environmentally friendly methods. Where this is not the case, the Conservancy Councils may seek to enter into management agreement schemes with owners and occupiers; the latter may also at any time approach the relevant Conservancy Council to enter into such an agreement. If landowners do carry out forbidden operations, English Nature does have legal powers of enforcement through what are called Nature Conservation Orders. And as a last resort English Nature has compulsory purchase powers (Reid, 1994).

Traditionally, management agreements have compensated landowners/farmers for profits that could have been made by using the land to its full agricultural or forestry potential. So for an owner wanting to carry out an operation that might be profitable but is a PDO, the payment is essentially re-imbursement for profits foregone. Since the early 1990s English Nature has sought to change its approach by concentrating more on positive nature conservation management and it started two new schemes - the Reserves Enhancement Scheme (RES) - launched 1992, and the Wildlife Enhancement Scheme (WES) - launched 1991 (EN, 1996a). RES helps voluntary conservation groups to make effective management plans. Where WES is taken up, signatories to agreements receive financial support for positive nature conservation methods. At 1998, the two schemes cover only about 28,800ha. By 2000, the WES area was up to 137,977ha while the total SSSI area in England is 1,053,796 ha (EN, 2000), so the WES still only covers a small percent of SSSSI land. This must be balanced against changing practice with individual management agreements in the rest of SSSI territory -where also the more positive aspects of management (as in WES) are increasingly being stressed (M.E.Massey, RES Project Manager 1997, personal communication).

English Nature also have programmes aimed at the recovery of plant and animal species that have declined, programmes which can make a positive contribution to habitat management. These programmes are not restricted to SSSIs. The Species Recovery Programme, initiated in 1991, consists of a range of partnership projects that aim to restore, maintain or enhance populations of plants or animals that are in severe decline or currently under threat of extinction. The more recent Species Action Grants Scheme can provide funding for work in connection with already costed Action Plans for the conservation of threatened species from a list of priority species prepared by the UK Biodiversity Steering Group. Grants are to assist with site management, species management, research and monitoring, and publicity. Any organisation or individual who can demonstrate that their project will contribute to a particular action plan is eligible for assistance.

Limitations to the SSSI scheme

In the past, it has been generally agreed that there are severe limitations to the value of the SSSI scheme:

a) It may be important, but difficult, to establish 'buffer zones' round SSSIs. These may not themselves contain anything of scientific importance, but unless they are established, the SSSI may be vulnerable to damage. This is particularly important when an SSSI is small and isolated, as is often the case. For example where SSSIs are located in fens, water abstraction nearby can easily damage the SSSIs.

b) Often the list of PDOs is formidable. They can give the landowner the impression that he cannot do anything with his land without infringing a PDO requirement, including things that he has been doing for years. So the relationship between Conservancy Council and landowner can start on a very poor footing.

c) If the owner or occupier of the land wishes to carry out damaging operations, the authorities (Conservancy Council) can delay the work for four months. But unless the authority succeeds in arranging a management agreement with the owner, or can successfully apply for further legal controls through the imposition of a Nature Conservation Order, they cannot stop the operations taking place. A Nature Conservation Order applies to all people in the area - not just owners and occupiers. But it is a complicated business getting an order into operation, and if there are any objections the Secretary of State must hold a local enquiry or hearing. And such orders have run into difficulties in dealing with attempts to control existing operations.

d) The planning authorities under the town and country planning system have great powers over a piece of land that is or contains an SSSI. Such planning authorities have various interests to balance, and nature conservation is only one of these. There may be economic and social interests that the planning authority considers are more important. Should that be so, the planning authority has the power to allow any PDO. So development on a site can take place, which would totally destroy the value of the site. However, local planning authorities are required to consult English Nature about any proposed developments within SSSIs. And since the publication of Circular 1/92 "Planning Controls over Sites of Special Scientific Interest" in January 1992, such authorities must also consult English Nature about proposed developments in the areas around SSSIs (in so-called 'consultation areas'). This has the potential at least to offer some protection in buffer zones (point a above).

e) Restrictions on activities in an SSSI (except if a Nature Conservation Order is in place) only apply to the actual owners or occupiers of the land in question. They do not and cannot apply to other people – e.g. cannot be used to control the activity of visitors to the area, including vandals.

f) SSSIs often include agricultural land. Now farmers can get subsidies for production, which exceed any financial support they may be offered under SSSI agreements. Unscrupulous farmers may then plough up valuable wildlife sites. In one SSSI in an area of chalk grassland which supported a rich variety of wild flowers, one owner was paid £40 /hectare for maintaining the sward. But if he were to plough and plant a flax crop, he could receive £591/ha subsidy under the flax regime of the Common Agricultural Policy (CAP) of the European Union. The farmer decided to do this and notified English Nature of his intention. Unfortunately there was no mechanism for ensuring that landowners who deliberately damage or destroy SSSIs within their estate can be denied access to such payments. After four months of negotiation with English nature, 15 hectares of the SSSI were still ploughed up. This is ironic when one realises that for five years the owner had been receiving money to conserve the area, money that came from the public purse! (WWF, 1997). The whole problem of agricultural subsidies will be discussed in the section on the CAP.

g) English Nature is handicapped in that its officers have, unlike pollution inspectors, no automatic right of access to private land, which would be very useful for monitoring SSSIs.

h) The whole original basic approach when the SSSI system was introduced was negative rather than positive - preventing particular damage rather than creating positive management. Now the vast majority of sites are not climax vegetation - vegetation that has evolved without any interference from man into a stable state - but rather areas subject to mans activities for a long time and requiring positive husbandry to maintain them. So merely preventing damage to a site is not enough - the value of a site can be diminished through neglect, e.g. down grassland destroyed by invading scrub.

Recent proposed improvements to the SSSI scheme

The Government, responding to criticisms from English nature and other bodies, has recently proposed significant improvements to the legal framework of SSSI protection. These improvements are contained within the new Countryside and Rights of Way Bill, principally through modifications to The Wildlife and Countryside Act of 1981. Unfortunately, at the time of writing, there are serious doubts if the Government will find sufficient time to take this Bill through parliament. I will refer to this bill in relation to the points a) to h) above.

Some of the most important changes concern the ability of Conservancy Councils to prevent damaging operations within SSSIs (point c above). The changes are brought in by substituting a new Section 28 for the Section 28 in the original Act. It will now be much more difficult for an owner/occupier to carry out damaging operations. The new section 28C says that an owner/occupier may not carry out an operation specified in the sites notification unless written consent has been given by the Council or the operation is in accordance with terms of agreement of previous Acts or a management agreement. 28I gives the Council authority to serve a management notice, which requires the owner/occupier to carry out certain work on the land. And section 28L gives the Council the powers of compulsory purchase when the owner /occupier refuses to enter into a management agreement or is breaching an existing agreement. 28M provides hefty fines for violations of section 28C.

Another very important improvement of the law comes over the question of right of entry (point g above). This is brought about by amendment of Section 51 of the 1981 Act. Council officials now have a right of entry which should make monitoring of land management by the owner/occupier much more effective - for example, they have a general right to enter to assess the condition of the flora, fauna, geological or physiographical features. And they have the right to enter to see if management agreement conditions are being complied with.

The criticism (point h above) that the management approach was preventing further damage rather than more positively managing the site, is dealt with under Section 28H. This states that management schemes may not only be to conserve the flora and other features, but, also, specifically, to restore them.

The least satisfactory part of the Bill as far as SSSIs is concerned, is I think, the section dealing with the powers of Planning Authorities (PAs) (point d above). Protection of SSSIs is slightly increased here. Now the PAs must not only consult if they want to carry out a PDO. They must give written notice (Section 28F). The Council then can issue a notice saying that they do not consent to the activity. However, provided the PA then gives 28 days notice of commencing operations, they can still do so. The most valuable part of this section of the Bill relates to point a) above (the need to create buffer zones). For the first time, the law recognizes the value, to maintaining an SSSI, of the land immediately adjacent to it. Clause 28F speaking of damage to flora, fauna etc, within an SSSI, says that a PA must give written notice even if the operations would not take place on land forming part of the actual SSSI.

Assessment of the SSSI scheme

English Nature has been criticised for not doing enough to legally enforce SSSI protection; indeed, despite the fact that severe damage to SSSIs continued to take place, as at 1998, there had only been two prosecutions during the previous five years; English Nature is also accused of failing to designate sites which are important for wildlife (even sites that qualify for SPAs -see below). And WWF had to threaten English Nature with legal action before it agreed to notify one very important site (WWF, 1997).

English Nature periodically issues information about damage to SSSIs. It said that during 1991-95, one site was completely lost, 14, partly lost, many were damaged. The biggest cause of damage was agricultural activity. For the 1995/96 period alone, there were 163 damaging incidents affecting 121 SSSIs, 4.2% of sites, 0.3 % total area. Agricultural activity accounted for 82% of this damage by area. Excessive grazing was the main component of this agricultural related damage (on upland grasslands, in mires and woodlands) (EN 1996b). The En (2000) report gives an overall area assessment of al SSSIs at the beginning of the new millennium, classified as follows:

Favourable	43.21 %
Unfavourable, recovering	15.55 %
Unfavourable no change	29.60 %
Unfavourable declining	11.20 %
Part destroyed	0.43 %

Interesting observations on the state of the SSSI programme come in a recent research report by English Nature (Solly et al,1999). While this was concerned only with woodland SSSIs, it does reach some conclusions which may have wider implications. The study was based on 150 randomly selected woodland SSSIs, carried out by questionnaire to the site owners/occupiers and site visits. 28% of the sites were improving. But nearly a quarter of the sites were in an unfavourable condition and neither improving nor declining, while 10% were in an unfavourable and declining condition. Lack of coppicing and grazing was thought to be two of the major causes of unfavourable condition, emphasizing the need for the positive management of SSSIs. The report found that cost was a major obstacle to the implementation of adequate management. Further, more than 5% of respondents to the survey were not even certain of the nature conservation objectives for their woodlands.

Such assessments do not suggest the SSSI scheme is being very effective in safeguarding habitat.

In the past, EN has been criticised about lack of consistency in its monitoring and because it had never conducted a thorough survey of the effectiveness of SSSIs for conservation over the whole period since SSSIs were established. But in 1997 EN started a programme to systematically monitor SSSIs using a set of common standards. For this purpose each SSSI site is subdivided into smaller areas called monitoring units. The plan is to assess every SSSI at least once every six years. This programme started in April 1997. The EN 2000 report says that 55% of the assessments have been completed, and the remainder will be completed by March 2003. In my view, this programme is quite inadequate in that a six yearly inspection, even if achieved, is far too infrequent for checking on adverse developments that may take place.

G. Decline of wildlife

Over 100 species of plant and animal have become extinct in the UK this century - for example, five% of butterfly species were extinct by 1996 (WWF et al, 1996). There have been major changes in density and distribution of many plants and animals, including some serious declines, and a useful summary of these changes is given by DoE (1996c).

Field areas in arable land have 30% fewer plant species, and in grazing areas 14% fewer species, in 1990 compared with 1978 (CPRE 1995a, referring to a DoE report). A study of 12 species of arable land flowering plants recorded presence /absence in the number of 10km grid squares, comparing 1930-60 with 1986-1989. Big reductions occurred in all species ranging from the Cornflower (*Centaurea cyanus*) with the largest reduction (264 to 3 squares), down to Pheasant's Eye (*Adorus annua*) (36 to 12 squares) (CPRE, ibid reporting work by P.J. Wilson).

One of the most studied animal groups, and therefore one of the groups we know most about, is birds. Further, since birds are near the top of the food chain, they are a useful indicator of biodiversity in general. A spectacular example of decline is the Barn Owl (*Tyto alba*). Since the first census of this species in 1932 the population in England has fallen by 70% (CPRE ibid, data from the Hawk and Owl Trust). Information from the British Trust for Ornithology, Irish Wildlife Conservancy and Scottish Ornithologists Club, show that for the UK, there have been considerable changes in farmland birds during the last 20-30 years. 24 species have declined, often massively, five have been stable, eleven have increased. The biggest decline were the Tree Sparrow (*Passer montanus*) - 89%, Grey Partridge (*Perdix perdix*) - (82%), Corn bunting (*Emberiza calandra*) - 80%, Turtle Dove (*Streptopelia turtur*) - 77%, Bullfinch (*Pyrrhula pyrrhula*) - 76%. The smallest declines were with the Starling (*Sturnus vulgaris*) - 23% and Yellow Hammer (*Emberiza citrinella*) - 17%. The biggest increases were Collared Dove (*Streptopelia decaocto*) - 860%, and Stock Dove (*Columba oenas*) - 246%. The range of the collared dove has increased enormously this century -it spread westwards over Europe and eventually reached and spread in the UK (Campbell and Cooke, eds, 1997).

In contrast to the situation with most farm birds, some species of birds of prey have increased in numbers since the 1970s - merlin (*Falco columbarius*), red kite (*Milvus milvus*), marsh harrier (*Circus aeruginosus*), osprey (*Pandion haliaetus*) and white-tailed eagle (*Haliaetus albicilla*), buzzard (*Buteo buteo*) and sparrowhawk (*Accipter nisus*). This is partly caused by the withdrawal of certain pesticides in agriculture and consequent recovery of populations, partly through strenuous conservation work including nest protection and re-introduction of stock, partly through reduced persecution (RSPB, 1999).

The Government has recognized that bird populations provide a useful indication of the state of wildlife. For a "radical step forward" as the RSPB put it, was taken when it included a wildlife indicator based on populations of breeding birds in its set of indicators of sustainable development (UK Gov., 1999b) based on data supplied partly by the RSPB, BTO and the DETR. This showed the decline of woodland species since the early 1980s and the much bigger decline in farmland species. And now the RSPB (ibid) report that these declines are continuing.

What are the prospects for the future? A pessimistic note was struck by the RSPB (ibid) in relation to the Governments Biodiversity Action Plan (BAP). This set targets for the short and medium term recovery of bird species. The RSPB conclude that less than 25% of the BAP species are likely to meet their short or medium term targets. They add the comment that to date, the major bird conservation success stories all involve rare or scarce species.

Invertebrate animals, especially insects, spiders and harvestmen (relations of spiders), are important food items for many bird species, so it is interesting to see what changes have taken place in this part of the animal kingdom; unfortunately, data is very limited. On farmland, most invertebrate groups have either declined (including several insect groups, spiders and harvestmen) or remained stable (Campbell and Cooke eds, ibid).

One group of insects that has been studied more than most other invertebrate groups in Britain is the Lepidoptera - moths and butterflies. Here the best-studied county is probably Warwickshire. One study of butterflies involved sampling all the 2 km squares in the County and in addition sampling at all the known sites of the rare species (Warwickshire Branch of Butterfly Conservation, 1997). It covers the 25 years before 1995, and the 43 species previously recorded in the County. Of these species, two had apparently become extinct before the 25-year period started. In qualitative terms (presence or absence of species), in terms of the remaining 41 species, only one species increased its range. Twenty species declined (recorded in fewer squares or, with the rare species, fewer of the known sites). Of these twenty, four had apparently become extinct, seven had suffered a decline of 30% or over. In quantitative terms, things looked even worse – there were massive decreases in population density of the commoner species. Ironically, urban fringe habitats (waste ground) often supported the best butterfly populations. Most agricultural areas in the countryside were in effect butterfly deserts.

There can be little doubt that decline of landscape features such as hedgerows and orchards (most of the orchards of Warwickshire and Worcestershire have gone), has caused decline of insect species. And there is no doubt that the spraying of pesticides has dramatically reduced populations of insects and flowering plants within fields used for growing crops. With cereals the field may be sprayed twice with herbicides, three or more times with fungicides. The extent of insecticide spraying will vary with incidence of pest outbreaks, but is likely to be at least once. Such fields, as distinct from any field margins or set-aside land that there may be, are virtually dead for most of the time except for the chosen crop plant. Since agriculture accounts for most rural land, and the actual cropping area accounts for most of the area of arable farms, one can see that the effect on flowering plants and insects in the countryside as a whole is colossal. Nevertheless, insects reproduce quickly and can spread from refuges; flowering plans disperse readily, and there are some havens at least in what limited non-crop land remains.

As far as birds are concerned, can one really be sure that changes of agricultural practice, especially pesticide use, have been the cause of bird population decline? Certainly the changes in agricultural practice since the Second World War have gone on concomitantly with the decline of bird populations. So a reasonable hypothesis would be that the former has caused the latter. The evidence for an overall causal relationship comes from within-region comparisons of 'organic' farms with conventional farms. The former do not use pesticides and artificial fertilisers, and use a range of management techniques such as crop rotation and use of biological control, which are less commonly used on conventional farms.

One study was carried out between 1984 and 1987 in Denmark by the Danish Ornithological Society - a comparison between 31 organic farms and an equivalent area of intensively managed, conventional farms. 24 of the 35 species studied had higher numbers on the organic farms than on the conventional farm area, including Lapwing (*Vanellus vanellus*), Sky Lark (*Alauda arvensis*), Swallow (*Hirundo rustica*), Whitethroat (*Sylvia communis*), Linnet (*Acanthis cannabina*), Corn Bunting and Yellow Hammer (all these were among the species that declined in the survey mentioned above, except the Whitethroat which was not listed) (FoE, 1991). A similar study, the Organic Farming Project, was carried out by the Institute of Arable Crops Research and the British Trust for Ornithology in the early 1990s on farms in a wide area of southern and eastern England. This likewise demonstrated higher numbers of some bird species on organic farms than on conventional farms. It also showed a higher breeding density and productivity of the Sky Lark on fields in organic farms (Campbell and Cooke, ibid).

A comparison of organic and conventional farms has also been made in studies of invertebrates (Cobb et al 1999). The study was carried out in southern England, using across-farm transects. Butterfly abundance per kilometre per farm, was significantly higher on the organically managed farms than on conventionally managed farms. Comparisons between organic and conventional farms were also made for surface-active spiders in winter wheat fields. Significantly more spiders, and more species of spider, were captured from the organic than the conventional fields. The authors however caution against assuming such differences will always be found between the two farming systems.

It would be useful to know how the various individual aspects of changed farm practice have contributed to farm decline, and in particular, how important has the use of pesticides been in this respect. It should be noted here that the interest in pesticides has shifted in recent decades away from possible direct effects, to indirect effects. Decades ago there was evidence of direct effect of pesticides on birds (poisoning of adults, egg thinning and therefore breaking, infertility), and these concerns were widespread in the developed world. The publication in the USA of Rachel Carson's (1962) book "Silent Spring" which documented the effects of insecticides on man and animals played an important role in bringing about the taking out of use since the 1960s of the most harmful compounds like the organophosphates, and their replacement by less harmful compounds, many of which are more selective in target. Prior to the banning of such insecticides there was a widespread destruction of grain-eating birds and birds of prey in Western Europe, but the populations recovered after the banning of the above insecticides (Gardner, 1996). More recently the concern has been on the indirect effect of pesticides - killing off plants and animals (invertebrates) that provided birds with their food.

There are two major difficulties in trying to make such an assessment of the role of pesticides in bird population decline. The first is lack of adequate data on wildlife. Despite birds being a relatively well-studied group of animals, there is far less accurate information about them than one would like. And there is little information about long term trends of abundance of plants and invertebrates, which provide food for the birds. The second is that pesticides are applied in the same areas where other aspects of modern farming are also practiced, rather than in different areas. For example, both spraying of pesticides and hedgerow removal have taken place in the same areas, and we know that hedgerows are a haven for many bird species so their removal might have a big effect on some bird populations. So this makes it difficult to disentangle the contributions of different aspects of farming practice to bird decline. Then again, information is available about the growth in use of the different categories of pesticide over the decades since the Second World War. There is a rough correlation between such usage growths and the rates of decline of particular bird species. But then again, other aspects of modern intensive farm practice were also developing during the same time period, so in any analysis their effects would be confounded with the effects of pesticide usage growth.

The only way to solve this problem is to experimentally manipulate the different aspects of conventional farming practice. The most convincing study here was one carried out by the Game Conservancy on the Grey Partridge and its food items in a 29 square km area in Sussex over a period of nearly 30 years. This study included experimental manipulation of pesticide use. One conclusion of the study was that partridge chick survival was reduced by the indirect effects of insecticides and herbicides (as reported in Campbell and Cooke, ibid).

While it is generally agreed that pesticide use is one factor responsible for wildlife decline, other farm practices are also implicated. For example, in upland areas, the change from late hay making to earlier silage making has meant that habitat for breeding of such birds as the Lapwing and Skylark has been seriously disturbed, leading to reduced breeding success. The change from spring sowing to autumn sowing of cereals has meant the disappearance in many areas of winter stubble fields, which previously provided food for many birds, and a habitat to live for small animals.

As my last example of change in groups of organisms, I take changes in mammal populations (UKBSG,1995; Harris et al ,1995). While a large number of studies have been carried out on mammals, many conclusions about populations can only be tentative because of lack of data. In particular, there is a lack of basic data on population densities for many, if not most species of mammal in Britain.

The Biodiversity Steering Group prepared a list of 125 species of threatened plant and animal species (species which had declined seriously in numbers or range, or were found in only a few small areas, etc.) Of these, ten species of mammal had declined in numbers or range by 25-49% during the last 25 years in Great Britain, including several bat species, the water vole (*Arvicola terrestris*), dormouse (*Muscardinus avellanarius*), brown hare (*Lepus europaeus*) and red squirrel (*Sciurus vulgaris*). Harris et al (ibid) summarised the known/believed changes in population size and degree of population fragmentation in Britain over the last 30 years: 2 species became extinct, 14 species declined substantially, 9 species declined to a lesser degree. 8 increased substantially, 9 increased to a lesser degree. Of the species increasing, several are considered actually or potentially damaging to agriculture, including rabbit (*Oryctolagus cuniculus*) and red deer (*Cervus elaphus*), but, fortunately, several of the increasing species are species of concern to conservationists because they had previously been reduced to very small numbers, including the otter.

As with birds, it is usually difficult to specify the precise causes for increases or decline and the relative importance of different causes. But the general intensification of farming practice including habitat loss is probably the greatest general cause of decreases. According to Harris et al (ibid) many species are threatened, the major causes being thought to be:

Cause	No. Species
Competition	7
climatic change/adverse weather conditions	7
disease	4
population fragmentation/other habitat isolation	7
habitat changes	31
inter-breeding	5
deliberate killing	18
pesticides/pollution/poisoning	25
predation	4
road deaths	7

Examples of factors causing or probably causing decreases are:

Water vole, *Arvicola terrestris*
(1) Loss, fragmentation, and disturbance of habitats.
(2) Predation by mink.
(3) Pollution of watercourses.
(4) Poisoning by rodenticides

Brown hare, *Lepus europaeus*
(1) Conversion of grassland to arable land.
(2) Loss of habitat diversity in the agricultural landscape.
(3) Changes in planting and cropping regimes, such as moving from producing hay to producing silage, and autumn planting of cereals.

Pipestrelle bat, *Pipistrellus pipistrellus*
(1) Reduction in insect prey abundance, caused by high intensity farming practice and loss of insect -rich habitats.
(2) Loss of winter roosting sites in buildings and old trees.
(3) Disturbance and destruction of roosts, including the loss of maternity roosts caused by the use of toxic timber treatment chemicals.

The effects of pollution on wildlife will be discussed in Chapter 8 Section 4 and Chapter 7 Section C.

Finally, we may ask the question – to what extent have designated nature reserves in the wide sense of that term, had an impact on wild life populations? There can be no doubt that at a local level, they have made significant contributions to conserve the flora and fauna. And they have contributed to the increase of certain rare species. However, one may question whether they have had any more general effect. For there is a stark contrast between two facts.

First, the number and extent of areas that were designated to protect wild life habitats and wildlife in England have increased very considerably in recent years. Thus the area of National Nature Reserves increased from under 45,000ha in 1991 to approaching 80,000 ha in 1999. Over the same period Local Nature Reserves increased from about 11,000 ha nearly 30,000 ha over the same period (EN, 1999). And SSSIs, which amongst other purposes protect flora and fauna, have increased in total area also. Second, as already mentioned, there is a continuing serious decline in the populations of a range of wild bird species, which collectively can be regarded as indicators of the state of biodiversity in England.

H. Wildlife on 'waste land' and in suburban gardens

As we saw in Chapter 3, general planning policy is moving in recent times towards preventing encroachment on countryside land for housing and other development by making maximum use of existing previously used land in towns and even in more rural areas. In general terms, this must be a good thing. However, this policy needs some modification. The health of wild life populations to a large extent depends on the health of populations of invertebrate animals, since they are a fundamental part of the food chain. Now as Chris O'Toole of Oxford University commented to me: modern agriculture has almost wiped out such populations widely in the countryside. In contrast, derelict building sites, old railway sidings, chalk and gravel pits, now usually have a far better invertebrate diversity (spiders, beetles and wasps etc.) than agricultural countryside. It would be better O'Toole commentated, to build houses in the countryside than on such sites. In fact the wild life potential of derelict land has been known for a long time (Handley, 1996), and we saw in the previous Chapter how advantage of this has been taken in Sheffield.

Suburban gardens together, cover a significant part of the total land area of England. They have therefore, a great potential for wild life conservation. But what is the wildlife status of gardens at the present time? My own feelings are that the value of gardens for wildlife is very limited, but I wanted to know more about this. . So I wrote to the RSPB the following letter:

"I write to enquire about the RSPB's perception of, and possible research into, the value of suburban gardens for wildlife, and in particular, birds.
Gardens are sometimes regarded as havens for wildlife. Now I accept that gardens have a great potential in this respect, but at the same time I do not think this potential is being much realized in typical suburbia.

I say this because of my own experiences, which are I think to some extent unusual. I was born (1931) and brought up in Sheffield, my parents house being in middle suburbia, adjacent to a public park.
I distinctly remember in the years around and during the Second World War, that the gardens in my immediate neighbourhood were rich in bird life. A typical spring morning would bring the calls of a few different song thrushes competing with each other, as well as blackbirds doing the same. And also I would hear the hedge accentor (dunnock), wren and robin. From the park came the voice of the mistle thrush.

My experience is somewhat unusual because I left Britain in 1961 to go to Africa. My visits back to the UK became less and less frequent and shorter in duration. I finally returned to live in the UK in 1993. And I came back not just to my own city, but the very house in which I had been brought up. This has enabled me to compare and contrast, as two stills taken from a cinematographic series, what things are like now with what they were like before I left. The comparison is depressing.

Now on a spring morning, I may hear only a solitary blackbird. I don't here the song thrush. Occasionally I might here a mistle thrush in the park. I still see the occasional robin and wren. And tits visit the garden as before. But the contrast is enormous. <u>Dawn chorus was really a chorus. Now early morning is mainly silence.</u>

But I notice something else. The gardens around my own have changed somewhat in character. A few of the hedges have been replaced by fences (presumably because that involves less maintenance). There seems to be an increase of manicured lawns and of paving stone covered areas. Many or most gardens seem to be prettified extensions to internal living space – flower borders round lawns. I must be careful not to exaggerate the changes and in any case I have no concrete evidence to support my memories on the last point. But what I do know is that there has been a big increase in the number of cats in our neighbourhood (and I had to go to a big expense to keep them out of my garden). Naturally I wonder if the changes I observe and remember could be at least partly responsible for the decline of birds.

What I suspect, but cannot prove, is that there has been a big increase in the use of slug pellets and other anti-'pest' chemicals (were pellets even invented in 1950?).

And so I arrive at the following hypothesis which I extend beyond my own neighbourhood to the whole national main suburban housing area (leaving out gardens of the very affluent outside the main city areas):

The decline of suburban birds has been caused by increased use of chemicals, increased ownership of cats, and a change to a less labour intensive gardening practice.

I am aware from comparisons between organic and conventional farms, that it is possible to achieve a local increase in bird life despite prevalence of 'bird deserts' in the surrounding areas. So an ancillary hypothesis is the following:

The decline of suburban birds has not been caused by the intensification of agriculture, even if agricultural land might be fairly close to some but not most suburban areas.

Now it seems to me, that if gardens were managed properly (as I try to do in my garden) – some organic food production, wildlife areas, pond, hedges of hawthorn and other wild species, reduction of lawns and letting these become wilder in herbage height and species composition with no chemical treatment – we could bring about a massive restoration of wildlife.

Now where does the RSPB fit into all this? Specifically can you please answer the following questions?

1)   Does the RSPB regard the mass of suburban gardens as an actual as distinct from potential haven for birds?
2)   Does the RSPB know of any research on the possible effect of cats, slug pellets and other garden practice, on bird populations?
3)   Has the RSPB sponsored or carried out itself and published, research in this field?
4)   Does the RSPB think there has been an increase of cat ownership nationally in recent decades?
5)   What are the RSPB's views on the hypotheses I advance?
6)   If the RSPB does in fact agree with my hypotheses, has it campaigned to change gardening practice?
7)   Likewise, has it campaigned against cat ownership?

Your attention to my queries would be much appreciated".

I received the following reply from the RSPB's Senior Research Biologist:

"Your reflections on the changing numbers of many bird species in suburbia are in accordance with the experiences of many others. Long-term monitoring of garden bird populations by the British Trust for Ornithology through their Garden Bird Feeding Survey and Garden Bird Watch has shown fairly clear cut declines of birds such as song thrush, blackbird and house sparrow. Others have increased (e.g. collared dove, magpie, greenfinch and blue tit) but are perhaps not such voluble contributors to the dawn chorus! You might wish to contact BTO to obtain more information on these surveys; they can be contacted at BTO, The Nunnery, Thetford, Norfolk 1P24 2PU (01842-750050).

Although I am not aware of any hard data to test this, my personal experience on the changing management of gardens concurs with yours; greater use of 'non-living' surfaces such as paving, and a more manicured approach to what remains. This may well entail a greater use of the same pesticides in gardens whose use we are striving to control on farmland. Modern houses are, themselves, usually designed to exclude rather than offer accommodation to bats and nesting birds such as swifts, martins and house sparrows, so the problem of 'modern design' in suburbia may well extend beyond the garden. Cats are known to be major predators of birds, but it is not known whether the mortality they cause is a direct cause of population declines. Overall then, I would regard your first hypothesis as reasonable but largely untested.

With regard to your second hypothesis, there has again been no detailed research to examine the interaction between suburbia and surrounding farmland in determining bird populations. My own view is that, if anything, suburbia may help to support bird populations in neighbouring areas of intensive agricultural land, and that a recent tendency for farmland birds such as yellowhammers and reed buntings to begin to visit gardens in late winter (when seed supplies on farmland are at their lowest) is no coincidence.

To try to answer your specific questions:

1. RSPB regards suburban gardens as actual havens for birds, but nonetheless as a habitat which could be improved. For example, our current research on the ecology of song thrushes in Sussex and Essex shows that villages and gardens consistently hold high densities of these birds relative to surrounding farmland yet nonetheless BTO data show that garden populations, nationally, are declining.

2/3. There is no research which shows whether or not either cats or slug pellets are directly responsible for the long-term decline of bird populations, and RSPB has not (yet) carried out or sponsored research in this field. However, RSPB does adopt the precautionary principle. For example, we might recommend the fitting of bells to domestic cats to reduce the rate at which they catch birds (we are aware of some recent experimental research which confirms this), and the use of non-toxic alternatives to slug pellets.

4. Recent research by the Mammal Society suggests an increase in cat ownership. You would need to contact them for details.

5/6. My responses to your ideas are outlined above. RSPB has not yet campaigned on the general issue of gardening practice but we do offer advice on ecologically sustainable and 'wildlife friendly' gardening through our Wildlife Enquiries service and offer a wide range of information leaflets and publications on this subject in our shops.

7. The RSPB does not campaign against cat ownership. This might change if evidence came to light that they were playing a significant role in causing the national population decline of any species. Even then our activities would probably be directed more positively towards finding ways to reduce the predatory impact of cats, rather than against their ownership. Personally, however, I find it unlikely that cats are a primary cause of national population decline of any bird species and believe that managing to provide the habitat and food that birds need in gardens, as in other habitats, is the most likely way forward.

Overall, you may feel that RSPB has been less active in researching the impact of management of 'suburban habitats' on birds than it might. I would agree. However, in recent years, our research resources have been stretched across a wide variety of other very important issues (notably the impact of agricultural change on birds). In the future, and in the light of recent declines of species such as house sparrow, I believe that increasing research attention will be paid to suburban habitats, and that RSPB will play a role in that work.

Yours sincerely   ...."

I decided to take this matter further, so contacted the Mammal Society (MS). They kindly sent me details of their findings in relation to cats, from which I abstract the following salient points.

The MS had conducted a survey of the kinds and numbers of animals that are killed by domestic cats, in a survey that was carried out during five months in 1997. The survey yielded results for nearly a thousand cats, and over 14,000 prey items.

From this result, the MS did the following calculation.

The mean number catches/kills per cat over 5 months was 16.7.
So average annual catch estimated to be 40.
Estimated number of cats in Britain (pet industry estimates) is 7.5 million.
Conclusion: The British cat population could be killing at least 300 million animals and birds every year.

The MS add the comment that this figure does not include a) animals eaten away from home; b) animals killed by the estimated 800,000 feral cats believed to be living in England.

The survey found that large numbers of toads, newts, lizards, slow-worms and grass snakes were amongst the prey items. 3,383 birds were taken by cats in the survey (over 20% of the total catch).

There were 13 bird species in which more than 30 individuals died. The biggest numbers of kills here were for the house sparrow, blue tits, blackbirds, starlings and thrushes (few cat owners differentiated song from mistle thrush) and robin.

The MS commented on the results. They thought it unlikely that cats alone would cause many species to become endangered in Britain. But for those species already under pressure for other reasons, such as grass snakes, slow worms, thrushes and harvest mice, cats could produce significant effects. And although only a few bats were killed, bat kills could be serious. British cats could be killing 230,000 per year; and bats are slow to reproduce, having on average less than one young per year.

Now in the face of such evidence, which dates from several years ago, one is entitled to wonder why the RSPB is not taking a more active line on cats. I am also puzzled by the statement in the RSPB letter that recent research suggests fitting bells to domestic cats might reduce kills. For the MS reported on this question: Of the 740 cats for which bell records were available (cat reported as having or not having a bell), 232 were bell wearers, 508 were non-bell wearers. The mean kill rate for bell-wearers was 19, for non-bell cats, 15. These results do not suggest attaching bells to cats has a beneficial effect! The MS raise the question – are bell wearers better hunters because they have to be stealthier in order to keep their bells quiet? Now it may be that the RSPB has some other more recent evidence on this point, although the RSPB does not specify the evidence.

I would have thought that the evidence from the Mammal Society is strong enough to make campaigning on the cat issue a priority for the RSPB. And why, when suburban gardens occupy such a significant part of land area, has not the RSPB researched suburban gardens even if this meant some reduction on research on other issues? *I advance the following hypothesis. Many members and supporters of the RSPB will be cat owners (I would not be surprised if the figure was as high as 50%). To research on, and possibly campaign on, the effect of cats on wildlife populations might then result in a massive fall away of RSPB support. This comment can be linked with my criticism of NGOs at the end of Chapter 10.*

One final comment. The BTO seems to regard gardens as providing a very useful support for bird populations in winter. And they note that in the winter of 1998/99 five species exceeded all-time 'high' levels of feeding attendance. These were the collared dove, woodpigeon, jackdaw, goldfinch and pheasant. But two widespread species dipped to an all time 'low' – house sparrow and starling, as also did two less frequent visitors to gardens, the reed bunting and the fieldfare (BTO News 224, Sept.-Oct. 1999).

I. Climate Change

It is now generally accepted that global warming is taking place, which is due, at least in part, to the increased concentrations of greenhouse gases in the atmosphere, caused by man's activities. In England, our climate seems to be changing, and four of the five warmest years in the 340-year long record occurred in the last decade (Cannell et al 1999).

Climate change may bring with it an increase in extreme weather events such as heavy rainfall and droughts. In the UK it is expected to have profound effects on the countryside and its wildlife. Global warming, as well as bringing an overall warming of the UK atmosphere is likely to cause decreased precipitation in summer, increased precipitation in winter. Drier warmer summers will keep soils drier longer, reducing the recharge of aquifers, the principal source of water in much of the English lowlands. Heavier and more intense winter rainfall may lead to greater volumes of surface runoff over a short period, reducing groundwater recharge and causing increased flooding (Wade et al 1999).

The amount of water used to irrigate crops is expected to increase because there is an increasing pressure from retailers to produce the high quality crops grown under irrigation. Further, increased evaporation (resulting from higher temperatures) and lower rainfall could lead to increased water abstraction for irrigation. Hot dry conditions may well increase in the summer, and this would increase the incidence of fires, which damage the habitat.

The densely populated South East Region of England is a focus for concern over the effects of climate change. One of the greatest challenges for the region will be balancing the supply and demand for water, bearing in mind that already, the Region has the highest demand for water per head of any UK region. More reservoirs may have to be built, and increasing amounts of water transferred from other regions, especially if water levels in the Regions rivers and wetlands were to be maintained. At the same time, water supply will interact with other environmental problems arising from climate change. There may be increases in soil erosion, and elevated nutrient enrichment or elevated pesticide levels through changes to agricultural practice. The overall result would be that important aquatic habitats like the River Itchen might be subject to lower flows of water but higher concentrations of pollutants. There is the threat of large areas of lowland Britain being inundated unless there is a massive increase in spending on sea defences (Wade et al, ibid).

The changes in climate will have a profound effect on the composition and distribution of the flora and fauna in Britain. Species are adapted to a range of climatic conditions, some being more restricted than others. There is likely to be a northward movement of distribution of some species, which will be frequently hampered by he discontinuity of habitat, and an increased invasion of Mediterranean climate species into Britain. Just to give one example of the likely effect of global warming – the health of beech trees. One measure of this health is the density of foliage – 'crown density'. There is a strong negative correlation between the percentage of beech trees with over 25% crown reduction and average rainfall the previous July. It is thought that if summer droughts become more frequent in southern Britain, beech trees there will become less healthy and suffer dieback (Cannell and Sparks in Cannell, ibid).

For the present writer, one significant feature of the whole discussion of global warming scenarios is that little is said about the significance of the high density of our human population and future population growth, for our future water supply. Likewise in all the discussions about immigrant flows and the value of immigrants to or economy and society, what is rarely even considered is the fact that increase in population will put increasing stress on our water supplies. In the overall balance of things, an increase in population could be the last straw that breaks the camel's back and we will become unable to cope with the effects of global warming.

Chapter 6

The Changing Countryside, part 2.
Agri-environment Schemes and the Common Agricultural Policy

It is widely thought that the European Common Agricultural policy (CAP) has been instrumental in causing the damage to landscape and decline of wildlife described in the previous chapter. At the same time, various schemes, which fall under the umbrella of the CAP, have the potential to secure environmental improvement.

A. Agri-environment schemes

In recent years a number of schemes have been made available to farmers that can bring environmental improvement to the countryside. These schemes are voluntary; farmers are compensated for production foregone and/or environmental benefits provided. These schemes were largely developed and implemented in intimate relationship with the development and implementation of the Common Agricultural Policy (CAP) of the European Union, which will be discussed in the next section.

(i) Details of the schemes

Most of the schemes are operated and controlled by the Ministry of Agriculture Fisheries and Food (MAFF). The schemes are listed in the box below.

Of the schemes listed in the box, seven were either revised to become part of, or introduced as part of the UK's 'agri-environment package' which was introduced as part of the 1992 reform of the European Unions Common Agricultural Policy, under Council Regulation 2078/92 (see next section). These seven are: ESA, CA, M, H, NSA, OA, and CS (the UK package includes one more scheme, Tir Cymen, which is the Welsh Stewardship Scheme and so lies outside the scope of the present enquiry). The term 'agri-environment scheme' is often used just to cover these schemes, i.e. it is used in a more restrictive way than it is used in the present chapter.

The OA scheme was replaced by the Organic Farming Scheme (OF) in April 1999. Enrolment in the FCG scheme closed in 1996; the H scheme closed to new applicants in December 1999, elements of it are now integrated into CS. The M scheme closed in 1998. SA was introduced to reduce arable crop production, but can have real environmental benefits so is included in the list. CA was introduced to improve access to the countryside but is also included in the list because such access could lead to

---

SCHEMES

The tabulation indicates when each scheme started and the period of time in years that the agreement signed by farmers covers.

1. MAFF schemes

Environmentally Sensitive Areas (ESA)	1987 effectively five yrs
Set-aside under arable payments (SA)	1988 one or five yrs
Farm Woodland Premium (FWP)	1988 twenty or thirty yrs
Farm and Conservation Grant Scheme (FCG)	1989 ten yrs
Nitrate Sensitive Areas (NSA)	1990 five yrs
Countryside Stewardship Scheme(CS)	1991 ten yrs
Countryside Access Scheme(CA)	1994 five yrs
Habitat Scheme (H)	1994 ten or twenty yrs
Organic Aid Scheme (OA)	1994 five to nine yrs
Moorland Scheme (M)	1995 five yrs
Arable Stewardship Scheme (AS)	1998 five or six yrs

2. Forestry Commission

Woodland Grant Scheme (WG)	five or ten yrs

greater appreciation of, and support for, the environment.

The NSA scheme closed in 1998; it had been designed to reduce the extent that nitrates could get into rivers, in areas where nitrate concentrations in sources of drinking water were high. Now compulsory restrictions on the use of nitrogenous fertilisers have come into force under the EC Nitrate Directive (91/676/EEC) in what are called Nitrate Vulnerable Zones (NVZ). These are areas where land drains into waters with high or rising levels of nitrate. The total NVZ area is bigger than the total NSA area, and all NSAs are within NVZs. The UK Government apparently misunderstood the Nitrates Directive, and only paid attention to land near to drinking water sources, whereas the Directive is meant to apply more widely; consequently the Government was referred to the European Court of Justice. The Government now intends to designate further nitrate vulnerable zones. Now there are large areas of agricultural land that will still lie outside designated vulnerable zones once the new zones have been chosen. High nitrogen fertilizer input, with consequent risk of pollution, even if this be only the release of nitrogenous gases into the atmosphere, is very widespread in agricultural land, and will not be affected by the Directive. The WG scheme is successor to schemes going right back to the 1920s.

Detailed descriptions and evaluations of the schemes were given in Barker (1998). Here only schemes that will be referred to in some detail later in this chapter, or in later chapters, are described. These are SA, ESA, CS and OA.

Set-Aside.

As we will see in the next section, under the Common Agricultural Policy, in the arable sector, farmers receive support payments based on the area on which crops are being produced. To receive such payments, farmers have to take a small percentage of their crop area out of food production, i.e. set aside a portion of the land. The minimum proportion (percentage) of the total area that must be set aside, is decided yearly. It has varied over the years between 5% and 15%. Currently it is 10%. The scheme is only technically voluntary, because most farmers need to get the support payments.

Certain basic features of the set-aside scheme are 'environmentally friendly'. Thus on the set aside land farmers may not apply any fertiliser, manure or organic waste with the exception of on own farm holding generated slurry, manure or organic waste (e.g. from draining ditches); fungicides and insecticides may not be used. A green cover must be established on set-aside land, either through sowing a suitable cover or through natural regeneration, and such a green cover is thought to reduce nitrate leaching. And set-aside land may be managed for specific conservation ends such as providing sites for ground nesting birds or creation of wildflower meadows. If set-aside land is placed next to woods, hedges or rivers, set-aside will act as a buffer zone between the natural feature and the crop growing land. Setting aside field margins and headlands might serve to link up useful wildlife habitats like small woodlands, and provide access for better maintenance of hedgerows.

On the other hand, with most of the set aside land, farmers may, if they wish, rotate the land set aside from one place to another, in which case long-term recovery of habitat is not possible. There has also always been the danger that farmers would compensate for production losses incurred through set-aside by intensifying production on the land remaining in production.

Environmentally Sensitive Areas Scheme.

This scheme was proposed to the EEC by the UK; in CAP development, the concept was introduced during the 1985 review of agricultural policy (Woods et al 1988) and was first implemented in the UK in 1987. This scheme is offered in areas defined as having special landscape, wildlife, or archaeological interest. The ESA scheme is supposed to address the problem whereby the shift from mixed farming and traditional stock farming to intensive livestock and crop farming has resulted in loss of hedges, hay meadows, heather moorland, etc. So the scheme was supposed to encourage farmers to maintain, or to re-introduce, traditional, environmentally friendly land management practices. Farmers are offered financial incentives to follow prescribed farming practices, which vary from one type of land to another. Examples are reducing or excluding stock from overgrazed woodland; and with unimproved grassland, not increasing the use of fertilizer beyond existing levels, and not applying fertilizer to any area where non was applied at the time. Various 'tiers' of agreement are offered to farmers, which demand progressively greater departures from conventional farming practice, the lowest tier demanding the smallest change.

Countryside Stewardship Scheme.

Unlike ESA this scheme is not restricted to certain defined areas of England, and its flexibility allows it to give priority to target some of the most traditional English landscapes and their wildlife and historical/archaeological features. The scheme was designed by the Countryside Commission (CC) on the basis of its own pilot scheme that started in 1989. It was also run by the CC until it was handed over to MAFF in 1996. In developing the targeting process the CC entered into discussions with various other bodies to try to ensure maximum impact for the scheme -e.g. discussions with the Nature Conservancy Council (now English Nature), wildlife trusts and local authorities. As originally conceived, it was a scheme complementary to ESA - targeting of C.S. meant that there was very little area overlap with ESA.

The scheme aims to conserve and restore traditional landscapes and wildlife habitats, conserve archaeological sites and other historic features, create new wildlife habitats, and improve public access. Examples of the various landscapes targeted are chalk and limestone grassland, waterside land, uplands, and the coast. One example of the measures promoted will illustrate the general approach. On Chalk and limestone grassland, the CC (now the MAFF) looks for proposals which:

a) conserve and improve grassland and archaeological sites by reducing grazing and fertiliser application, or through scrub control;

b) restore traditional stone walls and hedges;

c) return cultivated areas to characteristic down land;

d) improve access and promote educational visits.

While the mix of farming and conservation practices advocated in different landscapes varies, certain basic requirements apply to all areas, including avoiding overgrazing, not applying organic or inorganic fertilisers, lime or slag, and certain limitations in the use of herbicides and pesticides.

Two other features of the scheme should be mentioned. First, although the schemes guidebook lists the sorts of improvements sought after, these are not laid down as a rigid set of requirements. Proposals can be made to the authority, and priority in deciding acceptances is given to applications offering the best cocktail of improvements. So acceptance of a proposal is discretionary. Second, the scheme is not limited to farmers, but is open to anyone who can enter into a ten-year agreement - e.g. voluntary bodies.

Organic Aid Scheme (now the Organic Farming Scheme).

Financial Aid is available for farmers wishing to convert from conventional to organic production methods. Aid is available both to farmers wanting to extend the area they already have in organic production (but not to assist them on land already in organic production), and to farmers who wish to begin to convert to organic production.

Organic farming works as much as possible with, makes maximum use of, the processes by which natural ecosystems are regulated and sustained, for example, by encouraging the basic biological cycles which involve a) soil components - minerals, organic matter, micro-organisms, soil flora and fauna, b) plants and animals. It is a low input system in that it avoids the use of inorganic fertilizer and nearly all synthetic pesticides. For fertilizer, only animal manure and vegetable waste is used. For pest control, pest incidence is minimised by farming practices such as crop rotation (which minimises the build up of pest populations); where active pest control is needed, biological control methods are adopted; in livestock farming organic farming usually involves relatively low stocking densities and a careful attention to animal welfare. valuable wild life habitats like hedges are maintained. Generally, organic farming is carried out within the framework of mixed farming (combining arable and grassland farming).

Organic farming in the European Community is largely subject to a regulation introduced in 1991 - Council Regulation no. 2092/91. This regulation is intended to ensure that organic farming methods are carefully defined, and produce accurately labelled, so as to ensure that organic farmers are protected from unfair competition, and consumers know that when produce is appropriately labelled, they really are getting products produced by organic methods, and especially that synthetic chemicals have not been used in production. Each country/language has a single word denoting the organic status, for example "organic" in English, "okologisch" in German, "biologique" in French.

Annex 1 of the regulation summarises the principles of organic farming under two headings:

1) The fertility and the biological activity of the soil must be maintained or increased, where appropriate, by:
a) cultivation of legumes, green manures or deep-rooting plants in an appropriate multi-annual rotation programme;
b) incorporation in the soil of organic material, composted or not, from holdings producing according to the rules for this Regulation.

2) Pests, diseases and weeds shall be controlled by a combination of the following measures:
choice of appropriate species and varieties; appropriate rotation programme; mechanical cultivation procedures; protection of natural enemies through provisions favourable to them (e.g. hedges, nesting sites, release of predators); flame weeding.

The Organic Aid Scheme was replaced this year with the Organic Farming Scheme, which has a higher rate of payments than the former scheme.

(ii) How effective have the schemes been?

One thing that stands out when one begins to examine the agri-environment scene is that there is a plethora of schemes, rather than an integrated strategy for environmental improvement. While recently the number of schemes listed at the beginning of the chapter has been reduced, further countryside schemes have been introduced in relation to the Rural Development Regulation that will be discussed later. This variety of schemes has created confusion and excessive amounts of paper work for hard working farmers, which is not conducive to successful implementation of an agri-environment policy. These problems have been recognised for a long time, as reported in detail in Barker (1998).

The overall impact of the schemes depends on two conditions. *First*, the extent that schemes have been implemented over the whole agricultural area (percentage of total agricultural land covered). It is important to keep in mind here that the overall area of agricultural land in England is over 18 million hectares, or leaving out common rough grazing land, over 9 million hectares. So any scheme that only covers a few thousand hectares will not by itself have much overall impact. This first condition itself depends on two factors: (i) the area of land over which the scheme is offered to farmers (referred to as the 'eligible area'); (ii) the extent that farmers operating within the eligible areas have in fact entered land into the schemes ('uptake'). The *second condition* is the extent that scheme requirements change the conventional farming practice and restore habitats - what I will call the within - scheme area scheme 'efficacy'.

Some schemes are applicable widely in England (e.g. Countryside Stewardship, and even there, lack of funds means that actual agreements can only be made for very carefully selected key habitats). Others have very restricted eligible areas (e.g. NA). Uptake of schemes has been very variable. It has been very wide, in arable areas, for set-aside (simply because set-aside is a pre-requisite if farmers want to claim arable payments). At the other extreme we have the habitat salt marsh option, which by 1998 had only been taken up on 59 acres! Overall, uptake has only affected a small part of total agricultural land. Now the two schemes with by far the greatest uptake (and biggest budget provision) are ESA and CS. All other schemes cover much smaller areas. By 1944, the area of land covered by management agreements under these two schemes was only four percent of the total agricultural area of England (Baldock et al (1996). And by 1999, these two schemes together have been taken up in 676,384 ha - a far cry from 9 or 18 million hectares! (statistics about the schemes in this section were supplied to the author by officials of MAFF).

The important ESA scheme was first offered in 1987. There are now 22 designated areas in England. As at 6th October 1999, the total eligible area was 959,918 ha, the uptake area was 523,545 ha, 55% of the eligible area.
However, uptake has been very variable between areas. At one extreme were West Penwith (eligible 171,518 ha; uptake 95,663 = 91%) and North Peak in the Peak District (eligible 50,300 ha; uptake 43,980 ha =87%). But at the other extreme were Breckland (eligible 54,100 ha; uptake 7,210 ha =13.3%, and Essex Coast (eligible 22,000 ha; uptake 3,970 ha = 18%). It is worth noting here that Breckland was introduced right back in the 1987/88 period.

 We turn now to the efficacy of the ESA scheme. In each ESA area, the scheme is offered in a series of 'tiers'. The lowest tier requires the smallest number of alterations to conventional farming practice; higher tiers require progressively more alterations, offering a greater environmental impact. For example, in the Pennine Dales ESA, the number of conditions imposed for tier 1A is nine. Tier 1B requires the farmer to observe the nine conditions of tier 1A and adds a further 19 conditions. For tier 2A farmers must observe all the conditions for tiers 1A and 1B, together with either a further three, or a further two conditions, depending on the programme. Of course it is not just the mere number of conditions, but what those conditions are. Taking this same Pennine Dales ESA, I look at one aspect that we have seen in an earlier section is an important aspect of intensification - the application of fertilizer, and hence the yield that can be obtained. The only condition relating to this aspect in Tier 1A is condition number one - "do not exceed your existing application rate of inorganic or organic fertilizer". For tier 1B, this condition is tightened by conditions 16, 17 and 20. Condition 16 reads "do not exceed your existing level of inorganic fertilizer and in any case do not exceed 25kg of nitrogen, 12.5kg of phosphate and 12.5kg of potash per hectare per year or the equivalent in artificial organic fertiliser. This must be applied in one application". Condition 17 reads "do not apply slurry or poultry manure". Condition 20 reads "do not exceed your existing level of farm yard manure application on any fields. In any case do not use more than 12.5 tonnes of farm yard manure per hectare per year and apply in a single dressing. Farm yard manure produced off the farm may only be used with the prior written approval of the Project Officer and must be well-rotted". In each of the two alternative Tier 2 levels (2A and

2B) the restriction is further tightened - in 2A the farmer must not apply any inorganic or artificial organic fertilizer. In 2B, no organic or inorganic fertiliser may be used.

Now if one looks at the statistics, and considering the whole ESA scheme one finds the uptake is greatest for the lowest tiers. So uptake of tier one (the tier providing the least environmental benefit) is greater, often very much greater, than uptake for tier two (some schemes have a third tier). And this is despite the fact that higher tiers tend to get higher payments.

For example, with the Cotswold Hills scheme uptake (as percentage of eligible area) is as follows:

Tier 1: 73%; tier 1B: 62%; tier 1C: 60%; tier 2: 6%

The conditions operating with this Cotswold hills ESA are illuminating.
One needs to remember that this area was traditionally a sheep grazing area with unimproved, plant species-rich limestone grassland. Vast areas of this grassland have been lost to arable production. This change has been accompanied by removal of dry stone walls, banks and hedges. Now Tier One of the scheme is primarily concerned with ensuring that the bad effects of intensive farming are not actually accentuated. So farmers are actually paid, for example, for not increasing the area of arable land, not increasing the rate of application of fertiliser, not removing walls and hedges! It is not until one gets to Tier Two that the issue of reverting arable land to extensive permanent grassland is addressed.
With ESA in general, researchers have concluded that Tier 1 payments have attracted farmers because they do not demand extensive changes to management practices (e.g. Hird, 1995; Whitby 1996a), in other words, farmers take up lower tiers because of "ease of compliance" (Whitby and Adger, 1993). Bearing in mind that a farmer does not have to enter all his land into the scheme if he decides to participate, Hird (ibid) adds the point that the low level of payments compared with CAP support means that marginally productive land tends to be protected, while habitats associated with very productive land tend not to be entered.

In early February 1988, the Ministry of Agriculture, Fisheries and Food announced modifications to the scheme, which it claimed would improve the conservation value of ESAs, especially wetland habitats, heather moorland and woodland. First, in six ESA regions, there would be increases (usually moderate) in payment rates. Second, in eleven ESA regions the number of farm management options would be increased.

The *Countryside Stewardship Scheme* is widely recognised by conservationists as a valuable scheme. The way that it targets valuable habitats and the flexibility of the system whereby proposals are evaluated, are highlighted as features of particular advantage. As at 31st march 1999, the uptake can be summarized as follows:

Area under agreement (hectares):	152,839 ha
Arable margins (kilometres):	9,636 km
Length of linear features (kilometres):	10,506 km

In mid 1997 the scheme covered roughly 100,000 hectares. So in terms of area covered, it is next in importance to ESA. The scheme seems to be having an appreciable impact overall in the areas where it has been taken up, and many environmentalists consider it the most effective of the schemes. However, one should distinguish between two aspects of habitat restoration. First, preventing now existing habitat types from degenerating further, and gradually improving them, and second, restoring habitats that have been lost through the spread of agriculture or forestry e.g. lowland heath which has been converted into arable land. In terms of the different management practices advocated overall, Country Stewardship is weighted more to the former than the latter. And the actual uptakes tends to reinforce this disparity. Thus with lowland heath land, in 1997 agreements for presently existing heath covered approximately 6,900 ha, while agreements to re-create heath covered just under 600 ha. The corresponding figures for upland moorland are approximately 4,200 ha and nearly 94 ha!

The *Organic Aid Scheme*. In England some farmers were already farming organically before the Organic Aid Scheme was introduced. By 31st August 1997, the total organic area in England was 27,337 ha (this includes 20,528 ha already fully converted to organic methods, the rest was in the process of being converted). But of this total, the Organic Aid Scheme has only contributed 6,130 ha - 2,118 ha in 1994/95, 2,555 ha in 1995/96, and 1,457 ha in 1996/97. However, by the time the scheme closed in 1999, the total uptake of the scheme was approximately 19,000 ha. The new Organic Farming Scheme proved immediately popular. As at 31st march 2000, the uptake area was estimated as 100,000 hectares (information supplied to the author by MAFF).

In terms of efficacy, we have already seen that organic farming is beneficial to wildlife, partly at least through its ban on most pesticides. A MAFF report (Unwin et al, 1995) concluded that organic farming causes less water pollution than conventional farming, is likely to increase earthworm numbers, and usually increases soil organic matter content.

The still small area of organic farming in England is a matter of concern. One factor, which inhibits farmers from converting to organic methods, is the fact that the transition demands the restructuring of the whole farm business, a complex process that requires the farmer to be willing to learn about the relevant techniques and to be innovative. Advice to farmers on conversion in England has been limited, and mainly in the past provided by a very limited number of private sector consultants, although now there is free government-funded advice for farmers entering the organic aid scheme. There are considerable costs involved when converting to organic production. For example, during the transition period, farming tends to become more extensive (stocking rates decreased, area under crops decreased) while at the same time produce cannot be labelled and sold as organic. Labour costs might increase. Sometimes organic farming requires the purchase of different machinery. And there may be increase of infrastructure costs (e.g. new stock proof fencing). Calculations suggest that the total costs may not always be covered by the aid from the Organic Aid scheme (Cobb et al 1999).

One criticism of the agri-environment scheme system concerns the long-term effects, or durability of the schemes. Farmers enter into agreements for a limited period. During that period some positive improvements of the environment will have been produced, and we may think of this as an increase in the natural capital of the areas concerned. Now at the end of the agreement period, farmers may, particularly if changes in market incentives encouraged them, revert to the intensive farming practices that they practised before entering into agreements. The natural capital would be destroyed. Now environmentalists would argue that this should not happen; after all, society has paid, through its taxes, for this increase of natural capital, so farmers should not be free to dispose of it. However, if this ever came to a test, existing law would probably support the farmer in most cases (Whitby 1996a and b).

A basic feature of the agri-environment scheme system is that the schemes are *voluntary*. This means that the extent that schemes are actually taken up does not depend on the degree of local need for the environmental improvements that the schemes bring; rather, apart from a few farmers who have very strong conservation ideals, uptake depends on farmers assessment of the financial benefit to them of enrolling or not enrolling for the schemes. There is a widely held view that farmers are custodians of the countryside. The low uptake of some schemes in many areas does not fit squarely with this idea. One fundamental problem is the level of financial incentive provided by the schemes compared with the level of subsidies for agricultural production simultaneously offered to farmers (overall, far larger funds are available for the latter than for the former). So with individual schemes, payments offered have sometimes provided insufficient inducement for farmers to enrol. For example, under the former Habitats Scheme, a farmer of arable land could receive payments for converting some land to saltmarsh. But the payments foregone for production under the Arable Area Payments Scheme would mean the farmer ended up with a loss of £500/ha (Hanley et all 1999). Various authors, e.g. CC (1993), have also commented that compensation payments on set-aside were higher than the incentives for many environmental schemes, despite the fact that the management required, and the public benefit obtained from set-aside is considerably less.

It is worthwhile at this point to look at property rights. All the schemes operate on the basis of a contractual management agreement between the farmer and the government. Underlying the whole system are farmer property rights: farmers have the right to maximize profits on their land, irrespective of damage to the environment that this may entail. So, if farmers are to be asked to farm in a more environmentally sensitive manner, and to do so reduces the farmer's profits (through decreased yields or costs of making specific environmental improvements), then society must compensate the farmer for financial loss. Put another way, Society does not have any prior property right to environmental outputs, but must subsidise farmers to produce them! (see for example Hanley et al ibid, who refer to writings of Hodge and Bromley). The system bears additional costs as occur with any policy that arranges the transfer of property rights - transaction costs. If landowners had to pay these costs, they might be deterred from entering the schemes. Consequently, besides trying to minimize these costs, government normally covers them.

We see here conflict with a fundamental element in the strategy developed by environmentalists for dealing with the whole environmental problem, the so-called 'polluter pays' principle. Briefly, this principle states that the person or business that causes pollution damage should have to pay for removal of the pollution and compensation for those people affected by it. As a corollary, and in the industrial field, companies are expected to install machinery, which will reduce polluting effluents. Both the British Government and the EU accept this principle. Now elements of modern farming practice cause pollution - for example pollution of waterways and the atmosphere with nitrogenous substances. The polluter pays principle would have farmers paying for the damage caused (we leave aside the difficult question of how to precisely assess that damage). Instead of doing this, we have in some schemes the situation where farmers are compensated for reducing or abstaining from, polluting practices. The offering of such compensation implies that the farmers have the right to pollute (Whitby, 1996a).

We will return to property rights in Chapter 12 Section C. Assessment of the environmental value of agri-environment schemes is taken up again in the following section.

B. The Common Agricultural Policy (CAP) of the European Union

Farming in the UK in recent decades has been much influenced by the Common Agricultural policy, to which we now turn.

(i) Origins of the CAP

The Common Agricultural Policy of the European Union evolved at a time of changing demand for agricultural products and changing market conditions. The Second World War and the rapidly rising human population created the need to increase agricultural production. Advances in technology made it possible to satisfy this need. But beyond a certain level, continued technological advances create problems. Production tends to outrun demand, so unless products can be sold cheaply on the world market, prices would fall, with adverse effects on the farming community. At the same time, short-run supply variations (caused by adverse weather conditions and disease) leads to price variations, which particularly hit those farmers who can neither increase inputs nor reduce costs. But the distribution of such farms within the European Union varies from region to region; areas of predominantly small farms on relatively infertile land will have a high percentage of such farms (Brassley, 1995).

These and other considerations led governments in continental Europe, most of whom would be founder members of the European Community, and during the years leading up to the formation of the community, to incorporate in their own agricultural strategies systems of price support and import controls; in this way they tried to maintain prices and thus protect their farming communities, and maintain chosen self-sufficiency levels. These features of market control would be incorporated in the CAP. At the same time, there were variations from region to region, and country to country, in the cost and efficiency of the agricultural sector. Such variations could undermine the idea of having an overall common European economic policy. Therefore the exclusion of agriculture from the general common market was impossible. The Community required a common agricultural policy (Brassley, ibid). There was also continued concern that western European countries were still quite heavily dependent on agricultural imports (even in 1962, i.e. a few years after the European Community was formed, the Community was only satisfying 80% of its consumption needs). So a basic goal of the developing agricultural policy was to expand production and so reduce dependence on imported food as well as cutting down the Community's import requirements in energy, raw materials etc (EC 1996).

The European Community (EC) was establish by the Treaty of Rome, signed in March 1957, the Community actually coming into being at the beginning of 1958. The original members were Belgium, France, West Germany, Italy, Luxemburg and The Netherlands. The UK did not join until 1973, long after the CAP had been designed and put in place. Articles 38 -47 of the Treaty of Rome are the articles applying directly to agriculture. Article 39.1 sets out the main objectives of agricultural policy:

a) to increase productivity by promoting technical progress and ensuring the rational development of agricultural production;
b) thus to ensure a fair standard of living for the agricultural population;
c) to stabilise markets;
d) to guarantee a secure supply of food;
e) to assure reasonable retail prices to consumers.

Article 40 laid down broad guidelines about how the objectives were to be achieved. Article 43 indicated the procedure to be used to reach agreement on CAP details. It also required the European Commission to submit detailed proposals to the Council of Ministers. Tentative more detailed shape to the CAP was then given by the 1958 conference at Stresa (Italy), and the Commission produced its proposals in 1960. The CAP was then put in place during the next few years. Central to the whole CAP is the price mechanism which was supposed on the one hand to protect farmers against excessively low prices and thus guarantee them an adequate livelihood, and on the other hand to protect the consumer against excessively high prices.

Farmers receive a guaranteed price, set yearly by EC farm ministers, who are under pressure from their farming constituencies to set high prices. Since the demand for farm produce is relatively constant, when an excess supply is produced, prices tend to fall. This is mitigated by a system called intervention - the EC buys up farm produce when prices fall below what is called the intervention price. If prices subsequently rise, this stored produce can be released onto the market again. The whole system is further complicated by trade with countries outside the EC. World prices tended to be lower than internal prices, so exporters would suffer losses. To deal with this, exporters are refunded the difference between the internal price (the price at which they purchase the produce) and the lower world market price; these export subsidies are called export restitutions or refunds. At the same time it was necessary to protect the community from flooding by low-priced imports. These low prices were caused by a) lower production costs; b) subsidies from the governments concerned. So a system was introduced to subject imports to variable levies (Leonard, 1993; Brassley, ibid). In should be noted that although the UK did not join the EC until 1973, a guaranteed price system had been in operation in the UK for many years. So it can be seen that the EC, from its early days, aimed to support the incomes of farmers through two main mechanisms:

> (i) buying up the surplus supplies of products on the internal market when prices looked as if they might fall below agreed minimum (intervention) prices;
> (ii) applying levies and customs duties at the Community frontiers so that imports could not be sold into the Community below the desired internal market price (Agra Europe, 2000). This desired price is termed the 'target price' with cereals, the 'guide price' for beef.

When the CAP was first introduced it was reasonably successful. But during the next few years, problems developed. As already mentioned, the guaranteed price system for farmers was set yearly by farm ministers who were under pressure from farmers and from the fertiliser and pesticide industries to set them at a high level. So there was a constant stimulus to over-production. The policy of only importing food, which cannot physically be produced in the community, further stimulated home production within the community (self-sufficiency rose to well over 100% for most products); and technological improvements resulted in increasing yields. This combination of factors led to the accumulation of massive agricultural surpluses (Whitby and Adger, 1993). These were very expensive to store; some of them were destroyed, ploughed into the ground, some were converted - for example, some wine was converted to industrial alcohol. But much surplus food was exported onto the world market using prices made artificially low by use of export refunds. This antagonised traditional food exporting countries (Leonard, ibid).

A process of reform of the CAP began, and is still continuing. The most immediate problem in the late 1970s was milk surpluses. In 1979 a co-responsibility levy was imposed on milk producers to help meet the cost of disposing the surplus and to reduce the incentive to produce more milk. This did not prove to be effective. So in 1984, milk quotas were introduced to limit total milk output. Every farmer was given a production quota, the size of which depended on the yield in 1981 which was called the 'base year'. But the problems were not confined to milk, and in 1984 a ceiling was put on agricultural spending, and a stabilizer system was introduced which allowed for reduction of support prices if a maximum guaranteed quantity of production was exceeded (Brassley, ibid).

Subsidies however remained, and radical reform was clearly needed. The Commission recognised this need and in 1991 presented proposals to deal with the situation. However, only a watered down version of the proposals were eventually accepted (Ockenden and Franklin, 1995). The final package was adopted in 1992; it is sometimes known as the MacSharry reform, after the Commissioner who at that time was in control of agriculture. We will return to the 1992 reform shortly.

Now the CAP as originally conceived caused environmental problems. The price mechanism produced the situation where the more farmers produced, the more support they received. The results were:

> a) farmers started to use land that would otherwise have been left uncultivated, to increase production - moors and heaths were 'reclaimed', wetlands drained, hedges removed;

> b) farmers saw that fertiliser and pesticides would increase yield per acre and so they increased their use of these chemicals.

Now there was no specific reference to environmental aims in the articles dealing with agriculture in the Treaty of Rome. However elsewhere (article 130r) environmental protection was mentioned as a component part of Community policy. Gradually, however, environmental concerns arising out of the changes just briefly described, became in theory at least, more integrated into agricultural policy. The EC's first Action Programme for the Environment, published 1973, recognised the need to tackle emerging problems of agricultural pollution, which the Second Action Programme four years later re-iterated. The EC's Third Action Programme went further, recognising there was a need to promote an overall strategy that made environmental policy a part of economic and social development, and enhanced the positive, and reduced the negative effects of agriculture on the environment. In its 'Green Book' of 1985 the European Commission made the point that environmental policies must set the framework within which agricultural production takes place. And also in 1985 Article 19 in EC Regulation 797/85 led to the introduction of the first agri-environment measure, the Environmentally Sensitive Areas scheme that was mentioned in the previous section (Baldock and Lowe, 1996; Whitby 1996a). The 1987 Single European Act created the legal requirement to integrate environmental protection into other EC policy areas. The need for environmental integration is stressed in the Fifth Environmental Action Programme, and a more comprehensive legal basis was given by the Maastricht Treaty on European Union, signed in 1992. Finally, the changes just outlined paved the way for environmental aims to be explicitly incorporated in the 1992 CAP reforms to which we now turn.

(ii) The 1992 CAP reforms

The reforms were designed primarily to reduce prices, reduce production and bring it more in line with demand, and focus support for farmers on those farmers who needed it most. Some attention was also given to the need to make farming more environmentally friendly. The reform package eventually adopted had the following elements:

(i) Cuts in the prices of the main products in surplus over a few years, so as to bring prices closer to, but not right to, world prices (the Commission had originally proposed going even closer to world prices). Thus, cereal prices were to be reduced by 29% and beef by 15% by 1997.

(ii) Farmers were compensated for the loss of income caused by reduction of prices. At the same time measures were brought in to reduce production. In the arable sector, compensation payments were based on the *area* of farmed land, the rate being fixed using historic average yields. To some extent then compensation was 'decoupled' from production - a farmer could not claim more if he increased his yield per hectare. All but the smallest farms were required to take an annual proportion of their land out of production as 'set-aside' (discussed in previous section) - in other words, there was an intended bias in favour of the 'small' farmer. Further, an upper limit, or ceiling, was put on the amounts of payments available in each region. England forms one regional area.

(iii) With the livestock sector production was also to be reduced, extensification encouraged. For farmers to receive headage payments (payments on the number of animals kept) they must conform to a system that set ceilings on stocking densities and sets quotas of livestock per farm. Quota is attached to the *Suckler Cow Premium Scheme* (SCPS) for cows used for rearing calves for meat, and the *Sheep Annual Premium Scheme* (SAPS). Farmers were eligible for an extra extensification premium is they adopted certain practices to reduce production. In both arable and livestock sectors then, compensation took the form of *direct aid payments* for losses incurred. Milk quotas would continue.

(iv) Introduction of agri-environment schemes, under Council Regulation (EEC) 2078/92 as one of three so-called 'accompanying measures' (the other two being an early retirement scheme and a forestry aid scheme).

Regulation 2078/92 stresses the need to make agricultural production compatible with environmental protection by encouraging farmers to use environmentally sound production methods. The encouragement takes the form of payments, which in part compensate farmers for losses incurred through adopting less intensive methods, and in part pay for positive environmental improvements:
"Whereas the measures provided for in this Regulation must encourage farmers to make undertakings regarding farming methods compatible with the requirements of environmental protection and maintenance of the countryside, and thereby to contribute to balancing the market; whereas the measures must compensate farmers for any income losses caused by reductions in output and/or increases in costs and for the part they play in improving the environment".

The scheme works with farmers on a voluntary and contractual basis. Baldock and Lowe, (ibid) list the aid schemes that the regulation permits and espouses. These include schemes which bring about a significant reduction of polluting inputs like fertilizers, pesticides, and herbicides in crop production; maintenance and introduction of organic farming; with livestock farming, reduction of livestock density so as to reduce damage caused by sheep and cattle overstocking; ensure the upkeep of abandoned farmland and woodlands, etc. In the In the first section of the present chapter we looked at the schemes adopted in England.

(iii) Effects of the 1992 reforms

The reforms did result in a decrease of production, at least initially. It proved possible, over the first few years, to reduce intervention stocks; but then there was a renewed upswing trend in cereals, dairy products and beef (EC, 1995; Winter et al, 1998).

Perhaps the most important question to ask is - did the reforms lead to any reduction in the intensity of farming?
As far as the arable sector is concerned, the reforms did not lead to any big change in farming intensity. There was a succession of good harvest years, culminating with bumper harvests in 1996. At the same time, continued advances in farm technology allowed an increase in yield (tonnes per hectare). Cereal prices rose above the intervention price partly because of higher world prices, and green pound devaluations (the green pound is the currency unit used within the EC) favoured our farmers. So there was no incentive for farmers, who like to maximise their profits, to reduce the intensity of farming. While set-aside did reduce production, and trends in production largely mirrored the set-aside rate, in 1996, although the *area* of cereals was 3.8% below its 1992 level, *production* of cereals was 13.5% higher than in 1992. All this points to the fact that trying to achieve production targets by restrictions on area of land in production (set-aside) is very difficult.

Measures of farming intensity are provided by the amounts of fertilisers and pesticides used. Now with *arable farming*, as far as fertilisers are concerned, most farmers had not changed the amount of nitrogen they applied to their crops after the 1992 reforms; where changes were made, there were more farmers who had increased their nitrogen applications than farmers who had decreased them (Winter et al, ibid).

From the wildlife point of view, pesticides pose a greater threat than high levels of fertiliser use. It had been thought that decreases in prices under the 1992 reforms would lead to reductions of pesticide inputs, especially through set-aside. But it appears that there was probably only a reduction of 3.2% stemming from the 1992 reforms. And while set aside played a part, the reductions seem to have been principally caused by the introduction of new, low-dose chemicals. Further, it is possible that lower prices could induce an increase of relatively chemically intense crops (Falconer and Oskam in Brouwer and Lowe, 2000). And the European Commission itself has conceded that the overall usage of agro-chemicals has not been greatly affected by the 1992 reforms (Lowe and Baldock in Brower and Lowe, ibid).

In the beef sector, in a farmers survey reported in Winter et al (ibid), only 11% of beef producers said that the way they managed their livestock farming had been affected by the introduction of the new stocking density regulations. Of this 11%, three-quarters said they now managed their stocking density more carefully, but only about a quarter had actually reduced stocking densities. Fertilizer is applied to grassland to increase yield and quality for silage. Now such fertilizer applications have changed little since the reforms came in with four out of every five farms in the survey. It was concluded that stocking rate rules and extensification payments had had only a minimal effect on land management.

The introduction of stocking density rules in the Beef Regime was really a means to reduce total costs rather than reducing stocking densities per se. Under the rules It was perfectly possible for a farmer to claim for a number of animals - even extensification premiums - which kept the density within prescribed limits, but then also additionally graze non-eligible animals which meant there was no actual reduction in stocking density. In England and Wales the regional Ceiling for total numbers was exceeded each year until 1997. And several commentators have argued that the stocking densities set by the policy were too high to produce much real effect. Some farmers indeed found themselves with stocking densities already below the required densities. Thus in a survey of 389 beef farmers in the UK, only 9.6% were affected by the stocking density regulation. Of these farmers that were so affected, only 18% actually made any reduction in stocking density (Andersen et al in Brouwer and Lowe, ibid).

In the Sheepmeat and Goatmeat Regime (the latter of little importance in the UK), breeding sheep numbers had risen rapidly in the EU between 1983 and 1992, with the growth in the UK being above the EU average. And during the 1992 review it was noted that this upwards trend was leading to a considerable drop in prices, seriously affecting market balance, and the increase in production was causing a steady increase in the bill for support. Consequently, limits on the numbers of animals to be supported were introduced (quotas). Since the 1992 reforms, breeding ewe numbers have in fact declined in all EU states except Italy. Although in principle, reducing stock numbers should reduce grazing pressures and help improve biodiversity, there is in fact uncertainty about the actual environmental benefits achieved. The situation here is complex. Restricting the number of animals supported can cause market prices to rise, which in turn reduces the level of the annual ewe premium support payment. This is likely to lead to producers maximizing yield (increase number of lambs or volume of dairy products sold). In order to achieve this maximization, producers may increase inputs of purchased feeds, fertilisers and veterinary products, use more intensive forage conservation methods and make more intensive use of sheep housing. Such changes are likely to increase risk of pollution and habitat damage - i.e. have effects opposite to what would be produced by decreased grazing pressure (Ashworth and Caraveli, in Brouwer and Lowe, ibid).

In general, as far as stocking densities are concerned attention has been focused on average stocking densities - densities over the whole grazed area. Such limits are themselves inadequate particularly where large areas are grazed. Extensification may have taken place; but what also matters here are the local stocking densities, in particular parts of the farm, where stock may still congregate causing soil erosion and habitat destruction; it is in fact difficult to design regulations to deal with this aspect of the problem (Whitby, 1996a, partly drawing on the work of I.Delpeuch).

What about the effect of the agri-environment measures?

Much concern here has focused on the amount of money that was made available to implement the agri-environment schemes, which is a measure of the extent that the EU takes environmental problems seriously. Now the reform introduced an important shift and improvement in policy. As we saw earlier, agri-environment schemes started before the 1992 reforms (with ESA), but the funding came from what is called the 'guidance section' of CAP funding, which has a very small budget and was quite separate from the much larger 'guarantee section' which is the fund for supporting the CAP market measures, such as export refunds and intervention purchase. Now with the 1992 reforms, it was decided to provide the funding for the accompanying measures including the agri-environment schemes through the Guarantee rather then the Guidance fund. This was of symbolic significance in that it showed that the agri-environment scheme was to be incorporated within the core of CAP. Furthermore, the Guarantee Fund is not subject to the same budgetary restrictions as the Guidance Fund so the funding for the agri-environment scheme was not limited from the beginning by a fixed annual ceiling The reality however, has been that the budget for the agri-environment schemes has only been a tiny part of the total of the Guidance and Guarantee funds-for example, 4% by 1996 (Baldock and Lowe, ibid; Whitby 1996b; Buller, in Brouwer and Lowe, ibid).

The impact of individual agri-environment schemes on the environment was discussed in Section A of this Chapter. More generally we can say that some real environmental improvement has resulted through the application of these schemes. On the other hand, the limited uptake of schemes has limited their effectiveness.
They have failed to have a big impact on overall pollution (fertilisers and pesticides). Thus has partly been because relatively few of the schemes are directly concerned with reducing farm pollution, and partly because
uptake of the schemes has often been low. And the reason for the low participation in the schemes is that many farmers would have experienced a drop in farm income: subsidies and direct compensation payments to farmers have often been high compared with payments for environmental improvement with the agri-schemes. And by 1995, the farm survey mentioned earlier showed that only 7% of farms in the survey had joined an environmental scheme that was part of the agri-environment measure package (Winter et al, ibid; Buller, ibid).

Now the organic aid scheme is particularly important, because it is a radical whole-farm scheme with major impact on fertiliser and pesticide use. Now since 1985 there has been a rapid growth in the organic farming sector in the EC, especially since the implementation in 1993 of the EC regulation 2092/91 defining organic crop production. The achieved percentage of total agricultural land managed organically by 1997 varied considerably between Member States of the EU, from less than 1% to over 10%. Austria, Italy, Sweden and Switzerland did particularly well. Great Britain only managed 0.34%. France achieved 0.55, Germany 2.25. However, one cannot consider organic farming in isolation, because with a limited total budget, each Member State had to decide on the spread of monies between different schemes under Regulation 2078/92. A low expenditure on one scheme might be balanced by a comparatively high expenditure on another scheme which produces some environmental improvement. However, most observers consider organic farming as the scheme with the highest potential for giving environmental benefit (Lampkin, in Brouwer and Lowe, ibid).

Finally, concern has been expressed about the *possible adverse environmental effects of EU enlargement*. The countries now recently admitted, and those seeking admittance, are mainly from eastern Europe. These countries are undergoing modernisation which will include raising technical performance and productivity in agriculture and it seems likely that this phase will have to be passed through before they will begin to show a serious interest in, and concern for the environment. Further, the general low levels of income in such countries and their heavy dependence on agriculture as a productive sector will mean that there entry to the Union will add further to the budgetary pressures within it (Whitby, 1996).

(iv) Further reforms proposed in 1997.

In July 1997, European Commission President Jacques Santer, announced proposals for further reforms of the CAP. The document released ("Agenda 2000 agriculture") indicated that the Commission considered that the 1992 reform had brought considerable improvement of market balances and a decrease in surpluses; further, with cereals, set-aside had helped to keep production under control. There was now a "more rational use" of fertilisers and pesticides. However, further reform was needed and the reforms initiated in 1992 should continue to be developed, especially the move to reducing price support towards world prices.

If present policy remained unchanged, it was observed, cereal intervention stocks could reach 58 million tonnes by 2005; as far as beef was concerned, the BSE crisis and other factors should lead to short term reduction of stocks, but intervention stocks would then increase and could reach 1.5 million tonnes by 2005. Further, if set-aside were to be retained as a major part of the stock reduction mechanism, the areas of set-aside would have to be very substantially increased. The Commission admitted that market prices for cereals had improved much more than expected which had led to "over-compensation of producers (i.e. farmers) in the last few years". And the Commission also comments "the scale of support still provided through prices and crop specific payments.... may discourage farmers from committing themselves to more extensive practices or dedicating land to environmental purposes". The Commission also admitted that agricultural market policy was not properly integrated in to overall rural policy, and the whole CAP system was complex and lacked overall coherence. And "too many programmes and measures can apply simultaneously in the same area under different policy headings, affecting consistency".

The Commission made a number of proposals including the following:

- The shift from price support to direct payments should be continued. The cereal intervention price should fall from 119.19 ECU/tonne to 95.35 ECU/tonne (20% reduction). With beef, the price should fall from 2,780 ECU/tonne to 1,950 ECU/tonne (30% reduction). A non crop-specific area payment would be established; any set-aside areas would get this payment.

- Introduce a ceiling on the total of direct income payments that can be paid to a farmer - remember the large farm profits mentioned in an earlier section. This is technically called 'capping', a form of 'modulation' (see Box X).

- Compulsory set-aside should be abolished (in the CAP jargon, fix the reference rate for compulsory set-aside at 0%).

- Increasing attention needs to be given to rural development. Here agri-environment schemes will play a prominent role in supporting sustainable development in rural areas, and responding to society's increasing demand for environmental services.

- Agri-environment measures should be strengthened through providing for a bigger budget and allowing member states to increase their co-financing contributions. The measures should be targeted, and most relevant here are services which call for an extra effort by farmers, such as organic farming, maintenance of semi-natural habitats, traditional orchards and hedgerows. . But member states would be enabled to make all direct payments for arable crops and set-aside conditional on the farmers taking positive steps to improve the environment ('cross-compliance' see Box Y).

Significantly omitted from the proposals was the idea that compensation payments to farmers (production subsidies) should be time limited, thus making more money available for social, economic and environmental improvements in rural areas.

Many commentators thought that these proposals were too weak to make much difference to the environmental situation. Thus while direct subsidy from price support would be reduced, it would still be substantial; in other words direct payments would not be completely uncoupled from production so the incentive to increase production would not be eliminated. Further, the price support reduction is accompanied by compensatory high non-crop specific area payments, which would make it more difficult to find funds for the agri-environment schemes. And the proposals do not effect a proper integration of the environment into agricultural policy since the agri-environment schemes are still treated as a separate entity from general agricultural policy. These and other points are made in Birdlife International (1997).

(v) Final agreed Agenda 2000 proposals.

The publication of the Santer proposals was followed by a long period of discussion and bargaining among EU member states. Final agreement was in two stages. First, the farm ministers of the Member States met late
February in Brussels and early March 1999 and finally agreed on a reform package. This was then presented to the meeting of Heads of Government in Berlin who made some alterations to this package, finally adopting a modified

---

BOX X   Modulation

By this is meant modifying subsidy systems so that instead of spreading subsidy evenly in terms of hectarage or headage, its distribution is skewed in favour of the particular group concerned, in other words, the subsidy is targeted. There are two main forms of modulation:

(i) placing a ceiling on the total subsidy for any individual farmer/farm holding - called 'capping'.
(ii) reducing support the bigger the farm or the larger the production level - called 'tiering' (conversely, increasing support the lower the production level).

A good example of tiering is provided by Norway (Ross and Turner, 1995). The price support system in dairying targets support to the smaller producers in marginal areas. The support is in effect tapered according to dairy 8herd size. In terms of maximum annual production in litres, the maximum payment per litre is given for an annual production of less than 30,000 l, a reduced payment for 30,000-40,000 l, and the lowest payment for over 40,000 l.

Now modulation already existed in the UK before the further CAP reforms. There was capping in the BSPS (part of the CAP headage payment system), since farmers may only claim on a maximum of 90 animals in each age category (8 - 21 months, and 21 months and over). The organic Aid Scheme had elements of both forms of modulation. The first five hectares received an extra payment, but there was a ceiling on payments at 300 hectares. And in Chapter Three we saw that with CAP payments to arable farmers, the smallest farmers could apply for payment without having to set aside any land. But all these measures are rather minor examples of modulation.

BOX Y   Cross-Compliance

This term is discussd in detail by Baldock and Mitchell (1995) on which the following notes are based.

One way to make agriculture under the CAP more environmentally friendly would be to require farmers to observe certain environmental conditions if they are to receive support payments such as arable area payments. This is termed cross-compliance or the 'red ticket' approach. Such mechanisms serve to bring a degree of integration between environmental considerations and basic CAP agricultural production policy. A degree of cross-compliance was already in place before further reform of the CAP. For example, certain livestock headage payments required that the land be not overgrazed (although the conditions attached have not in fact done much to prevent overgrazing). Cross-compliance could be expanded as a tool to improve the environment. For example, direct payments could be made conditional on the conservation of field margins: In arable farming, farmers would be obliged to create conservation field margins for arable fields where direct payments are being claimed. In livestock farming, the obligation to establish such field margins could be attached to the forage area for livestock premia.

Another example is to link eligibility for CAP support payments to farmers' acceptance of one of a menu of agri-environment schemes (the menu would be developed from the existing suite of agri-environment schemes).
This proposal has been termed the 'orange ticket' approach and was advocated by the RSPB (1994; 1996). Depending on the precise requirements, introduction of more comprehensive cross-compliance could increase the competitive position of organic farmers since they are already incorporating environmentally friendly practices into their farming

The term cross-compliance has had a wider connotation in the USA where it has sometimes been used to include the situation where, in addition to farmers not receiving support payments unless they observe certain environmental conditions, farmers may become eligible for higher levels of support if they comply with further environmental conditions (the 'green ticket' approach). With this definition, payments under agri-environment schemes would be covered by the term 'cross-compliance'. It is better to restrict the term cross-compliance to the narrower meaning.

We have seen that many argue agricultural support in general should decrease. If this happens, as seems likely, this would reduce the financial penalty for non-compliance so that the incentive to comply with cross-compliance would be eroded. Not surprisingly then, support for cross-compliance is not unequivocal as far as environmental organisations are concerned; indeed some people argue that attaching environmental conditions to support payments might give few benefits in practice while at the same time providing a justification for maintaining high total subsidy levels (Baldock and Mitchell, ibid).

BOX Z   Regulation

This term will be used here to mean any measure that requires farmers to observe environmental conditions irrespective of whether or not they are receiving support payments or belong to any agri-environment scheme. This then covers EC and National Legislation on the environment which is not tied to support payments or agri-environment scheme payments, for example, the EC Nitrate Directive which requires certain minimum restrictions on farming practice in the 'nitrate vulnerable zones'.

---

package on the 25th of March. The original Santer proposals, which many environmentalists considered did not go far enough anyway, were watered down at both stages of the final decision making process.

The reason why the Heads of Government made the final alterations was primarily the desire to cut total CAP expenditure, including putting restrictive limits on the amount of money that could be spent on rural development and the environment. Heads of Government however, disagreed as to how the target of ECU 40.5 billion per annum for the main CAP budget could be achieved. One group of nations, including France and the UK, wanted to gradually reduce the level of direct payments to farmers, with some of the savings transferred to the rural development budget (which includes the agri-environment schemes). This approach is termed the principle of 'degressivity'. This was opposed by some member states including Germany who proposed the alternative method of reducing expenditure: postpone the reform of the dairy regime, increase the price cuts for cereals and retain set-aside. It proved difficult to work out a way to implement degressivity that would be acceptable to all Member States so in the end the idea was abandoned (Lowe and Brouwer, in Brouwer and Lowe, 2000). Further, no commitment was made to eventual reduction of prices to world market levels.

The final proposals included the following (Santer and Brussels proposals mentioned for comparison).

1) Price support to be reduced

Cereals
Santer: A 20% reduction in the intervention price in one step in the year 2000.
Brussels: The same reduction but phased in over two yearly steps.
Berlin: Intervention price reduction of 15%, phased in as suggested in Brussels.

Beef:
Santer: A 30% reduction in intervention price two years.
Brussels: Intervention price reduced by 20% over three years.
Berlin: Similar.

Dairy products:
Santer:.Intervention price for butter and skimmed milk reduced by 15% over four years
Brussels: Intervention prices for butter and skimmed milk powder reduced by 15% over three years, but only starting from the 2003/2004 milk marketing year.
Berlin: As Brussels, but the reform further delayed - to start in the 2005/2006 milk marketing year.

2) Compensation - Direct income payments. The above price reductions will be partially offset by an increase in direct aid payments. In the final agreement the area payments for *cereals* will be increased in two steps, which represents a 50% compensation for the overall price cut. But it is expected that the internal market prices will stay above the support price level. In the beef sector, the direct aid payments (the special premium for males and suckler cows) to be increased over three years, and a new slaughter premium introduced. In the dairy sector, a system of aids will be introduced increasing over three years in line with the price reduction.

3) Over the question of whether or not there should be a ceiling for direct income payments (*modulation*), the following changes occurred:

Santer: There should be a ceiling on the total of direct income payments that can be paid to a farmer (capping).
Brussels: The ceiling proposal deleted. However, member states my introduce some modulation: a system whereby member states may be authorised to modulate direct payments per farm, within certain limits, in relation to employment on the farm, overall prosperity of the holding, or the total amount of aid paid to the holding. Direct payments should be gradually reduced (degressivity)
Berlin: Similar on ceiling proposal and modulation. Degressivity abandoned.

4) Compulsory Set-aside (in the arable sector)

Santer. Rate set at zero.
Brussels: Set at 10% 2000-2002, then zero after that.
Berlin: Set at 10% 2000 to 20006 - i.e. maintained at a high level.
(This rate is termed the 'default' rate. This means that the Council has the option of agreeing a higher or lower rate for any given year, on the basis of a commission proposal).

5) Extensification. Under the 1992 reforms, extensification premium were offered in the livestock sector. This was hoped to reduce production, and also reduce overgrazing. Farmers could claim this premium on the number of animals that would keep the number below a certain level (expressed in livestock units). There was nothing however to stop extra animals being kept on the land, provided no claim was made for them. So little extensification was achieved. Under the final Agenda 2000 Agreement, premium can only be claimed if the stocking level taking into account *all* the farmers animals, is below the stipulated level. An interesting feature with the beef regime is that of the 'national envelope'. A small proportion of the direct payments in this regime may be distributed by Member States at their discretion, to give greater flexibility for dealing with regional disparities and to encourage extensification.

6) Agri-environment measures and rural development.

Santer:These Agri-environment schemes should be developed in relation to overall rural development.
Brussels: Agri-environment schemes should be incorporated into a new rural development programme. Member States should define appropriate environmental measures that farmers must adopt if they are to receive direct payments on production (cross-compliance).
Berlin:Agri-environment schemes should be incorporated into a new rural development programme. Member states *may* attach appropriate environmental conditions to direct payments. A new Rural Development Regulation will

be introduced. Member states must draw up Regional Development Plans. These must contain agri-environment schemes. Member states have the option to introduce young farmers and early retirement schemes.

One of the most significant features of the final agreement was the considerable latitude given to Member States over the issues of cross-compliance and modulation. It would be up to member states to define both the particular environmental measures that farmers would be expected to adopt, and the penalties they would pay if they did not, which could involve the reduction of direct payments. The modulatory elements would be discretionary. Funds made available through aid reduction following cross-compliance or modulation are retained by the respective Member State to be used for agri-environment measures, assistance to Less Favoured Areas, early retirement, afforestation and rural development. And the optional nature of some schemes has just been mentioned.

Subsequent legislation has put in place the mechanisms for implementing the Agenda 2000 agreements. Particularly interesting are the regulations governing direct support schemes and rural development. The latter will be dealt with later. As far as the direct support schemes are concerned the key regulation is Regulation 1259/1999.

Regulation 1259/1999   *"Establishing common rules for direct support schemes under the common agricultural policy"*. Regulation 1259/1999 deals with the question of possible general mandatory environmental requirements and cross-compliance (introductory paragraph 3 and Article 3 "environmental protection requirement") and modulation of direct CAP subsidy payments (introductory paragraph 4 and Article 4 "modulation").

Article 3 says that where agricultural land and agricultural production is subject to direct payments, ".... Member States shall take the environmental measures they consider appropriate..." and goes on to list what these measures may include:

(i) support in return for agri-environment commitments;

(ii) general mandatory environmental requirements;

(iii) specific environmental requirements constituting a condition for direct payments.

Category (i) would cover the *agri-environment schemes*; category (ii) concerns possible *regulation*; category (iii) concerns *cross-compliance*.

Article 3 then, indicates considerable member state discretion in introducing or maintaining existing measures ("... Member States shall take the environmental measures they consider appropriate...)". This discretion is also extended to penalties for non-compliance for measures introduced, as section 2 of Article 3 says: "Member States shall decide on the penalties that are appropriate...".

Modulation. The purpose of modulation is stated to be stabilising the employment situation in agriculture by taking account of the overall prosperity of holdings, so as to secure a fair standard of living for the agricultural community (para 4). Article 4 says modulation may be introduced when:
the labour force on a holding falls below certain limits - in other words, modulation is to help in the retention of agricultural workers;
where the profit margin or total income of the holding exceeds certain limits -i.e. to modulate payments in favour of the small farmer.

However, once again, individual member states are given considerable latitude over the whole question of modulation. Member states *may* decide to introduce modulation; if they introduce modulation, they can determine its actual extent. The only limit is that the reductions of payments should not exceed 20%.

(vi) Criticisms of the final Agenda 2000 agreement.

It seems to be agreed that the agreed price cuts will mean that some food prices will fall; indeed the EU claims, on the basis of economic evaluation studies, that a large proportion of the effects of reduction should be passed on to the consumer with a drop in the consumer price index by 33% in 2006. This might benefit UK consumers to the tune of £1 billion/year. However, customers will still pay more than they should for their food because of the continuation of price support (HoL, 1999). As might be expected, farmers (unlike environmentalists) are pleased that the proposal to set a ceiling on the total of direct income payments that can be paid to a farmer has been dropped (Farmers Guardian, 2nd April).

The CAP will still entrench economic inefficiency. Subsidies paid to farmers will continue to result in the production of goods whose value is less than the cost of inputs used. This is particularly so for hill farmers -the price they can get is very low (recently sometimes £5 per head) while the sheep annual premium is £30 per head. This continuation of support means that trade of the EU with the rest of the world is still distorted - prices remain above world prices, so export restitutions and variable levies are still used, and so developing world countries still face subsidised competition. And there is no commitment to end production subsidies even in the long run (HoL). So the Agenda 2000 agreement is likely to be fiercely challenged in the forthcoming World Trade organisation discussions (Lowe and Brouwer in Brouwer and Lowe, 2000).

Subsidising food production tends to result in more food being produced than can be sold, and so set-aside is needed to reduce production (HoL ibid). However, as we saw earlier, set aside, if properly managed, can be advantageous for wildlife. The price support system also makes more difficult the planned enlargement of the EU by adding countries from central and eastern Europe to the club. Agricultural prices in these countries are generally lower than in the EU, so it would be extremely expensive to extend the existing EU support regimes to these other countries. And rising prices in these countries will lead to an increase in output and therefore even bigger surpluses. (HoL ibid)

Although the final Agenda agreement came in for a lot of criticism, the Rural Development proposals (discussed in more detail in the next section) have received a cautious welcome by environmental groups, as providing at least some possibility of a positive impact of the CAP on the environment. However, although the incorporation of agri-environment measures into the overall framework of rural development can have positive effects, through cross-compliance, these measures appear as if grafted on to production based payments - which have quite different objectives to the agri-environment schemes. This attachment illegitimately dresses up production subsidies in environmentally friendly clothing. So the Rural Development Regulation 'remains in the shadow of agriculture' and does not introduce a real coherence to total rural policy for rural communities (HoL ibid).

Rural policy has been described in Commission circles as the 'second pillar' of the CAP. But in fact, it is a very weak second pillar. In the first place, studies had indicated that a critical component of funding rural policy would need to come from a steady reduction of production subsidies; funds thus released being used for rural policy support. But such a steady reduction was not included in the Agenda 2000 proposals. Second, both the Rural Development Regulation money and the commodity support money come from the same funding source - called the EAGGF (FEOGA) Guarantee Section. This might suggest that under appropriate conditions, funds could later be transferred from commodity support to rural development. However, decisions made at the Berlin Summit in effect segregated these two expenditures, which will prevent any transfer (Lowe and Brouwer, ibid).

As far as the actual agri-environment component of rural policy is concerned, agri-environment expenditure as a component of the Rural Development Regulation is in principle frozen at existing levels until 1996, whereas following 1992, expenditure was allowed to rise year by year in response to the take up of schemes by Member States.

As far as biodiversity is concerned, environmentalists are agreed that the reforms will not really halt the decline of wildlife. The CAP promoted intensive farming, which has been the single most destructive force for the countryside environment and wild life. Now the UK government signed up to support the Biodiversity Convention at the Rio Earth Summit. But such commitments are not worth the paper they are put on if governments subsequently fail to put environmental concerns at the front of their thinking. Abandoning a radical reform in favour of a minimal one, means that biodiversity will continue to suffer (Coward, C. 1999).

Worth noticing here is the reaction of English Nature to the Brussels proposals -i.e. before the whole CAP policy had been yet more watered down by the Berlin Summit. The press release of 12th March was entitled

"Timid CAP reform sounds death knell for England's wildlife"

English Nature's Chairperson, Baroness Young said of the Brussels proposals:

"This is tragic news which demonstrates a lost opportunity. Despite all the warnings and advice proffered by English Nature and others for truly radical reforms that would have reversed the damaging impact of the CAP, wildlife will continue to be seriously damaged by the intensive farming practices that the CAP supports. Our farmland animals and flowers will face the same pressures that have contributed to the dramatic declines in farmland birds, our native

bumble bees, and the losses of downland and meadows".

(vii) The Rural Development regulation introduced as a result of the Agenda 2000 agreement

The Rural Development Regulation introduced following the Berlin Summit aims to make the CAP more supportive of rural communities and less damaging to the rural environment. It is clearly going to be very important for the future of the countryside, and so we will now look at it detail; then we will examine the proposals put forward by the UK government for implementing this regulation in England.

The EU regulation.

As far as rural development and agri-environment schemes are concerned, the Agenda 2000 agreements were brought into force through regulation 1257/1999 concerning support for rural development (regulation 1750/1999 lays down the detailed rules for application of this regulation).

Regulation 1257/1999 *"On support for rural development from the European Agricultural Guidance and Guarantee Fund (EAGGF) and amending and repealing certain Regulations".*

The introductory paragraphs and Article One of the regulation state that one aim of the regulation is to bring about a simplification and closer integration of rural policies.

Article 2 sets out what activities are eligible for support within the rural development framework, with the aim of increasing farming activity and hence rural development. Amongst other things, are encouragement of non-food production, diversification of activities, development of economic activities and creation of employment, the maintenance and promotion of low-input farming systems and "the preservation and promotion of a high nature value and a sustainable agriculture respecting environmental requirements".

Article 22 expands on 'agri-environment' aspects. It starts with the aim of supporting agricultural production methods designed to protect the environment and to maintain the countryside. Support should promote:

- ways of using agricultural land which are compatible with the protection and improvement of the environment;
- environmentally favourable extensification of farming and management of low-intensity pasture systems;
- the conservation of high nature-value farmed environments;
- the upkeep of landscape and historical features;
- the use of environmental planning in farming practice.

As far as the actual 'accompanying measures' are concerned, the three existing ones (agri-environment schemes, early retirement and afforestation) are retained and are to be supplemented by a scheme for less-favoured areas and areas 'with environmental restrictions' (introductory paragraph 10).

The regulation promotes the 'setting up' of young farmers (introductory paragraph 20 and article 8), vocational training to improve the competence of farmers (introductory paragraph 21,22 and article 8). It also promotes (article 10) the early retirement of farmers with a series of objectives:
- to provide an income for elderly farmers who decide to stop farming;
- to encourage the replacement of such elderly farmers by farmers able to improve, where necessary, the economic viability of the remaining agricultural holdings;
- to reassign agricultural land to non-agricultural uses where it cannot be farmed under satisfactory conditions of economic viability;
- early retirement support may include measures to provide an income for farm workers.

Finally, the regulation requires member states to apply minimum standards regarding the environment (articles 5, 8 and 26.

(viii) The response of the UK government to the Agenda 2000 agreement - the production side.

We deal first with the response of the Government on the agricultural production side, then on the response to rural development and agri-environment schemes.

As we have seen, the recent reforms give the UK Government quite a lot of leeway in the way the reforms are actually implemented. As far as *regulation* goes, the Government sees this tool as primarily to be used to implement existing EU and national law, rather than using regulation as a means of a radical pathway of change.

The UK Government proposes to *modulate* direct aid payments to UK farmers (compensatory payments in the arable and livestock sectors). The percentage will go from 2.5% in 2001 to 4.5% by 2006. The monies so retrieved will be used to protect the rural environment, to develop the rural economy, and to convert farms to organic production (Agra Europe, 1999, and the Rural Development Plan of the following section).

With *cross-compliance,* the UK Government decided to seek further advice before deciding on the use of cross-compliance. The DETR commissioned the Institute for European Environmental Policy (IEEP) to undertake a study on its behalf (this is the same Institute, which produced the Baldock and Mitchell 1995 publication that was referred to in the box on cross-compliance earlier in this chapter). The Institute identified 30 possible options for cross-compliance in England, and evaluated these options against a set of criteria, concluding that a few of the options would meet the criteria used. These include a) requiring adherence to existing Codes of Practice, b) the requirement to have simple farm plans, and c), the creation of arable field margins (Dwyer et al, 2000).

As far as Farm Plans are concerned, three types are considered. First, a Farm Waste Management Plan, which would define where it was suitable to spread farm waste and the spreading rates, and ensure storage facilities are safe. MAFF already has a booklet dealing with such plans, which is being used in a few targeted areas. The plan would be used to minimise farm -caused pollution. Second, a Farm Nutrient Plan/Budget. Farmers would have to do soil testing to determine the nutrient status of their fields and determine the nutrient content of all materials applied to the fields. The aim would be to ensure certain nutrients were not applied in excess and to balance input to crop needs. This could reduce pollution risks and could reduce input costs. Third, a Whole Farm Conservation Report along the lines of reports prepared for ADAS in its conservation schemes would be prepared. The report could be tailored to deal with the specific environmental problems of the area concerned (e.g. soil erosion). One function of all three types of farm plan would be to raise farmer awareness of the environmental impact of their practices and encourage them to do something to mitigate their harmful effects.

The IEEP report thinks that the arguments in favour of such plans are particularly strong for the first and third types (the report does say the second type (Farm Nutrient Plan/Budget) would require more work by the authorities than the first type of plan). The response of the Government is now awaited.

(ix) The response of the UK Government on the Agenda 2000 proposals affecting rural development and agri-environment schemes.

Each member state Government has to prepare its own proposals for implementing the Rural Development Regulation. As far as England is concerned, The UK governments proposals are set forth in *England Rural Development Plan 2000-2006* (MAFF, January 2000). This consists of two parts, first the National Framework, second, proposals for the different regions (taking account of the Regulations policy of following the principle of subsidiarity- policy should be as decentralised as possible).

Chapter Six sets out the Government strategy. The vision is of

- a living countryside with thriving rural communities where all residents are included;
- a working countryside, contributing to national prosperity as part of a competitive economy, with a balanced mix of businesses (including land-based industries) jobs and homes, reducing the need to commute long distances;
- a strengthened interdependence of town and country;
- a countryside in which the environment is properly protected;
- a countryside for all -'plentiful access'.

This vision is then elaborated through what the document terms 'national priorities'.

Later in the chapter there is a summary of the action the government intends to take:

- retain the existing agr-environment schemes (ESA,CS,OC), together with the FWPS and the WGS;
- introduce the hill farm allowance scheme;
- re-introduce a processing and marketing grant scheme;
- introduce three new schemes - rural enterprise scheme (RES), energy crops scheme (ECS) and vocational training for people in farming and forestry(VTS) scheme.

However, the government will not introduce aid schemes for either the early retirement of farmers and farm workers, or for setting up young farmers.

The <u>rural enterprise scheme</u> promotes a large range of activities, which seem to cover almost all aspects of rural development. Thus the RDP lists 13 different activities eligible under the scheme, ranging from land reparcelling, through providing basic services for the rural economy and population and diversification of rural activities, to protection of the environment in connection with agriculture, forestry and landscape conservation. The scheme provides a national framework, which will be implemented and administered on a regional basis. The scheme is project based - individual schemes proposed would compete for support on the basis of their merits and the contributions they are judged to make to the achievements of the targets within the regional strategies. So in this sense it is like the Countryside Stewardship Scheme.

The <u>energy crops scheme</u> aims to promote short-rotation coppice and *Miscanthus* planting, with the aim of increasing the amount of electricity generated from renewable sources and creating jobs. Energy crops could make a significant contribution towards reductions of the greenhouse gas carbon dioxide.

The <u>vocational training scheme</u> is introduced because the government considers improving the skills base in rural areas is vital for strengthening rural economies. A series of priority areas are identified, including, for example:

    business/marketing skills;
    countryside and environmental skills;
    development of innovation.

As already mentioned, the government is continuing to refuse to implement an early retirement scheme (ERS). It gives its reasons for not implementing both this and the scheme for setting up young farmers in paragraph 28 of chapter Six. There was mixed support for the ERS during consultations; and the costs of running the scheme would outweigh the benefits; further, it would, the government claims, have been difficult to target those most in need. As for aid to young farmers, the levels of aid available would have been insufficient to 'deliver real benefit'; one wonders however, if this were true, why such a scheme was included in the regulation at all. Paragraph 28 goes on to explain the governments strategy to assist young farmers - they intend to provide the 'right economic climate', and target measures they will introduce under other schemes where appropriate.

The Rural Development Plan adapts the overall strategy to the varied needs of the different regions of England (sections 6.1.4 and 6.1.5). Each Region decides what are its priorities, and this is discussed in the Regional sections of the Plan. For example, in the Yorkshire and Humberside Region, diversification of agricultural activities has high priority while management of agricultural water resources has a low priority (both these come under the Rural Enterprise Scheme). In terms of schemes, the RDP says the ESA scheme, aid for conversion to organic farming, and compensatory allowances for the LFAs will be operated on a national basis, others, while operating within the national framework, will have regional discretion in deciding the targeting and funding priorities. These are the CSS, the FWPS, the WGS and support for energy crops. Finally, some schemes will be operated regionally, including the Rural Enterprise scheme.

Mention was made in section A of this chapter of the problem arising from the multiplicity of schemes available in the countryside, and the need to create a single agri-environment scheme. While the latter may not be fully realisable under present CAP regulations, it is disappointing that the Government does not seem to have attempted closer integration between schemes. Further, under the Rural Enterprise Scheme, one topic that can secure funds, as already stated, is protection of the environment in connection with agriculture, forestry and landscape conservation, and the other topics listed overlap also with other schemes. Now although the RDP says this measure excludes those activities covered by the main environmental schemes, one cannot help thinking of the difficulty of individuals, organisations and companies who will have such a variety of scheme options to consider and the potential for administrative confusion and high administrative cost inherent in the approach.

After minor modifications, the Rural Development Plan was finally accepted by the EU and launched by our Agriculture Minister Nick Brown on the 3rd of October 2000.

Chapter 7

Case Study 2. The beleaguered pocket handkerchief -the Peak District National Park

A. Personal experiences

As a young person in the 1930s, 1940s and 1950s, I spent a lot of time walking in the Peak District. My parents and I went walking there practically every weekend. We made use of the excellent tram and bus service to get us to a starting point; regularly we would walk ten miles or so before Saturday afternoon tea. In my teens, a friend of mine and I would walk the Peak district at weekends or in holidays, sometimes sleeping in barns. Later as a botany student, I went out into the Peak District to study the flora. I then spent over thirty years away from England, and returned six years ago and recommenced my walking. I am then, in the position of being able to compare what the Peak District was like decades ago, with what it is like now. And of course I can try to assess personally the extent that the Peak District shares the features of environmental degradation dealt with in the previous Chapters. What follows are a few brief observations on these matters.

When I was young, you did not come across many walkers, and on the high moors, you often had the land to yourself. Walking once remote paths is often now like strolling in a city park. One used to be able to walk along country roads in tranquillity. There were of course fewer people then, and so less pressure on the countryside; also there were hardly any cars. I occasionally walked from the bottom of Monsal Dale down the main road to Ashford near Bakewell (the A6 road). Now it would be extremely dangerous to walk the first part of this stretch of the road because of the traffic. Other parts of this road are also dangerous, the worst bit being in Wye Dale where the road comes right down into the valley and goes under the railway bridge (see photo page 142). But it's not only the main trunk roads that are dangerous. Several other major roads have an almost continuous flow of cars in good weather, and of course vast numbers of freight vehicles, and even minor roads have many vehicles passing along them.

People had to make a real effort to get into the countryside, as my family did, which in my view was a good thing. Now, with the motorcar, no real effort is required. Just like most suburban gardens, the countryside has, for a significant segment of the older population, come to be an extension of the living room – get in the car, drive out into the countryside, sit and read the newspaper in the car. But walkers also use the car more than they do public transport to get out into the countryside. At the same time, you find that most buses in the countryside are usually almost empty.

People pressure on the high moors has increased. A popular walk for me as a young person going out alone, was to take the bus from Sheffield to Castleton, walk over to Edale, go up Grinds brook (taking its right hand fork near the top) and over Kinderscout to Kinder Downfall. Often you saw no one on Kinder. I particularly remember one snow covered misty winters day approaching the downfall and being surprised to encounter a couple of people looming out of the mist coming the opposite way! But there is something else that sticks in my memory from that time. That was the terrain on this last bit of the outward walk – across Kinder. One crossed a stretch of heather moor, then came to a steep-sided dyke. You jumped down into this, crossed a narrow 'valley' and jumped up the other side, and so on to the downfall. It was firm underfoot. I don't recall on this particular route, any big bare areas, or much in the way of boggy dykes. When I went this route a few months ago (it is not the usual way I go over Kinder now) things were quite different. Part of the moor was now grass and sedge land rather than heather moor. There were bare areas, and boggy dikes. I know that memory can be faulty and incomplete, but I am convinced that this particular route shows recent deterioration.

A way across part of Kinder that I have done many times in the last five years but I don't think I did as a young person, although it is close to the above route, is to go up the brook from Kinder downfall where it gradually turns southwards, and then cross over to Crowden Brook. It looks awful. Vast bare areas. Now I am told that bare areas have been here for a very long time. But the point I want to make is that footprints are everywhere. And if it's a sunny summers day you are liable to find three or four other people traversing the same bit of land on a wide front.

Villages too have change. They used to be quiet places. Now the roads are lined with cars. Pubs used to be quiet places where, going for a lunchtime drink of mild beer and snack of cheese and pickle, one could, for a short while, imagine oneself blending into the rural community. Now they are crowded, noisy places, filled with townsfolk eating pseudo-traditional rural meals.

The Peak district has been mined and quarried for centuries. Wherever you go, you see the signs. In many fields, you come across little mounds and hollows which are all that is left of the surface of mine workings. For a long time they have been grassed over, and are often habitat for interesting plants. In the steep sides of some limestone valleys you see what appear to be cave entrances which often on examination show themselves to be the entrances to old mines. Quarrying has removed whole hillsides, and left big holes in the landscape. Quarrying still continues. In a couple of places smoke rises continually from tall chimneys of works associated with the quarries. In recent times there has been a row over a proposed extension of quarrying on one prominent limestone ridge, which, if allowed, will destroy habitat, damage the view, and cause added noise and congestion on the roads from the big vehicles used to move the stone - which is apparently to be used for yet more road building! This same ridge contains a great open gash from discontinued quarrying (see photo page 145), but at its upper end it is being partly filled in with all sorts of uncovered rubbish. A little further along, deep narrow gaps have appeared in the surface through blasting for mining in the rocks below, and there are 'danger' and 'keep out' signs and fences.

In the northern part of the Park there are steep narrow valleys (cloughs) leading up into the high moors. One sees the occasional scattered groups or single holly, alder and birch trees, retaining a precarious foothold. But while some may be protected by fencing, the majority are not and they can never regenerate now because there are sheep everywhere. 'Up on top' some moor areas are now badly overgrazed by sheep, and along part of the Pennine Way route large areas are almost completely bare of vegetation, the exposed peat being covered with boot prints; however, in recent times steps have been taken to reduce sheep numbers.

In various places in the Peak district, you can come across little patches of woodland - a pine wood on the edge of moorland here, a little mixed deciduous wood there, and a mature little oak wood on a bank near a river not far from one of the major villages in the Peak district (see photo page 142). The majority can never regenerate. Sheep or cattle are everywhere. So tiny saplings within these patches of woodland cannot grow, and where these bits of woodland are too dense perhaps for internal regeneration, they cannot regenerate around their peripheries for the same reason. Why cannot these little areas be fenced off for ten or twenty years so they can regenerate? The loss of grazing area would in most cases be small

One can find old cartways, which have on one or both sides a straggling row of hawthorn trees. These were obviously once hedgerows, and the trees are the remnants; in wintertime they are home to flocks of fieldfares. These hedgerows can never themselves regenerate because there are sheep everywhere. And the local farmer or landowner obviously could not care less and does no replanting. I found myself getting very annoyed when I passed along one of these tree rows, which lines the track in the lower part of one of the most beautiful and least spoilt of the valleys in the Peak District (a valley where many of us had recently signed a petition against development). Here the stony track is very wide, ample room for the biggest of farm vehicles. Yet someone has gone along last year and flayed the whole row, cutting off branches, leaving the usual ragged ends. Why? The branches were not in the way

In lower altitude areas, hedges mark field boundaries. In some areas the hedges are regularly flayed very low. Why on earth must farmers do this! If these fields were used for growing crops, then one might think that farmers thought, mistakenly, that they were bad for pest control. But these fields are used only for stock rearing. The hedges as I knew them were appreciable taller, and not so closely cropped, making much better habitats for birds than the present hedges. A very common sight in the Peak District National Park is hedges that are 'gappy', often the gaps crossed with barbed wire, and sometimes the gaps are longer than the hedgerow stretches. In more high altitude areas field boundaries are marked by stone walls. Almost everywhere these walls are in various stages of collapse. This process had already been going on for a long time when I was young; now it is worse.

I am often overcome by a sense of the neglect of the countryside. No doubt farmers here as elsewhere are short staffed, and perhaps a few take conservation seriously. But the general high degree of countryside dereliction strongly suggests that most farmers are not genuinely concerned to protect the countryside. In upland areas where there are still gates, they are more often than not just tied up with an old piece of coloured twine. Often the gates have disappeared entirely, leaving one or both gateposts, and stock ambles from one field to another. On the occasional farm the occupier seems to have just discarded odd bits of machinery, old tyres etc. anywhere. It is refreshing to come to a well-managed area like the Duke of Devonshire's Chatsworth Park.

There is a field by a major river, and the path from the river crosses this field. When I started writing this book, way out in this field there was a complete but totally redundant stile –redundant because there is now no hedge (since then most of the stile has been removed, but remnants remain – see photo opposite). An uneven line of grass on either side of the style suggests where a hedge once was that must have been grubbed out. Ironically, at the far side of this field is a hedge under active regeneration control. There is barbed wire protecting recently planted shrubs. I wonder if one and the same farmer first of all got financial assistance to grub out one hedge, and is now getting assistance to regenerate another hedge!

In upland parts when I was young, flocks of lapwings seemed to be very widespread, and the song of skylarks dominated

Remains of redundant stile. Once upon a time there was a hedge, home to bird and beast. And our farmers claim to be custodians of OUR countryside!

Car Park between Toad's Mouth and The Surprise on the approach to Hathersage from Sheffield. Such car parks well inside the park are an essential part of the National Park Authorities policy to encourage people to use public transport!

all the upland fields. Now you can walk all day and see no lapwings, and hear only a couple of skylarks. Many of these fields are now bright green - full of lush planted rye grass or perhaps rye mixed with timothy grass and white clover; nothing seems to be living there except the grass. Everywhere on farms, instead of haystacks you see the round silage bales stacked. While some of these are encased in a dark greenish plastic, others stand out like a sore thumb - they are black, or occasionally very light coloured plastic.

It is true that conservation activities in the broad sense do take place in the Peak District. Some walls have been re-built. You will find small areas where trees have been carefully planted (but sometimes these have obviously not been looked after subsequently and some have died). But overall, the writer's impression is that far too little has been done. The Peak Park authorities seem to have given much higher priority to maintaining pathways and renewing signposts than they have to protecting woodland, planting new woodland and other positive conservation measures.

There is a side valley to a botanically rich dale (Coombs Dale) where I frequently walk. At the bottom is a relatively recent wooden style giving access to a path that goes up the lower edge of the west side of the valley -a slope covered in what in modern parlance is called unimproved hill grassland. Plenty of room, an easy path to walk on the gentle slope, and good views. This side of the valley is separated from the other side by an old wall, now with some barbed wire atop. Roughly half way up this side-dale, the path crosses to the other side over a good wooden style (probably put up not many years ago). This other valley side is dominated by woodland at the main Coombs valley end. Higher up, the steep limestone scree slope is scattered in its lower parts with sloe, elder, and blackthorn trees, and patches of hazel and hawthorn (trees are thinning out by the time the path cross-over point is reached). These trees can never regenerate because livestock have free access. The trees look old, lots of dead wood lies on the ground. Top priority should be given to excluding livestock. But if people and their dogs also scrabble around on this slope, things will get worse. Now very recently, a path has been opened up on this side of the wall, complete with styles and signposts. A totally unnecessary path! And the style halfway up which provided the crossing point has been partly dismantled. This and the new path on the other side are close together - in places not more than ten metres apart! What makes matters worse is that this area is part of an SSSI!

When I first saw these changes a year or two ago my immediate reaction was that this new path must be the work of the Peak District National Park authorities. My subsequent enquiries showed that it was not as simple as that. There apparently used to be a path on the east side – clearly here my memories from my youthful days are deficient. The Ramblers Association wanted this path cleared of vegetation and re-opened. The Peak Park Authorities acceded to this, providing assistance to the Rambler Association people who did the work. When I talked about this to one Rambler Association member he said he thought that ramblers would prefer to walk among the trees on this side, rather than walking up the grassland on the other side! Exactly – prefer! Is not this the problem? **In this densely populated land of ours, we simply cannot let people always have what they prefer.** In my opinion, this action by the Ramblers Association was stupid. Dedicated members of the Association might not wander from the path, but parents will allow their children and dogs to scrabble up and down the scree slope, causing further deterioration of habitat.

B. General Introduction

The Peak District National Park occupies the greater part of what is commonly called the Peak District, which in turn occupies the greater part of the southern end of the Pennine chain of uplands. It is in effect a tiny pocket-handkerchief, wedged between two of the most densely populated areas of our little country – the Manchester conurbation in the west and the Sheffield area in the East. One could comfortably walk the length of it (north-south) in four days, walk across it (west-east) in one. Its actual area is 1,438 km ^{2}. The National Park was designated in 1951.

The National Park Authority (NPA) here is the Peak Park Joint Planning Board (PPJPB), a public body consisting of members and officers. The members are responsible for determining policies and priorities, controlling resources and finance. Collectively they are like a company's board of directors. There are 38 members, none of them directly elected. They are representatives of country, district, city and borough councils and other organisations in the whole Peak District and surroundings; a few of them are appointed by the Secretary of State. The officers are employees who carry out the work of the Authority. The PPJPB produces both a Structure Plan (SP) and an area-wide Local Plan (LP) for the Park (see Box in Chapter 3 Section B).

The 'statutory purposes' of the Authority are:

> (i) to conserve and enhance the natural beauty, wildlife and cultural heritage of the area;
> (ii) to promote opportunities for the understanding and enjoyment of the park's special qualities by the public.

The Authority also has a 'duty':

> to seek to foster the economic and social well-being of the communities within the National Park.

In order to fulfil its duties, the authority provides a range of services, including the Farm and Countryside Service (for farmers) and Rangers (to liase with the general public); it has a residential study centre running courses in the field of environmental education. Its Ecology Service carries out research and provides advice and coordination on ecological issues. There are also other services such as the Built Environment Service.

The Peak Park Authority employs about 300 people. For the year ending 1999, the Gross Expenditure of the Authority was nine and a half million pounds. It generated about three million pounds income, so had a net expenditure of about six and a half million. It is funded by Central Government and Local authorities in the ratio of 75:25. The Authority sets forth its plans for park management and future development in its Structure Plan, the current one adopted 1994 (PPJPB, 1994a) and in its accompanying Local Plan (presently being revised).

The National Parks Authority is far from being the only authority with jurisdiction in the Park. It does not have authority over farming and forestry which come under MAFF and the Forestry Commission respectively. The situation is further complicated here in that the Peak Park is divided between three MAFF Regions, each with its own offices and staff. National schemes for environmental improvement are controlled by EN (the SSSIs) and MAFF (the agri-environment schemes). Transport matters (roads, trains, buses) are primarily the responsibility of various national, regional and local authorities. The Park Authority only owns a small part of the total park area (4.1%). Major landowners include water companies - Yorkshire Water, North West Water and Seven Trent, the National Trust (e.g. Kinderscout) and Sheffield City Council. Then there are some big private estates like the Chatsworth Estate. So the Park authorities have to cooperate with various other authorities and owners in attempting to achieve Park objectives.

Like all other Planning Authorities, the PPJPB has to work within the framework of national legislation, which may not always be entirely consistent with the objectives of the PPJPB. Also, once the PPJPB has, following public consultation, produced its Structure and Local Plans, the Secretary of State has the power to make changes prior to the final adoption of the plans. Now the Current Structure Plan was finally adopted in 1994. The Local Plan reached its deposit stage in 1997 and July of the present year (2000) saw the production of the Provisional Adopted Version. However, the Secretary of State subsequently directed the PPJPB to make small changes to both the Conservation and Waste Management Sections of the Plan, which may have the effect of making it more difficult for the PPJPB to achieve its first statutory purpose. In the present writer's view the alterations to the Conservation Section are probably more serious than those to the Waste Management Section, so I take the former by way of illustration of the general problem of intervention by the Secretary of State.

The directed changes concern what is termed the 'natural zone', that is those parts of the Park like the gritstone moors that lie outside the built up areas, enclosed farmland and plantation woodlands. The PPJPB had wanted to say that development in this zone would only be allowed in exceptional circumstances, which would concern developments essential for the management of the area (for example, a new river weir). The Secretary of State directed that in order to fully reflect national and regional policy the Plan must explicitly leave open the possibility that as an exception to the main policy thrust, "development which is essential in the national interest (for example, that which is required by *national considerations of mineral supply*" might in rare cases be allowed, likewise "a development that is essential for the conservation or enhancement of the National Park's valued characteristics (for example *specialist building stone* required for conservation)" (my italics).

The implication of these alterations is obvious: it will be more difficult for the PPJPB to restrain quarrying and mining in the Park. One Park official commented to me it is suspected that powerful business groups had successfully lobbied the Government to make these alterations.

In the Peak Park there are many villages, and one town (Bakewell). The Park, like other English rural areas, has seen a decline in services over the years. Surveys carried out by the RDC in 1991 and 1994 in 56 of the parishes in the Park (the majority of the parishes containing settlements) showed a decline of food shops by 5% (some parishes lost their only food shop), non-food shops by 11%, and general stores by 35.3 %. As far as bus services were concerned, there was a slight increase in the number of days when bus services were available, yet the 1994 picture was stark indeed. In these 56 parishes, many had infrequent bus services (PPJPB, 1994b):

Number of days on which bus services operated

0 days	1day	2days	3 days	4 days	5 days	6 days	7 days
4	4	5	2	0	3	15	23

The gross topography of the National Park is determined by the underlying geology, and the action upon this of ice movements in the last ice age and subsequent wind and water erosion. In cross section from west to east the Peak district is the centre of a dome of rock (anticline), which extends down to Manchester in the west and Sheffield in the east. In northern parts the surface rock is millstone grit underlain by coal measures, but in southern parts these layers have been worn away exposing the underlying carboniferous limestone. However the millstone grit extends southwards on either side of the limestone dome so we get the Bamford, Stanage and Frogatt Edges in the east together with the Eyam to Abney area, and Stanton Moor, and in the west, millstone grit down to the moors north of Leek (the Roaches).

The millstone grit areas are known as the 'Dark Peak' (although popularly this term is often restricted just to the northern parts of the Peak District) since they are dominated by dun coloured moorland and slightly lighter coloured upland pastures with dark stone walls (although I shall qualify the pasture colour later on). The limestone areas are referred to as the 'White Peak' and are dominated by grassland, pale coloured stone walls, hedges, woodland and occasional bare limestone rock.

Apart just possibly from isolated small areas like remnants of older woodland, the landscape features are the works of man – human settlements, quarries, overgrown surface spoil from mine workings - especially the so-called lead rakes, plantations, pasture land and moorland, hedges and stone walls.

In terms of major land use type, the National Park consists of:

Farmland	77,520 ha
Moorland	50,929 ha
Woodland	11,155 ha

As in most of Britain the vegetation is then largely not the original vegetation or what that vegetation would be now if man had not come on the scene. Before Neolithic times, the whole area was largely wooded (part of the 'wildwood'). Removal of trees by man, and subsequent livestock grazing and arable agriculture has produced the present day vegetation cover; probably none of the original wildwood remains. If man did not continue to manage the countryside, it would probably once again become predominantly woodland covered.

For example, on the moorlands, current management practice for grouse shooting and sheep grazing tends to maintain areas covered in heather and associated plants; if left alone, these areas would once again probably largely become forested. And in certain areas limited re-afforestation is taking place - possibly for example, the stand of birch trees near the junction of the B6054 and B6055 roads on Totley Moor south east of Sheffield. However, the thick peat layers that have accumulated since ancient times on parts of the moorland would probably prevent tree colonisation in some areas.

Now National Parks Status is meant to conserve landscape. So a legitimate and important question to ask is - to what extent has this status actually helped to stem the tide of landscape deterioration that has characterised much of Britain since the Second World War?

A superficial examination would suggest - not much. As elsewhere in Britain, Peak National Park landscape has deteriorated. In lower lying parts there has been considerable loss of traditional hay meadows, with their rich variety and seasonal variation of colour. Higher up, conversion of soft pastel coloured rough grassland fields to seas of bright green rye grass has been extensive; denudation of moorland and expansion of erosion gullies has taken place. Upland stonewalls have continued to deteriorate. In lowland areas, many hedgerows have been lost and many remaining ones become increasingly 'gappy'. Small settlements have expanded, and although new building has perhaps usually been carried out in a way that fits more or less with the surrounding buildings, the built up area has increased. And the streams of cars and other vehicles are unfortunately now part of the landscape. National Parks are meant to protect landscape. If landscape is protected, wild life is protected in good measure. For example, unimproved grassland has a variety of species of plant, and is home to a lot of animal life; ryegrass meadows are practically sterile.

C. Millstone grit moorlands

Forest cover spread upwards following the last glaciation and came to dominate the whole area. Lower slopes were covered with ash, lime and alder, middle slopes more with oak, pine and elm, upper slopes and much of the plateaus were scrub vegetation with birch, hazel and willow, so much so that actual moorland as we now understood it would probably have occupied only a small fraction of its present area (Anderson et al, 1997). The activities of man have transformed the upland areas to the moorland we know.

The characteristic moorland vegetation is dominated by varying combinations of ericaceous plants (ling, bell heather, bilberry), crowberry, cloudberry, grasses, cotton grasses (which are sedges), mosses and lichens. This vegetation overlies a layer of peat. Such peat forms in areas with high rainfall, frequent mist cover and poor drainage. The peat is anaerobic and acidic, preventing the breakdown of the dead vegetation of which it is composed; it is also low in plant nutrients. Consequently, the vegetation growing upon it characterised by plants adapted to high pH and low nutrient levels. The peat varies in thickness but is commonly two metres or more thick on the plateaus (see colour photo page 170).

This peat has always been subject to erosion, due in part to the harsh climate of these regions. And deep gullies, or dykes, one product of erosion, have probably existed for many hundreds of years. On a shorter time scale, the survey of Moss (1913) showed the widespread occurrence on the Kinderscout plateau of patches where all the vegetation had been lost, leaving areas of bare peat. He also notes however, evidence of recent deterioration on moors dominated by cotton grass, in the 'cutting back' of streams at their sources. Comparing older and more recent maps he concluded that streams at the time he was writing were on average 0.4km longer than they were in the 1870s, which were in turn 1.2 km longer than they were in 1830. He notes that the banks of these streams are often sloping banks of peat. And after rainstorms the streams are rapid torrents of brown peaty water. Every storm, he comments results in quantities of peat being carried away, so the stream comes to penetrate further and further back into the peat and the stream channels become wider and deeper.

Until recent times erosion was probably largely balanced by natural renewal of the vegetation. Mans influence during the last couple of centuries, and especially since the Second World War, has tipped the balance towards overall degeneration. Moorland vegetation stands on a deep peat layer. Loss of surface vegetation cover has led to peat erosion. Now almost all the peat cover is suffering from erosion. Survey results published in 1981 reported there was 6.5 km^2 of totally bare and eroding land, and a further 26.8 km^2 of vegetated ground that was partly bare or very fragile. Studies since this time, show that deterioration has continued (Anderson et al, 1997). Extensive areas of bare peat can today be seen especially on Black Hill, Bleaklow and Kinderscout (see colour photo page 170). So that, for example, the areas of bare peat on Kinderscout are more extensive than they were at the time of Moss's survey. Erosion of peat (and the underlying mineral layer) has serious consequences beyond the question of moorland landscape. Much of the eroded material, transported by water (and wind) ends up in reservoirs, reducing their capacity, and also discolouring the water supply. So at the Bamford water treatment works, vast quantities of peat slurry are produced through flocculating out the peat; this slurry cannot be used for gardens because of the chemical treatment used, so, ironically, peat that was a covering of the plateau rocks, ends up in landfill sites.

Man has caused moorland deterioration through various agencies - (i) air pollution, (ii) fire, (iii) overgrazing (mainly sheep) and (iv) human trampling, and then wind and rain, especially flash floods, has extended the deterioration caused by man. The effects of these individual agencies, and the complexities of their interactions, are by no means fully understood. But the following conclusions would probably be agreed by the majority of workers in this field.

(i) Air pollution. The following notes are based predominantly on S. Caporn, in Anderson et al, (ibid). The industrial revolution led to atmospheric pollution with particulates and sulphur dioxide and it is thought that this pollution was responsible for the massive decline in mosses (*Sphagnum*, etc) that took place two hundred years ago. While sulphur and soot emissions have decreased since the late 1960s, nitrogenous gases and volatile organic compounds have increased, mainly through increased road traffic, and from increased uses of nitrogenous fertilisers in farming.

Pollutants have direct and indirect effects on plant life. The plant life of the moors is adapted to low fertility of the substrate (low nitrogen content etc), and increased concentrations of nitrogenous compounds can have harmful effects. While heather growth may be promoted, it appears that after some time, the shoots are damaged, which may lead to an opening up of the heather canopy allowing grasses etc. to invade, and lichens and mosses disappeared from experimental plots. High nitrogen concentrations also seem to inhibit *Sphagnum* regeneration. Pollution (from sulphuric and nitric acids) has produced acidification of rain and mist, which has very harmful effects on vegetation. The moorland peat substrate is naturally acidic, so plants are adapted to a relatively acidic soil. But acidity has increased. Heather itself seems relatively tolerant of high acidity, but growth of some other plants seems to be inhibited. The moors are often immersed in cloud cover, and acid mist is thought to be a real threat to the aerial parts of plants.

Acidification has indirect effects. Where peat has been eroded away, exposing the underlying rock, acid rain can lead to the release from the rock of toxic metals (aluminium and manganese). Aluminium damages root tissues and reduces the uptake of nutrients by the roots. The secondary pollutant (see Chapter 8) ozone has increased in recent times and the air close to the ground may have high concentrations for several days at a time in the summer. Ozone is thought to damage plants on the moors, partly probably by making plants less tolerant of frost.

Pollution not only damages the existing vegetation covered area, it also has a harmful effect on the re-colonisation of bare areas. As already noted, pollution has reduced mosses and lichens, and they are important parts of the re-colonising flora. Finally, we may note that in terms of critical loads (Chapter 8), concentrations of oxides of nitrogen, total nitrogen deposition, ozone and cloud water acidity, are close to or in excess of critical loads.

(ii) Fire. Major fires have been responsible for producing some of the worst now existing patches of damage on the moorland. Some of these fires occurred before the opening up of public access - from wartime training in the Pike Low area, and the Broomhead Moors patch from a bad fire in 1947 (Yalden, in Phillips, J et all 1981). Indeed some bare ground seems to have originated with fires up to 200 years ago, for example, an area at Holme Moss. However, more than 300 'wildfires' were recorded from the Peak District moorlands from 1970 to 1995. The more severe of these fires extended over tens or even hundreds of hectares, and often the underlying peat was destroyed (Tallis, 1997).

Controlled burning is a technique widely practised to stimulate new growth for grouse and sheep. However, such fires occasionally get out of hand to produce serious burns. However, when the location of all fires is mapped, it is seen that they are concentrated in areas such as the Chew, Bleaklow, Kinderscout and Stanage areas, areas which are most frequented by people (there is a general concentration along the Pennine way, the most important of all the footpaths). In statistical terms, the 1970-95 data showed 45.4% of the fires were close to footpaths or roads. Most of these fires probably arose due to carelessness (cigarette ends etc.) but some were probably arson (Anderson et al, 1997).

(iii) Grazing. Sheep have been grazed in the uplands for a very long time. Traditional practice has been to keep stock in the upland pasture below the moor and then to also let them out onto the moorland higher up (a practice that was severely disrupted in areas where reservoirs were built).

Sheep numbers were fairly stable between the two world wars. Then came the general intensification of agriculture. By 1965 the numbers doubled, and numbers continued to increase during the 1970s, and at a slower rate in the 80s and early 90s (Anderson et al ibid). The result has been overgrazing.

The problem is not just one of overall stocking density, it is also a problem of sheep distribution. On the moors, the sheep, if left to themselves, do not spread evenly across the moor. They form loose social groups of often related individuals, each group concentrating on one particular part of the moor, called a heft (and they also often tend to keep on returning to the particular area in which they were born). Within this grazing unit the sheep will favour certain vegetation types - they have grazing preferences, which are determined by a) nutritional value, b), digestibility, c), availability. In general they prefer grasses and sedges to dwarf shrubs like heather and bilberry. However, there is seasonal variation. Thus mat grass (*Nardus stricta*) is really only palatable briefly in spring. The grasses are not growing in the autumn and winter, and sheep tend more to eat heather and bilberry during these times. Left to their own devices then, sheep can cause localised overgrazing. To prevent this, active shepherding is required.

Across the moors as a whole one can distinguish the following vegetation types:

> (i) mat-grass with bilberry;
> (ii) acid grassland;
> (iii) areas where heather is sub-dominant;
> (iv) areas where heather is dominant;
> (v) cotton grass bog;
> (vi) bracken

Studies on the dark peak moors show that sheep tend to concentrate most heavily on the first two vegetation types, and to a lesser extent on the third. Consequently, if left untended, they tend to congregate around the discontinuous heather along the edges of the moors. They graze grass patches very short, and their feeding on flowering shoots of heather and bilberry reduces flowering and seed production (important in maintaining the vegetation). One result has been the conversion in many areas of bilberry and heather moorland to grass dominated moorland. Furthermore, bare ground is disturbed, accelerating peat loss through rainfall, and preventing seedlings from recolonising these patches.

The seasonal variation of the vegetation means that stocking density is more critical in some seasons than in others. In summer time grass growth may be great enough to support a relatively high sheep density. But by autumn, favoured grasses will have been eaten; flowering shoots will be increasingly eaten in autumn to spring, when no new growth is taking place; this means plants cannot then flower and set seed the following season

In the past, sheep on the moors were actively shepherded, which tended to secure a more even grazing over the moors. A return to active shepherding could therefore much improve the present situation (although the only way to deal with persistent homing sheep is to sell them out of the whole area). It has been alleged that farmers would rather stay home and watch television than get up onto the moors and shepherd the sheep. Whether this is true or not, many farmers have less time available now than formerly, for shepherding, since many farmers keep sheep elsewhere, sometimes much further away (one extreme case as far as the Solway Firth), so some farmers spend a lot of their time driving round in landrovers rather than looking after their sheep on the moors (one MAFF official, in conversation with the author).

Comparison of fenced (sheep excluded) and unfenced plots has shown that sheep will prevent the regeneration of vegetation on bare ground, and so that to re-vegetate large bare areas, it will normally be necessary to exclude sheep completely by fencing. In places where the slope is not too severe, active repeated shepherding of sheep out of the area to massively reduce stocking levels might sometimes be adequate to allow regeneration, as might complete removal of sheep during winter. However, in the most severely denuded areas, it will often be necessary to supplement fencing with other measures such as applying fertiliser, or reseeding the area (Anderson, ibid; Tallis, ibid).

(iv) Human walking. The number of hikers who visit the Dark Peak Moors in peak summer weeks is very large. In a single July week in the late 1980s it was probably over 50,000. A direct effect of this human traffic is that the width of paths in the moorland areas has increased. Thus with the main north south path is the Pennine Way. The mean bare width of the stretch of this path from Edale to the Snake summit changed from 3.54m in 1971, to 14.28m in1987 - an increase of 300%. The number of paths has increased in some areas (Anderson, ibid).

As a cause of the overall deterioration of millstone grit moorland, most observers, while agreeing that considerable damage has been done in the neighbourhood of paths, do not see trampling as a major cause of moorland deterioration. However, causing damage is not the same as maintaining the damage. In my own experience as a walker, I would think that human trampling is a major factor preventing moorland regeneration in bare areas. In recent times when I have traversed the higher part of Kinderscout, wherever there were extensive bare areas, there were frequent signs of human trampling. Footprints, some quite recent, holes produced by hikers boots sinking in to the wet peat. When you look for a place to traverse a deep dyke, you find others have been there before you, causing masses of peat to slip down towards the gully floor. I find it difficult to believe that such areas could ever regenerate with present day people pressure, even if we could permanently stop fires, remove all livestock, and by waving a magic wand get rid of all pollution.

But people pressure does more than damage vegetation and peat. It scares off birds and interferes with their breeding, as conservationists have pointed out. If you go out for example, on a sunny weekend in spring or summer, often even in autumn or winter, to the Stanage edge - Toads Mouth area, there are so many people around, one cannot imagine some moorland bird species would ever remain and even less breed in such an area. This raises the whole question of access to moorland and the countryside in general. In my view it is dangerous nonsense to advocate open access. There are just too many people. I own a small piece of land, which includes my garden. I don't exercise my right to walk over my vegetable patches!

In early April this year, in the Mount Famine to Jacobs Ladder area (SW of Kinderscout), within the space of a quarter of an hour, I saw four people with a dog not on a lead, sometimes the dogs were running all over the place. This sort of thing must disturb birds that are preparing to breed. On this walk, and the vast majority of all walks I do in the Peak Park, I do not see any Park Ranger. Then again, in May I am walking on a path in the Goyt valley near Buxton. A dog comes bounding along and up at me, its owner a short distance behind, shouting to it. 50 yards after I passed the man a prominent

Sign in Goyt Valley

Danger road. I am sitting precariously on a low stone wall very close to the A6 near where it passes under a railway bridge in Wye Dale.

Small mature oak wood between Baslow and Calver. Regeneration is unlikely as the area is unenclosed.

Post World War Two housing estate. Fulwood. Telephoto from the south (Ringinglow Road).

notice requesting people to keep dogs on a lead!

In my opinion, officials of the National Park Authority and of the National Trust (which owns a large part of the Peak District) tend to under-estimate the impact of human trampling, because it is politically easier to take this line than to face the facts. A few months ago I attended a meeting in Sheffield at which one of the speakers was an official from the National Parks Authority. His talk was based on a slide show of the Peak District. One of his photos was taken from a moorland area – I think it was Kinderscout. The biggest part of the land in the photograph was bare peat. The speaker talked about causes of bare peat. Quite correctly he discussed air pollution and overgrazing by livestock. But the most obvious feature of the photograph was that the bare peat was covered with footprints! No mention of the effect of human trampling was made at all. This strikes me as a thoroughly dishonest way to go about things.

D. Other habitats and landscape features

Heath land
Heather is found as isolated patches scattered in the White Peak area. This might seem surprising since heather is a plant of acidic soils, and limestone provides a base rich substrate. However, leaching of minerals from the limestone together with the deposition of wind borne glacial deposit, has created acidic soils in big areas.

These heaths today cover only a tiny fraction of the whole White Peak area -100 ha, which is 0.002% of the 528.6 km² of the whole White Peak natural area. After Neolithic period removal of woodland, heather-bilberry moorland would have been the dominant vegetation type in most of the White Peak area. Already by the beginning of the Second World War, most of this heath land had disappeared. But some quite big areas of heath land were lost since the second world war in the Hucklow area and adjacent to the present Longstone Moor, (Buckingham et al, 1999a), and I note that most of this loss was after the Peak National Park was established.

Some of the present heath land areas are relicts of the earlier more extensive heath cover ('primary heath'); but other areas are where new heath land has developed on previously disturbed sites such as lead rakes (see later) and abandoned sand pits (secondary heath). The main cause of heath land loss has been the desire of farmers to improve the productivity of the land. This has been done by applying lime, artificial fertilisers, and manure, often accompanied by burning the heather, and ploughing followed by reseeding with productive grass seed. Heath land has also been lost to quarrying, mining and landfill sites (Buckingham, ibid).

Lead rakes
Lead mining in the White Peak destroyed some of the heath land. One set of remnants of this activity are the numerous 'lead rakes' - surface workings and spoil heaps in long lines, long since largely overgrown by vegetation (see colour photo page 171). However, by destroying part of one habitat, this activity created another. There are unique and sometimes species -rich plant communities on these rakes, with some lead tolerant species that are sometimes uncommon elsewhere, such as the Spring Sandwort, *Minuartia verna*. And the vegetation has been recognised as internationally important by the European Habitats Directive. Consequently, it is now important to preserve these lead rakes.

Unfortunately lead rakes have continued to be lost in recent decades for two reasons. Some are being worked for fluorspar, barites and calcite, which are of considerable economic importance. Others are being ploughed up, and agriculturally 'improved' with fertilizer and herbicide so as to add a little more land for stock rearing. Study of aerial photographs has shown that in some areas, up to three-quarters of surface remains have already been destroyed. The Peak National Park has an on-going project to botanically survey these rakes and promote their retention. Work started in the Bonsall Moor area (WNW of Cromford near Matlock). Various estimates show that on this moor very roughly a third of the lead rakes have been lost (Buckingham, ibid). The survey work has been extended to other areas like Castleton and Bradwell, and continues.

Hay meadows
Before the modern intensification of agriculture, the hay meadow was one of the most common habitat types in the Peak District, dominating the lower parts of many valleys, and much of the upland in the White Peak. But since the second world war, farmers have been seeking to improve the productivity of meadows by adding fertilizer, improving drainage, ploughing and then re-seeding with productive grass species (some to mono-cultures of rye-grass), and changing management practice from hay production to silage (see colour photo page 171). Despite the landscape conservation status of the Peak National Park, this loss of hay meadows took place within the park at an alarming rate. Consequently, in 1994, the Peak National Park Authority set up the Hay Meadows project, to find out more about the nature and extent of the decline, and to try to arrest it. What follows is based on the project report Buckingham et al (1997b). Part of the work was based on comparisons of data collected by the project, with data from the 1980s. This is not a straightforward matter because the methods of data collection in the earlier surveys were not uniform. However, some conclusions could be made.

The traditional hay meadow was species rich. Farming 'improvements' have reduced the number of species. For the purpose of the project, meadows were classified into four categories:

         A. Flower rich meadows of high conservation value.

         B. Meadows of lower value than A, but still with some conservation interest.

         C. Meadows of limited value but with potential to increase in conservation value
         with appropriate management.

         D. 'Improved' meadows of no conservation value.

Putting categories A and B together to make a super-category 'flower rich meadows', it was concluded that there was a 50% loss of remaining flower-rich meadows between the mid 1980s and 1995-97. In a further 26% of meadows there was a "decline in interest". This loss then occurred after the National Park was established.

Loss of meadows and meadow quality occurred at different rates in different parts of the National Park. For example, no Category A meadows remained in the 1990s in the Peak Forest area, while 37% remained in the Bradwell area. Such variation can probably be at least partly understood in terms of sociological, economic, geological and topographical factors. Thus at Bradwell, many fields are still owned by part-time farmers who are not solely dependant on farming activity for their income, and so these farmers may have felt less pressure to intensify their farming. And then at Peak Forest, farming is dominated by relatively large farms on comparatively flat land where the large fields are accessible to modern machinery. Here it is easier to intensify production.

Besides investigating overall meadow quality, the project also looked into the loss from individual meadows of key species, using data from 436 meadows. It was found that some species have been much more affected by meadow decline than others. The worst affected were plant species that are particularly associated with calcareous soils - there were some staggering losses. Thus between the two survey dates, the Hoary Plantain was lost from 95% of the meadows, Lady's Bedstraw from 94%.

Woodland

Woodlands include some moderate sized conifer plantations in the northern valleys and elsewhere, ash tree dominated woodland in valleys in the White Peak, some other fairly large mixed woodland such as that on the hills behind Chatsworth House and Lady Manners wood close to Bakewell. There are also numerous small bits of woodland. Some tree planting has been taking place in recent times, for example, as part of the landscaping round quarries. And recently, a 20 ha area of oak woodland is being re-created by planting acorns and young oak trees in lower Bretton Clough (a co-operative venture between the owner, the Forestry Commission, English Nature and the Peak Park authority).

Some of the woodlands in the Park are actively managed, but one occasionally comes across a bit of woodland which is clearly not being managed, and where stock are not excluded so regeneration of such small areas of woodland is unlikely to take place. An example is a conifer plantation on the hill slope near Stanage House on the Sir William Hill. Perhaps more important, because it concerns native oak woodland rather than plantation, is a small area of mature oak woodland west of the Derwent river just north of Baslow (see photo page 142). This latter example is on a fairly steep slow, and you can see signs of substrate damage by cattle. The amount of land that would be lost from cattle/milk production by enclosing this wood and a little of the surrounding land, would be minimal.

Trees are an important aspect of landscape in the park, not only where present in woodland, but equally important from the landscape point of view, where they occur as isolated trees along field boundaries, usually in or near a hedge or stone wall, and also sometimes away from field boundaries. Many of these are old, and it seems that when they die or are badly damaged by lightning, they are often not replaced. This process leads towards a general reduction of the tree component of landscape. The 1997 ADAS report on the North Peak ESA (a report dealt with more fully in Section J below) records that 89% of isolated trees were 'mature' or 'old', only 2% were saplings. The report euphemistically comments that with this low percentage of saplings and their low potential for survival, long term future of isolated trees may not be secure.

Hedgerows and Stone walls

Hedgerows and especially stonewalls are characteristic and widespread features of the park landscape. According to the latest yearbook of the park authority there are 1,710 km of hedgerows, 8,756 km of stonewalls and banks.

We saw in Chapter 5 Section E, that common features of landscape deterioration in England are the loss of hedgerows and the loss of continuity in remaining hedgerows. The Peak Park has not escaped such deterioration. In the opening section of this chapter I mentioned one place where a hedge has been removed. And if one walks in the Peak District one comes across many hedges, which are very gappy indeed. Sometimes sheep wander freely from one field to another through the gaps. Sometimes strands of barbed wire prevent stock movement. If you take a walk from Hope up Lose hill, you will see many examples. Sometimes the hedgerow has become a tree row, usually very gappy - take the path round the hill

Inside the big quarry near Eyam. Why are such major destructive activities allowed in such areas of "natural beauty, wildlife and cultural heritage"?

Same quarry Removing the stone. Stand on this road a short while and you will realise how much stone is being taken away.

Deep Rake, Longstone Edge. Yes, its been going on for a long time.

from Edale old village to Barber Booth and you pass a good example (see colour photo page 172). Go to lower Alport dale, and you see another gappy tree hedge. Elsewhere, for example, near Bakewell, you see hedges which are carefully trimmed both very neatly and very low, altering their former characteristic appearance and very much reducing their value for wildlife.

Walls are one of the most characteristic landscape features of the Peak district, along with stone-built village houses. In some places like Chelmorton you see the regularly aligned walls that mark the boundaries of earlier field strips that stretched out from settlements (see colour photo page 171). Elsewhere you see the stone walls that divide up big areas of what would have been heathland. And in the Dark Peak you see walls extending up to the edge of the moorland proper (see colour photo page 169). Some wall rebuilding has recently been taking place, and the Countryside Stewardship Scheme has been used to help preserve walls, especially the field strip type. Many walls, especially in the Dark Peak area are broken down and gappy and farmers make little or no effort to do anything about it.

Rivers, Reservoirs, Ponds

The principal river systems in the National Park are the Derwent –Wye and the Dove-Manifold systems, the former associated with two of the major reservoirs that are found in the Park – the Derwent and Ladybower reservoirs. Every valley in the Dark Peak has its river or brook. But in the White Peak some valleys /sections of valleys are dry.

It is worth noting that the building of water reservoirs has had a dramatic impact on landscape, as well as disrupting farming activity as already mentioned. During the twenty years after the National Park was designated in 1951, six new reservoirs were built. But reservoirs, once constructed, have to be maintained. And in recent times it was realised that the Ladybower Dam wall needed refurbishment and reinforcement, which would require a large quantity of stone. Different possible sources of the stone were considered. Finally the choice was narrowed down to two possibilities. First, extraction of rock from below the top waterline on the flank of the dam; second, opening a temporary quarry within the conifer plantation along the side of the dam. The latter proposal was the one finally accepted, and work has started. So now there is more quarrying within the Peak Park, albeit the site is small, and 'restoration work' will be carried out afterwards.

Ponds were in the past a significant component of landscape. Changing agricultural practice has led to the loss of many of these ponds. The Peak National Park Great Crested Newt and Pond Conservation Project, using sample areas in the White Peak, found a 50% loss of ponds between 1970 and 1985.

Even tiny 'ponds' can provide valuable habitat for wild life – for example a tiny wet area that has formed above Eyam on what is probably old mine-workings (see colour photo page 172).

E. Quarrying and mining

The following account is based primarily on the Peak National Park's own Mineral Extraction Fact Sheet number eleven.

Quarrying and mining have been going on for a very long time in the Peak District. It is known, for example, that the Romans mined lead in the region, and by late Anglo Saxon times lead extraction was extensive. Lead mining is now no longer carried out, although some lead is obtained as a bi-product of fluorspar processing (see below). Quarrying for limestone and gritstone has left big marks on the landscape, and quarrying still continues. Most of the limestone being produced is used for road building and repair. The second biggest use for the limestone is in making cement. And one of the first views of the interior of the Peak District when one travels from Sheffield via Fox House and down into the village of Hathersage on the A625, is partly spoilt by the tall (130 metres) chimney of the Hope Cement Works, at the south-western end of the whole valley system, pouring out 'smoke' (it is actually steam). The photos opposite show the Works viewed from high ground east of Bradwell and the quarry which services the Works.

Besides defiling the landscape, quarrying creates atmospheric pollution, dust on surrounding vegetation, and considerable noise, both from the actual quarrying processes but also from the large lorries that carry much of the rock away. There are now fewer quarries in the park than there were earlier this century, but they are much larger. And quarrying, far from abating after the National Park was designated in 1951, showed a great increase in the output of limestone and fluorspar (by volume, limestone is by far the rock type most removed in quarrying in the Peak Park):

Limestone production (million tonnes/annum)

1951	1961	1971	1981	1989	1990
1.5	2.2	5.4	4.0	7.4	8.6

When the National Park was designated, its boundary was so set as to exclude much major quarrying near Buxton. That is why if you look at a map of the National Park you see this curious large indentation around Buxton. However, the Tunstead quarry near Buxton, which is one of the largest quarry systems in Europe, was granted planning permission in 1980 to extend into the National Park on the north-east side of this indentation, at the area known as Old Moor.

One of the worst quarries in the National Park itself, in terms of size and effect on the landscape, is the one that lies between the village of Eyam and Coombs Dale (see BW photo page 145 and colour photo page 170).

Gritstone is also still quarried, for the purpose of producing building stone, from about a dozen medium to small quarries in the park. Fluorspar is obtained from three different operations. First it is obtained from open cast mining, at a variety of sites ranging from large open pits such as Dirtlow, on Bradwell moor, to small sites worked by a few men. Second, it is produced from underground mining - the main current mine is under Longstone edge. Third, it is obtained by reworking old spoil heaps, including the Lead Rakes already mentioned. Fluorspar is used for a variety of purposes - making steel, refrigerants, solvents, etc. The major company involved in mining and processing fluorspar produces 80,000 tons annually from its plant near Stoney Middleton. This is 70% of the total British production. Unfortunately for the Peak District, almost all (98%) of the high quality 'acid grade' fluorspar is found in that district.

Unfortunately too, the processing of the fluorspar, by crushing the ore finely and separating out the minerals, leaves a waste (slurry), which has to be disposed of, in what are called 'tailings lagoons'. So if you look down on upper Coombs Dale you see a large lake - this is where the slurry from the mill near Stoney Middleton is deposited. Other minerals also extracted in the Peak District include barites, calcite, fireclay and sand.

F. Visitor pressure on the vegetation and wildlife

The number of visitors to the Peak District National Park has increased enormously in recent decades. Brown and Shepherd (1991) report on work by P.E. Yalden and D.W. Yalden in 1988, concerning visitors at the Snake Summit, especially on the Pennine Way. During the bird-breeding season, they reported that 7,800 visitors accompanied by 300 dogs went north along the Pennine way from the main road. 60 % of the dogs were unleashed and 25 ran wild. Weekend use was 2-4 times as heavy as during the week. On paths as a whole in the region, where there were good paths, there was little disturbance over the moor away from the path, but where the paths were poor or diffuse, much disturbance was recorded more widely.

Considerable damage has been caused to the vegetation through trampling, and soil erosion has sometimes been caused. One frequently finds that paths are indistinct, leading to a proliferation of paths. But an even bigger cause of path proliferation in my experience occurs in those very frequent areas where the ground is almost always wet. Trampling of the vegetation here, leads to water submerging the path, so people try to get round the wet areas, thus enlarging the path and creating new paths. The Peak Park authority has dealt with this on some stretches of the main paths, by laying down a pavement of massive stone slabs. This has successfully encouraged people to keep to the path. At the same time such a path destroys the wild feeling of tramping on the moors.

We know that changing agricultural practice has been a major cause of the decline in bird numbers. But it is not the only cause. Although it may be difficult to prove, it seems most likely that heavy visitor pressure in certain areas may deter breeding by some ground nesting birds and raptors. Ring ouzel populations declined in recent decades, and an ADAS monitoring report of 1997 notes that this has been attributed to increased use of its breeding habitat for recreational purposes, particularly rock climbing (ADAS, 1997a). And it is a fact, that almost all the escarpments in the Peak district have a path going along the top and climbers use most of the rocky areas. Uncontrolled dogs can also seriously disturb ground-nesting birds including grouse. Many of the moorland birds are ground nesting, and the very presence of people can cause birds to fly up, wasting energy, preventing brooding so that the chicks get cold and wet and attract predators. While it is true that most walkers keep to the paths, not all do, and dogs can be a real menace (people with dogs put significantly more birds off eggs than walkers alone).

However, definite evidence about the possible effects of visitor pressure is very limited and to some extent conflicting. As we will see later, there was no evidence of decline of bird species (apart from the dunlin) in the twenty years prior to 1991 in the northern Peak area (Brown and Shepherd, ibid). Yet the intensity and extent of recreational disturbance has greatly increased in this area. On the other hand, golden plover have decreased in the Snake Pass summit area. Now the Snake pass summit is a focal point for walkers going north-south up the Pennine way, which crosses the main road at this point. It seems likely that visitor pressure has had an effect here. And Yalden (reported in Brown and Shepherd, ibid) found that in the Derwent valley, although the number of the common sandpiper remained stable from 1979 to 1982, there were changes in the siting of their breeding territories which could be related to changes in the pattern of human disturbance over the same period.

G. People pressure and transport issues

Enormous numbers of people now visit the Peak National Park. Thus a 1986-87 survey estimated there were 18.5 million visits during the year. The breakdown of this figure into components illustrates the significance of car transport: The 18.5 m estimate was made up of 16 million car-born visitors, only 1.5 million arrivals by public transport, and 0.5 million arrivals on foot. By 1996 the total number of visits per year was estimated to have risen to over 22 million (PDNP, 2000 Year Book). There is a massive car park provision to cope with this car (and coach) borne visitor pressure. 1995 figures showed that if one considers public off-street car parks, there were over 100, varying in car capacity from 10 to 750, with a total of 17 with a capacity of 100 or more. There is private off-street parking (pubs etc.) at nearly 90 sites, with a capacity varying from 6 to 130, mostly between 20 and 50. And then there is on-street parking in settlements. And still one gets many vehicles parking at the roadside away from settlements (data supplied to the author by the Parks Transport Policy Service.

Private visitor traffic is however, only one component of road traffic. Very many people travel between areas outside the park by travelling through the Park. Thus between Sheffield and Manchester, much used routes are the A628 (Woodhead) in the north, the A57 (Snake Pass) through the middle of the park, and the A623 (Stoney Middleton) a little further south. This pressure on trans-park roads is to a small extent alleviated by use of the Sheffield to Manchester (via Edale) rail system; on the other hand, the closure of the Woodhead railway increased the pressure on trans-park roads.

Commuting traffic for employment is another major component of road traffic. Some residents in the park travel between one settlement and another within the park for their employment. More significant in terms of total commuter traffic is probably commuting between the park and surrounding areas. This has two components - park residents who work outside the park, and people who live outside the park but commute in to work in the park. The Special workplace Statistics based on 10% of the 1991 census returns (PDNPA, 1996), shows that the Park had about 16,800 residents in work, of which about 6,450 (about 39%) worked outside the Park. And the number of people who come into the Park to work was 4,260. Now some commuters use public transport (train/bus), others travel by road. The twice-daily heavy commuter traffic, mainly cars, on major roads crossing the Park boundary, such as the A625 to Sheffield suggests that a large proportion of commuters travel by car. So what proportion of commuters use the roads? Unfortunately statistics are not available. In the summer of 1999, two surveys were carried out – the Hope valley rail user survey, and the Hope valley Bus Users survey (the railway connects Sheffield and Manchester, with stations along the Hope valley), but these surveys do not answer this question.

The surveys were carried out by the Hope Valley Community Rail Partnership – a group consisting of representatives of the Peak District National Park Authority, Derbyshire County Council, North Western Trains and various local groups. The aims of the Partnership are first, to increase use of the Hope Valley rail line and so reduce car travel: second, to link the railway system more effectively with the local communities to increase their economic, social and environmental well-being. The Partnership is partly funded by the European Union.

The Hope Valley Rail User Survey was carried out on ten days, and there were over 500 responses to the survey. Persons were asked what was the purpose of their journey. The most common purpose turned out to be visiting the countryside, especially at the weekends. 'Travel to work' came second during the week, 'visiting friends' came second at the weekend. On weekdays, 'Shopping' came third. Passengers were also asked where they lived, and what was their destination station. The highest proportion of passengers lived in Sheffield. In terms of destination, Sheffield was the most common destination for passengers overall, by far the commonest destination on weekdays. But Edale (at the foot of Kinderscout) was the second most common destination overall. This is particularly significant because Edale is the main entrance point for the uplands of Kinderscout.

The survey also asked the question "could you have used a car to make this journey instead of the train?" For weekday journeys, a majority said "yes". For Saturday, about half said yes, and for Sundays a majority said "no". Overall, this suggests that the railway has made a significant contribution to reducing visitor and road commuter traffic.

The Hope Valley Bus Users' Survey was carried out on four days, and was confined to the two main bus services connecting the Hope valley to Sheffield (273, 273/4). Once again, 'visiting countryside' came top of the list. 'shopping' came second. The authors of the survey concluded that both bus services were important to give valley residents access to Sheffield shops. On the question about availability of a car for the journey, a majority of users of the 272 service said "yes", but a majority using the 273/4 service said "no". Once again then, the bus services do make a contribution to reducing road traffic. However, neither this survey nor the rail survey really enables one to gauge the importance of public transport in total transport provision. *If the Peak Park Authorities take the issue of promoting public transport seriously, it is surprising that it has not itself carried out surveys on the relative extent of use of car and public transport by commuters.*

Road freight is another major component of road traffic. Part of this is trans-park traffic (e.g. Sheffield to Manchester). Part of it is connected to quarrying and manufacturing within the park, and service provision. The 1997 Survey of employers in the Peak District by the Park's Research and Monitoring service (PDNPA, 1997) provides very interesting information. During the 1990s there has been an increase both in the number of lorry movements, and the size of vehicles servicing premises. It seems likely that manufacturing firms will use bigger lorries in future. At the same time, rail transport was used much less by manufacturing and mineral industries than road transport (roughly 4% using rail, 96% using road).

Where then were the markets supplied by these two industries? For both, the vast majority were outside the Park (only 15-20% within the Park), and many markets were even outside the country (about half the markets with manufacturing, about a quarter with minerals). Data was also available for the location of suppliers for manufacturing. About half were not only not in the park but also not even in the region – they were elsewhere in the country or abroad. Now while it could be argued that mineral industries don't have any option - they must be in the park because that is where their materials come from, the same cannot be said for most manufacturing. Manufacturing accounts for about 20% of jobs in the Park. I calculate from the data in the Workplace Statistics that over 60% of these manufacturing jobs are held by people living outside the Park. Why have so much manufacturing within the Park so far away from supplier and customer? Most of this manufacturing is not intimately linked with agriculture or other traditional rural activities! This topic will be returned to in Chapter 12.

All this road traffic has reduced the quality of the countryside in the Park (sight and noise of vehicles, pollution, traffic congestion, dangerous roads for walkers and cyclists) in much the same way as it has reduced countryside quality elsewhere in England. Ironically, the designation of the area as a National Park, and the promotion of the park as a place of beauty by the park authorities and other agencies will have, in the writer's view, been one cause of the problem- the situation may be worse inside the park than outside it.

Road traffic in the Park seems likely to increase during the next 20 years unless very radical national and local polices were introduced. Considering the Peak National Park with immediately surrounding areas, it has been predicted that the traffic growth 1994 to 2015 will be at least 30% and possibly as high as 70%.

How has the Peak Park responded to the various transport pressures that have developed over the years?
The Structure Plan (SP) states clear objectives for transport:

> "To manage the demands for transport in and across the Park; to seek to alleviate the problems caused by traffic, so as to protect and enhance the valued characteristics of the Park; to support the provision of public transport between the towns, villages and recreational areas of the Park and from the urban areas around the park; and to improve conditions for non-motorised transport and for those transport users with mobility difficulties." (Structure Plan para 9.3)

The Transport Chapter of the SP emphasises that road traffic between points outside the park (for example, freight transport between different urban areas), should go round the Park rather than through it. Within the Park, investment on road maintenance and improvement should be focused on the 'strategic network' of the major transport routes already used by cross-park traffic, avoiding investment on other roads which might generate increased traffic on these roads. The Plan advocates the re-opening of the Matlock to Buxton and Woodhead railway lines as transport alternatives to roads.

In practical terms, measures adopted by the Peak Park Authority include the following:

> 1) It has usually opposed road 'improvements' (widening, straightening) within the park, hoping to discourage people wishing to travel between destinations outside the park from using trans-park routes and use routes outside the park instead. While some road alterations have been prevented, it does not appear that people have been discouraged from trans-park travel. Road improvements are also opposed so as to try to preserve the rural quality of roads. This has succeeded in the sense of retaining the winding nature of many of these roads, but traffic has increased on most of them, damaging quality in terms of safety and quietness.

> 2. It has tried to improve road safety and reduce conflict with other road users (cyclists, walkers) by introducing speed restrictions on some roads (e.g. 50 mph on parts of the A623). In major villages it has attempted traffic calming by an increase in the 30 and 40 mph sign posting and more and clearer road markings. These measures have probably had some beneficial effect, although many drivers largely ignore the 50 mph rule and seem to interpret 30 and 40 mph as 40 and 50 mph respectively. Some roads are highly dangerous to walkers as was mentioned earlier this chapter. A short while ago I was on a bus travelling north through the small village of Stoney Middleton. This is a village with a narrow winding main street. The bus driver ignored the 30 mph restriction. A lorry coming in the opposite direction at speed was driven by a man who was holding a mobile phone to one ear while steering the lorry round a corner with the other hand!

> 3. Weight restrictions have been introduced on many roads, which has stopped some through freight traffic on some roads.

> 4. It has introduced cycle hire schemes to encourage cycle rather than car use; cycle hire is popular, and will probably have had some effect in reducing car use for short trips within the park.

> 5. In order to improve access but at the same time discourage car parking haphazardly along roads creating congestion, increased danger, and visual pollution, it has allowed or encouraged the development of car parks (see photo page 135).

> 6. The Peak Park has introduced the 'park and ride' scheme seasonally or at weekends at Fairholmes in the Derwent valley and at the Roaches in the south west of the Park for certain times. It also uses the scheme for particular events like the Bakewell show. However, it has not used the scheme in connection with any of the major road entrance routes into the park, so the park and ride idea has had little impact on general Peak Park traffic.

> 7. In terms of transport provision for visitors, useful recent developments have been the summertime bus service between Edale station and Castleton, and the bus service from Sheffield to Stanage Edge.

Public transport provision must surely be a key factor in any planning for the future. And the SP says:

> "The Board (i.e. the PPJPB) continues to reguard improved public transport as a major part of its efforts to reduce car usage and as a vital part of life in the Park".

That being so, you would think then that the Peak Park would develop an overall scheme for public transport in the park. According to a senior official, it hasn't. Qualifying this I was told that bus services are the responsibility of the various local authorities. The Park authorities do consult with these authorities, but is the pig in the middle. In contrast, Derbyshire County Council has produced a very good, regularly and frequently updated, Peak District bus and train timetable, complete with map and other useful information. I have found this very helpful in my own hiking in the Park, although it is very sad that most of the buses I have used are practically empty.

Road pricing could be an extremely useful tool for reducing car traffic and encouraging public transport use. Now the Peak Park Structure Plan has a Transport Policy 8, which deals with traffic management and parking. It says that where appropriate various measures will be introduced in pursuit of the policy of making the best use of the road network, improving road safety, environmental and traffic conditions. The list of nine specified measures includes restraint on the volumes of traffic entering the Park by means including signing, parking provision and pricing. However, road pricing has not been introduced at park entrances. Within the Park one trial scheme is being considered at Derwent. It is true that in the past, national legislation to promote road pricing has been absent. But the Authorities of the National Parks might have pressed government to sanction such measures, at least within the Park, or could have itself promoted a private members bill in parliament to introduce road pricing in the Peak District. Now that Government policy is moving towards the idea of limited adoption of road pricing , it is disappointing to note that the latest version of the Local Plan (the Provisional Adopted Version July 2000) says the PPJPB is not proposing general road pricing in the National Park; if road pricing does come about it will probably need to be introduced by Central Government. The PPJPB is then relinquishing the opportunity to take the lead to introduce such a radical measure. In the writer's view this is a paradigm of Authorities being conservative and unwilling to advocate radical measures (as we have already seen in the First Case Study, Sheffield (Chapter 4).

H. Counter-urbanisation

The following account is based mainly on the 1979 and 1994 Park Structure Plans and 1995/96 housing statistics, together with discussions and correspondence with officials, and was previously reported in Barker (1998).

National Parks, are not, according to national policy, meant to contribute to the general national provision of housing, including that arising out of counter-urbanisation, but rather, to provide just for the needs of people living within the parks. National policy is re-enforced as far as the Peak Park is concerned by the governments Regional Planning Guidance for the East Midlands which concludes that no target for housing provision should be given for the Peak Park, implying that the land for housing demand would need to be found outside the Park's boundary. In England as a whole, a Structure Plan area (structure plans determine the amount of housing that should be provided - see Chapter Four) that includes a National Park, normally covers a whole county, and thus covers areas outside the National Park as well as the park itself. This means it is possible to consider relieving the pressure for housing development within a park by catering for extra housing provision in areas outside the park boundary. The Peak Park, however, is placed in a peculiarly difficult position. The Structure Plan covering the park is unique - it covers only the National Park. The Planning Board of the park has no jurisdiction over areas outside the park. So it is unable to relieve pressure for housing development in the way just described.

Now it would theoretically be possible for planning authorities in areas surrounding the park to assist the park by adding to their own allocation for housing, a component to assist the Peak Park. Some authorities have agreed to help in this way. However, some of the authorities have green belts going right up to the Peak Park boundary. These authorities are under great pressure to avoid building in the green belt. So it is unlikely in practice that these authorities could do much to help the park.

I wished to examine two aspects of housing and population, first the actual amount of building inside the park compared with that outside the park; second, the extent and character of counter-urbanisation inside the park compared with outside the park. I have not yet been able to take the study of the first aspect very far because it has proved very difficult to get the necessary statistics from outside the park for the comparison. I had in fact imagined that a study such as I had in mind, must have already been carried out for all National Parks, if government is really serious about limiting development in these parks, and wanted to monitor the situation. However, neither the Town and Country Planning Association nor the Head of the Planning and Research Centre at Anglia Polytechnic University know of any such study (personal communications). So I have limited my investigation to the second aspect - counter-urbanisation, its extent and nature.

The population of the park fell by almost 2,000 in the twenty years from 1951, falling especially in more remote areas. But from a level of about 37,500 in 1977, the population rose to a little over 38,000 in 1981. The population seems to have remained roughly at 38,000 since. The trend of population decrease in the years before the 1979 Structure Plan was prepared, was however, not universal. Populations actually increased in a few parishes - mainly five in the Hope and Derwent valleys. These valleys are within easy commuter distance of urban areas like Sheffield. Relatively wealthy urban people moved into these parishes, and this was linked with rising land and property prices, which helped to force many local people out of these areas. In and out migration left its mark on the age structure of the Peak Park population by the time of the 1979 Structure Plan was completed. Of the total of 70 parishes within the park, only 21 had a population structure approaching the national average. Other parishes had a higher than average number of the over 45 and the 30-40 age groups and a lower proportion in the under 29 age group. It is clear then, that general national tendencies of urbanisation and counter-urbanisation have been reproduced, at least in part, within the Peak National Park. The 1979 plan comments on the cycle of changes, which result in the decline of rural areas. The imbalance in the age structure mentioned above, makes it difficult to provide a normal range of community services; services like primary schools and public transport decline, which in turn favours further loss of the native population.

From January 1977 to March 1991, new housing provision (new build plus conversions, but excluding holiday homes) was 1,443 dwellings; 114 more dwellings were under construction, and there were outstanding permissions for 480 dwellings. From 1981 to 1991 the total housing stock in the park rose by about 9%. Of housing development permitted, conversions consistently accounted for a large percentage - about 39% over the plan period. Conversions were mainly of redundant farm buildings. There has been a striking increase in the number of permissions for holiday accommodation, from an average of 9 units permitted per year from 1978 to 1983, to an average of 37 from 1984 to 1989. Between April 1991 and March 1994 an average of 31 holiday units have been permitted per year and by March 1994, 96 holiday units were outstanding. Some figures are available for the percentage of park dwellings that were used for second and holiday homes during the 1979 plan period and since.

The 1981 census found that about 2.6% of household spaces in the park were for holiday cottages or second homes. But the 1991 census found that the figure had risen to 4.9%. If we consider the 'replacement structure plan' period beginning April 1991, by the end of 1995/96 19% of all dwelling completions and commitments over the plan period were for holiday accommodation. The trend then seems to have been towards an increase in the proportion of holiday accommodation. The 1994 structural plan says that about 1,000 more dwellings will need to be built in the period 1991 -2006; some of these will be covered by existing commitments.

Now the 1994 Structure Plan makes the comment that the National Park was not designated to be a high quality residential district. But to a large extent, this seems to be what it has become. Now it is worth remembering here that Park policy is subject to national law, and there is no law which might be used to prevent private housing that has no restrictions placed on it being taken up for second homes, holiday homes, or retirement from urban areas.

Most new conversions come onto the open housing market. And most of the existing housing in the Park is in private hands and so can come onto the open market. The overall outcome has been that many conversions, and many sales of existing housing stock, were to urban people who were retiring or wanted a second/holiday home. As one Park planner unofficially said to me, this was the way the park played its part to help with general national housing demand. Land for housing in the Peak Park is strictly limited. The free-market caused land and house prices to rise. There was intense competition for the available land, and owners usually sold to the highest bidder. Further, developers found it most profitable to build houses for the upper range of the market rather than houses more directly related to the needs of local residents. Consequently, local people were being forced out of some areas by lack of affordable housing, a subject to which we now turn.

At Bamford there was an old derelict mill by the Derwent River. Below the dam weir are many boulders, and an abundance of small bushes, and flowering plants. A little wild life paradise. Now recently the mill has been converted into flats, and a few new dwellings added. One can imagine that when people live here, the little wild life area is likely to be despoiled. A few days after I had walked this area I returned to the site, posing as a potential buyer, and let myself be shown around. Before I left, I casually asked the woman who was showing me round - are the people buying flats mainly people who are retiring? The woman replied that it was more a case of people buying second homes - in one case a third home of someone who did not normally even reside in Britain. I came away having been given a glossy brochure and having enquired about prices. £100,000, £150,000 ...these are certainly not properties that ordinary local folk could ever hope to buy (see photo opposite).

In response to protests that local people could not get homes, the Peak Park's Structure Plan published in 1976 contained a series of policy statements limiting new housing to local needs. However, these statements were not accepted by central government. Peter Shore, the Labour Secretary of State, proposed to delete them from the plan. Subsequently Michael Heseltine, the Tory Secretary of State did so - he struck out the social criteria for housing policy but retained the aesthetic ones. Both Secretaries insisted that under the Planning Laws extant, planning applications must be decided by the merits of the proposed use, not by reference to the user. The Peak Park Board commented on the situation in the 1979 plan, saying that it had found it difficult to ensure that when land is approved for private housing, the local people are the main beneficiaries. They acknowledged that they had often appeared to favour new comers at the expense of local people, while in fact this was contrary to their stated policies and was caused by factors beyond their control. The consequence of all this is that people who have moved into the park have been relatively wealthy. The parks market town - Bakewell - mirrors this wealth. You will find there, for example, food shops serving a very high quality and variety of foods, shops it would be difficult to find in the nearby city of Sheffield (in fact I know only one - in one of the wealthiest suburbs)!

People look to housing authorities and housing associations to provide low price housing. Now as at 1991 only about 11% of the households in the park lived in accommodation that was in the control of such authorities and associations, or otherwise subject to an occupancy constraint. The current position about housing association activity in the Park is that it is very limited compared with the national level.

The 1979 plan notes that there was at that time a shortage of both public and private rented accommodation. Only three parishes contained council house provision above the national average of 30%. The figure for the Park as a whole was 12%. Some parishes contained no council housing. At any one time, only a small proportion of local residents faced problems, but to the individuals concerned, the problem was a very real one, and over time a substantial proportion of the community could be affected. The affordable housing situation was made worse in 1980, when authorities were required to sell Council Houses as the new Housing Act came into force - something which apparently took the Park planning authorities by surprise.

A large proportion of council houses within the Park were sold off during the plan period, with no conditions attached that the housing should remain affordable. The 1994 plan notes that in two villages in the Park, more than 80% of council housing stock had already been sold. This meant that affordable housing decreased; housing lists grew, although not dramatically so, during the 1979 Structure Plan Period. It seems ironic that conversions of farm buildings, instead of being used to provide dwellings for long time Park residents, were instead used to house wealthy people from urban areas, many of whom then had two homes. When such former council housing is sold on, it becomes prey to the free-market situation already described.

Now the 1994 structural plan states that new dwellings in the park during the period of the 1979 structural plan accommodated enough people to match the reduction in average household size (reduction of household size is dealt with in the next chapter). And as already mentioned, the 1994 plan says that about 1,000 more dwellings will need to be built in the period 1991 -2006; some of these will be covered by existing commitments. But the question clearly arises, did new housing in the past really meet locally created need, and will it in the future, or does it rather provide housing for well-to-do people from outside?

While as I said at the beginning of this section, I am not in a position yet to compare building within, with building without the Park, there are certain known facts that are worrying.
The actual provision of new housing in the Park (new build and conversions of non-housing buildings), vastly exceeded

the figure in the 1979 structural plan - in fact house building exceeded plan provision by 76%. This excludes holiday accommodation. If that is included, the figure is 94%. If un-taken up commitments to build are also taken into account the figure rises to 148%(without holiday accommodation) and 183% (with such accommodation)! The Peak Park then joins numerous other authority areas where housing provision greatly exceeded plan provision. Not only were the structure plan provision of housing figure greatly exceeded, the plans attempt to divide new stock between different parts of the park also failed. The park had been divided into a small number of areas, with a tentative assignment of amount of house building to each. In the face of market demand, it became impossible to stick to the planned division (remember it was pointed out earlier that there had been population increases in two of the Park valleys).

The overall tentative conclusion from my study would seem to be that despite the Peak Park having a special countryside status, and although proliferation of new housing might have been less than in neighbouring rural areas, there is not otherwise a great deal of difference between development taking place within the Park to development taking place outside it. Thinking in terms of the general urbanisation and counter-urbanisation trends, the Peak Park does not stand out as an area resisting such a trend. Wealthy urban people have been enabled to appropriate pieces of the countryside. The rural character of Park communities has been diluted by urban immigrants. Some rural people have moved to towns (some probably in effect forced out of rural communities).

There is probably a very ironic twist to this story, and that involves local authorities whose green belts meet the parks boundary. By applying their own strict green belt policy, which is desirable from the point of view of their own residents, they are perhaps encouraging their own relatively wealthy people, who are unable through this policy to purchase a dwelling on city outskirts, to move out into the Peak Park, and if these people are still in business in urban areas, this will contribute to the growing and damaging rural-urban commuter traffic!

I. Changes in bird and mammal life in the park

Various surveys have been carried out on birds in the Peak National Park. Unfortunately, these do not allow anything like a full analysis of changes in bird populations over the years. In the first place, quantitative studies have mainly been carried out in very recent decades, so do not provide information on changes in the first few decades after the Second World War. In the second place, most studies have concerned particular parts of the Peak District rather than the Peak District as a whole (e.g. the South West Peak District, or the Dark Peak moors). Some others concern only one or a few species. Further, ideally, one would like to see for any given area, a survey repeated at regular intervals by similar sampling methods, covering all recent decades. While some repeat surveying has been carried out, this falls far short of such regular interval surveying. Another problem with comparisons between bird surveys, at least over a small number of years is this. Even if successive surveys showed no decrease in the numbers of a given bird species, this would not necessarily mean that this species was not badly affected. Some birds are long-lived, and return yearly to the same site to breed. They may return year after year to breed, even when each year they fail to do so.

Nevertheless, there is evidence of species decline in the south-western parts of the Park over recent decades, which seem to mirror national changes. And as elsewhere in the country, these declines can largely be ascribed to changes in farming practice. This evidence comes from surveys carried out on the North Staffordshire moor area, most of which lies within the Peak Park boundary. The moors are a mosaic of upland and upland fringe habitats - heather and grass moor, unimproved and improved pastures, hay meadows and rushy patches. There were large population declines of curlew, snipe, lapwing, golden plover and ring ouzel between 1985 and 1992, and all these species suffered further large declines between 1992 and 1996. So that between 1985 and 1996, curlew suffered a 59% decline, snipe 73%, lapwing 72%, golden plover 92%, ring ouzel 92% decline. These declines were attributed to the intensification of agriculture - sheep overgrazing, ploughing and re-seeding with rye grass, stimulating vigorous grasses at the expense of upland herbs by fertiliser application, switching from hay to silage production and the draining of pastures (McKnight et al, 1996; see also ADAS, 1997a)

Studies on moorland birds reported by Brown and Shepherd (1991) present a rather different picture as far as the Peak Park as a whole is concerned. They reported on work over the whole South Pennine moors, from Skipton (Yorks.) southwards, so the total area included many areas besides the Peak district. A study carried out over the whole area in 1990, compared several different surveys of parts of the whole area from the previous twenty-five years by D.W. Yalden and others, for selected species. For the whole study area it appeared that there was little evidence for decline for most species studied. Some of the earlier studies allow comparison for particular species for the Peak National Park or part of it. The results here largely mirrored the conclusion from the whole study area. However, there appears to have been a significant decline in dunlin in the whole Park area since 1974. Also, there was evidence that both red grouse and golden plover had declined in the South West Peak Area. Many observers think that the ring ouzel, a bird associated with cliffs, crags, and other broken ground, has declined in recent decades. However, Brown and Shepherd concluded the evidence was inconclusive.

A 1997 report on the breeding birds of the Dark Peak compares monitoring surveys carried out during 1994 and 1996 (ADAS, 1997b). Most of the species occurring were monitored in a random sample of 4km² sampling units (called 'tetrads'). In terms of both number of tetrads in which species were recorded, and also total numbers of each species recorded, the comparison suggests that overall there was no decline, rather some increase in populations. However, it must be emphasised that this report only covers a very short time period, so tells us nothing of any long-term trends.

One other survey provides information on the birds of the moors on the eastern side of the Peak District. This was commissioned by EN in 1998 and compares 1990 and 1998 data. This shows an apparent increase of several species, but a decline in the golden plover and possibly the twite.

Various observers have commented on increased presence of the raven in the Peak District. This bird only returned as a regular breeding bird since 1992 and by 1997 there were 6-10 pairs ((Anderson, et al, 1997). It is generally thought that this increase is related to changing farming practice: the large increase in the number of sheep on the moors in recent decades, combined with reduced activity of shepherds, has led to an increase of carcases which are important food for the raven. Changes in farming practice and decline in sporting management have affected mammal populations. Crows and foxes have increased (P.Linley, in FRCA 1999), one specific reason for the latter is the movement for foraging of urban foxes into the countryside near by, according to one MAFF official. Of particular interest on moorland is the mountain hare. This was introduced into the Peak District from Scotland in the second half of the last century; by 1984 its population was probably about 500 animals. There have been numerous other small populations in Britain but these became extinct, which serves as a warning about the vulnerability of this population (Anderson et al, ibid).

Finally, surveys apart, one indication of changes in bird populations comes from peoples experience over a long period of time. My own experience, as I said in the first section of this chapter, is that lapwings and skylarks, two of the characteristic species of the Peak District, have declined considerably since the Second Word War. I also think that some finch species like the chaffinch and linnet were commoner in the Peak District around the time of the Second World war than they are today, although I have no quantitative data to support my view.

J. Specially protected areas - SSSIs and Agri-environment Schemes

The National SSSI programme operates within the Peak District National Park, as do the national agri-environment schemes ESA and CS. In addition, the Park Authorities started their own National Park Conservation Scheme with the purpose of supplementing the National schemes operating in the Park.

(i) SSSIs

It should be born in mind that the SSSI programme protects not only sites of biological interest, but of geological interest also. Some sites are consequently classified as 'geological', others as 'biological' and some as 'mixed'.
In 1999 there was a total of 50 SSSIs in the National Park, of which 8 were cross-Park boundary. Of these 17 were classed as geological, 3 of which were cross-boundary. So the biological and mixed categories amounted to 34, of which 5 were cross boundary. Now in 2000 there are 52 SSSIs (information supplied by EN). Many areas of land within SSSIs are under CS management, and some under English Nature's WES scheme. So there is overlap between the SSSI programme and the CS scheme. Furthermore, there is overlap between the areas covered by SSSI programme and the ESA scheme. In particular, the very large Dark Peak SSSI, covering most of the Dark Peak moors, lies within the area of the North Peak ESA, and several SSSIs in the south west Peak District lie within the South West Peak ESA.

As with SSSI sites elsewhere in the country, the features of special interest which caused the area to be designated are listed for each site in the site description.   For example, with the Castleton SSSI in the 'mixed' category, the special interest features are:

Geological:	Inland outcrops and stream sections
	Active process geomorphological sites
	Caves and Karst
Biological:	calcareous grassland
	Cultivated /and disturbed land –ephemeral and short perennial plant communities

We have seen in Chapter 5 that nationally, deterioration has taken place within some SSSI sites, and the same applies within the Peak Park. Here are two examples that I noticed in walking the Park. I referred to the first one in the opening section of this chapter – the Coombs Dale SSSI, and specifically a scree slope there. The shrubs which have been dying off cannot regenerate. Now this SSSI belongs to the 'bio' category. The features of special interest centre on a) woodland, broadleaved and semi-natural; b) grassland, acid unimproved; c) grassland, calcareous unimproved. Admittedly the area I discussed is only a small part of the area and I have not surveyed the whole SSSI. However, since SSSIs are usually only small areas anyway, one cannot afford degeneration on even a small part.

The other example is in the Hamps and Manifold valleys SSSI. If you stand on the south-western slopes of Oldpark Hill and look across the Hamps river (where that river makes a sharp bend towards the south-east) towards the land south of the village of Grindon, you see a devastated area of woodland. Again, only a small part of the total area, but small parts count.

EN claim that considering the Peak Park SSSIs together with other Derbyshire sites outside the Park, there is a smaller percentage of upland heath in an unfavourable condition than the national average, but a larger percentage of bog habitat in an unfavourable condition than the national average. Apparently they are unable to do the analysis for Peak Park sites alone. They have spread sheets giving detailed information about Peak District sites, but have not apparently produced monitoring reports on individual Peak District SSSIs (correspondence with Peak District and Derbyshire EN team). This lack of proper reports, which makes it difficult for people to form an opinion on EN's work, contrasts sharply with what ADAS has done (see below).

(ii) Agri-environment schemes

ESAs

The ESA scheme operates in the Park. The total eligible area covers very roughly half the total Park area. There are two schemes – the North Peak ESA and the South West Peak ESA. The former scheme was launched in 1988, the latter scheme in 1993. The following table summarises the overall position at March 2000 (data supplied the author by MAFF):

region	eligible area	uptake area	uptake (% of eligible)
North Peak	50,300 ha	43,980 ha	87
South West Peak	30,500 ha	22805 ha	75

Uptake of the schemes has therefore been high in both ESAs. However, they differ in the extent that tier 2 options were taken up (tiers were discussed in Chapter 6 Section A). In the North Peak ESA there was only a low uptake of tier 2 (which included a moorland enhancement by exclosure option). But in the South West Peak there was a high uptake for two of the tier 2 options – traditional hay meadows and traditional pastures.

The North Peak ESA covers the Dark Peak Moorland, and is made up predominantly of moorland habitats, but it also includes, in the valleys, a variety of grassland habitats and some woodland. In contrast, only about a fifth of the South West Peak ESA is actual moorland, grassland habitats predominating. About 2/3rds of the North Peak ESA is also SSSI designated, a smaller part of the South West peak is also SSSI, including most of the moorland.

Agricultural production in the North Peak ESA is based exclusively on extensive livestock systems. Virtually no arable crops are grown. The main farming enterprise type is the keeping of hill sheep flocks on the moorland. Most of the moors are also used for grouse shooting. The South West Peak ESA has traditionally been managed for livestock farming.

The two ESAs are monitored for MAFF and the results published in reports by ADAS, on which the following notes are based. Since the South West Peak ESA was established much later than the North Peak ESA, monitoring there has been carried out over a shorter period than with the North Peak ESA. We deal with the North Peak ESA first (ADAS 1997b,c, d and e) then the South West Peak (ADAS 1997a).

The North Peak ESA

On the issue of grazing pressure, the scheme requires farmers to accept certain stocking levels and in winter (the time when sheep concentrate their feeding on the heather as pointed out in Section C), remove 25% of their sheep from the moor area. In calculating the extent of grazing pressure, samples of heather vegetation were examined, individual shoots being examined to determine the proportion grazed. This data was used to calculate an index of 'Biomass Utilisation' (BU).

Some reduction in the level of grazing took place between 1993 and 1996, although this was not a smooth decrease – the level went up again in 1995. There was a strong correlation between BU and actual stocking densities. There was a difference between moors managed primarily for grouse shooting, and moors managed primarily for sheep. The former tend to have lower grazing levels; the causal relationship here is probably at least partly rotational burning, practised on grouse moors. This increases the amount and spread over the moors of young heather which is the sheep's preferred eating heather type. Heather burning is part of the prescribed management for Tier 1C, and has increased overall in the whole ESA since 1988.

It was mentioned in Section C that active shepherding is required to prevent sheep congregating locally and causing overgrazing. Studies showed that sheep were not evenly distributed, rather they formed clusters, and there was no change in these patterns over time, suggesting there had been little change in shepherding practices. This despite the fact that the management plans agreed with farmers under the ESA agreement "must also include the extent to which shepherding practices are to be implemented to minimise localised suppression of the heather margins and regenerating moorland vegetation".

One of the problems in this ESA region, and (other areas containing moor fringes) is the extent that bracken has spread, reducing the area of heather moorland and rough grazing grassland. Bracken is of little value to wild life and is avoided by sheep. So one objective of this ESA is to reduce the area of bracken by spraying. This had met with success, and some concomitant regeneration of characteristic moorland species has taken place (although a limited amount of re-colonisation by bracken took place through inadequate re-spraying).

Hedges, and more particularly, stone walls, are characteristic landscape features in this ESA, which therefore has preservation and restoration of these features as another objective. The majority of these features are not on the open moorland, but rather on the moorland fringes and in the valleys.

In 1993 hedgerows made up roughly 10% of linear features in the ESA. For monitoring purposes, hedgerows were classified into the categories continuous, discontinuous, derelict and trace. In terms of total length of hedgerows, this declined slightly between 1993 and 1996. However, this masks an improvement in terms of categories. There was an increase in both continuous and discontinuous hedges, matched by a decrease in derelict and trace hedges. Improvement in hedgerow continuity was greater on land under agreement than other land.

All this sounds quite good, but it must be kept in perspective. If you walk the Dark Peak area, you still see today very many gappy hedges, as was mentioned earlier in this chapter. The changes described by the monitoring process may have significantly limited further loss of hedgerows but they have only produced a very marginal net increase in the whole area. Some of the figures give indication of this. For example, on agreement land there was a net increase in the length of continuous hedgerows of 115% between 1993 and 1996. But this was caused by a net increase of just four hedgerows in the discontinuous class totalling 0.44 km, and small net decreases in the length of hedgerows in other continuity classes. As at 1996, within the samples used for monitoring, continuous hedgerows made up only 12% of all hedgerows (including trace hedgerows), or 18% (excluding trace hedgerows from the total).

Stone walls were classified into the same four categories. Over the period 1993-1996 the total length of walls decreased slightly. In terms of categories, there were increases in both continuous and trace walls, decreases in discontinuous and derelict walls. If one considers each wall category, land under agreement had different changes to land not under agreement. But if one thinks only in terms of improvement (moving up or down categories) there was little difference between land under agreement and land not under agreement.

Isolated trees. There was insufficient data to establish if there had been any changes between 1993 ad 1996. However, as reported in Section D, the majority of trees were in the older age classes. So we can expect a slow decrease in wayside trees unless active measures are taken to ensure replacement.

One of the serious problems in the Peak District as elsewhere in England is the loss of unimproved grassland through intensification of farming. Inadequacy of survey data prevented an assessment of possible changes attributable to ESA status. However, there are provisions for protecting and enhancing grasslands in the North Peak Tier system. Further, although these provisions did not originally include an option for dealing with semi-improved grassland, provision has been included for this category in the revised prescriptions for this ESA. Other recent additions to the suite of options available to farmers are the Traditional Hay Meadow Supplement and the Wet Area Supplement.

The South West Peak ESA

Grazing pressure was assessed by similar methods to those used in the North Peak ESA. Levels of heather grazing did decrease from 1993 to 1996 on the six monitored grazing units, as did the level of heather suppression. However, there was considerable variation between years. Also the sampled grazing units are not representative of all the moorland. In particular, they did not cover most of the peripheral areas or areas with very small blocks of heather – probably the areas most severely threatened from overgrazing. So the authors concluded that they could not extrapolate the result with the grazing units samples, to the whole heather area.

Furthermore, the recorded variation in stocking densities across the grazing units did not appear to have any obvious effect on the overall grazing levels, and the similarity of grazing levels that were found between agreement tiers is in their view, a reflection of this. Statistical analysis was carried out on the extent that Biomass Utilisation (BU) was spread evenly over the moors: The results suggest that if anything, grazing pressure has become more localised, not less, in 1996 compared with 1993. As with the North Peak ESA, the conclusion was that shepherding has been ineffective in dispersing sheep away from the most vulnerable areas of heather.

As was mentioned in an earlier section, controlled burning is a valuable method of moorland management as it encourages new shoot growth. Three burning seasons were monitored, and heather burning fell well below the levels really needed in all three seasons.

Monitoring of the bird populations was carried out in collaboration with the RSPB. The main results were reported in an earlier section – principally a decline in bird populations. Significantly, the ADAS report concluded that none of the changes in bird populations between 1996 and 1996 were related to the agreement status of the land.

As in the North Peak, stone walls (58% of all linear features in 1993) and to a lesser extent hedgerows (23% of all linear features) are characteristic landscape features. So hedgerows are a larger component here than in the North Peak ESA.

Changes in walls and hedgerows noted were quite similar to the changes reported above for the North Peak ESA.

The total length of stonewalls decreased slightly between 1993 and 1996. A similar proportion of walls were lost on agreement and non-agreement land. With the four wall continuity classes, there were increases in both continuous and trace walls. But the increase in the continuous wall category was mainly due to the renovation of one 5.1 km stretch of discontinuous wall (total wall length over all wall categories was 106.5 km in 1993).

With hedgerows, there was a slight overall decrease in total length between 1993 and 1995. There was a slight increase in the continuous hedgerow category. However, to put this in perspective: total hedgerow length in 1993 was nearly 43 km; the increase in the continuous category was only 0.2 km.

The overall conclusions of this monitoring report were stated quite bluntly, and amount in my view to an overall failure to improve the environment. These conclusions were as follows (in the light of what was written above, we may query whether the increases in stock proof walls are 'notable'!):

Objective 1. To maintain the wildlife conservation value and landscape quality of semi-natural upland vegetation and grassland. The objective has not been met.

Objective 2. To enhance the wildlife conservation and landscape value of semi-natural moorland vegetation. The objective has not been met.

Objective 3. To enhance the wildlife conservation value and landscape quality of species-rich meadows and pastures. This objective could not be assessed.

Objective 4. To maintain and enhance landscape quality through management of characteristic landscape elements.   This objective has been met through notable increases in the length of stockproof walls and to a lesser extent of hedgerows, and through smaller increases in other landscape elements.

Objective 5. To maintain and enhance archaeological and historical features. The objective has been met in part.

Countryside Stewardship Scheme (CSS)

The Country Stewardship Scheme is widely acknowledged as conferring real environmental benefit to the countryside (see previous chapter). And in the Peak District National Park the scheme has been widely taken up throughout the Park outside the ESA areas, although most of the agreements cover only small areas of land.

The agreements up to 1998 classified by landscape type are as follows (information supplied the author by MAFF):

Lead Landscape description	No. of Agreements	Area (ha)
Chalk & limestone grassland	77	1715.53
Field boundaries – hedges	2	11.34
Field boundaries – mixed	3	24.15
Field boundaries – walls	16	42.52
Historic landscapes – other	3	47.24
Historic landscapes – Park	2	41.22
Lowland Heath	1	83.99
Old meadows and pasture	21	330.53
Traditional buildings	2	
Uplands	95	2770.19
Waterside land	2	44.48
Total for Park	224	5111.19

Stated in the above form, the field boundary information is a bit misleading. The areas presumably mean the areas on farm under agreement on which there are these features.

Woodland Grant Scheme (WGS)

The National Parks authority signed an agreement with the Forestry authority in 1996, so that applicants to the national Woodland Grant Scheme are guided in their applications by the Farm and Countryside Service. The purpose of this is to try to ensure the agreements contribute most effectively to he achievement of Park objectives. The agreements made in 1997 and 1998 should see the creation of about 70 ha of native woodland.

The National Parks own scheme

The Farm and Countryside Service of the Park Authority is consulted on many aspects of the development and management of the national Schemes (ESA, CS, WGS) to try to ensure that the schemes address the particular needs of the Peak District. However, these national schemes still leave gaps in critical areas. So the Service has introduced its own scheme to supplement national schemes – the National Park Farm Conservation Scheme. This offers agreements with farmers and landowners of various durations up to 10 years. This scheme is offered when the Peak Park has been unable to broker agreements using the National Schemes. The Rates of grants and payments have been set in order to complement national Schemes payment rates. The 1999 Annual Review of this Service (PDNPA, 1999a) provides some indication of the scale of the Parks scheme. During 1998/89, 181 Farm Conservation Agreements were concluded. Work being carried out under these agreements is supposed to achieve:

      1) 13,260 metres of drystone walling;
      2) 1,827 trees and shrubs planted;
      3) 2,921 metres of hedgerows planted or restored;
      4) 46.29 hectares of grassland safeguarded.

Over the period 1988-1999, the 1999 review lists the following 'achievements':

      1) drystone walling - 227,259 m;
      2) tree/shrub planting – 76,282;
      3) hedgerows – 33,768 m;
      4) ponds – 51;
      5) grassland and moorland   about 1,902 ha.

Mention as made earlier of an important habitat – the Lead Rakes. It would be difficult to deal with these with the national CS scheme because they are narrow strips of low hectarage, while the CS scheme normally deals with whole fields. Now the Farm and Countryside Service has currently got a consultant looking into the issue of lead rake protection. Meanwhile, some agreements covering lead rake areas have been secured, although the Service prefers to secure these in relation to whole farm agreements. The situation is made more difficult by the fact that their are mineral rights on lead rakes, and these rights are often not held by the farmer, but by big landowners who have leased the rights to mineral companies.

The Service also sees its Scheme as potentially useful in preventing further intensification of farming practice, which might occur when a farm changes hands. Thus if a farmer wants to retire, the new owner might want to intensify production. If the Farm and Countryside Service can persuade the present owner to make an agreement before sale, the new owner will have to comply with the conditions.

Finally mention should be made of the possibility of the Park Authority purchasing land to ensure conservation and enhancement of the environment. This option has not been used much. But recently, using Heritage Lottery money, the Park has purchased nearly 100 acres of land above Sheldon (west of Bakewell). This area has 13 hay meadows and some lead rakes, small plantations and ponds. They bought this land because someone had bought the neighbouring land and 'improved it' and the Park Authority thought the same thing would happen to this other area if they did not purchase it. The Park Authority intends the area to be farmed by a tenant who will have to observe covenant conditions.

K. Conclusions. Do we need a National Park Authority?

To a degree, the aims of the National Park are contradictory. On the one hand the Park should conserve natural beauty and wildlife, on the other hand it should promote opportunities for public enjoyment of the park. This problem is stated, in relation to road traffic, by Government circular 125/77 (Department of Environment and Department of Transport, 1977), which follows on the report of the Sandford Committee that reviewed National Park policies. The circular states that much can be done to reconcile public enjoyment and preservation of natural beauty; this can be achieved by good planning and management. Nevertheless, the circular concludes, there will be situations where the two purposes are not reconcilable. Significantly, the circular states that where this is the case, priority must be given to the conservation of natural beauty.

Now that was right back in 1977. Since then the population of England has grown considerably. Developments on the transport front (new motorways, increased car ownership) mean that more people now travel to the Parks, and are prepared to travel greater distances to reach them. Increasingly, this has heightened irreconcilability of objectives. And when you consider the present extent of road traffic and parking in the Peak Park and concomitant noise, and the pressure put on the habitat, wildlife and peacefulness of the countryside by walkers and those pursuing a variety of recreational pursuits, one may doubt if the above stated priority has indeed been achieved.

However, to the extent that the assessment of the situation assumed by Circular 125/77 is now out of date, and the extent that the circular was perhaps over optimistic about the powers of planning and management, it could be argued that it was an unrealistic expectation that the Park Authorities could fulfil their obligations to reconcile conflicting aims. Radical strong measures need to be introduced at National level – an illustration of the proposition that we need radical measures as mentioned in the Introduction of this book – but such measures have not been introduced. Nevertheless, why did the PPJPB not avoid putting any car parks well within the Park, instead putting them all just inside the boundary, and then making arrangements with Derby County Council and other authorities to service these car parks with buses?

It seems reasonable to conclude from the evidence given in this chapter, that although environmental deterioration has been slowed or halted in some respects, and some restoration of landscape and habitat features has taken place, overall, the countryside in the Peak District National Park has deteriorated in recent decades in a similar way to the deterioration in England in general.

Further, in so far as environmental improvement has been achieved, prime responsibility for this has not been with the Peak District National Parks Authority, but with other bodies, particularly MAFF and EN. It is these other authorities, which control national agri-environment schemes. Furthermore, while the park authority has its own National Park Conservation Scheme, the greater part of the money used by the Farm and Countryside Service for all its activities comes from national bodies – the Forestry Commission, English Nature, and most importantly, the Ministry of Agriculture, Fisheries and Food (MAFF). While the Park Authority through its services attempts to coordinate the environmental policy of these outside bodies, surely such coordination is needed in all parts of the country. There should be the equivalent of the Park's Farm and Countryside Service in every region of Britain!

In terms of stated purposes and objectives, the Park authority seems to have been successful in promoting the enjoyment of the park (with the concomitant increase in motorised traffic and noise in the park, and damage to natural habitats through trampling and disturbance). It may well have also had some success in promoting understanding of the park's special qualities, through its Farm and Countryside Service, Rangers, and Study Centre, although I have not included the latter in my study through time constraints. It may also have had success in promoting 'economic well-being', if by that is primarily meant start up and maintenance of business activity in the park, irrespective of whether that business is primarily concerned with traditional rural activities.

But in terms of conserving and enhancing natural beauty and wildlife, it does not seen to have been very successful. And in terms of fostering social well-being, it does not seem to have been particularly successful either, except in relation to those affluent people who have emigrated into the Park, thereby contributing to rising house prices, making it difficult for local people to obtain housing, and disrupting village communities.

One may then legitimately raise the question, should we have a Peak National Park Authority at all? Would it not be better to abolish it, and allow National and Regional authorities to take over completely, responsibility for the Peak District? This would mean some loss of jobs, although Park staff carrying out basic work such as ecology etc, as distinct from administrators, could probably be recruited by the authorities taking over from the Park Authority. And there would be a saving in the region of six million pounds annually – money that it may be argued, would be better spent by other authorities. Such a move would promote an improvement of environmental strategy because it would encourage the integration of park area strategy with regional strategies.

Now Park officials, in defending the work of the authority, rightly point out that their work has been made very difficult because of divided authority over the area, outlined earlier. They also rightly point out that EU and National Law is weak in some respects for achieving genuine environmental improvement. Degradation of agricultural land may be largely blamed on agricultural policy beyond the control of the Park Authorities. And when one reads ADAS and other reports one keeps coming on statements that access to a particular piece of land was not given to Park researchers by the landowners/tenants, which does not help the monitoring process. But one is left with the nagging doubt – could the Authority not have done a great deal more if it had really put concern for the environment at the centre of its efforts.

The approach of the Park Authorities is to build partnerships with the people who live and work in the Park, recognising the need for trust and understanding (Peak Park, 1999b). This is however the now universal rhetoric of all authorities – it would be endorsed by the National Government, City Councils, Uncle Tom Cobbly and all. One is left wondering if this is not often a cloak – here and elsewhere - for avoiding what would be absolutely necessary confrontations if environmental improvement were to be attained, and at the same for assisting business and other interests in such a way that officials secure their own prospects for the future.

The alternative to abolishing the Park Authority would be for the government to nationalise the Park – to purchase all the land, by compulsory purchase if necessary. And then to insist on applying existing environmental measures fully, at the same time, of course, as improving environmental law.

Chapter 8

Town and country, transport and pollution

A. Introduction

Increase in road transport has had various disastrous environmental effects. Road building has taken large areas of green land. Often this land has been especially valuable for wild life, or has been good quality agricultural land. In rural districts the desire to improve vehicle flow has led to straightening and widening of country lanes, destroying much of their essentially rural, and local character; increasing vehicle flow in rural areas has made it not only less pleasant, but positively dangerous to walk or cycle along roads. And through vehicle noise road transport has destroyed the peacefulness of vast areas of rural England (various publications of CPRE such as 1996b). Road transport has increased atmospheric pollution enormously, and we shall see later (section E of this chapter) that this affects the countryside as well as urban areas. Increased private car transport has adversely affected the health of the people not only through atmospheric pollution but also through depriving people of the exercise necessary to maintain health. Road transport dominates the land transport scene, both for freight and people. And with people, private car transport dominates over public bus transport. In terms of energy conservation this is unfortunate since rail transport is more energy efficient than road freight transport, and bus transport than private car transport.

For a long time there has been a call for an integrated transport policy. Such a policy would have two overall aims:
1) to integrate together the different modes of transport; especially to integrate road transport with rail transport (road with rail haulage), and integrate private and public transport (private cars with buses and railways, one aim being to reduce car use); 2) to integrate transport development with all land use planning, to ensure the contiguity of housing with services and centres of employment, thus reducing the need for car travel. It is in connection with this last aspect and the question of freedom of mobility that a slogan has become popular in the policy debate - 'accessibility rather than mobility'.

The development of transport policy until recent times was reported in Barker (1998), which made use especially of CPRE, 1992a). I pointed out there that many of our present day problems were with us a long time ago. In particular I noted how in the 1963 "traffic in towns" report of Colin Buchanan and others (SWGMT, 1963), attention was drawn to the already existing traffic congestion in towns, highlighting the urgency of the need to solve traffic problems. Indeed the report said "The problems of traffic are crowding in upon us with desperate urgency". This report pointed out that there are absolute limits to the amount of traffic that can be accepted in towns and noted that the motorcar has a tendency to disperse development. This was because a car-based society needed more space per person (the spatial demand of vehicles for circulation and parking) and because the car increased facility of movement, making out-of-town car-based shopping centres and work places more feasible and therefore more attractive to developers. The report goes on to sketch out the way to develop a transport policy, which is very similar to current thinking. It mentions the importance of urban form for minimising traffic movement; it notes that one must influence demand for car use, and mentions the options: permits or licences to control entry into defined zones, road pricing, parking policy, subsidising public transport so that it offers considerable financial advantages over the use of cars. It concludes that in the long run, the most potent factor in maintaining a 'ceiling' on private car traffic in busy areas is likely to be the provision of good, cheap public transport, coupled with the understanding of the public about the position. All this was said nearly four decades ago!

B. Land lost to roads and parking

Road building has made a major contribution to the loss of green land to development. By 1995, the area of land allocated to roads was, according to the Council for the Protection of Rural England, already 1,456 km^2 in England, and 2,848 km^2 in the UK as a whole. I calculate that the England area is roughly four times the area of the city of Sheffield (which of course contains a large area of roads), and CPRE calculate that the UK figure is larger than the whole of Leicestershire (CPRE, 1995b). Motorways are especially land greedy. Each km of road takes about 7.5 ha land. But road construction does more than remove greenland, it also causes damage to other land. For rock has to be quarried to make the roads. Thus each km of motorway uses 120,000 tonnes of quarried aggregate (CPRE1992b). To the area of land lost to roads themselves, must however be added the area lost to parking provision. CPRE divide parking space into a number of categories, such as supermarket parking, parks and schools and hospitals, etc. The category using the most land was residential parking, and the next biggest category, heavy goods vehicle parking. Taken together, CPRE estimate that the area in the UK given over to parking is over 590 km^2 - an area of land twice the size of Birmingham (CPRE, 1995). Over half the land lost is agricultural land. Many locally valued wildlife sites are lost or damaged. In 1991 the then Roads Minister listed 27 SSSIs and 12 AONBs that would be adversely affected by trunk road improvements alone (CPRE 1993). WWF et al (1996) claims that 69 SSSIs were threatened by the then government road building programme.

C. Increase of road traffic

There has been a steady and massive increase in road use in recent decades. For example, traffic grew by roughly 40% between 1984 and 1994.

Private car use has increased greatly in recent decades. So that by 1998, travel by bus and train accounted for less than 10% of distance travelled in Britain. As far as freight is concerned, the proportion of freight carried by road has steadily risen, for example from 53% to 63% during the eighties (CPRE 1992b). Forecasts suggest that road traffic will more than double on rural roads by AD 2025 (CPRE 1996a). The 1989 National Road Traffic Forecasts suggest that if the proportion of freight carried by road continues to increase, light goods vehicle traffic will rise in line with growth in GDP up to 2025; heavy goods traffic will also increase but more slowly, but could be as high as an increase of 140% by 2025. The increase in freight transport in recent times is not just a question of there being more vehicles on the roads. It is also a question of the distance travelled by vehicles. This can be seen using the measure tonne kilometres, which is the weighted total of the distances travelled by each vehicle load of goods. Over the last 30 years the total tonnage of goods carried in Britain has not varied much. But the trend in tonne kilometres is different. There was slow growth in this measure in the 1950s, but it rose more rapidly to 1993, actually an increase of 141% on 1952 (this increase parallels the growth of Gross Domestic Product). The increase in average freight trip length was from about 37km in 1952, to 84km in 1993. By 1993, road was the predominant form of freight transport, accounting for 63% of the total tonne kilometres. The rest of tonne kilometres in 1993 were accounted for by coastal shipping, 25%; rail, 6.5% and pipeline, 5.5% (UKRTSD, 1996a). This low contribution by the rail network is very worrying in terms of traffic congestion, and also in terms of energy use since rail transport is more energy efficient.

D. Energy use by transport

The need to conserve natural resources makes it very pertinent to compare the energy consumption of different modes of transport. Here, car travel is less efficient than other modes, although relative efficiencies vary with occupancy rate. FoE (1994), using information from the European Communities, gives the following information. Energy consumption was given in mega joules primary energy/passenger/kilometre. The following transport modes were compared:
a) petrol car,<1.4 litres; b) petrol car >1.4 litre; c) diesel car <1.4 litre; d) diesel car >1.4 litre;
e) rail (suburban electric): f) bus (double decker).

The 25% occupancy figures were:
a) 2.61; b) 4.65; c) 2.26; d) 3.65; e) 1.05; f) 0.7;
the 50% figures:
a) 1.31; b) 2.33; c) 1.13; d) 1.83; e) 0.59; f) 0.35;
the 75% figures:
a) 0.87; b) 1.55; c) 0.75; d) 1.22; e) 0.35; f) 0.23;
the 100% figures:
a) 0.62; b) 1.16; c) 0.57; d) 0.91; e) 0.26; f) 0.17.

Another way of looking at relative energy efficiency of different modes is to compare on the one hand, their shares of total UK energy consumption for transport, with, on the other hand, their shares in the movement of people and goods. Road, rail and water use respectively 94%, 2.4% and 3.5% of the energy consumption by surface transport in the UK. But their shares of net mass movement by UK transport are, again for road, rail and water, 69%, 7.5% (7.8% for goods and 5.7% for people) and 24%. To complete the picture, we compare walking, cycling and motoring in built up areas. A 70 kg person walking uses 0.14 mega joule/km; using a 20kg bicycle, 0.035 mega joule/km; but cars use 2.8mega joules/passenger/km during commuting in urban areas (RCEP, 1994). These facts are very interesting in connection with the campaign to persuade people to walk or cycle rather than drive in towns.

E. Pollution

(i) From transport

When fuel (including petroleum) is burnt completely, carbon dioxide (CO_2) and water result. So carbon dioxide is one emission from vehicle engines. However, engines are never 100% efficient, so there are by-products that are pollutants, to which must be added impurities in the fuel used. So Exhaust fumes include sulphur dioxide (SO_2), oxides of nitrogen (NO, NO_2, NO_3, collectively called NO_X), volatile organic compounds (VOCs), carbon monoxide (CO), lead, and particulates ('black smoke').

What share of total UK airborne pollution is attributable to transport? The following percentage estimates for 1992 are from RCEP (ibid):

carbon monoxide	90 (91)
nitrogen oxides	57 (61)
volatile organic compounds	38 (48)
particulates	48 (48)
sulphur dioxide	4 (7)

The figures in brackets include transport-related emissions from oil refineries and power stations.

It can be seen that transport makes a major contribution to pollution. If terms of the different components of transport (road, rail, air, shipping), road is by far the biggest contributor to the totals with carbon monoxide, nitrogen oxides and VOCs. The only major pollutant that transport makes only a very small contribution to is sulphur dioxide. Most of the atmospheric sulphur dioxide comes from fossil fuel combustion, especially coal, with power stations making the largest contribution.

Pollutants are strongly suspected of causing diseases, such as respiratory diseases, cancer, and now, heart attacks. Correlations between high pollutant levels and diseases are well established (for example, the growth in emissions of NOxs from traffic is strongly correlated with the increase in the number of asthma cases). But association, or correlation, is not the same as causation, and in general, it is proving difficult to actually nail down particular pollutants as causes of particular diseases, although we know for example that benzene, one of the VOCs, is one of many causes of cancer; there is evidence that tropospheric (near ground) ozone, the production of which is stimulated by NO_2, increases susceptibility to infections, and like some VOCs irritates mucous membranes and damages lung function.

There is evidence that both vanadium and nickel inhalation causes asthma, both cadmium and arsenic various cancers, chromium and very fine dust particles, cancer of the lung, heart damage, and other effects. We know that lead adversely affects the brain. carbon monoxide and/or hydrogen sulphide can damage red blood cells, may affect the brain, and block an important metabolic pathway in the liver, which is the body's pathway to detoxify pollutants inhaled and swallowed. One piece of telling evidence that pollutants cause disease comes from studies, which relate disease incidence to the distance from particular (types of) pollution source. Normally here, if you plot incidence on the Y axis and distance on the X axis, you find a peak incidence at a distance from the polluting source –which for example if you are considering vehicle emissions is close to the roads, but if you consider incinerator emissions, is further away - and then the disease incidence gradually falls away over distance (one of the points that the medically qualified environmental campaigner Dr. D. Van Steenis makes in his talks to local groups up and down the country. And the information in the preceding paragraph came from his unpublished papers (Van Steenis, 1999a and 1999b).

In general terms, where are the concentrations of pollutants greatest? Common sense would suggest that the highest concentrations are in urban areas. However, the situation is not quite as simple as that, and we shall see that to take this matter further one needs to distinguish between what are called primary pollutants and secondary pollutants. Primary pollutants are those substances originally emitted from the polluting source, be it a car engine or any other source. Secondary pollutants are formed in the atmosphere through interaction of the primary pollutants with each other and with other components of the atmosphere, assisted sometimes by energy from sunlight. The chief secondary pollutants attributable to transport are nitrogen dioxide (NO_2) and ozone (O_3).

As far as primary pollutants are concerned, the highest concentrations are found where emissions are greatest. High in urban areas, they are two to three times the general urban 'background' level alongside major roads. Samples of air taken from inside vehicles travelling on major roads have even higher concentrations. The increased health risks are obvious.

With secondary pollutants, the situation is more complex (RCEP, ibid). Small amounts of NO_2 are found in vehicle emissions, but much more is rapidly formed in the atmosphere through the oxidation of NO emitted from vehicles by ozone ($NO + O_3$ gives $NO_2 + O_2$), or by the hydroperoxy radical ($NO + HO_2\cdot$ gives $NO_2 + \cdot OH$). So NO removes ozone. But in the atmosphere, this NO_2 is the main precursor of ozone! The energy of sunlight converts NO_2 to NO and $O\cdot$ Then $O\cdot + O_2$ gives O_3. The air masses drift away from urban areas, so the highest concentrations of ozone are usually found in rural or suburban areas (this account is a simplification of the situation which is described more fully in the Royal Commission report).

Ozone is not of course the only pollutant that is so blown over into rural areas. So although pollution may originate primarily in towns, it comes to be spread around the country (and as we shall see later, abroad). Now many pollutants directly, or indirectly (for example by causing acid rain), damage vegetation, although again, as with the question of the causation of human disease, it is still proving difficult to sort out the relative contributions of different pollutants, and the mechanisms of their action (Mansfield and Lucas, 1996).

Vehicle emissions make a major contribution to global warming (the 'greenhouse effect'). The so-called greenhouse gases include water vapour, carbon dioxide, methane and nitrous oxide, and the latter three have significantly increased in the atmosphere through human activity. Carbon dioxide has made a much bigger contribution to the greenhouse effect than the other gases (estimated as 65% in the 1980s). Of the UK's carbon dioxide emissions, 21% come from surface transport, and road transport accounts for 87% of transport related emissions (RCEP, ibid). Carbon monoxide indirectly contributes to global warming: methane (produced for example when cattle belch and fart, but vehicle emissions only contain a little) is another greenhouse gas. methane undergoes oxidation in the atmosphere, but CO interferes with this oxidation, thus raising atmospheric methane levels.

Vehicle emissions contribute to depletion of the ozone layer by the action of NO_xs in the stratosphere (upper atmosphere). More significant however, for this effect, are the chlorinated fluorocarbons (CFCs) used as coolants in refrigerators and air-conditioning systems, as propellants for aerosol cans, and to produce the bubbles in some plastic foam containers. These have been largely banned in the developed world, although still allowed in the developing world; but now there is evidence of import for illegal use in Europe of CFCs manufactured in Russia, China and India (BBC news 3rd September 1997 reporting on work by the Environmental Investigation Agency). CFCs are also greenhouse gases.

How have levels of atmospheric pollutants varied over recent time, and what are the prospects for the future? As far as changes in the concentrations of traffic generated pollutants in recent decades are concerned, there has until recently been little long-term monitoring of many of these pollutants. However, it is likely that concentration in urban areas of NO_xs, CO, VOCs and particulate matter have increased during the decades after the Second World War (Holman, 1996). There have however been reductions in some pollutants during the last decade (DETR 1999c). Most vehicle emissions may be gradually reduced in the near future since controls over emissions are being progressively tightened under EU regulations (UKRTSD 1996a -but see below). One of the most spectacular changes that has already taken place is the decrease of lead. Two factors have been responsible - a) reducing the permitted lead level in fuel; b) encouraging the use of unleaded petrol. Sales of unleaded petrol have risen from almost nothing in the mid-1980s to over 65% by 1996. The result is that lead concentrations were down to about 20% of what they were in the 1970s (Holman, ibid; HMSO, 1996). Emissions of SO_2 have decreased fairly steadily from 1970 onwards, but are still very high (in 1994 the level was a little under three million tonnes) (HMSO ibid).

What about CO_2? According to government sources, emissions have decreased (not very steadily) from 1970 onwards. And the government claims, Britain will be one of a handful of developed countries who are 'on course' to meet commitments made at the 1992 'earth summit' in Rio where the Framework Convention on Climate Change was signed (HMSO, ibid). Emissions are however, in absolute term, enormous. Further more, there are tendencies working to at least partly vitiate attempts at reduction of emission levels. The number of vehicles on the roads still increases. Tightening controls on vehicle emissions mentioned above are not expected to reduce road freight emissions without radical policy change. At present, it is estimated that in Europe, lorries are responsible for only about 4% of human activity caused CO_2 emission. But according to current forecasts the growth of road freight transport will increase CO_2 emissions by approximately 30% relative to 1990 by the year 2000, and 60% by 2010 (UKRTSD, ibid).

(ii) from agriculture

The pollution of rivers, groundwater, lakes and estuaries, even seas, is now a major problem in Western Europe. Effluent from intensive livestock production has now taken over from the chemical industry as the chief source of both river and groundwater pollution; pollution from intensified arable agriculture has also made a big, but lesser contribution to this water pollution problem. The increased use of fertiliser in both arable and grassland areas, and vastly increased animal wastes (from cows, pigs, etc) has led to increased concentrations of nitrates and phosphates in the soil which leads to run-off into, and pollution of, water channels. And it is estimated that 5-6 percent of the European human population is now being supplied with drinking water which contains more nitrate than the permitted EU maximum of 50 mg NO_3/litre, and 25 percent of the population is using water with a level greater than the optimum of 25 mg/l. Consequently, water supply administrators are finding it more and more difficult to control nitrate levels (Gardner, 1996).

Agriculture accounts for 60-90% of ammonia emissions in Britain. It is produced by animal waste decomposition, mainly in livestock holding buildings, waste stores and in slurry spread over the land. The ammonia contributes to the formation of acid rain and this leads to acidification of freshwater. Deposits of ammonia as a gas or as ammonium salts in the soil has a damaging effect on vegetation and alters the vegetation composition of some habitats (Baldock et al 1996; MAFF, 1992). Inorganic and organic nitrate and phosphate running off into waterways leads to a process termed eutrophication. These substances cause increased plant productivity - a bloom of plant life. But it leads also to a massive increase in microorganisms, which use up oxygen in decomposing organic materials. Cattle and pig slurry and silage effluent in particular create very high oxygen demands. In extreme cases, oxygen depletion in waterways can lead to death of aquatic animal life including fish (MAFF, 1993).

Agriculture is a major producer of greenhouse gases. While it only contributes a share of about two percent of total UK carbon dioxide, it contributes 32% of the methane and 17% of the nitrous oxide. The methane comes largely from farm animals in their belching and farting and from stored slurry. Nitrous oxide comes from the reaction of nitrogen containing compounds in manures and soils, especially under anaerobic (absence of oxygen) conditions. These massive contributions to greenhouse emissions are caused by the intensification of agriculture already discussed. Pollution by pesticides is also a problem, and we have already seen the importance of this for wild life. As far as human health is concerned, it has proved difficult to evaluate the impact of pesticides. Apart from accidents or wilful misuse, the threat to life itself is probably not a serious one, and pesticide residues in average diets, according to authorities referred to by Gardner (ibid) are well below "acceptable daily intakes". However, a fundamental problem remains, namely, that no one knows what the minimum (threshold) concentration of various substances are if possible long term health effects like cancer are to be avoided, or indeed if there is any threshold concentration.

(iii) Pollution in general

If we wish to consider the level and seriousness of pollution we have to recognise the significance for impact, of basic facts about the human population - its size and density. In the first place, the amount of waste generated is linked to population size. Second, the impact of pollution on a country as a whole will depend partly on the density of the population - for a given population size, the impact on the total environment of the country will clearly be less if the population is sparse (the country relatively large) than if the overall population is dense (the country small). Unfortunately for us, England is in a disadvantageous position on both counts. We have a large and dense population. But much of continental Europe is densely populated also, and Gardner (ibid) states that the pollution concentration in the northwestern countries of Europe is among the highest in the developed world. The amount of pollution generated also depends on the affluence of the population. To take an obvious example. As a country becomes more affluent, more people are likely to own cars, and hence vehicle emissions rise. And finally, the amount of pollution depends on the degree of technological development in the country. A primitive society, while it may contribute to global warming through using wood fires for cooking, has no ability to produce pollutants like SO_2 from power stations since it does not have these. On the other hand, technological innovation can reduce pollution levels, and the developed world tends to employ cleaner technologies for power stations and other facilities than the developing world.

The environment, or any subdivision of it, seems to be able to cope with a limited quantity of pollutants, and to some extent neutralise, transform or utilise them. Consider CO_2; this is abstracted by green plants in the process of photosynthesis. Clearly, however there are limits to the quantity of CO_2 that plants can remove. Soils too play a major role in removing pollutants. But these pollutants can pass on into surface waters or ground waters, and the extent that this occurs depends partly on the nature of the soil. Clay soils are especially good at removing and retaining pollutants: they have a low permeability and contaminants become absorbed on to the tiny clay particles. However, if the soil cracks in dry weather and subsequently there is heavy rain, pollutants such as pesticides can drain rapidly into surface waters. In contrast to clay soils, soils with much higher particle size - soils with high sand or gravel content - allow water to flow through much faster and may have very little capacity for absorbing pollutants. Even clay soils cannot go on absorbing pollutants indefinitely. Sooner or later there is likely to come a point- perhaps triggered by changing conditions, when the soil ceases to be a 'sink' for pollutants and becomes a 'source'. And the term 'chemical time bomb' became used to refer to the accumulation and later release of phosphates and heavy metals from heavily manured agricultural soils. There is now considerable pressure to make use of derelict land which may be contaminated, Now as mines become disused, water pumping may be ended. Such changes can trigger off the release of accumulated chemicals. In ground water, some absorption of pollutants takes place by the rocks through which the waters pass. But dispersal and dilution, which helps to clean surface waters, occurs much less in ground water, and such waters can become unfit for public supply (RCEP, 1996).

Acidity is one of the determinants of what types of plant grow where, and acidity varies naturally from one area to another Thus soils and waters in upland areas of Britain tend to be relatively acidic. Now air pollution leads to increased acidification of soils and waters. And increased acidification can in turn lead to the release of metals into water, metals which may be harmful to plant and animal life. Conifer afforestation seems to be also implicated in causing increased acidification in some areas. These plants have the capacity to actively absorb pollutants directly from the atmosphere. Recall (Chapter 5) that the area of Britain covered in conifers has increased since the Second World War.

Some recent changes in the distribution and abundance of plants and animals are attributed to changes in acidity and/or the release of metals. So, for example, in upland areas of Wales, there has been a decline in plants requiring less acidic, more basic soils. In general, acid deposition in soils has a bad effect on most soil organisms (bacteria, fungi, etc) - organisms that are essential for the proper functioning of soil. In Wales, trout populations in an estimated 12,000km of rivers and tributaries have been reduced or even eliminated by acidification (RCEP, ibid). Sphagnum moss has declined in areas like the southern Pennines. This was attributed to atmospheric SO_2. However, since the 1950's atmospheric SO_2 concentrations have fallen considerably and yet the sphagnum has not recovered. It is thought that this is due to increased concentration of nitrogenous pollutants (Mansfield and Lucas, 1996).

The fact that beyond certain limits, pollutants can harm plants and animals, has led to much attention to be given to explore what those limits are; this has been spurred on by the need to establish air quality and soil quality standards. In this connection, researchers refer to critical loads and critical levels of pollutants. These terms relate to the level of pollution below which significant adverse effects are not observed (critical loads), and above which they are (critical levels). While present data is very limited, it was concluded in 1996 that the critical levels of all the major pollutants except ammonia was exceeded in some part of the UK during the previous five years, the biggest offender being ozone (Mansfield and Lucas, ibid). Work carried out by the Critical Loads Mapping and Data Centre show large areas of the UK where critical loads are exceeded RCEP (ibid).

What are the prospects for the future? Both the European Community and the United Nations Economic Commission for Europe recognise the dangers of pollution. They have both set targets for reductions of emissions of sulphur and nitrogen, and the UK is committed to reach these targets. However, RCEP (ibid) concludes that these limits are inadequate to prevent critical loads being exceeded. For example, it is likely that many SSSIs will still be receiving sulphur in excess of the critical loads for soil acidity in 2005.

Finally, atmospheric pollution demonstrates very clearly that one cannot isolate one country from other countries in considering environmental degradation. The prevailing south-westerly winds over Britain mean that atmospheric pollutants produced here are to some extent carried in the atmosphere over to the continent, contributing to the damage of forests and water life there. For example, a recent report from Sweden speaks of the widespread acidification of Swedish forest soils and concomitant leaching out of mineral nutrients, caused by a high level of air pollution combined with the low buffering capacity of the soils. The report states that this pollution mainly originates abroad. Critical loads have been exceeded for both sulphur dioxide and nitrogen dioxide. It concludes that air pollution poses a serious threat to the forest ecosystem (SI, 1996).

On one of the main routes to Kinderscout. On the way to Jacob's Ladder from Barber Booth

Looking towards upper Lathkill Dale from the SW, showing the vegetation differences between valley slopes and the 'improved' meadows above this limestone area.

Looking towards Edale Moor and Kinderscout from the Lose Hill ridge, showing the Edale Valley and, on the slopes, the boundary between enclosed land and open moorland.

The big quarry south of Eyam, looking from the North, and showing also the path to Black Harry Gate and upper Coombs Dale.

Bare peat on Kinder Scout.

Showing how deep the peat can be on the moors - on the way from Kinder Downfall to Grindsbrook.

Narrow regularly arranged stonewall bounded fields are characteristic features of some parts of the White Peak. The walls mark the boundaries of medieval agricultural strips which were not individually bounded.

Lead rakes are common linear features in the White Peak. Tideslow Rake near Little Hucklow.

Upland meadows in the White Peak have been transformed by intensification of farming practice. A field full of rye-grass near Priestcliffe.

Hedgerows can become tree rows; both can become 'gappy'. This row of hawthorns is alongside the path between Edale and Barber Booth.

A little pond that has formed in old mine workings on the hillside above Eyam. A small but very valuable wildlife site.

Wetland habitats at Blackburn Meadows, Sheffield. Developed at a former sewage farm, this area is now a valuable wildlife site; businesses like to locate near such pleasant landscapes.

Chapter Nine

General strategy and a long-term goal

A. General strategy

It is universally recognised that mankind's impact on the environment is excessive, and we saw in Chapter 1 that this impact has three causal components, expressed in the Sustainability Equation I=PAT, or I=PCT. The logical thing to do would be to try to directly ameliorate the effects of all three components. However, as I also said in Chapter 1, most environmentalists do not advocate taking direct action on population.

One of the reasons that environmentalists do not advocate such a population policy is that they consider it would be politically impossible to achieve. Yet most environmentalists do advocate a reduction of the material standard of living in the developed world (reduction in the A or C component of the sustainability equation). Now society in countries like the UK is dominated by self-interest, with everyone wanting an even higher standard of living than they have at present. So is it not just as impossible to persuade people to bring about a reduction of the C or A component of the equation, as it is to persuade them to take direct action on the P component?

I argue that the environmental situation is so serious that we will have to attempt the impossible, and take action on all three impact components directly. The next chapter explores action with population.

B. Strategy should be based on a carefully defined long-term goal package

Environmentalists recognise we need to take a long-term perspective in considering the environmental problem, maintaining indeed that sustainable development requires such an approach (e.g. Blowers, 1993). And they also note that while the environmental problem requires long-term solutions, political and economic decision-making is dominated by short-term considerations (e.g. WWF, 1994). Nevertheless, the emphasis in most of the writings of environmentalists is on short and medium term measures. When long-term goals are mentioned, they are usually of a general nature. I suggest that we need to focus our attention much more on long term planning if we are really serious about our responsibilities to future generations of mankind. We need to develop a vision of what England should be like several or even many generations ahead, a vision which integrates all aspects of the environment and of our society in a long term goal package (Barker, 1998).

The attention of planners seems to be focused on the medium term future. Consider a topic right at the heart of the present book – the loss of green land to housing. If you read the literature you will find that there is a general vague goal of reducing the rate of loss of greenland to development (for example, CPRE 1993), but attention is most commonly focused on how much green land will be lost to housing by say 2021 (see Chapter 2), almost as if all the processes causing green land to be lost to housing will suddenly stop at such a date. Adopting this approach absolves us from considering uncomfortable questions, of which the most important I think concern possible future population growth.

The approach leads to an underestimation of the value of greenland, and the need to retain it. For example, we find the TCPA (1997b) declaring that for development decisions, land per se has no privileged place. It is just one element in the total ecosystem. Rural land, once urbanised, is unlikely to return to rural use; but this is not necessarily a key consideration, provided the remaining rural land is capable of yielding equivalent amounts of renewable natural resources, and as long as the effect on the total ecosystem (for instance in terms of photosynthesis) is not adversely affected. The paper goes on to suggest that the most important concern about rural land use is not about the land itself, but rather the fact that development in rural land might stimulate motorised travel with concomitant high consumption of non-renewable resources (fossil fuels) and high levels of pollution.

Such statements hardly seem to recognise the danger to quality of countryside of reducing the finite and small area of green land left in England. Over the medium term, the loss of countryside area might not be great, but if current trends continue, this loss would be very large in the long term. And the choice of examples (renewable natural resources, photosynthetic activity) conjures up the picture of a future countryside given over to plant production for purely utilitarian purposes - food production, coppice willow for fuel, a sink for removal of excess carbon dioxide (through photosynthesis). It is difficult to square this TCPA statement with their other assertion that they are committed to maintaining and increasing biological diversity, and encouraging wildlife. And the approach seems to completely ignore aesthetic considerations - what about the value of the countryside as a haven of tranquillity, and of beauty arising in part out of the peculiar mix of different land uses that we associate with our countryside? Finally, many feel, as the present writer does, that nature, that wildlife, have rights too, in other words the world about us does not just exist for our support and pleasure. The present writer asserts then, that land should have a privileged place in any policy/planning process.

Focusing on the medium term has another disadvantage: past experience shows that policies are rarely completely implemented, targets rarely met in full. Each medium term period ends with at best a very incomplete realisation of the aims adopted at the beginning of the period. This might not be very serious for one time period; but over a succession of periods these short falls accumulate with devastating effect.

I argue that we need to develop a detailed long-term vision of our country and use this to inform and control all policymaking. We need a goal package, which specifies for some date in the long-term future the desired total population size, the allocation of land for various functions, and all aspects of the economy. Only in this way will we be able to achieve sustainable development, and more particularly, safeguard our countryside. Only if we hold in our heads such a vision will we realise that very radical measures are needed now, and summon up the courage to advocate them whole-heartedly.

The lack of a detailed long-term vision hampers any attempt to get the necessary support of the people of the land for adopting radical measures. In the prologue to this book, I referred to the phenomenon of the debasement of human expectations. Successive generations of people may adjust to the debasement of the environment, because their own experience of this debasement only covers a small part of the total debasement time span so they have no real experience of what the environment was at a healthier early stage, and therefore do not realise what they are missing, what they have lost.

Clearly one thing we can do is to draw peoples attention to the positive features of our past environment, make them understand just how far things have really gone on the pathway of environmental degradation. Hence the need to draw the attention of people to analyses like the one I make in the first part of this book. But we should be doing a lot more than that. Besides showing what we have lost, we need to put before people a vision of the ideal future state, a vision that involves a lot more than a collection of positive past environmental features. This vision would be based on our understanding of the potentialities of man, including our admittedly imperfect understanding of the potentials of our technology. This vision would make people far more discontented with the present situation and inspire them to take an active part in changing it. In this way we might secure the support of the public for radical planning measures. Likewise if we want planners to take their environmental responsibilities seriously, they must have constantly before them, the vision of the long-term future state. Adequate short and medium term goals will not be devised without such a vision.

There are obvious objections to the long-term goal package proposal. In the first place, it can be argued - what right have we now, at the beginning of the new millennium, to dictate to future generations how their society shall be shaped? And definitions of sustainable development seem to imply future generations setting their own goals:

"Development that meets the needs of the present without compromising the ability of future generations to meet their own needs".

This often quoted definition seems, in my view, to weaken our responsibility for long term planning now, particularly when the end of the definition is modified to..."to achieve their own goals", a definition which WWF (1994) accepts. It is as if people were saying that what we have to do is simply to get the environment into a reasonable state now, so that future generations can decide what to do when the time comes. But unless we take long term planning more seriously now, the range of options of future generations might be greatly curtailed. For example, while current projections have our UK population peaking about AD 2036 (Chapter2), there is a very real possibility that it might continue to grow beyond that date. People in AD 2,100 might be faced with a much larger population, with all the implications that has for greenland loss etc. They would not thank us for failing to take control of population size change now.

In the second place, it can be argued that we simply do not know enough about long-term trends to create a clear long-term goal package vision. We simply do not know:

a) whether or not the human population will decline anyway, and if so at what rate;

b) the extent that future advances in agricultural science and medicine might revolutionise agriculture, and human survival;

c) the extent that new methods of sustainable energy production and recycling may alter the requirements of environmental programmes;

d) the extent and effects of climate change.

However, as far as the first of these points is concerned, this is something we could know about in that we could control human population size change. The second point also concerns something that could be controlled if we so desired to do so: we could control the direction of research, and we have the ability to decide how new knowledge is applied. In agriculture for example, we could set the goal of extensive farming world-wide. We would then focus research on achieve biological control of existing crop pests under a less intensive production regime, and cease to develop higher yielding and more disease resistant strains; and we can make the decision not to foist GM crops on the world.

Nevertheless, uncertainty about future trends is a serious problem to setting an integrated set of specific goals for any far distant date. However, with the human population controlled, and clear stated general aims for each aspect of the environment and the organisation of society, it should be possible to achieve a fair measure of precision in defining the long-term goal package. Our future descendants will not respect our generation, if we are unwilling to take up the challenge to do this.

C. Developing the long-term goal package

I shall argue in the following Chapter that we need to aim to drastically reduce the human population of England. The long-term goal package would be developed around the desired end point population size, which I think is the most important component of the goal package. This goal population size will be discussed in the following chapter. Sufficient here to note two things about it. First, the goal population must not be greater than the Carrying Capacity (Chapter 1), and, taking into account mans broader aspirations, it would probably be much smaller than the carrying capacity population.

Second, although the population size aimed for is the central parameter in the whole goal package, this does not mean that somehow a figure is arrived at and then all other components of the goal package are adapted to it. On the contrary, all other aspects of the goal must be jointly considered in arriving at a suitable goal population. Thus Day (1992) in discussing the concept of the optimum population argues that this is not an end in itself, but rather a means of achieving social goals; and it cannot be determined on purely economic criteria. Man does not live by bread alone. To be fully human man requires serenity, dignity, order, leisure, peace, beauty, elbow room.

In the goal package, the total population would be distributed through the country in a specified way - specified both in terms of the division, town and country, and in terms of regions of England. Categories of employment (for example, farming, different components of manufacturing, different components of service industry, etc) will also be laid out in the spatial plan of England. The design of every city and town will be specified. The distribution of all conservation areas, future as well as present, will of course be laid out on the map. The economic and monetary policies of this future society will be stated, and will of course be environment centred.

To achieve this visualisation, a model would be specified containing tentative goals for each aspect of the society and environment, stated in general numerical terms ("of the order of "); then using computer generated iterative processes, these goals will be integrated and made more precise. Computer models such as the present day Land Use Allocation Model of the Centre for Agricultural Strategy at Reading University (Jones et al 1995) could perhaps form a basis for the study. A few different scenarios, with different numerical values put to the various goals, even varying sets of goals, could be experimented with, leading to a small series of different visualisations of this future society.

The goal package would be gradually evolved in relation to a series of future dates, which might for example be AD 2050, AD 2,100, AD 2,200 and possibly finally AD 2,300 (the final date would correspond to the final desired much reduced population size and the rate at which this goal population was approached).

Initially the final goal package would be very vague. Only population size itself would be precisely stated. For the penultimate date, the vision would be a little clearer; more components would be added and some more quantitative detail. For the AD 2,100 package the vision would be more detailed still. And the AD 50 package would have a fully worked out, but obviously tentative goal package. As time went on, the whole process would roll over so that gradually the AD100 package came to be fully detailed. We would be helped here by the fact that as far as climate change is concerned, we are likely to be in a much better position to predict the future in a few years time when there has been time to test and refine current climate change models.

Chapter 10

Control of the human population

A. The Global perspective

In Chapter One I described the growth of the human population, and argued that this growth is a major factor causing the world's environmental problems. I also described how policy makers hope to slow the growth down. Their approach is an indirect one, focusing on meeting the wishes of individual people. It is by no means certain that the approach will work. And do we not need to reduce world population, rather than just slowing growth down and stabilising total world population at some level above the present size?

The scientific approach to any environmental problem is to identify the causes and then mitigate them. If the idea of population reduction did not provoke such opposition as it has from human rights and religious groups, the size and growth of the human population would, in the writers opinion, have been labelled the biggest and most dangerous cause of our present environmental problems, and steps would have been taken world-wide not just to slow growth, but to reduce population size by the curbing of reproduction.

Should not more attention be given to deciding on a population size goal, and then to concentrating all our efforts to reach it? In doing this, should we not be willing to consider far more radical policies? Various Asian countries have tried out what Concepcion (1994) describes as intervention schemes to modify reproductive behaviour. These consist of combinations of incentives and disincentives to discourage large families. Should we not strive for a universal application of such schemes? China, with one fifth of the world population, already enforces a one-two child policy, and is one of the few countries to achieve a spectacular reduction in population growth. Would it not be best to try to extend this policy globally? Such a radical policy would go directly against what is widely regarded as the fundamental human right of freedom of reproduction. But thinking about this right, we need to ask ourselves two questions:

1) What 'human rights' have the millions of people (by no means all refugees) who are already experiencing extreme poverty? Would they not gladly exchange this reproductive right for even a very modest secure standard of living?
2) Suppose that the continued exercise of this right of freedom of reproduction by people now, significantly contributes to a failure to reduce population growth below the latest projection, and this in turn leads to such severe degradation of the environment world-wide that all mankind's descendants for all time are deprived of those 'rights' we have now - the right to live in a world that still has vast wilderness areas and high biodiversity, a world where widespread non-intensive, wildlife-friendly agriculture still remains an achievable goal, a world with the potential for allowing all people to have a decent standard of living. Can responsible people risk such a possibility? Is not this a problem where we should apply the precautionary principle? Should we not then stop insisting on this reproductive right?

It would be extremely difficult to implement a radical population control policy, not just because it would infringe human rights, but also because it would disadvantage developing regions compared with developed regions of the world. Since agriculture is much more labour intensive, and health care and old age pension schemes much less available in the developing world compared with the developed world, young people are in greater demand for agricultural work and providing for elderly relatives in the former than in the latter world. A policy to limit the number of children would therefore have a more serious effect in developing countries than it would in developed ones. However, these difficulties could be alleviated if the developed world was prepared to accept more responsibility towards helping the developing world to overcome its problems - problems at least partly caused by the developed world's exploitation anyway. The developed world would have to undertake to very significantly improve its technical and financial assistance in fields such as developing public health facilities. It would also help if governments in the developed world could be seen to be introducing measures to drastically reduce the C in the I=PCT equation.

Finally, to encourage developing world countries to adopt radical population policies, it would have been helpful if debt cancellation, at present tentatively under way, had been made conditional on adopting such policies.

B. Why we should control and reduce the population of England

We saw in Chapter 2 that contrary to what many people think, the population of England is not only still increasing at present, but it is projected to continue to increase for decades to come. Indeed it is thought that the population of England will grow by about 5 million before it commences to decrease, if indeed it does decrease at all, since there are considerable

177

uncertainties about the extent of future net immigration. We also saw that the proportion of the population that consists of ethnic minorities is projected to increase considerably. It is against this background that I argue for population control and reduction, and control of ethnic balance.

Before however, we consider reasons for reducing the population of England, there are a few of more general points about population control and reduction that are worth making.

First, reducing the population implies control of mortality, fertility and immigration.
Population control would make it possible to achieve a stable age distribution, and this has economic benefits, namely, making it possible to plan well in advance, educational provision for the young and health care for the aged. The un-forecast increase in fertility rate after the Second World War, with the baby booms, created problems when it became necessary to increase educational provision, which would have been avoided if population control had been practised.

Second, concern has been expressed that where a population is declining because of a below replacement level of fertility, as would occur if population size were to be deliberately reduced, the population continues to age, exacerbating the existing problem of provision for the aged. However, this process of ageing would not go on indefinitely. With a constant fertility rate, (and a constant mortality rate), it will normally not take more than two or three generations to produce a stable age structure Day (1992, referring to work by S.H. Preston and colleagues).

Turning now to the reasons for population reduction, I argue that such reduction is a necessary condition for achieving significant amelioration of the general environmental situation in England, saving our countryside and enabling our country to play its proper part in improving the environmental situation worldwide. More specifically, population reduction is required for:

(i) preventing green land loss to housing and other development;
(ii) significantly reducing pressure for intensive food production and significantly reducing resource depletion, pollution and landfill of waste products;
(iii) reducing people-pressure on the countryside;
(iv) preventing deterioration of city life;
(v) enabling England to move towards its carrying capacity.

(i) Preventing green land loss to housing and other development

Population growth leads to an increase in the number of households. It is true that there are other causes for the increase in the number of households, as described in Section H of Chapter 2. But we saw there that increase in the adult population has been accounting for a little under half of the total increase in the number of households in the recent past, and is projected to account for well over half in the future. So population growth is a major cause of increase in the number of households, which in turn leads to increasing need for housing, which in turn means more housing on greenfield sites, which in turn means loss of countryside land to housing (see Fig.11 page 194). Now in Chapters 3 and 11, I describe how loss of green land to housing can be minimised by densification of housing in existing urban areas. But there is a limit to which existing urban areas can go on absorbing more households. Maximising use of existing urban areas for housing only delays the eventual loss of countryside to housing if population continues to increase.

(ii) Reducing the pressure for intensive food production;
reducing resource depletion, pollution and landfill

We saw in Chapter in Chapter 5 that the chief underlying cause of the decline in the landscape and wildlife quality of the remaining countryside has been the intensification of agriculture. This intensification was initially promoted to feed the growing population of England; it is also now maintained as a way of boosting agricultural exports. We also saw that this same intensification, being continued through further advances in technology, has reduced the total area of land that is needed to be kept for food production. However, food production remains, and will remain, the chief use for countryside land, and the only way to improve this land is by making production less intensive which will require an extension of the area of land used for food production. This will be considerably hampered by further use of greenland for housing caused by increase in the human population. Further, although extensification of agriculture should be the top priority in improving countryside land, there is also a need to use more land for energy crop production, and the creation of wildlife areas (Section E of Chapter 12). The possibilities of these changes in land use will also be inhibited by further loss of greenland to housing.

As far as resource depletion, pollution and landfill are concerned, it is well known that we can considerably reduce these problems through modern technology and a different approach to the question of re-use and recycling (see Chapter 3, Section A). Solutions, or partial solutions are then available, but the problems of implementing the necessary measures - financial and political, have so far meant that totally inadequate progress has been made. The problems of depletion, pollution and waste disposal are exacerbated by continued population growth. I suggest that a completely satisfactory solution to these problems will not be attained without a considerable reduction in total population size.

Clearly reducing the human population could reduce the pressure to use non-renewable and renewable resources. Attention is usually focused on the former, but we need to be careful about the latter also. With renewable resources, we need to ensure that the harvest rate does not exceed regeneration rate, otherwise our stock of the resource decreases. Furthermore, while a given stock is potentially renewable, it may be depleted to the point where renewal is impossible. This applies for example to stocks of some fish species which if reduced below a certain critical level, may never recover: this is a pressing concern in the oceans and seas of the world at the present time, including the seas round the UK, which fishermen exploit to feed the large and still growing populations of the UK and the rest of western Europe. Turning to land, we may note that soil is a renewable resource, but it is only renewed at a very slow rate. If you remove topsoil, and rains wash subsoil away, restoration of the soil becomes problematical. The more people there are, the greater the pressure to use intensive agricultural methods which lead to soil erosion. So there are limits in connection with renewable resources as well as with non-renewable ones.

(iii) Reducing people pressure on the countryside

People pressure on the countryside has caused considerable problems – damage to habitat, the scaring off of birds in the breeding season, the loss of that remote quiet feel that the countryside used to provide, as was discussed in Chapter 7.

Problems over access are I think already acute. However much one might want to increase public access to the countryside, one has to face the fact that uncontrolled access can have a deleterious effect on vegetation and animal life. It would further disturb breeding birds along rivers (would the Kingfisher and Dipper ever survive if the margin of every river in England became a public path?), on moors (Curlew etc.) and elsewhere. It is likely to cause increased soil erosion, especially around towns and in favoured countryside areas such as some parts of the Peak District National Park. It is true that even ardent advocates of open access recognise that certain areas of land would have to be either temporarily or permanently closed to the public. Nevertheless, providing access to the public always has the tendency to damage the environment. Consequently, I regard the Governments Countryside and Rights of way Bill (apart from its last section on SSSIs) as a thoroughly foolish and harmful piece of proposed legislation. Be that as it may, the main point I want to make here is that the more people there are, the worse the damage to the countryside is likely to be. The corollary is that a massive reduction of the human population would improve the situation enormously.

If people are to become more concerned about the environmental situation and especially the need to conserve the countryside, it is important that their isolation from the environment is broken down and they really get to know not just the countryside landscape, but the plants and animals of the countryside. So we need to encourage people to wander from the beaten track. It is no use simply obeying the sort of notice that has appeared in some areas - "please keep to the path; you can see all the flowers from there" (e.g. Dove Dale in the Peak District). In the first place this statement is untrue; many plants may be so small that they are obscured from view by other plants. In the second place, you can't really get to know plants by looking at them from a distance; you have to get right up close to them. So it is ironic that at a time when we should be encouraging people to wander from the track, it is necessary to strictly limit such wandering. It is no use saying that the sort of situation just described only applies to a small part of the countryside that is particularly rich in wild life, because that is the particular part of the countryside where people really need to roam to see things properly. The human population is just far too big.

It is now impossible in most parts of England to find somewhere that one can go and have complete peace and quiet. Even in a relatively remote corner of a nature reserve one can hear, and often see, the traffic on nearby roads, and find oneself constantly bumping into other people who are also wanting to 'get away from it all' but may be chattering loudly to each other or their children. Now we are told that it will be possible in future to greatly reduce car noise. And if policies to control private transport were introduced, we could have the situation where many cars are replaced by fewer buses. But the high density of people in these 'natural' areas would remain. Peace and quiet, and the sounds of nature. Just some of the qualities that one cannot put a monetary value on. Yet the present writer would argue that they have an indispensable role to play in keeping any society sane and healthy. Do we want a sane and healthy society? To fully retrieve the peace and quiet of the countryside would require a massive reduction in population.

(iv) Preventing deterioration of city life

Turning from the countryside to urban areas, we may note that the words 'city' and 'conurbation' conjure up a variety of images, but one of these is a picture of masses of people crowded together, high traffic and noise levels, high levels of social delinquency, streams of ugly worn faces, in other words, a place of low 'quality of life', or low environmental quality in the broad sense. The ways that conditions can be improved have been often rehearsed: better city design, including of course an integrated transport policy, reducing unemployment, reducing social inequality (Chapter 3). But as cities get bigger, are these methods adequate to prevent further deterioration of the quality of city life? While it has been suggested that there may be no limit to how big a city can grow and still function efficiently in economic terms at least (Lowry, 1991), the nagging doubt remains that cities have become too large. If city size could be reduced considerably, this would probably make it easier to solve environmental and social problems.

As population density in cities increases, there will be a tendency for freedoms to be restricted -freedom of movement, freedom from noise. And one might expect that as population density increases there would come a point at which conflict becomes more common (this argument is sometimes advanced as an underlying rationale for being careful not to try to increase city density unless big efforts are simultaneously made to improve urban design).

Parsons, in his study of population aspects of freedom (Parsons, 1971) notes that the larger the population, the bigger the city, the easier it is for someone to gain anonymity and relative freedom from informal social control, with a corresponding increase in the freedom to behaving differently. He goes on to speculate that this might be the basic reason underlying the high crime rates in the larger cities, in which the informal constraints on individual behaviour operating in small groups, from people who know you, are absent.

The possible relationships between crime rates on the one hand, and city size and population density on the other, are complex, and no doubt much disputed. However, there is at least some evidence suggesting a correlation between city size and crime rate. Parsons (ibid), reports on evidence that comes from studies of crime in the cities of the USA. He tabulates crime records against city population size, using the population size categories a) under 10,000, b) 50,000 to 100,000, c), over 250,000. He shows a positive correlation between urban crime rates (crimes per 100,000 population) for the various forms of crime. For all categories except larceny-theft (where the greatest rate was for the intermediate size category), the rate gets progressively greater across the three categories. For example, the figures for murder and non-negligent manslaughter are 2.7, 4.2, and 5.5 respectively. For rape the figures are 7.0, 9.3, and 23.7; and for burglary, breaking in and entering, 313.3, 474.6, 574.9.

All this leads, I think, to the conclusion, that there might be considerable benefit, crime-wise, if we could reduce the total population of the land and hence the size of our urban populations.

There would also probably be benefit for future city life if the immigration component of population growth were to be reduced. Level of conflict in cities probably has several causes. But one possible cause is social and racial heterogeneity, a topic also explored by Parsons (1998) He writes:
    " In a society that is rapidly becoming still more heterogeneous and concerned with group rights and political correctness, it seems quite possible that competition in terms of number-power- including competitive breeding proper – will increase considerably". And elsewhere he says he has long suspected that the colossal amount of violence and crime in the USA (said to be the country's biggest 'industry') must in part be caused by sheer heterogeneity and lack of shared values.

This raises the possibility that in England, as the total ethnic minority share of the population increases (which it is doing), at the same time that different ethnic minority groups retain different shared values, which may also be different from the shared values of the white majority, conflict will tend to increase. If the Government adopted the precautionary principle, it would seek to limit immigration not only because of the need to reduce further total population growth per se, but also to prevent a possible increase in racial conflict in cities.

A word more on shared values. There is much talk of how the sharing of values between communities could be an invigorating process for society. However, the majority of non-European immigrants seem to be primarily concerned about maintaining the values of the communities from which they came. I suspect the majority are not the slightest bit interested in English values, except in so far as they guarantee them safety and a decent standard of living. And we see in London, the practical out workings of attitude to community values – the development of a series of rather closed ethnic group communities. If present day minority groups came to be a majority in England (which is possible), I wonder if they would be concerned to maintain the rights of the white English majority to the same degree that they loudly demand their rights are upheld now.

Another area where relationships with population factors are complex and controversial is unemployment. Since the vast majority of people live in cities, any problems in the employment field will be felt most in urban areas.

Now many studies in the USA have failed to show any impact of immigration on either wage levels or unemployment, according to Nigel Harris, an economics professor at London University (in the discussion about immigration, BBC current affairs, 16-12-99).
Further, unemployment in England is at present at a low level. However, we need to remember that in the European Union as a whole as it is now, there are an awful lot of unemployed people, at the same time people have the freedom to move between countries and apply for jobs in other countries within the EU. We cannot just consider the unemployment in the

UK at the present time in isolation from employment levels in other EU countries, or possible changes in unemployment levels over future time. We have also to face the possibility that the movement of industry and commerce, and therefore jobs, from Europe to the Pacific Rim will continue, creating more unemployment.

The population of Europe is still rising and may well probably continue to increase for a couple more decades at least. At the same time we are living in an age where modern technology reduces manpower needs, so that part time employment is becoming ever commoner. There is a real danger that unemployment might increase, and reducing unemployment in a growing population is rather similar to trying to run down an upward moving escalator when it is outpacing you (Ashmead, 1997). And almost weekly we are hearing on the BBC news of some factory or other closing down and putting hundreds, often thousands of people out of work. This might well continue. What is the attitude of those workers laid off, to immigration? They, and many other ordinary people, will be unlikely to be convinced by evidence such as that of Prof. Harris cited above. They fear that immigrants will take jobs and thus deprive them of a livelihood, and this could lead to rising racial tensions.

Consequently, the precautionary principle would suggest we severely curb the immigration component of population growth.

(v) Enabling England to move towards its carrying capacity

I now turn to the concepts of carrying capacity and ecological footprints that I introduced readers to in Chapter 1. I concluded there that on a global basis, the human population exceeds the carrying capacity.

Now various workers have concluded that the population of the UK and England considerably exceed carrying capacity. For example, even if we adopted a modest footprint (keeping the European lifestyle except greatly reducing use of fossil energy), the Optimum Population Trust estimates that the carrying capacity of the UK is only 23 million (present population nearly 60 million) (Willey1999c).

The 1995 report of the Institute for Environment and Development (commissioned by the Government) reported on Britain's ecological footprint (IIED, 1995). This made use of the concept of 'ghost acres' - the land required to supply the country's import of food, animal feed and fish, that is land abroad on which we depend in addition to our own land.

The report contains four footprint studies, one of which is forest products. This particular study points out that wood products come mainly from renewable forests, but some from deforestation (non-sustainable production). From the former, 6.4 million hectares throughout the world are more or less permanently taken up in providing wood products for the UK; for the latter, 67,000 hectares are either deforested or so severely degraded that they will become deforested. The total footprint is 3 times the UK's own area of productive forest and woodland.

One may attempt to calculate what the UK population would have to be to reduce our ecological footprint in a given way that is to make the UK more self-sufficient. A decade ago one calculation gave the following results amongst others:

Then current population	57 million
Agricultural self-sufficiency under intensive cultivation	41 million
Agricultural self-sufficiency under moderate cultivation	35 million
Self-sufficiency for forestry and wood needs	15-25 million
Self-sufficiency for energy (using Renewable energy)	15-20 million

(work of D. Richardson reported in Myers, 1993b).

Such results suggest that at present, the UK greatly exceeds its carrying capacity.

Finally a word about population density which links together the concept of carrying capacity and the idea mentioned in the previous section that as population density increases, conflict is more likely. We are really a very densely population country: the UK is slightly more densely populated that Germany, over twice as densely populated as France and well over ten times as densely populated as Sweden!

C. What should the goal population size be? How quickly should we approach it?

In Chapter 9, I argued that our vision for the future should be developed in relation to a particular goal population. What should be the size of this population?

I think that the 'bottom line' - or perhaps we should here say the 'top line'! – should be the population that corresponds to the carrying capacity. If we accept the modest footprint idea and the estimates of OPT, then we would say that the maximum population we would allow would be 23 million – the size of the UK population shortly after the middle of the last century. This would be our top line.

At the other extreme, there must be a minimum population size. There needs to be a certain number of people in an area to provide the necessary goods to society and maintain social cohesion, in other words to maintain a good quality of life, and adequately provide for the defence of the society. There are also economies of scale to be considered. Thus, were a population very small, an increase in population size would allow more scope for the specialisation of labour and equipment and therefore increase efficiency. And a very small society would not be able to afford to produce and sustain certain very useful things like public transport (Parsons, 1971, Willey, 1996).

Since the great majority of people live in cities, working out the population goal must take into consideration the desired size of cities. A city needs to be big enough to fulfil uniquely city functions, but small enough to avoid depriving people of the conditions necessary for the healthy life. This is a question that Schumacher (1973) addressed. Rather than considering how big a city could be from the economic point of view, he points out that above a certain size, nothing is added to the virtue of the city. He suggested that while one cannot judge this matter with precision, the upper limit of what is desirable might be around half a million. Schumacher also discussed the question of minimum size, pointing out that the finest cities in history have been very small by 20th century standards. It is perhaps worth pointing out here that Plato thought the ideal city state would have 5,040 citizens proper, and together with non citizens, a total population of 60,000 (reported in Parsons, 1971).

Schumacher acknowledges that the basic instruments and institutions of city culture do require a certain accumulation of wealth. But just how much wealth is needed depends on the type of culture desired. He points out that art, philosophy, and religion, cost very little money. Some types of what may be called 'high culture' such as space research or ultra-modern physics cost a lot of money, but then they are really remote from the needs of most people. We could add that such research is increasingly done by groups of nations rather than individual ones. Clearly then, it would be possible to massively reduce the total population and still retain sufficient cities which can provide essential city functions.

Somewhere between the maximum and minimum population there will be the 'optimum' or 'best' population. The problems of defining an optimum population are considerable, as Parsons (1971 p. 290) wrote:

> "We have to ask best for what, best for whom, best how, when, where and why? We must not forget to ask in addition 'how does our society decide these questions – who decides, and by what social mechanism? "

However, Parsons goes on to say that difficult as the task is, we should try to define the optimum population. And then he goes on to discuss the topic in relation to liberty, as we will see in Section A of Chapter 13.

If we take into account all the reasons advanced in the previous section for reducing the population, I considers it would be good to aim eventually to reduce the population by perhaps as much as 90%.

How quickly should we try to reach the final population size goal?
Ideally the process of population reduction should minimise any possible economic and social instability caused by population reduction. This minimisation might be achieved if TFR remained close to what it has been in recent times, rather than changing it in a drastic way. For that would require the minimum interference with reproductive preferences. So at the beginning of the process of selecting a target population size for say AD 2,300 (Chapter 9), we should ask the question - what would the population size be by that date if current Total Fertility Rate (TFR) continued? Would this lead to the order of population decrease we are looking for? Day (1992) calculated that continuing the 1985 TFR from a base year of 1985, would bring the UK population down to its pre-war level by about AD 2,053, a roughly 20% reduction. And it would be possible now to calculate what the population size would be by say AD 2,300, under specified net immigration conditions, if the current TFR were maintained. I am not going to attempt the calculation: I merely indicate a way forwards.

There is another reason for not drastically altering (reducing) fertility rate, and that concerns a topic we will consider further later in this chapter: ensuring we have a sufficient work force to maintain the economy and provide for the increasing old age population. Coleman points out that the root cause of the ageing of the population is not lack of immigration but rather below replacement level fertility, and to ameliorate the situation in the long run, women should be enabled to have more than one child and bring the fertility rate approximately up to replacement level Coleman 1992, 2000a, 2000b). The corollary of this is, I think, that the further we move fertility rate below replacement level, the greater will be the pressure to increase immigration with the dangers to social cohesion that this brings (see later in this chapter). Consequently, I argue that we should keep fertility rate as high as possible consistent with our planned long-term population reduction.

D. What will have to be done to achieve the required population reduction?

If we are to reduce the population we must control fertility and immigration.

(i) Control fertility at below replacement level

A 'stick and carrot' approach might be adequate to maintain the desired fertility level. Irvine and Ponton (1988) suggest elements of this approach: There could be tax benefits for families with fewer than two children, sterilization bonuses, withdrawal of maternity and similar benefits after a second child, larger pensions for people with fewer than two children; there could also be payments for periods of non-pregnancy.

(ii) Eliminate net immigration

We have seen in Chapter 2 that the most significant cause of population growth in England during the next few decades at least, is likely to be net immigration. And uncertainties about the future mean that immigration pressure might be at least as great as it is now for many decades to come. So immigration must be curbed, indeed I suggest it should be stopped completely, by whatever means are necessary. The UK would have to change some of its own laws, abrogate some EU and United Nations Agreements, and refuse to sigh up to any international agreement which would limit its sovereignty on this population issue.

Perhaps most important of existing laws is the 1951 UN Convention relating to the Status of Refugees, extended in application by the 1967 Protocol relating to the Status of refugees. From this Convention stems our policy of offering sanction to people who are being persecuted. This Convention defines a refugee as a person who:

> "... owing to a well-founded fear of being persecuted for reasons of race, religion, nationality, membership of a particular social group or political opinion, is outside the country of his nationality and unable or, owing to such fear, is unwilling to avail himself of the protection of that country; or who, not having a nationality and being outside the country of his former habitual residence.... is unable or, owing to such fear, is unwilling to return to it"

Abrogation of this Convention will become more and more urgent, if, as seems very possible, political stability worldwide breaks down further, and the many oppressive regimes become even more oppressive. We may then be faced with floods of genuinely persecuted people clamouring for admission to our country.

E. Have we then no responsibilities to other peoples in the developing world?

Eliminating immigration does not mean that we turn our back on the needs of the rest of the world.

You know, it is so easy to salve our consciences! - help refugees by letting them into our country without really thinking through the consequences, and of course, in the knowledge that they are unlikely to come to live next door. So easy, in Church, to listen with compassion to details of third world debt and misery and then feel exonerated by putting money in the collection plate for Christian Aid or Oxfam. What we put in the collection plate probably will make little difference to our own standard of living; at the most, it might make us take just slightly fewer holidays abroad. All most of us are doing is like the Victorian man who gives to the beggar as he walks down a city street.

And of course it cost nothing really to make public pronouncements about the evils of our immigration system and related matters – it even seems to make people feel good, and might win votes at elections!

Our problem is much deeper and much more serious. What should we really do? We should be prepared to drastically reduce the luxury in our lifestyle. It sounds so banal and simple, yet it would be so difficult to achieve. Reduce the A in the I=PAT equation. It would involve genuine sacrifice, and genuine long-term commitment. It would not however make us less healthy - I would contend it would do just the opposite. And I think it could actually make us happier. And people in the developing world might just respect us, which they largely do not at the moment.

We do have responsibilities outside our shores. But we will not ultimately help the world if we let out country deteriorate drastically, which will happen, I believe, if we do not control population and population composition. As many countries as possible should try to achieve sustainable development. This will not only make a direct contribution to ameliorating global problems like global warming and resource depletion; it will also ensure that some countries at least retain the capability to help the rest of the world.

F. Objections to a policy of population control and reduction

There are various objections to introducing a population control policy ranging from objection to any form of control, to objection to the more specific aim of reducing the population or controlling immigration. The bases for these objections range from misunderstanding of the facts to moral principles. I will discuss each in turn.

(i) Our population is already decreasing. Therefore, even if we thought that the present population is too large we certainly do not need a policy to reduce population.

In Chapter 2, I showed that the premise here is false. Our population is increasing and will go on increasing for some time to come. An example of belief in this false premise is given in Section B of Chapter 13. I believe this premise is widely accepted in England.

(ii) Population growth is levelling off and the population will then begin to shrink, so we do not need a policy of population reduction.

Here, as is clear from what I wrote in Chapter 2, the premise is not false as much as overstated. Current projections do have the population decreasing, although not until shortly before mid-century. However, as I argued in that same chapter, uncertainties about future population size are very great. It is certainly very possible (not remotely possible) that population will go on increasing beyond mid century. It is even possible that migration flows will increase and population growth not even slow down but accelerate. Unless it is argued either that it does not matter if population increases further, or that we need considerable further population increase, the precautionary principle would suggest we should bring in a population control policy.

(iii) Population growth leads to increasing economic prosperity. Therefore we should not try to reduce the population.

Some people would extend this to say that if the population is decreasing, we should introduce measures that would lead to population expansion. The falsity of this claim has been exposed by various authors including Ehrlich and Ehrlich (1990). If economic growth is measured by an indicator like GDP then one could defend the proposition. But if we enlarge our method of assessing economic performance to take into account depletion of resources such as groundwater, soils, forests, fisheries and wildlife, the basic premise cannot be sustained.

(iv) Our population is ageing, so we should allow population increase through immigration in order to boost the workforce so as to maintain the economy, and more particularly, support the increasing proportion of the population that is in the non-working elderly category. Therefore we should not adopt a population reduction policy.

One variant of this argument would add therefore we should relax on immigration control.

And the basic argument is sometimes stated slightly differently:

If we stopped population growth we would create a population with even fewer young people and a bigger preponderance of older people who needed supporting.

This argument revolves around the concept of support ratio. Most commonly this term is used to indicate the ratio of working people to elderly non-working people that is required both to sustain the economy in general, and to provide adequate support for the elderly in particular. I think the arguments can be answered as follows.

(a) The whole argument seems to ignore the fact that there must eventually come a point when population growth must cease. At the most absurd visualisation, population growth could not go on to the point when all physical surface space was used up and we were standing shoulder to shoulder! But leaving aside the absurd, even the most ardent supporters of immigration must surely realise that there are capacity limits. One may not accept some current carrying capacity estimates. But one must accept that there is a limit to the number of people the land can support. So eventually, one would have to stop immigration, if, as is possible, people were still wanting to immigrate into the UK. Consequently, adopting a policy of allowing continued population growth only postpones the age composition problem. Eventually, the problem of too many old people would strike. This has been argued for a long time by Ehrlich and others (for example, Ehrlich and Ehrlich, ibid).

Day (1992) also makes the point that immigration is at best a merely temporary expedient. He reported on research carried on in Australia by C. Young and published in 1989. At that time overall fertility was slightly less than replacement level, and the Government was supporting immigration as a solution to population ageing. The research showed that if the current immigration rate was continued, this would result in the population age structure becoming more distorted but the proportion of old aged people in the population would only be slightly lower. The study also investigated what would happen if immigration rate was maintained at 50,000 or 150,000 annually (even 50,000 is quite high compared with the then recent trends). By mid century (2046), the lower rate of immigration would have produced a proportion of elderly people of 21.4 %. The higher rate would have produced 19.55% – so only a very little difference. Furthermore, supposing no immigration was allowed at all, the elderly population would have reach 23% - not much difference from the other figures. But, the 50,000 immigration rate would have raised the total Australian population by 38%, the 150,000 rate by 90%!

(b) Allowing a flow of immigrants does not guarantee that you will get the sort of people you need. Day (ibid) thinks the benefits go to quite a narrow range of the host population – building contractors, developers and ethnic leaders (presumably meaning the support for these leaders policies) rather than the economy as a whole. And at the same time such immigration could have the effect of increasing ethnic and religious animosity.

(c). If we were to try to maintain support ratios, we would have to let in a very large number of immigrants. A recent United Nations Report (UN Population Division, 2000) says that to keep the support ratio at its 1995 level, the UK would have to admit 59.8 million migrants between 1995 and 2050, which would be slightly more than one million migrants a year! So we would have to roughly double the population. Even to keep the UK population at its present size (assuming decline in the absence of change in immigration levels) we would need to admit about two and a half million migrants by the year 2050.

(d) Do we need immigrants anyway? Could not the ever-increasing elderly population supply all the workers that are needed? Most elderly people remain healthy for at least a decade after retirement and many much longer. At the same time much less of the total country's work is now of the heavy manual kind that it was in the past, and you do not need to be extremely physically fit to work with a computer! We would both solve our labour need problem and reduce old age support if we, for example, raised retirement age by 10 years. At the very least we could do much more to create the circumstances which encouraged older people to go back to work. And the United nations report mentioned earlier, in fact comes to the conclusion that we could obtain in 2050 the same potential support ratio observed in 1995 in the United Kingdom by raising the upper limit of working-age to 72 years.

(e) The focus of attention for those advocating immigration is on the proportion of elderly people to working age people. This neglects another very important dependency - the child dependency ratio, that is the ratio of children to adults, the ratio of the non-productive segment of the population (children) to the productive segment (adults). Children create a burden both to parents (responsible for the provision of basic amenities of life) and to the state (responsible for the provision of health, education and other services needed by the children). While elderly parents are usually thought, per capita, to be about three times as 'expensive' as children, children are still very expensive. Now if you have a flow of immigrants, containing a higher proportion of people in the reproductive age groups than the native population, and with a fertility rate as high or higher than the native population, this will cause the child dependency ratio to be higher than it would be in the absence of immigration.

(v) Quite apart from the question of support ratios, we need immigrants to solve the problem of skills shortages.

To deal with this point we have to consider skill shortages in connection with unemployment. We also need to remember that unemployment levels are higher in some European countries than in the UK, but at the same time we have free flow of labour within the EC. It would be foolish to try to deal with our labour problems in isolation fro the rest of the EC. Now Coleman (1992) concluded that as far as economic and policy literature was concerned, the favoured solution for unemployment and skills shortages in the EC was not immigration into the EC but training and retraining, both of the unemployed and the existing workforce. And at the time Coleman wrote, he concluded that to reduce EC unemployment from 8% to 4% would require an increase in jobs of 12-15 percent, or 15-20 million.

Coleman pointed out that there was a large hidden labour supply. Within the working age population, there remain a large proportion of people who are economically inactive and are not seeking work although they are not debarred from doing so by disability or chronic disease. Further, most unemployed people were not being retrained. This inactive population arises from a number of factors. With the 15-20 age group, a majority are in full time education. The early retirement of men has provided a component. But the most important factor is the relatively low work force participation of women, especially married women. Coleman estimated that in the EC the hidden labour supply is about 15% of the working age population, that is 33 million people. That represents 23 % of the then current labour force. There was much variation between countries, for example, over 20% in Spain, under 10% in England.

Coleman concluded that "Europe has very substantial reserves of employable manpower which greatly exceed any short-term demographic deficiencies". And he points to the pressing need for retraining the unemployed and training young people and the existing work force for a more demanding skilled labour market in the future.

Although conditions may have changed somewhat since 1992, surely we need to concentrate our efforts for dealing with our specific labour shortages, by training and retraining of our own people, not by the opportunist and short term expedient of importing workers.

(vi) Reproductive freedom is a fundamental human right.

I have already written about this objection in the opening section of this chapter. And I will return to it again in Section A of Chapter 13. We have to balance the value of this freedom with the value of other freedoms, and in the context of a world of limited size.

(vii) Such population policies are racist. For both in terms of reproduction and of migration, any population policy would affect disproportionately groups other than the native English-speaking white group.

We need to distinguish here two possible types of policy. The first would simply be a policy to control total population size; the second would be a policy to control racial composition. In this respect the main contention of this book is that we need to arrest population growth as soon as possible and then ensure population reduction, irrespective of racial composition, for reasons of carrying capacity and loss of green land to housing.

However I have raised the possibility that if the proportion of minority groups increases in the total population beyond a certain point, that could lead to uncontrollable racial conflict breaking out. If that view were accepted, it would be sensible to adopt a policy that would prevent such a change of population proportions. One could go even further. One could argue that the feelings of the native population, in this case white people of English descent, are paramount. If there is a majority feeling in the native population against an increase of proportion of ethnic minority groups, for whatever reason, that feeling then should be respected.

At this point I should make my own position clear. I believe the most important thing is the size of the total population, irrespective of its composition, for reasons I have already made clear. But I do also think that an increase in the proportion of ethnic minority groups beyond a certain point might trigger off conflict, which must be avoided. And I do not believe that all the efforts by various organisations to inculcate racial tolerance could possibly prevent this. Consequently I believe a policy should be adopted to control the growth of ethnic minority populations.

I make the following additional points:

(a) I think we need a simple two pronged policy – maintain total fertility rate a little below replacement level, and stop all future immigration. There is no need to adopt a policy specifically for ethnic minority groups. On the fertility side, one should note that the policy would not simply differentiate between white English people on the one hand, and all ethnic minorities on the other hand. We have seen how fertility rate varies between ethnic groups. Chinese and Arabs apparently do not have a higher fertility rate, and West Indian blacks only a slightly higher fertility rate than the white population. Furthermore, there are many people in the white majority population who would want larger families than advocated by the policy, or at least feel very strongly on the fundamental human rights of reproduction issue (e.g. some Roman Catholics), so they would be affected by the policy as well as members of ethnic minority groups. On the migration side, it would not be a case of 'white' versus 'black', for the policy would apply equally to all potential immigrants, including whites (say from the Balkans).

b) I think it is very important to be clear what the term 'racism' actually means, and I also think that some refugee and human rights organisations subtly misuse the term. In the new Oxford Dictionary of English (Oxford University Press, 1998), racism is defined as follows:

Racism. **Noun** [mass noun] the belief that all members of each race possess characteristics, abilities, or qualities specific to that race, especially so as distinguish it as inferior or superior to another race or races.
. prejudice, discrimination, or antagonism directed against someone of a different race based on such a belief: *a programme to combat racism.*

© Oxford University Press 1998. Reprinted from The New Oxford Dictionary Of English (1998). by permission of Oxford University Press.

To take action that affects some races and not others, is not in itself racist. To be racist, an action must be promoted because of certain beliefs about qualities associated with particular races, especially belief about superiority/inferiority. I will return to the subject of racism in Chapter 13.

So to summarise. I do not accept the criticism that such policies are racist. That implies making decisions on the basis of a belief in racial superiority as the Nazis did, and I could not accept that. The sort of population policies I advocate would have more effect on some ethnic minority groups than others, and more than on the white native population, but I have given my reasons why I think this is absolutely legitimate.

(viii) Such policies are fundamentally against the whole Christian idea of compassion, and of responsibility for all peoples of the world.

I have answered this objection already in Section E of this Chapter.

G. The attitude of NGOs to the population problem

Many Non-Governmental Organisations (NGOs) campaign on environmental issues. What is the attitude of these organisations to the population problem? I decided I would tackle this directly by writing to some of the major NGOs operating in the UK to find out about their positions.

(i) Correspondence with NGOs

The NGOs I wrote to were mainly organisations with a world wide remit - Friends of the Earth (FoE), Greenpeace, Oxfam and Worldwide Fund for Nature (WWF). In addition I wrote to the Council for the Protection of Rural England (CPRE). Writing for Gaia Watch my letter was as follows:

> "It seems to us that human population growth is one of the underlying causes of world environmental problems. The depletion of non-renewable resources, the accumulation of solid waste and the release of toxic chemicals into the environment and the production of greenhouse gases leading to climate change, are all matters exacerbated by continued population growth. The need to increase food production to feed the growing population, with concomitant deterioration of the soil and the depletion of water aquifers on land, and depletion of fish stocks in the oceans, increases the prospects of long-term non-sustainable food production. The loss of green land to housing and other development worldwide, reduces the area of the globe which through the various natural cycles control climate. It also leads to loss of valuable wild life habitat. And as population density increases the potential for strife within and between nations increases, which in turn renders it more difficult for countries to develop their economies, sustain their food production, and enter into effective programmes of collaboration to deal with environmental problems.
>
> In trying to develop a way forwards on the whole population question, we would like to know what major environmental organisations think about these matters. We therefore would like to ask you – to what extent does ....have any policy advocating a) population stabilisation, b) population reduction, and does your organisation campaign on these issues? If such policy exists, we would be grateful if you could indicate to us any publication of your organisation which makes the relevant policy statement.
>
> Your response to this letter would be very much appreciated.
>
> Yours sincerely,"

(Looking back now at this letter, I think I should have added some comment about the possible relationship between the spread of infectious diseases and population density).

I deal first with the replies from the international organisations.

(a) Replies from International organisations

The replies I received were as follows.

FoE   (reply from information and enquiries assistant)

"Thank you for your enquiry regarding FoEs stance on population stabilisation and reduction.

Whilst we recognise that population growth puts pressure on the world's natural resources, in our view it is not the main cause of environmental degradation.

Friends of the Earth believes that environmental damage is not so much determined by how many people there are but by how much those people are consuming. It is affluent countries, such as the United Kingdom, whose high consumption levels are putting the most pressure on the world's forests, oceans and atmosphere. We feel that consumption levels in developed countries' must be reduced to allow developing countries access to their fair share of resources. Friends of the Earth believes that cutting rich countries' consumption to allow poor countries access to the resources they need, is a key way for these countries to tackle poverty and then to gain control of the size of their population.

The iniquities of the international economic system also need to be redressed, as current international economic policies can prove an almost insurmountable barrier for governments in developing countries struggling to provide for their citizens' health and welfare. I have enclosed a summary of our new publication "Tomorrow's World" for your interest.

Yours sincerely..."

From the letter we can take it that Tomorrow's world (McLaren et al, 1997) sets forth the FoE approach to population matters. And if we read the book we find the policy advocated on page 80:
"... the best way of reducing population growth is to create the social and economic conditions that provide people with the security they require to have smaller families". The authors go on to advocate increasing access to birth control methods, and focusing aid on education of women and girls to elevate their status and improve their access to employment. They consider that upholding women's rights is the best tool for reducing birth rates by reducing the desire for large families.

However, the book does not advocate any direct action to stabilise or reduce the human population. So in terms of the I=PAT or I=PCT equation, FoE sees the solution in reducing consumption and improving technology. Noting the great disparity of per capita consumption between affluent and poor countries, which reflects disparity of resource use, FoE says that affluent countries have the duty to change their consumption patterns and the levels of their resource use must be reduced.

Greenpeace (reply from the Executive Director)

"I was very interested to read your comments relating to the question of population control. Greenpeace doesn't currently campaign on this issue, and it might be helpful if I explain in some detail why this is.

Greenpeace started campaigning in 1971 against the atmospheric testing of nuclear weapons. Shortly after that, Greenpeace developed campaigns to protect baby seals from being killed for the fur trade, and also started to campaign against the commercial killing of whales.

Gradually, over the years, Greenpeace has developed a number of new campaigns, primarily focussing in the early years on threats to the oceans, and the marine life of the oceans. More recently, Greenpeace has campaigned against genetic engineering, the destruction of old-growth forests, against the nuclear industry and nuclear weapons, and also to protect the atmosphere from pollution, and from the threat of global warming.

Greenpeace is an international organisation, operating in 40 countries, and with around 2.5 million supporters worldwide. All Greenpeace campaigns are agreed internationally; before a campaign starts, there must be international agreement about the campaign objectives, and the international strategy which will be followed to achieve those objectives. In addition, Greenpeace as an organisation has agreed to campaign on only a limited number of environmental issues, believing that restricting ourselves to a few specific campaign goals will allow us to make the best use of the resources given to us by our supporters, and so help us achieve those campaign goals.

As a result of this, it is simply not possible for Greenpeace to campaign on more than a few, major, international, environmental issues. One of the issues the organisation has not yet decided to campaign on is population control. This is not, of course, because we think it unimportant, but rather because it does not link directly with any of our existing campaigns, and because a number of other organisations already work effectively on this issue. We also believe that it is not the kind of issue where Greenpeace's campaigning strengths, in particular the use of direct action, would be particularly appropriate. Naturally, we keep our campaigning plans under constant review, and this is certainly something that has been discussed.

It's worth stressing that there is some disagreement about whether or not the environmental problems caused by rapidly growing populations are symptomatic of a more fundamental underlying problem. Many commentators on population growth suggest that rapidly growing populations are a symptom of poverty, and that rapid growth in populations can only be significantly checked by removing the underlying cause, namely by increasing the living standards of the population concerned.

There is, of course, some evidence for this view in the fact that populations in many developed, western countries are either growing very slowly, or are static.

In addition, it's clear that growing numbers of people in particular countries are not the only cause of environmental damage, because environmental damage occurs in countries with static or very slowly growing populations - the UK and most western European countries would be examples of this. Nevertheless, population growth and the consequent demands made on the environment by our existing, environmentally damaging lifestyles are clearly a cause of severe environmental problems.

For this reason, as I've said, Greenpeace continues to discuss this issue, and I'm very grateful to you for writing to us to underline your own personal concerns.

Yours sincerely..."

Oxfam   (reply from Supporters' services)

"Thank you for your recent enquiry about population issues. We are glad to have this opportunity to explain Oxfam's position on this important subject.

Oxfam is concerned about rapid population growth in developing countries. Where increasing numbers of people are trying to make a living in a limited area, the result is often worsening poverty and environmental degradation. Moreover, women's health and lives are often at risk when they have frequent, unplanned pregnancies.

However, Oxfam does not believe the answer to these problems is forcible imposition of family planning, as some people have suggested. As an organisation which respects the right of people in developing countries to make informed choices about their own lives, this would be an inappropriate approach for us. In addition, recent history can provide many examples of enforced family planning in developing countries which have not succeeded in reducing population growth at all.

The issues are much more complex than they sometimes seem. Poor people have large families *because they are poor.* In rural areas people often have many children to provide labour for the home and farm, as security for their old age because there are no state benefits, or because they know that some of them will die from poverty-related diseases before reaching adulthood. In urban areas too, people living in poor conditions, without access to education or health services, and on very low incomes, are unlikely to be able to make informed choices about family planning, or to afford contraceptives.

So, to address population growth, we believe that we have to tackle *poverty.* We do this by funding development work which includes family planning and mother and child health care, but only as part of a broader initiative. Related work often includes helping people to become literate, so they can understand written medical advice, and enabling them to increase their incomes, so they can afford contraceptives.

In Britain, even within living memory, people had much larger families than they do today. The reduction in population growth here can clearly be related to an increasing standard of living, and advances in health care and education. The same thing could happen in developing countries, if they are given the chance.

This is the philosophy behind Oxfam's approach. As an example of how it works in practice, I'd like to tell you about a family planning organisation with whom we're working in Senegal. ASBEF - the Senegalese Association for Family Well-Being- is the longest established family planning organisation in the country, and has clinics in the capital, Dakar, and four other cities. They are setting up two more at present, and eventually hope to cover the whole of Senegal.

Each of the clinics has about 100 visitors a day – women, and men too, who come for advice about family planning. They discuss with clinic workers what the most appropriate contraceptive method for them might be. The clinic also provides advice on related health issues, for example mother and child health care, and sexually transmitted diseases, including HIV/AIDS.

Because ASBEF knows it can't reach everyone directly, through the clinics, it trains volunteer health workers who go into their own communities, educate people about family planning, and sell low cost contraceptives. They reach about 100,000 people every year in this way.

Last year ABSEF trained 60 women who are members of women's groups supported by Oxfam. In the first year they have been working in their communities, these women have sent hundreds of people to the ABSEF clinics – the scheme is working very well.

ABSEF uses imaginative methods to get its message across. For example, they asked one of Senegal's most popular and respected singers, Baaba Maal, to appear on a calendar which they have distributed widely. They use radio, TV, newspapers, concerts, and even celebrity football matches, to promote their work.

They focus particularly on work with young people. They organise conferences in secondary schools, and activities at the children's sports and cultural associations which are popular in Senegal in the school holidays.

Oxfam supports the work of ABSEF because it offers *appropriate* family planning services. It doesn't tell people what they must do, but provides them with information and advice so that they can make informed choices (just like family planning clinics in Britain).

The enclosed leaflet provides some more examples of Oxfam supported projects which include family planning. I hope you find it interesting. If you'd like to read more about population issues, you might like to obtain the Oxfam book Population and Reproductive Rights, ..." (details given) ......

"Thank you for taking the trouble to contact us about this. Please let us know if you have any further questions.

With best wishes...".

WWF (reply from the Supporter Care Executive).

"Thank you for your letter received in this office on 16 June and for telephoning last week. Mr Napier has asked me to respond to your letter and I apologise for the delay in my reply.

WWF-UK is aware of demographic impacts in particular in relation to our field programmes. We commissioned some research into this, and I enclose the report "Do Numbers Matter? Population Impacts on Environmental Projects" which I hope will be of interest.

WWF is also concerned about consumption rates and lifestyle patterns both here in the UK and in other developed countries. For example, our consumption work includes transport issues, toxics, the tourism footprint, climate change and fisheries overconsumption.

You may also be interested to know that WWF-United States have also worked on this issue and you may wish to contact them for further information. For your reference the contact details for WWF-United States are: ...." (details given)

"Thank you for your letter and your interest in WWF.

Yours sincerely....".

The "Do numbers matter?" document explains the position of WWF. It points out the contrary views on the root causes of today's environmental problems – on the one hand, the view that economic policy, poverty, bad resource management and natural phenomena are the causes, on the other hand, the view that the root cause is "the unprecedented rates of population growth". WWF considers that "...the truth lies somewhere in between" these two hypotheses. And it specifically says that it recognises the importance of population stabilisation. But it sees the way to accomplish this as better education and reproductive health care provision. Also, significantly for the concern I express in the present book about the dangers of immigration, it says, in relation to its project sites, that the two most common population factors affecting the sites are population growth and immigration.

(b) reply from the CPRE (reply by the Director)

"Thank you for your letter of 9 February.

CPRE recognises that population growth is a contributory factor to the projected increase in household growth. It is, however, the changes in household structure (the formation of single person households etc) rather than population per se that remains our priority in the important debate on the household formation figures. We have an important part to play in drawing this distinct focus to media, public and official attention.

It is not within CPRE's remit to campaign on population growth per se. Our focus in this important debate will continue to lie elsewhere.

Thank you for taking the trouble to write to us.

Yours sincerely"

(ii) Assessment of NGO attitudes

As far as the international organisations are concerned, we can see that FoE, Greenpeace, Oxfam and WWF all recognise that population growth is intimately connected with environmental degradation in the developing world. However, with the exception of WWF, they regard poverty rather than population growth as the underlying main cause of that degradation. Indeed only Greenpeace and WWF seem to recognise that population growth might even be a cause. In general the NGOs accept the general United Nations position described in Chapter 1- the way to achieve population stabilisation is through the elimination of poverty, and the spread of health education and contraceptives and improving the position of women in society. Direct action to stabilise population size is not advocated. So in terms of the I=PAT, or I=PCT equation, direct action is advocated on only two of the elements on the right side of the equation, which I argued in Chapter 1 is an irrational approach – if we have three factors causing a problem, why not do something directly about all three? All the organisations draw attention to the need to curb the excessive consumption patterns in the developed world, but do not then go on to deal with the other side of the coin – the need for developing world countries to take action to directly curb their population growth. I think the approach of the organisations considered here is adopted by the majority of environmental campaigners and environmental organisations worldwide.

One point in the Oxfam letter deserves special comment:
 "In addition, recent history can provide many examples of enforced family planning in developing countries which have not succeeded in reducing population growth at all". This at best is a one-sided view since it makes no reference to the biggest success story of them all – the population policies of China.

Turning now to the one NGO with purely local remit, namely CPRE, this organisations strategy on household growth is in my view illogical. After all for a person to form a single person household, he or she must be born first, and so the number of such people will be increased by population growth. The data and projections on household growth dealt with in Section H of Chapter 2, show that changes in household structure (which would come under components C3 and C4 in the table shown there) account for a far smaller percentage of the total household growth than do population factors, especially the growth of the adult population. Since the CPRE is very concerned about the need to build houses on greenfield land which depends on the growth in the number of households, why do they focus attention on household structure, when population growth is the more important factor in causing increase in the number of households? I will return again to the approach of the CPRE in Chapter 12 Section B.

I think that most smaller environmental organisations, like the big international organisations, do not advocate direct action to stabilise and reduce human numbers, indeed are opposed to such policies; but there are a couple of smaller organisations in England that are prepared to advocate such measures. These are the Campaign for Political Ecology (ECO), and the Optimum Population Trust (OPT). These organisations adopt the approach I have advocated earlier, namely, we need direct action on P, as well as A and T in the I=PAT equation. A third small NGO, the Population Working Group, a networking organisation, while arguing for the stabilisation and then reduction of human population numbers, has a membership which includes those people and organisations which broadly support the UN line, and those who believe that measures aimed directly at stabilising and reducing the human population need to be adopted also.

Why is there this almost universal unwillingness to consider population control? We know some specific and immediate reasons for this unwillingness, such as the teaching of the Roman Catholic Church. But is there some deep underlying reason? Some believe there is, and it has been named, by P.Demeny the Hardinian taboo, after the American ecologist G. Hardin. It is a sort of psychological failing, supposedly inherent in our psyche, that makes us unable to control our population numbers. It prevents us from considering rationally the significance of population growth. It is at its most obvious when people fail to recognise that a population (of a country or region) has already reached the point where it not only exceeds its carrying capacity, but it cannot solve the problem either by sufficient out-migration or by generating enough exports to pay for the necessary food imports – a condition known as 'demographic entrapment' (King, 2000). Some environmentalists consider that several countries have already entered this state.

I wonder however, if there is not another, if you like more practical or financial reason, as far as NGOs are concerned. I think that the supporters of major NGOs will include many individual people and organisations that oppose population control for one reason or another. So the people who run these major NGOs, would not advocate population control because the consequence of such advocacy would be that they would lose a major part of their support on which there existence depends. Stevens makes a similar point in relation to the very strong advocacy of FOE of consumption reduction in the developed world. She argues that developing countries fear that the strong advocacy of the developed world for environmental protection by promoting, for example, legislation to tighten emission standards, would make it even more difficult for people in the developing world to get things like refrigerators - the developed world countries would be pulling up the drawbridge on their affluent lifestyles. Therefore, FOE has to stress how the developed world countries can meet sustainability targets (Stevens, 1999).

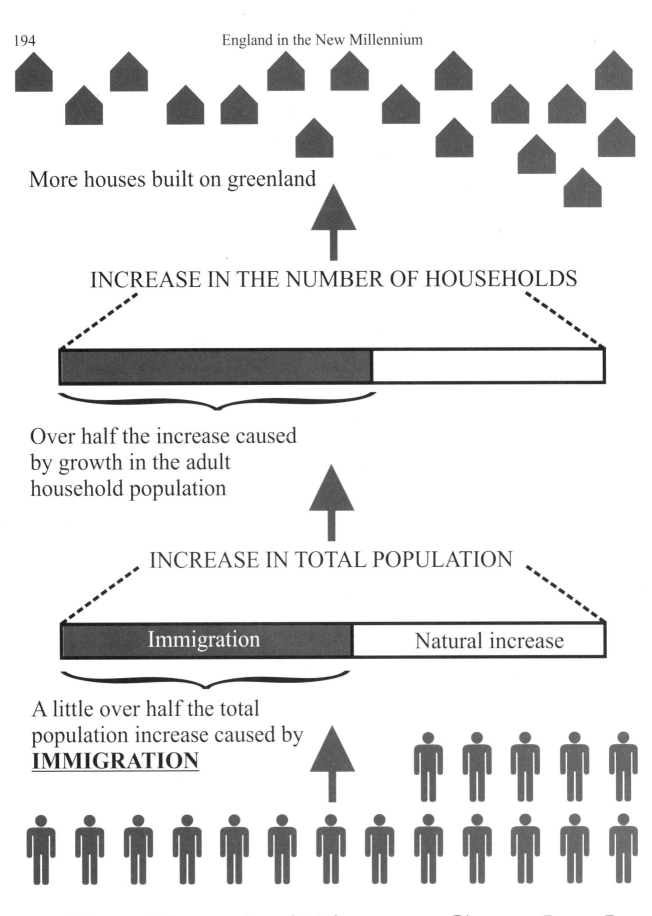

More houses built on greenland

INCREASE IN THE NUMBER OF HOUSEHOLDS

Over half the increase caused
by growth in the adult
household population

INCREASE IN TOTAL POPULATION

Immigration | Natural increase

A little over half the total
population increase caused by
IMMIGRATION

New Housebuilding on Greenland -
-The Population Connection
Fig. 11

Chapter 11

The transformation of the town

A central concern of this book is minimising green land loss to housing. Attention on this issue is usually focused on what we may loosely call urban form. In particular, attention is focused on 1) the extent that future housing can be accommodated within existing urban boundaries, and therefore on matters like the extent that brownfield land can provide the space for housing, and densification; 2) how we can make cities attractive places to live in, and so discourage counter-urbanisation.

However, there is another aspect to the problem, if we are thinking at the national level, as the Government recognises. This is the big variation between the regions of the country in the availability of brownfield land. Thus the National Land Use Data base has determined how much previously developed vacant and derelict land there is in each of the regions of England, and shown that the north of England, as was expected, contains much more of this land than southern England.

There is also big variation in employment levels and degree of economic development, and hence housing demand between the regions. So in large parts of the north it has proved difficult to attract business to urban areas, with concomitant greater pressure for development in the south, especially the South East Region of England. Therefore strategies must be developed which will spread development more evenly over the country. But it is not just a matter of North v. South. Every region has its own peculiar set of circumstances affecting investment and employment, affecting perceptions about the desirability of a place to live. All these considerations point to the need for some devolution of government to the regions, and the strengthening of regional authority by this and other means.

We need therefore, area-based policies. Such programmes are politically inescapable (Power, in Bate et al. 2000).

So we will first of all look at regional development, and then at urban form.

A. Recent developments on regional development and urban form

(i) Regional development

In Chapter 3, I explained how Government is wishing to break away from the 'predict and provide' approach to housing provision and move towards the alternative called 'plan, monitor and manage'. And I mentioned the new Government's February 1998 White Paper "Planning for the communities of the future" which said that the Government wishes to give more responsibility to the Regional Planning Conferences (regional groupings of LAs that have been in existence for some time and which produce Regional Planning Guidance). To further strengthen local and regional involvement in planning the government has now introduced two more bodies. I briefly discuss these in the next section.

Regional bodies

There are now within each region of England several organisations concerned with regional development. The situation is further much complicated by the fact that bodies of similar function have often been given different names in different regions! I shall not attempt to explore this latter complication in any detail in what follows.

For a long time there have been Regional Planning Conferences/ Regional Local Government Associations – conferences of the various Local Authorities. In the past, these have been the main bodies involved in producing the Regional Planning Guidance (RPG); this is however, now changing (see PPG 11 below). And the previous government, in 1994, established Government Offices for the Regions – one for each of the eight Regions. These are the civil service arm of government and are also involved in producing RPGs.

Now the new government, desiring to strengthen regional involvement in and control of development has established two more bodies -the Regional Development Agencies (RDAs) and the Regional Chambers RCs). The Boards of the Regional Development Agencies have eight to fifteen members, all appointed by the Secretary of State. The Statutory purposes of the RDAs was set out in the Regional Development Agencies Act (UKG, 1998) as being:

    (i) further economic development, social and physical regeneration;

    (ii) promote business support, investment and competitiveness;

(iii) promote employment;

(iv) enhance the development and application of skills;

(v) contribute to the achievement of sustainable development.

The Regional Chamber Boards vary in the number of members. Local Authority representatives take up most of the seats; but NGOs and other 'stakeholders' - business, environmental and community groups - are included (there is variation between chambers as regards which other organisations are included). Regional Chambers are described in the government White Paper "building partnerships for prosperity" as forums for consideration of issues of shared interest, such as transport and land-use planning, and economic development. Further, the White Paper describes the chambers as players in the Government's approach to 'regionalisation' based on decentralisation of power, partnership in decision-making, integration of policies across issues, and the need for clear leadership in spatial planning and economic development; RDAs are required to "take account of" the views of the Chambers. The CPRE considers that taking part in the activities of the RCs is likely to be an important way for CPRE regional groups to influence broad regional policies (CPRE, 1999a). We will return to Regional Chambers below (in considering PPG11).

The organisations just described are by no means the only ones concerned with regional aspects of development, and achieving sustainable development. Thus the new Countryside Agency (formed out of the former Countryside Commission and the Rural Development Commission) has offices in each region, and amongst the agencies objectives are promoting social equity and economic opportunity, and conserving and enhancing the countryside. Then there is the Ministry Agriculture, Fisheries and Food (MAFF) which operates through a series of regional centres, the Forestry Commission, English Heritage, etc. Finally new regional roundtables for sustainable development, involving NGOs, are emerging in most regions.

So many different organisations have an interest in regional development. And the UK Round Table on Sustainable Development (UKRTSD) has recently (July of this year) commented:

"Lip service is paid to sustainable development by most of the different bodies jostling in the regional market place, but no one body and no one political group is in a position to pull matters together and to take the leadership and responsibility for making it the key unifying concept at regional level" (UKRTSD, 2000).

It is far too early to assess if RDAs and RCs will fulfil their objectives. Will they be able, in conjunction with the other bodies, to bring about sustainable development? More particularly, will they be able to cause a re-direction of investment and employment across the country so as to maximise the urban capacities of northern cities for housing development or indeed, deal with the peculiar requirements of each region in these matters?

As far as the RDAs are concerned, the CPRE is sceptical:

" Primary CPRE concern is that RDAs may pursue crude economic growth (rather than sustainable development) tied to a rigid pursuit of Gross Domestic Product (GDP) targets. This could involve development of large 'greenfield' sites and road building, which pay little or token regard for environmental sustainability ... " CPRE, 1999b).

The Lord Rogers report

The Lord Rogers report, which I discussed in chapter 3, makes many specific recommendations that it considers, working with the grain of government policy (as the report puts it), will enable government objectives to be achieved. Some of these recommendations concern, or at least have major implications for, regional development. I deal with these now.

Chapter 5 makes the general point that a major reason for failure of urban regeneration has been government departmentalism. On the other hand, the report accepts the conclusion of the Joseph Rowntree Foundation that it is only at the local level that different facets of regeneration can be brought together in joined-up solutions. The RDAs have a vital part to play in translating national policy objectives of individual departments, into a coherent and integrated economic strategy for the regions. So government should strengthen its New Commitment to Regeneration programme endorsed in its 1998 local government white paper "in touch with the people".

Chapter 6 notes that while there are plenty of training courses in disciplines relevant to urban development (architecture, planning, landscape design, etc) a course that combines all relevant disciplines is usually absent. We need cross-disciplinary learning (the report commends the M.Sc in Urban Regeneration course at Sheffield Hallam university). The government should set up a network of Regional Resource centres to co-ordinate urban development training.

Chapter 8 notes that Regional Planning in the past has suffered from being fragmented – with general planning, transport and economic planning considered largely in isolation from each other. The government should strengthen regional planning by enabling RPG to provide an integrated spatial framework for planning and transport policies (integrated spatial planning was also mentioned in chapter 3).

Chapter 9 argues that the Regional Planning Bodies, could have a profound effect on the ability of the government to achieve its aims. The Government needs to put in place a long-term strategy for strengthening the Regional Planning Bodies including clarifying the statutory basis of the regional planning system. Clear regional targets for the re-use of recycled land and buildings must be introduced. And the Government must be prepared to give more money to Regional Planning Bodies - at the moment they are run "on little more than a shoe-string".

Chapter 13 observes that we have one of the most centralised systems of local government financing among western democracies. Within this system the current method of assessing need makes no explicit recognition of the management implications of maintaining declining urban areas where there are large tracts of derelict, vacant or under-used land and widespread land neglect. Arguing that public capital investment must increase, and noting that the government has announced a Revenue Grant Distribution review, the report recommends that spending formula used to allocate central resources to local government be changed to adequately reflect the financial needs of urban authorities in managing and maintaining their areas.

We can conclude from this section that the new regional agenda has great potential, but that aims and functions of the different organisations involved must be further clarified, their activities properly coordinated to produce a clear strategy for sustainable development, and more power given to the RDAs and the RCs to implement the strategy. The recent policy developments contained in PPG11 would seem to be a step in the right direction.

Planning Policy Guidance Note 11 Regional Planning

When I thought I had finished writing this book, the Government published its new PPG on Regional Planning (October 2000). This discusses the role of Regional Chambers. As we saw earlier, the production of RPGs in the past has largely been the responsibility of Regional Planning Conferences. Now this is to change (para 2.03). Regional Planning for London is to become the responsibility of the Greater London Authority. And in several Regions outside London, the Regional Chambers will become the bodies with the main responsibility for the production of RPGs. PPG11 has a strong focus on the necessity of involving other stakeholders in the production of RPGs. Here it specifically mentions the RDAs, statutory environmental bodies, business and commercial organisations, transport providers, education and health authorities. The planning bodies of neighbouring regions and bodies that may cross regional boundaries like some National Park Authorities, should also be consulted (para 2.07). Indeed, developing regional objectives should be based on the 'collective view' produced by this stakeholder consultation process (para 2.08). It would seem then that this change of policy emphasis has the potential to answer the criticism of UKRTSD mentioned above.

(ii) Urban Form

The review of literature given in chapter 3 shows that government policy on urban development has been gradually moving in the general direction of the ideal city, including minimising greenland loss to housing. Attention was given in that chapter to the ideas contained in the Lord Rogers 1999 Urban Task Force report Towards an Urban Renaissance, and I quoted the mission statement of the task force. From this statement and what follows later in the report, it is clear the underlying assumption of the Task Force's work was that if cities can be genuinely re-designed, people will want to return to live in them. This seems to be a widespread belief. I deal now with specific recommendations of the report.

The Lord Rogers report

a) Principles of planning and maintenance

Chapter 2 ("designing the urban environment") asserts that we seem to have lost the art of designing cities. This century cities have become more fragmented – a loosening of urban form with a growing segregation between different uses and different users. We need to integrate all aspects of urban development in order to produce the compact and well-connected city. The key here is the preparation of the spatial masterplan that I described in Chapter 3). The report recommends that making public funding and planning permissions for area regeneration schemes should be made conditional on the production of such a spatial masterplan. Local authorities should prepare a single strategy for their public realm and open space.

Chapter 4 ("managing the urban environment") observes that many people reject our cities and choose to live elsewhere because cities are badly managed and maintained. To rectify the situation, the government must realise that we have to manage the whole of the urban environment more strategically, which requires giving more powers and resources to local authorities to do the job, indeed a strategic role should become a clear statutory duty. Local authorities should be able to enforce more strictly against those who refuse to meet basic standards of maintenance, and be able to ensure that local landowners such as rail companies and hospitals maintain their land and buildings in good condition.

b) The report contains many recommendations that would help to make maximum use of brownfield land and empty property, and increase density of housing development. These are principally given in chapters 2, 9 and 11:

Chapter 2 observes that it is central government, which must draw together the existing policy threads on urban design, and create a national urban design framework. This then needs to be translated into revision of planning and funding guidance that would:

- discourage LAs from using 'density' and 'over-development' as reasons for refusing planning permission (all too often the words 'intensity' and 'density' have carried with planners the connotation of urban cramming);

- create a presumption in planning against excessively low density urban development;

- provide advice on the use of density standards.

Chapter 9 ("managing the land supply") asserts that the planning system should be the main tool for managing land supply, so should be strengthened to do this. This would make it easier to recycle previously developed land so that a greater proportion of new development takes place in existing urban areas. The sequential approach (described under PPG3 in Chapter 3) should be formally adopted, and planning changed from 'predict and provide' to 'plan, monitor and manage'.

Now LAs need to know what spare capacity for development exists in their areas. The tool for achieving this is urban capacity studies. In practice, however, LAs have often put such restrictions on these studies that they have failed to identify the total capacity. This is because LAs have failed to question existing planning policies on matters like design standards and parking provision. They also tend to underestimate the potential supply from windfall (that is, unforeseen development opportunities becoming available unexpectedly, which can be studied by looking at the past record of sites). So there needs to be a consistent approach to capacity studies which take this broader view. And the Task Force recommended that all LAs should be required to regularly carry out such studies.

The chapter identifies various ways that the proper use of brownfield land has been held up in the past, and proposes ways to facilitate brownfield use:

- Certain northern authorities, knowing how difficult it is to persuade developers to use derelict land, have not really tackled the regeneration of their urban heartlands, but rather made big allocations of land for house building on greenfield sites, thinking that this will overcome the low demand for housing in their area. This should be stopped. Recycling targets for areas of low demand in inner urban areas should be set "very high indeed".

- Former public utilities often have large land banks which they hold onto for 'operational purposes' without using it, and thus depriving LAs of the ability to use that land. The Government should make it a statutory duty for public bodies and utilities to release such land for urban regeneration.

- Different parts of urban sites suitable for development are often under different ownership. Many owners hang onto vacant land, partly because they think they may be able to get a better price for it later. Now at present, vacant land is exempt from business rates – there is no charge for keeping the land vacant. The Government should then prepare and use a system for taxing vacant land. The powers of LAs to enforce sale of land should also be strengthened.

- At the moment, owners of derelict land often earn money by allowing sites to accommodate temporary car parking and advertising hoardings, made possible by temporary planning permissions granted by the LAs. Government should alter the law so that such 'low-grade uses' are no longer deemed to have such planning permission.

- LAs do have powers of compulsory purchase but there is such a complex of legislation, government guidance and case law that LAs are often reluctant to use these powers. So Government should both consolidate and streamline the Compulsory Purchase legalisation (the report goes on to consider compensation for owners of property on such sites).

In the past, government household projections, which are based on past trends, have been used in a 'top down' approach to determine local provision for housing, and this has both perpetuated urban sprawl and discouraged investment. The new system – known as 'plan, monitor and manage' aims to break this 'predict and provide approach' by giving local authorities greater control of housing land allocation, and making much more use of local assessment of need in building up an overall national assessment of need.

Chapter 11 ("recycling the buildings"), deals with the fact that there are lots of empty or part empty buildings in our cities that could be used for housing. The chapter gives some facts. In 1998, nearly three-quarter of a million dwellings in England were empty. Some of this housing is social housing, which more affluent people could not use even if they wanted to since the housing is specifically for the poor. Many historic buildings are under-used; but technical and legal problems make it difficult for developers to take on such buildings for regeneration development. Big shops often have vacant floors over the ground floor. In 1998 it was estimated that in London alone, 73,000 additional residential units could be created in London from existing vacant or under-used shops and upper floors. LAs have often not made any big impact on the amount of empty space in cities. The chapter makes a series of proposals including:

- LAs must be legally required to produce, and maintain, an empty properties strategy which sets clear targets to reduce vacancy levels.

- Social housing should be thrown open to middle income people and students.

- New measures should be introduced to encourage the restoration of historic buildings including revision of the key PPG here (PPG 15 "Planning and the Historic Environment").

- More public assistance should be given for converting empty space above shops.

- At the moment, thee is no VAT charge on new house building, but refurbishment and conversion each carry full VAT (17.5%). The report recommends that there should be no Vat on conversions and refurbishments (but notes that EU law would have to be modified to achieve this).

- At the moment, some owners of empty dwellings where there is vandalism, or the owners deliberately do some 'deconstruction', are exempt from Council Tax. The report recommends that such owners should become liable to full payment of Council Tax.

c) Effect of development on the environment

One of the major concerns of environmentalists is that while businesses and industries benefit from exploitation of natural resources and development like house building, they cause much damage to the environment which affects the population at large, and for which they do not have to pay (these are termed the 'external' costs). Such external costs should be borne by the businesses causing the damage, which would encourage them to operate in a more environmentally friendly way.

Now under existing planning law, LAs can ask developers to use a portion of their profits either to provide/ improve facilities at the development site, or contribute to LA coffers – the so called planning gain. However, development causes wide environmental damage and the developer does not pay for this. The report lists these environmental impacts:

(i) increase in air pollution caused by increased road traffic use;

(ii) increase in energy use and greenhouse gas emissions;

(iii) loss of countryside;

(iv) damage to biodiversity;

(v) soil erosion;

(vi) increased pressure on the LAs waste and water management systems.

The report notes that there are very real difficulties in trying to make the developer pay for this damage. It nevertheless recommends that a system of environmental charges should be developed and introduced which would complement, not replace, existing planning gain.

(iii) Is the general approach advocated adequate to secure regional development and containment of urban expansion?

Let us return to a central concern of this book – minimising green land loss to development. How much of our countryside is going to be lost to housing?

Now the United Kingdom Round Table for Sustainable Development recommended the Government to adopt a Target of 75% new housing on previously developed land (UKRTSD 1997a). The Government however has adopted the target that by 2008, 60% of additional housing should be provided on previously developed land, (DETR, 1998b. See also PPG3). Now suppose the Government achieved its target of 60%. **That would still leave an awful lot of housing to be built on greenland!**

Government thinking on future housing development concentrates on the medium term. For example, DETR (Ibid) says that the housing projections then available implied that the housing needed for the additional households might be 175,000 homes a year up to 2016. However, population growth will not end in 1916 – the population is currently projected to go on rising into the thirties, after which it may decline. Now we saw in chapter 2 that net immigration projections have underestimated the actual flow of migrants in recent times. Furthermore, we saw how a few years ago, it was assumed net immigration flow would decrease fairly rapidly to zero, whilst the latest projections assume net immigration to continue at the same rate for the whole projection period. Now supposing that net immigration continues at the present rate indefinitely, or even increases, not just in the next couple of decades, but for many decades to come. This is possible. The precautionary principle suggests we should take this possibility seriously. Such continued influxes of migrants would mean continued loss of Greenland to development.

To return to the 60% target. The Lord Rogers report concluded that it was unlikely that the Government would achieve even its 60% target, under policies in place at the time the report was produced (introduction to the report by Lord Rogers and chapter 14). Even in terms of Government funding, this would have to be massively increased if the goal was to be achieved (p.286 in the report). The report clearly thought that most or all its recommendations would have to be implemented to secure the 60% goal. Thus chapter 16 comments that if significant policy changes in line with the recommendations in the report are made, the 60% target can be achieved.

However, on the 30th June this year the BBC reported that Lord Rogers, observing that we live in some of the worst cities in Europe, claimed that only a handful of the reports recommendations had been implemented, and that there was no realisation of the problems (of urban regeneration) across government departments. And the previous month the CPRE issued a one page study of housing provision in relation to Regional Planning Guidance, and concluded that collated over the whole country, and for the period 1996-2016, the Government would achieve only 56.7% of new housing on brownfield land.

If we are to secure urban regeneration, and redress the imbalance between north and south in terms of development, a lot will depend on the attitude and power of developers who will wish to work with the grain of market forces. Now the Lord Rogers report does come up with recommendations, which affect the power of the developer. For example, in relation to the aim of securing mixed tenure housing developments where developers are required to provide affordable homes, developers frequently either buy themselves out of the obligation or else design their way out by site layouts that separate the low cost housing from the rest. The report here recommends Government to review the mechanisms of planning gain so that developers have less scope to get out of their obligations.

However, the emphasis in the report seems to be on securing the cooperation of developers to bring about urban renaissance rather than on curbing their potential for hindering sustainable development. The big question is whether the strengthening of regional bodies proposed by the government together with the sort of modest changes in developer constraint of the sort contained in the Rogers report, will be sufficient to change a now long continued pattern of development where market forces have secured counter-urbanisation and disproportionate development in the south, and at the same time secure regeneration in the cities, especially in the north.

Underlying the evolving regional strategies is still the belief in competition as the, or at least a principle way to secure regional regeneration. The RDAs should strengthen competitiveness. But surely this means that a given RDA will complete with other RDAs; we must achieve regeneration in our region – the devils take the other regions! And we saw in Chapter 3 that city leaders in Sheffield think that enabling Sheffield to compete successfully against surrounding areas is the way forward.

Recent reports do not suggest any big improvement in the disparity between regions. The BBC announced 6th December 1999 that a new Government report showed big variations between Regions. The report noted that the International Labour organisation found employment rates in February to April 1999 varied from 3.7% in the South East to 10.1% in the North East Region. At the same time, there was big within-region variation. And now on 21ˢᵗ August 2000 the BBC reported that the Oxford Economic Forecasting Unit, in a survey commissioned by the Financial Times, showed that a slump in manufacturing industry has widened the gap between regional growth rates. The figures suggest that the South East of England will experience a 3.7% economic growth rate during the next year compared with a 2.7% growth in the North East. The employment rate is also set to go up in the south, while there will probably be little or no change in the north. The dividing line seems to be a line running from the Wash to the Bristol Channel. Such reports do not suggest that Government's Regional Strategy is going to produce any big changes at least in the short term.

Finally, as was mentioned earlier, there is an underlying assumption in the Lord Rogers report and elsewhere, that if we can successfully re-design cities, people will return to live in them. But no matter how radically we re-design cities, they can never be as quiet and beautiful as the countryside. It is therefore, I think, a dangerous illusion that improved city design will cause a significant number of people to return to live in cities. Most people will not return unless the Government makes them do so.

(iv) The Henry George Foundation on the subject of urban decay and unemployment

In the next section of this chapter I shall be concentrating on urban design as the way forwards to restrain the growth of built up land. I will not attempt to carry out any overall assessment of economic factors, mainly because economics is a technical, and to the layman, arcane subject requiring special training, which I have not had. However, I would like to mention one economic approach to the problems of cities, since it strikes me as an imaginative and radical approach, and I believe only radical solutions will suffice. It is also an approach to which, unfortunately, little attention seems to have been given, so I would like to draw the attention of readers to it. The approach is land value taxation.

In Chapter 1 Section 8 I explained that this idea was championed by Henry George, and I outlined the underlying philosophy of the idea. In England at present, the approach of Henry George is promoted and developed by the Henry George Foundation. Those readers who are interested in finding out more about this approach should contact the Henry George Foundation in London who can supply further information, such as the information I have used in preparing the following brief account (telephone: 0171 377 8885. e-mail: HGF_IGU@compuserve.com).

Underlying the proposals of the Georgists is the realisation that there are two quite distinct categories of taxation: taxes such as Income tax and VAT, which Georgists claim act as disincentives to production and trade, and taxes on land, which they claim have a stimulating effect on trade by encouraging productive efforts and discouraging the practice of holding land out of use. Now these ideas are applied to the problems of out cities.

It is generally agreed that the different problems encountered in cities cannot be solved in isolation, because they interact in complex causative fashion. We can mention urban decay- the existence of derelict land, badly maintained buildings, vacant property, unemployment, and inadequate wages at the lower end of the wage scale. To the Georgists, making rent of land the principal source of public revenue could play a decisive part in solving these problems. It is important first to realize just what the term rent means to an economist. It is payment for the use of land.

To understand how the system works it is best to consider an example. Bear in mind that the land owner will normally try to extract as much rent as possible from people who take a lease – up to about the level which would cause the shop keeper to go out of business and leave an empty property on the owners hands. Suppose a shopkeeper has a lease on a property and pays an annual rent and also pays for repairs, the rent to be reviewed every five years. But further development took place in the neighbourhood, with lots of house building. The shopkeeper benefited in that more people used his shop. But each five-year period brought a massive increase in rent, as rentable value rose, largely through the activities of the local builders and the activities of the numerous people who moved into the district. Since the shopkeeper in question was maintaining the building, the one person who contributed little or nothing to the enormous increase in rent was the landowner. The situation leads in some cases to such shopkeepers failing to make ends meet and having to leave.

The shopkeeper, in order to keep up with the increasing rent will innovate as much as possible to maximise profits. Suppose he reduces labour costs by changing to a self-service system. His profits will increase. But his success will get around, and competitors will appear who are prepared to pay a bigger rent. This will enable the landowner to increase rent. Generalising from this, one can say that in a freely competitive economy, the benefits from all technical progress will mainly end up as increases in the rentable value of land, which tends to stiffly increase. All kinds of improvement tend to ultimately lead to an increase in rent. The overall result is that in financial terms, the landowner is the cat that gets the cream. In cities, 90% of rent is collected by landowners. This suggests that there needs to be a way to ensure that all the cream goes collectively to those people who are performing a useful function and not to people who are merely deriving benefit from land and the exertion of others. The way is to tax land value.

A familiar feature of our cities is large areas of derelict land. The main reasons for this waste and neglect of inner-city spaces, is, in the Georgists view, land price inflation and land hoarding – land speculation. To understand land speculation, one must be aware that the land market is quite different from the market in consumer or capital goods. With the latter categories, the way the market responds is usually simple. If there is a glut, the price falls. If there is a shortage, prices rise. When prices rise, tomato growers or lorry manufacturers produce more, and prices tend to fall again. Alternatively, the producers or manufacturers simply move their goods from places where they are sold relatively cheaply to places where they are relatively dear.

The land market operates differently. For land is distinguished from other things – one cannot produce more land to satisfy increase in demand, and one cannot move it around from one place to another. If land prices rise, more people attempt to buy, which is just the opposite of what happens with consumer goods and manufactured products. . And where there is a big demand for land people do not bring it into use, but hold it back from use in the hope of even bigger increases.

To return to the derelict land issue. At an earlier stage in the development of the city, when population was growing and industry expanding, land was greatly in demand and land price rose rapidly. Owners of land then realized that they should hold on to land as an investment which would improve – they would wait to sell until price rose still further. However, even in times of recession and little development, people still buy land as it is the most secure of all possessions- it cannot be destroyed, and eventually it is bound once more to be in high demand – no one can manufacture more land. Hence we see one causative agent of inner city decay – land that is simply idle.

The tax system aggravates the situation. The owner of an urban site who neglects it is charged little or nothing in taxation (there is no business rate charged for vacant land). But the owner of a similar site who clears it, makes it safe for human habitation, and builds a factory or office block where others can find employment, is punished for his efforts by a hefty business rate charge. So business rates operate as a check on regeneration.

Now since the seventies, successive governments have made strenuous efforts to tackle the problem of urban decay. For example, they have moved government offices out of London to less prosperous areas. Money has been spent on Development and Enterprise Zones. New roads have been built, and grants given for land reclamation. Local authorities have been ordered to sell some sites and development corporations have been set up to simplify and speed up planning procedures. But all this has cost taxpayers money, and the landowners have benefited.

It can then be contended that the root cause of urban decay is land price inflation aggravated by an unfair tax system. The solution, to Georgists, is obvious: change the tax system so that it works to discourage the holding of land out of use and to encourage regeneration. This can easily be done by transferring the tax base from the value of buildings to the value of the sites on which they are built. Land of the same type in the same area would then attract the same level of taxation whether used or unused. This form of taxation is Land Value Taxation.

A lot of attention is given to the growing disparity between the rich and the poor, the division of cities into affluent and poverty stricken areas, and extensive unemployment. Various theories have been advanced to explain high unemployment. For example, increased mechanization reducing the amount of labour required. To the Georgist, none of these explanations are satisfactory. For example, new inventions of mechanization do reduce the labour required, but that does not necessarily mean there is a genuine superfluity of labour, for various wants of society, requiring labour, remain unsatisfied. The long period of full employment from the 1940s to the early 1970s was a period of rapid mechanization.

Unemployment is greatest for the unskilled – there are more of them in the market than there are jobs available. Consequently wages are very low, so many unemployed have not sought work, rather they have relied on unemployment benefits. To the Georgists the key is to raise wages. But employers say that high employment taxes make this impossible. They would have to raise prices to cover the extra cost, which would make them uncompetitive.

Now if taxes which fall on employment such as PAYE and national Insurance were greatly reduced, it would become possible for employers to increase wages. The money for this would come from the one source that does not affect production, which provides a totally unearned income – the rent of land. It seems likely that 20 to 30 percent of national GDP is currently really land rent. That is an enormous amount of money.

One can look at the unemployment situation also in its relationship to derelict and other brownfield land. Land speculation means that people are unable to use land to produce goods that will satisfy their own or other people's demands. This results in less demand for labour and hence unemployment. To, put it more succinctly – a site held out of use means that labour is deprived of an employment opportunity.

Another reason why city regeneration often does not take place is that there is a shortage of affordable land in places where people want to live and work. Once again, changing to the tax system advocated by the Georgists would largely, in their view, solve the problem. A tax on land values would make idle land a liability for the owner. Consequently, the flow of land onto the market would be increased. This would curb the increase in land prices, especially in areas such as the South East, and stimulate economic growth in other places (e.g. the North where unemployment is higher).

Such then is the way that land value taxation could, in the opinion of the Henry George Foundation, and if thoroughly implemented, vastly improve the possibility of regenerating our cities. And this ends my attempt to present the approach of the Foundation.

A very radical approach. And, like other radical ideas, it has not received a warm reception. Governments and powerful interest groups are usually wary of radical ideas. Whereas it is one of the themes of this book that only adopting radical ideas will allow us to save the world.

Now we saw earlier that one of the recommendations of the Lord Rogers report was that the Government should consider developing a scheme to tax vacant land. However, if one studies the section where this is discussed (p.224-5) it is clear that the report does not advocate the sort of radical approach of the Henry George Foundation, and I do not think this Foundation and Henry George are mentioned in the report.

B. Towards a Strategy for urban regeneration

Thinking in terms of the general approach to planning, there are two approaches.

The first approach, which is the one normally adopted, is to tweak the existing planning system, removing its most obvious defects, and consider what are the minimum further changes that need to be made in order to progress towards sustainable development (by planning system here I do not just mean town planning, but the totality of national planning – monetary, economic, social and environmental). The approach however, does not challenge underlying assumptions. In particular, it accepts that market forces, often partly globally or at least EU region determined, will provide the vehicle for progress. All that is needed is to apply minimum restraint to market forces so as to achieve small changes in direction. It is all rather like making minor alterations to a river system in a valley – you straighten sections here, put a barrier there, make small diversions of part of the waters for irrigation etc.

The alternative approach, in line with the strategy advocated in Chapter 9, is to start with a comprehensive and quite detailed vision of the future England. No constraints are accepted as inevitable. Then all attention is focused on achieving the vision.

(i) Control of Regional development

Rephrasing one of the basic ideas in Chapter 9, I suggest that the government needs to work out where it wants different types of economic activity, different business sectors and industries, to be situated in England. I mean here more than vague aspirations. Government should prepare a detailed Master Plan of England, showing the distribution of the different sectors first within regions, then sub-regions, and indicating the corresponding distribution of the total population of England.

In working out this masterplan Government would work closely with the recently created Regional Bodies and with National NGOs. At the same time as working out the masterplan, Government would need to modify existing laws so that it has the powers to implement the plan. We may note here that this big increase in Government control will not eliminate competition and the benefits which most analysts consider stem from competition. Rather competition would be re-directed. But it would be no longer possible for a given region to seek to simply attract as much business as possible, of whatever kind, and thus probably disadvantage a neighbouring region.

It will of course be objected that we just cannot tell qualitatively and quantitatively where we wish development to be focused. The rapid pace of technological change means that there will be changes in the means of production, in what we do produce, and in how we distribute products, which we cannot possibly foresee. But surely we can prepare the sort of distribution plan I mean provided it does not become a tablet set in stone. We have to think of the plan as something that will continue to evolve over time.

(ii) Control of urban development

This section is based on, and extends, a radical strategy for urban renewal that I proposed two years ago (Barker 1998). This started by stating *two goals*:

   *(i) **NO** more development on rural green land i.e. **ALL** development to be confined to existing built up areas, be it city, town or village;*
   *(ii) to gradually **REDUCE** the spread of built up areas - reduce the area of cities, towns and villages by successively removing peripheral building.*

Now discussion about urban renewal and future densification seems to have largely swirled around the periphery of the present suburbs - it has focused on inner city regeneration, development along what are termed 'transport corridors', and the building of new suburbs; it has usually either neglected existing suburbs, or assumed they can only make a marginal contribution to providing additional dwellings (see Box below). **Yet, in the present writers view, it is in the existing suburbs, especially the affluent ones, where the key to preventing urban expansion lies.**

Attitudes to suburbia

Curiously, existing suburbs seem to be largely regarded as somehow inviolable in their present form by the planning fraternity. The mainstream environmental movement and the coterie of town planners seems to have a decidedly middle-class ethos. Planning is for the rest of the population - those who cannot afford a large semi-detached house in the suburbs. One can easily imagine that the vast majority of planners and environmentalists live in outer suburbs or countryside villages and do not question their own right to the appropriation of a sizeable piece of ground for their own private occupation. It is true there has been some discussion about what I could call a limited tinkering with existing suburbia. Thus there has been discussion about very limited infill of small sites within existing suburban residential areas (for example, Llewelyn-Davies 1997). Occasionally there has been the hint that a more general densification of suburbs might be possible (for example, Elkin et al 1991). And in Chapter 3 we saw that the recent "planning for sustainable development: towards better practice" (DETR, 1998c), which took a more radical view on densification than previous publications, seems to suggest that densification might extend to existing suburbs.

The Lord Rogers report is tantalising in this respect. As you read it you think it might get there, but it never does. Thus in chapter 2 p.51, having talked in general terms about what needs to be done in terms of design, it goes on in the penultimate paragraph:

   "For some suburban areas this could involve 'retrofitting' or 'recycling' land and buildings to provide better local services at focal points, and improved public transport connections. It could also involve development densities and provision of facilities increasing in order to attract and integrate new residents within existing communities".

But that is where it stops. There is no suggestion of developing a policy for the gradual total transformation of existing suburbs.

An exception to the general approach that began this box, is some recent research sponsored by the Joseph Rowntree Foundation (Gwilliam et all 1998). The authors note that research on the contribution of existing suburbs to urban regeneration is a relatively neglected field of research. They find this disturbing since suburbs are a major part of our urban fabric both in terms of the amount of our population accommodated in them, and in the scale of land occupied (this was a basic point I made in my 1998 strategy). They conclude that selective densification of housing in suburbia is possible, for example round re-designed suburban centres. They also note that in some areas suburban housing stock is 'visibly ageing' and that in such situations replacement may be necessary, implying that densification would be possible in such situations. They conclude that over time, existing suburbs could make a significant contribution to meeting housing need. However, they also conclude (pages 65 and 69) that large scale physical restructuring of existing suburbs at least in the short term, would be impractical, both politically and economically speaking.

We can conclude from this little appraisal, that while planners consider existing suburbs could make a contribution to provision of extra dwellings, there is no strategy in place for a wholesale re-organisation of the suburbs.

If we look at a city from the air, one is struck by the fact that the greater part of the total expanse is residential suburbs. These often have a high proportion of terrace houses in the inner suburbs, semi-detached and detached houses in the outer suburbs. The 1991 classification of all housing in England by Dwelling Type shows terrace housing and semi-detached housing to be the preponderant types:

Percentage

Terraced house	29.4
Semi-detached house	29.5
Detached house	19.5
Purpose built flat	14.7
Converted flat/other	6.9

Source: English House Condition Survey as reported in SSE, 1996.

So suburban housing forms the greatest part of city area, and to the extent that it consists of semi-detached and detached dwellings, it is very inefficient from the point of view of economising space. Even in areas where terrace housing is dominant, where this in only two storey accommodation (or two stories and attic), density could often be increased without sacrificing environmental quality. So there is potential for increasing dwelling density throughout most of the suburbs.

Typically suburban housing has a small front garden, next to the street, sometimes merely a hedge and a piece of largely concreted ground round that quintessential English feature, the bay window, and a larger back garden. That other quintessential English feature of the suburbs is that most of the property is privately owned. As Cousins (1997) writes, there is a uniquely English fascination with home ownership as the most desirable form of tenure.

Currently around 70% of homes are privately owned (JRF, 1997b). The percentage of dwellings that are owner-occupied is much lower in France and Germany than in England, the percentage that are rented much higher. In 1991 the situation was England: 66%; France: 54%; Germany: 38% owner-occupied. But the proportion owner occupied has been rising in England in recent decades. The figures for 1971, 1981 and 1991 are respectively 52.1%, 57.0% and 65.9% (SSE, ibid). This difference between England and its two big north European neighbours can perhaps be linked to different cultural perceptions between northern Europe and the UK. In the former, town or city centre apartments are favoured more than suburban dwellings, although there are large public housing estates. "...The aspiration to an arcadian, single-use area, single-family house lifestyle is more developed in the Anglo-Saxon world than in Continental Europe. Builders in Britain would argue that suburbs, as they have been so far, are what the market demands" (Gwilliam et al 1998).

From the point of view of the strategy I wish to develop, the key features of suburbs are that suburban housing forms the greatest part of city area, getting on for a third of this housing is terraced housing and about half is semi-detached /detached; this is a very inefficient use of space. Most of the housing is privately owned.

Suburban housing developments are then, predominantly an inefficient use of space. There is potential for increasing dwelling density throughout most of the suburbs; furthermore, this could be achieved with little or no reduction in the total area of ground level green space, by using mainly 'middle-rise' instead of 'low-rise' buildings. We would need to use building designs different from those that have dominated our cities for so long. Two come to mind - the first a design from Sweden referred to by Ackerman (1979), the second a design by Sherlock (1991) also advocated by FoE (Elkin et al, 1991).

I take the Swedish example first. Ackerman explained that the dominant type of housing in Sweden at that time was three rectangular blocks ('loaves' is his word) - houses or flats - built at right angle to each other. He gives a pictorial illustration of one such grouping. The three 'loaves' form three sides of a rectangle. Each is three storeys high; each has the block composed of three vertical units, each with small balconies. He then gives an illustration to show what the architect P. Broberg did with this design, and comments:

"Broberg has totally changed the character by making the area denser, expanding the balconies to be truly useful, adding condominimiums on top of the houses, putting elevators on the fronts to make them operational for the handicapped, etc. The apartment space added is 40%. Suddenly a dead-dull block has become attractive, lively and changeable. It has become part of a living city".

There is still plenty of green ground space, and there are roof top gardens. The austere straight line and rectangle dominated scene is transformed into an intriguing and pleasant variety of shape and line (I reproduced the illustrations mentioned above in my 1998 book).

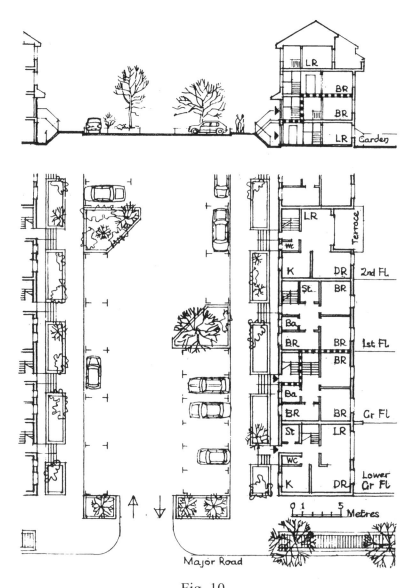

Fig. 10
From Sherlock(1991). Reproduced with the permission of HarperCollins Publishers Ltd.

The Sherlock design (Fig. 10) has as the housing unit a short terrace, four storeys high; in each section of a terrace there are two flats, one above the other, the two middle floors being where the bedrooms are located, so noise from living rooms and kitchens (top and bottom floor) are minimised. Each flat has its own separate entrance onto the street, which is broad, and has a similar terrace on its other side. When one considers that much terrace housing today is only two storeys, the Sherlock design, even with the gaps along the street between terrace units, could increase housing density appreciably.

Of course, other designs could be used for the new housing, but I just take the two types described above as examples.

The writer's proposal is then for a wholesale, universal replacement of all suburban housing (except that which has already been changed to a more modern design with denser form). This would involve eliminating semi-detached and detached houses (unless large and subdivided into flats), at least in their present largely two storey form, and redesigning most of the terrace housing, with the prime aim of housing densification.

There would even be a place in some areas for high-rise buildings. Many people following on the largely disastrous experiment with high-rise building post World War 2 have dismissed high-rise housing. But the failure of the high-rise experiment was not inherent in the concept of high-rise itself. It was more to do with the peculiar circumstances of the time, and the faulty way the schemes were often implemented. In Sheffield for example, slum clearance was also the break up of communities, as people were uprooted and dumped in the high-rise. Some people do not recognise the fact that communities did exist in the slums. People had a pride in where they lived. I remember a slum where as you walked down the street, you saw a row of carefully whitewashed front door steps. All was not dereliction.

High-rise housing can be viable, and desirable. For example, a report by Paul Brown in the Guardian Newspaper on 6th January 1999, explained the value of new surveillance technology in transforming high-rise blocks from half empty fear-ridden hulks to havens of security. The report also gave examples of successful high-rise projects like Trellick Tower in west London. And an interview with a resident in a Manchester high-rise block spoke of good views, quietness, and cooperation between tenants.

A later article in the Guardian (11th March 1999) gave details of the history of the Trellick Towers development. The article claims the architect (Goldfinger) who designed the building in the first place in the 1960s had at the heart of his thinking "the detailed consideration of the environmental conditions conducive to human welfare". The failure was not a failure of design. Various factors had probably contributed to the failure of the experiment, and the article singles out the action taken by the Greater London Council: the Council axed the plan to have a lobby concierge as such snoopers were "vessels of fascism". Denied necessary security, crime soared. In the 1980s a new residents association was formed, and a management group established. This began the transformation. Now the tower is one of London's most fashionable addresses

In re-organising housing, distinct solo-use housing areas would not be maintained. On the contrary, local facilities would be incorporated in developments, and indeed the urban village concept would guide overall design. In terms of building form, there would be a pleasing-to-the-eye variety of height and shape.

Implementing the proposal for widespread suburban change would involve demolition of most existing residential buildings, much at least temporary destruction of existing gardens (but not necessarily reduction of total green land area), change in the law concerning property rights, and behind all these things a fundamental shift in public opinion. The changes should be accompanied by a massive reduction in car ownership or at least car use. All these changes should also be accompanied by a determined effort to ensure that residents become involved, individually and collectively, in horticultural production with the aim both of satisfying all basic needs for vegetables for human consumption, and using urban food production as a means of both strengthening community spirit and re-establishing for city dwellers, a closer link with nature. Such food production is discussed in my earlier book; I did some calculations there which showed that provided car use was considerably reduced (therefore less parking space and suburban roads could be narrowed), and the 'front garden' of houses was used for food production, English cities could be largely self sufficient for vegetable production (Barker, 1998, Chapter 12).

A search would be made for the most run-down terrace and semi-detached housing. There is a lot of this around so such housing could be easily identified. Then one would narrow the search to housing with the lowest occupancy and where there was the highest unemployment - again it would be easy to find examples with at least one of these criteria well exhibited, and it should not prove too difficult to find some examples that fit both criteria. Local residents would then be approached and the basic idea outlined. Good artist-architect teams would construct not only coloured drawings of possible developments, but large-scale models. Residents would be invited to comment and take designs further. Once a design had been agreed, the local people would take the maximum part in physically breaking down the old, and putting up the new; and as far as possible, any people brought in from outside to assist would be selected by the local residents on the basis of their experience of such people. What should be avoided from the start is trying to make things easy by developing demonstration housing on derelict land, then inviting people to come and look. Right from the beginning the purpose would be to get people actively and sacrificially involved (after all, poor as their housing is, it is still their homes).

 So a ray of hope would be kindled in the lives of some of the most deprived of our citizens, and so underprivileged groups of people would set the example for the rest of our society. We only need one or two examples to set the ball rolling. Gradually, as attitudes changed, the new housing would spread though out suburbia.

The idea of stimulating interest in, and getting local people involved in, the construction of new housing, is of course not at all new. Various interesting urban-district renewal projects have already been completed or are being planned, in different parts of the world including England, and one intention with many of these projects is to stimulate public interest at large (and the interest of planners!) in alternative designs. For example, Dwelly (1996) describes the 'planning for real' process, which involves local people in decision making for major redevelopments, and uses three-dimensional models of the neighbourhood as a tool to this end (one such model is illustrated).

There are also very interesting models for urban villages. One very stimulating example is the Halifax EcoCity Project in Adelaide, Australia. This urban village is designed to accommodate 800 people, and its community facilities include a meeting hall, cafes, kindergarten, ecology centre, market place and other shops and services; it is car-free (parking is peripheral and underground). Construction uses green technology - e.g. non-toxic materials, solar aquatics septage systems, and there are roof gardens. The local community was involved with the project from the start - local business, trade unions, the indigenous Kaurna people of the Adelaide Plains, community groups and environmental groups. The whole project incorporates "principles of social equity, community enterprise and ecological responsibility" (Downton, 1997).

To change peoples' attitudes so that they accepted this new approach to housing, Government would need to mount a very radical and determined education campaign (see Chapter 13, section B). We need here to distinguish two aspects of the problem. The first is the desire people have for the semi-detached/detached house with its own garden. The second, is the desire for ownership. Some would argue that the only problem is persuading people to live in flats rather than in isolation, whether people own or rent the accommodation is not a critical factor. I however think we need a fundamental change on both these fronts. And The Town and Country Planning Association, in arguing that large scale transformation of suburbs is inconceivable, seems to think the basic problem is that most housing is owner-occupied (TCPA 1997a). We need to foster the idea of renting housing, rather than as at present, promoting home ownership. The education programme would also need to deal with the desirability of urban food production.

Where does the developer, the house builder fit into all of this? There would clearly need to be more control over their activities. It could be argued that given a new set of circumstances, competition would force developers to fall in line, and produce the sort of housing required. Past experience does not support this. There has been competition between builders. But this competition has been for development sites and for ways to produce the traditional housing types. So for example, we saw that in Sheffield, developers seem to have a catalogue of well-tried designs from which they can pull out the appropriate housing type (such as the 'Ebchester plus', or the 'Manchester plus' type) for a particular development. Competition has not generally stimulated experimentation over radical change of design, which is in fact what we will need.

It would not then be sensible for Government to leave it to developers to come up with the required types of housing. I would suggest the following way forwards, based on the fact that while there are already organisations that have produced more radical housing designs which might be more appropriate to a higher density programme, a lot of work remains to be done in this field. The Government should establish a Commission with the brief of producing a variety of appropriate housing types. It might also license appropriate existing organisations to be involved in producing suitable designs. Then Government would pass a law, which would require developers to adopt the designs, which its Commission and the already licensed organisations produce. These ideas could be linked to those put forwards in chapter 6 of the Lord Rogers report ('investing in skills and innovation'), especially the idea of creating Regional Resource Centres for Urban Development.

In order to ensure that no more house building is required on greenfield land, the use of previously developed land and vacant buildings must obviously be maximised, which is indeed Government policy. However, the efforts to reclaim previously used and sometimes contaminated land, and to convert vacant buildings would have to be intensified. It would be essential for LAs to keep an accurate tally on vacant properties and rooms, and probably rather more temporary renovation of property would have to be contemplated than at present. More radical action would also be needed with existing permissions for development. Many such permissions are for development that involves greenfield sites. While PPG3 advocates limited re-appraisal of existing planning permissions (see PPG3 in the Appendix of Chapter 3), we need to go further. All permissions for greenfield development should be abrogated.

The proposals outlined above would give greater freedom to planners through incorporating the whole of suburbia into what may be called the legitimate total planning area, rather than having a planning system which effectively leaves out of consideration large swaths of city, except for minor modifications. So the attempt to create 'nodes', 'sustainable urban neighbourhoods', 'urban villages', call them what you will, the attempt to create 'de-centralised concentration', would have the whole city as the legitimate area, and frequently, present residential areas would be broken up to make two or more such centres. This would facilitate maximum overall densification of housing. Then, as the whole transformation of suburbs takes place, it will be possible to find accommodation for all the new households without building on greenfield sites.

This conclusion assumes that population growth will cease around mid century. Should this not happen, either because of changes in attitudes to reproduction, or continued net immigration, greenfield land would eventually have to be used for housing. Likewise, only if population eventually decreases, which will probably in my view require a deliberate policy of population reduction, will it be possible to achieve the second goal with which this section started. As population size fell, some more peripheral urban villages would be dismantled, and the ground gradually returned to nature.

The proposals outlined above have another advantage. There is general agreement that we need to narrow the gap between the 'haves' and the 'have-nots', globally, nationally, and within each urban area. The writer mentioned earlier (see Box) that the whole present planning system seems to have a very middle-class ethos. It would perpetuate the above gap to a large extent. For on the one hand, it would create urban villages which would be primarily for the 'have-nots' ('primarily' because they would also provide accommodation for people like students, and lone mothers whether they be 'haves' or 'have-nots') and on the other hand, it would leave the classical middle-distance and peripheral residential suburbs for the 'haves'. Ironically however, from the non-material or 'values' point of view, if the ideal form of the urban village as a sociological entity, enunciated by people like Gorz (1985), was ever to be achieved, we would have the divided society where good social organisation based on a strongly developed community spirit was the privilege of the materially speaking 'have-nots', while the 'haves' would very likely continue as the majority of them are now - leading lives of splendid, selfish, suburban isolation!

We must, in these critical times, clearly distinguish between what people really need and what they want. For example, with transport, people might want to use their cars for shopping and visiting the countryside; what people need is to be able to get easily to shops and other facilities in the city, and to get out easily into the countryside for healthy relaxation. There is no reason why these needs should not be met by a properly developed system of public transport, integrating road and rail transport, and the appropriate provision of cycling tracks and footpaths. In terms of the long-term goal package, we could aim for an almost total abolition of private motorised transport. There would still be need for motor transport for certain categories of people - for example doctors, emergency services staff, possibly some categories of disabled people. The present writer's very recent experience is that it was perfectly possible to manage without a private vehicle, with little or no increase of travelling time, using the presently available public transport. And that is before any radical new transport policy has been implemented. This does not mean that everyone would be in a similar position - the writer does not have to commute daily into London!

We have in the writers view, a very simple choice. Either we adopt the above radical proposals, or we end up with an England that is largely just one gigantic suburbia, with the countryside, as it has been known for generations in the past, almost totally destroyed.

What sort of environment do we want for our great-great-great-great-great-great-great grandchildren - the offspring generation of AD 2300? Do they not have a right to a countryside as large and as varied and beautiful as it was up to very recent times? How can we allow the selfishness of a couple of generations of people to endanger the future for all subsequent generations?

I now turn briefly to the second goal stated at the beginning of the present sub-section.

Implementing the policy of population reduction (Chapter 10) will mean that the total number of dwellings needed in the country will decrease. I see the danger here, that as redundant housing is demolished, remaining dwelling units might be simply rebuilt, and the land associated with them extended in such a, that the total built up area of the country remains as it was at the time of maximum urban area expansion. This is what market forces of today's type would bring about. It would be a great pity, a great opportunity lost. Rather, urban compactness should remain the rule. As population decreases, each city would be re-organised so that peripheral urban villages would be vacated, the buildings and infrastructure all removed, and the land returned to nature.

Finally, no matter how well we re-design our cities, if people still have the freedom to take part in a counter-urbanisation stream, we will still lose our green land to housing. This matter is taken up in the following chapter.

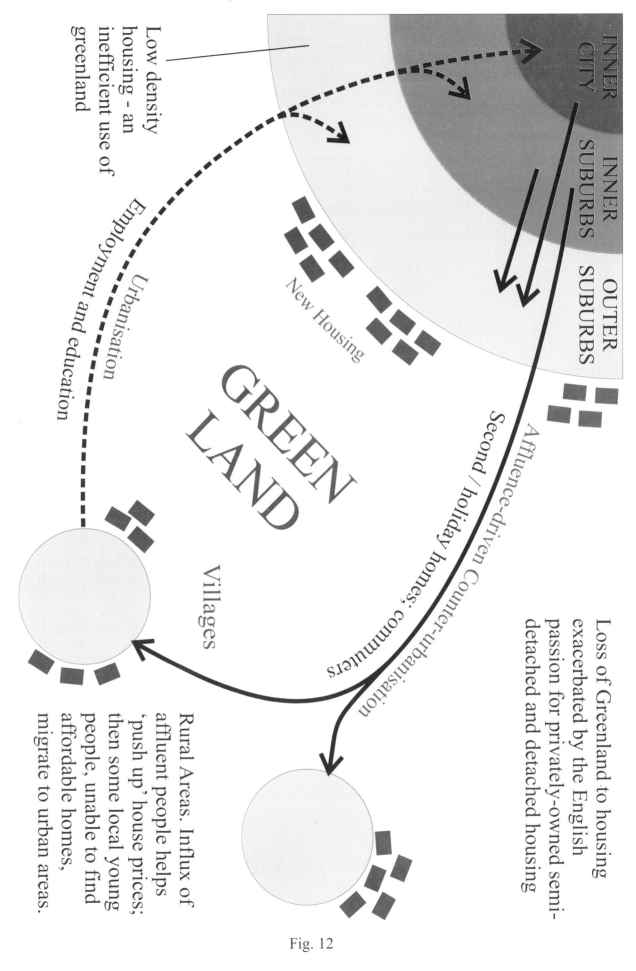

Low density housing - an inefficient use of greenland

INNER CITY

INNER SUBURBS

OUTER SUBURBS

New Housing

GREEN LAND

Villages

Urbanisation
Employment and education

Second / holiday homes; commuters

Affluence-driven Counter-urbanisation

Loss of Greenland to housing exacerbated by the English passion for privately-owned semi-detached and detached housing

Rural Areas. Influx of affluent people helps 'push up' house prices; then some local young people, unable to find affordable homes, migrate to urban areas.

Fig. 12

Chapter 12

The restoration of the countryside

It is widely considered that the countryside and rural society have deteriorated in recent decades, and Part One of this book documented this deterioration. What strategy can be developed to arrest and reverse this deterioration? This is the subject of the present chapter, which develops the analysis and strategy in Chapter 11 of Barker (1998).

A. Re-creating Arcady?

We have seen how conventional modern agriculture, with its heavy reliance on artificial fertilisers and pesticides and its increasing specialisation, has led to the twin adverse trends of (i) environmental degradation and destruction of wildlife; (ii) loss of jobs in the agriculture sector. This reduction in the agricultural workforce together with counter-urbanisation, has led to another trend, the gradual breakdown of traditional rural communities. I argue that a countryside strategy should be devised which reverses these trends, and it is in terms of such reversals that we may justifiably speak of 'returning to the past', or 're-creating the traditional rural scene', or 'putting the clock back', or 're-creating Arcady'. Now it is generally agreed that we need to revitalise rural economies and reduce the impact of agricultural practice on the environment. But the strategy advocated here differs in two respects from the strategies advocated by Government and most environmental NGOs, for they do not advocate reversing counter-urbanisation or re-creating traditional rural communities.

This does not mean that I think everything in the past was perfect. It obviously was not so in some ways, and we should be aiming for a countryside and an agricultural economy that is an improvement, both environmentally and socially, on the situation of the past. However, it should be said that some supporters of modern farming practice paint such a gloomy picture of agricultural economy before the Second World War as to discourage people from considering any return to the old ways. Typical of this approach is the following view of Soper and Carter (1991):

"However much some of the more extreme traditionalists may hanker after the weed infested fields, waterlogged pastures, overgrown hedges, rabbit-dominated downlands and bracken-covered uplands - so characteristic of the depression years in farming from 1880 to 1935 - these could not return to any significant extent, except possibly in a few areas where soil or climate render the land marginal for crops or grass. No country in the world can afford to waste its natural resources in this way...". When you think of how modern agriculture has destroyed natural resources, the last part of this statement is, to say the least, very ironical.

Harvey (1997) has a different view. He acknowledges that the popular view shared my most farmers today, is that the inter-wars period in Britain was a period of unmitigated disaster in agriculture; it was a time of decline and ruin, of mass bankruptcies and suicide, of families walking out of their farms in despair, a time of collapsed barns and weed-choked fields. But while admitting that the depression did affect agriculture as well as other sectors of the economy, and that its effects were ruinous for specialist cereal growers, he asserts that the above picture of the agricultural scene is a very misleading picture of the real situation. The mixed farming tradition saw the family farm through the worst of the pre-second world war depression. According to Harvey, studies have shown that overall farm production rose by 20% in the inter-war years, this at a time when British industry was deep in recession. And he gives some very telling examples of individual small farms using traditional mixed farming techniques, which, without the massive input of artificial fertilisers and pesticides which are so characteristic of present day farming and which produce such damaging environmental effects, gave high yields of healthy produce, and even in some cases increased yields and increased soil fertility over a period of years.

We now look at the various elements of the strategy.

B. Re-distribution of population and business

(i) Reversing counter-urbanisation trends

We have seen that during the second half of this century traditional rural community life has been shattered at the same time that expansion of rural settlements has taken place. Underlying both these changes have been the processes of urbanisation and counter-urbanisation, discussed in Chapter 2 and illustrated in Fig. 12. Rural people have moved to urban areas for various reasons (urbanisation), while urban people unconnected with the countryside in terms of employment and experience of the practicalities of rural living, have moved out into rural areas (counter-urbanisation). The result has been a dilution of the rural character, and a loss of integration, of countryside communities. In villages, everyone used to know everyone else; now frequently people do not even know their neighbours. And the newcomers, raised under urban conditions, have a very different outlook on life, and many still find their emotional centre in the towns. No doubt this loosening of rural community structure has been exacerbated by the now almost universal move towards a more self-centred or individualistic society. In recent times, counter-urbanisation has exceeded urbanisation, and this, together with continued population growth, has led to enlargement of rural settlements.

The whole process of counter-urbanisation is more than just a matter of moving from large cities to rural areas. It is a process in which there is a constant centripetal flow of people outwards from dense urban areas, filling in any vacant space. Within urban areas people move towards the periphery, from inner and middle-distance suburbs to outer suburbs. People move from large cities to small cities, from smaller cities to towns, from towns to villages, even villages to open countryside. It is a movement powered by affluence, encouraged by market forces including advertising, allowed by government, and socially divisive in that it accentuates the difference between the 'haves' and the 'have-nots'.

In recent times the flows of people in counter-urbanisation have been greater than the flows in urbanisation. This has increased the pressure to provide dwellings in the countryside, through conversion of existing buildings and the construction of new dwellings, leading to loss of greenland to development. The newcomers have been relatively wealthy, and house prices have consequently risen in rural areas. Planners have allowed developers to convert countryside buildings for housing, knowing at the time permission is given, that certainly, or almost certainly, these dwellings will not be affordable by the local rural people, and even that some will become second homes. This may not be the fault of planners (although the writer suspects that they could often be stricter). It is the fault of the whole planning system, and the legal system that underpins it, and changes in those systems are required. As a result of these changes, many young rural people have been unable to find accommodation that they can afford.

The developments just summarised have taken place within a very short time span - the lifetime of old people and even of middle-aged people who are alive today, people who therefore bear a large part of the responsibility for the changes. Are we going to allow these trends to continue? What sort of countryside do we want for our descendants?

If you examine the strategies of Government and environmental NGOs, you will find that the aim is a modest amelioration of the situation: we should try to limit further counter-urbanisation while at the same time encouraging a limited return of people to the cities. This can be done by making cities more attractive places in which to live and work. As the UKRTSD (1997a) puts it: "Conditions need to be created in which more people will want to live in towns. This means providing a variety of living environments and housing types: an improved urban fabric; more jobs; better education, health and leisure services; a fresh focus for civic pride to help overcome problems of crime, litter, and neighbourhood noise and disturbance; and help for local communities in urban areas in finding and implementing locally appropriate solutions".

Such strategies in the writer's view are unlikely to even achieve the limited objectives set. The TCPA is probably correct in its view that the majority of households will in fact continue to prefer to live in suburban and semi-rural areas (TCPA, 1997b). There is after all, no way to make a city as beautiful and quiet as the countryside.
So the pressure from people wishing to move dwelling from town to country will continue. Few retired people are likely to return to cities, so allowing the vast army of retired people to remain in the countryside means that a great deal of car movement, for shopping in neighbouring urban areas, will continue.

As far as the structure of rural communities and the rural economy is concerned, the strategies accept that not only the traditional rural community, but also the traditional distinction between town and country in terms of where different types of business are located, have gone forever. Revitalising the rural economy must proceed on that basis. This approach has I think serious disadvantages, which become clear if one looks a little deeper into the distribution of business between town and country.

We can think of all businesses as belonging to two categories. (1) Certain types of business must be located in rural areas, especially farming of major crops. Some other types of business, which can be located anywhere, are connected with rural activity, so would best be located in rural areas, for example animal feed manufacturing, and light engineering for the maintenance of farm vehicles (we saw in Chapter 5 Section C that such businesses are now often located in urban areas). (2) In contrast, activities like advertising could be carried on anywhere and are not particularly connected with rural activities. Developing integrated management plans for rural areas would surely be most easily achieved if all businesses of the first category were concentrated in rural areas, and the whole rural business scene was not diluted by non-rural related business.

There is another disadvantage to allowing business of the second category to locate in rural areas. This concerns travel to work. Many businesses in rural areas depend on a twice-daily movement of people over large distances, between homes in cities and the work place, mainly by car. Some of these businesses are rural activity related. But many are not, so this polluting, peace destroying movement of cars would be considerably reduced if all non-rural business re-located in urban areas. And the limited provision of business premises in rural areas, exacerbated through the uptake of premises by non-rural related business might deter some rural related businesses at present located in towns, from re-locating in rural areas.

I conclude that we need therefore a much more radical strategy than the one generally espoused. This strategy should reverse some urbanisation, and more particularly counter-urbanisation trends.

I start by stating two goals:

> **Goal One: to re-create the distinction between town and country communities;**

> **Goal Two: to stop any further loss of rural green land to development, and eventually, to reduce the area of countryside given over to urban-type development.**

To achieve these goals it would be necessary to:

> a) prevent any further movement of people not employed in genuine rural activity, from urban to rural areas;

> b) encourage people who have moved out of urban areas into rural areas , to move back again, unless they be employed in traditional rural activities;

> b) encourage the return to rural areas of rural people who moved to towns, provided they are then to re-engage in traditional rural activities;

> d) prevent first any further movement of non-rural related business from town to country, and second the creation of new non-rural business in rural areas;

> e) encourage existing businesses in rural areas that are not concerned specifically with rural activities, to re-locate in towns;

> e) improve the prospects for employment in traditional rural activities, especially farming;

> f) prevent further building development on green land in rural areas;

> g) eventually, as population size decreases, to remove some buildings in rural areas, decreasing the size of rural settlement.

A housing policy consistent with these aims must be developed.

Now people from urban areas who acquire homes in rural areas fall into the following categories:

(i) people with two (or more) homes, the main home in town, but a more recently acquired holiday home in the country;

(ii) people with only one home
> a) who move home from town to country in association with a change from employment in town, to employment in country in business that is not essential to rural life;
> b) as a), but to business that is essential to rural life;
> c) who move from town to country but remain employed in town;
> d) who retire into the country.

We may rank the legitimacy of rural home acquisition in these categories, on the basis of first, the grounds of social justice, and second, the above stated goals. On grounds of social justice, Category (i) is the most illegitimate. **Indeed it is an obscenity that anyone should be allowed to have a holiday home, especially one in the country**. In the world at large, there are millions of people who have no home at all. In England even, there are many homeless people. How then can we allow some people to have two homes, where it is clear that they actually only need one?

With Goal One as the criterion, the only legitimate category is (ii)b. The people involved may or may not be personally concerned about restoring rural communities. But they will indirectly help with that restoration through facilitating the development of genuine rural business/industry.

With Goal Two as the criterion, people in all the categories stimulate further housing development in the countryside.

However, Category (i) is the most illegitimate; for Category (ii) people do at least release a home in urban areas, which then becomes available as part of the housing stock which can accommodate the increase in the number of households. Within Category (ii) one could argue that Category (ii)a and (ii)b are the least legitimate; for besides stimulating loss of green land to housing, these people also stimulate loss of green land for setting up of business premises.

We could expand our legitimacy criteria to include two more criteria. First, effects on pollution and traffic congestion. Using this criterion, Category (ii)c is the least legitimate because of the effects of commuting. Second, employment. We could argue that people who move because of the need to secure employment, of whatever nature, have a more legitimate reason to move than people who are moving simply for retirement. So Category (ii)a is more legitimate than Category (ii)d.

We could then rank the categories in terms of legitimacy. One possible ranking, starting with the most illegitimate, would be:

(i) ..... (ii)d ..... (ii)a and c ..... (ii)b

The precise details of the legitimacy scale are not important at the moment, and could be worked out in relation to other policy matters. For present purposes we can use the scale given above.

If we are to prevent further loss of countryside green land to housing, then the only people who in future would be allowed to move residence town to country would be people in Category (ii)b. Sufficient people from other categories would have to be persuaded or compelled to relocate in towns to make room for category (ii)b people and remove the need to build more houses/convert more buildings for housing in rural areas. The pressure put on people to move back to towns would be graded according to the chosen illegitimacy scale. At the very least, all second homeowners would be required to relinquish their country home.

Just as we may think of illegitimacy of movement of people, we can also think of illegitimacy of presence of business and industry in rural areas. It should be made illegal to set up any business in rural areas which is not intimately concerned with rural as distinct from urban life and activity. Existing illegitimate business should be required to re-locate in towns. While this would increase the demand for urban land, and the imperative for densification, it could help to vitalise incipient urban villages. To achieve Goal One would require the re-creation of sufficient job opportunities in 'business essential to rural life'; so every encouragement should be given to those who wish to set up appropriate businesses or industries in rural villages. We will return to promoting rural employment in a later section.

Government needs to have a clear picture of where it wants business to be located not only in terms of distribution between regions (as argued in the previous chapter), but also in terms of urban -rural distribution.
Unfortunately, the present Government's policy, like the policy of the previous Government, would appear to be opposed to some of the proposals I have made above. In particular, the Government seems to accept that the change in the balance of economic activity between employment sectors in the Countryside (agriculture and other primary industries, different manufacturing sectors and Service sectors) is something which has not only helped some rural communities to survive, but has created an employment situation which has largely come to stay. It sees no need to segregate business into rural related business located in the countryside, and all other business located in urban areas, as the Rural Development Plan (RDP) makes clear. It is not that the Government does not want to support agricultural activities (and forestry). Indeed the RDP makes it very clear that the Government not only wants to support and develop such activities, but that this is an essential part of Government vision (see especially Section 6 of the Plan which describes the Governments strategy). And the Rural Enterprise scheme is very much geared up to supporting agricultural activity (Section 9) But the Government seems to accept that business that is not rural by nature has a valid part to lay in rural regeneration. The plan says the Government's vision includes..."a working countryside, contributing to national prosperity as part of a competitive economy, with a balanced mix of businesses (including land-based industries) jobs and homes, reducing the need to commute long distances". A 'balanced mix', and 'land based industries' just 'included'! And I note also that the objective of the Rural Enterprise Scheme is to support rural communities in part by creating more diversified rural communities. Finally, the RDP does not have a strategy to reduce counter-urbanisation.

It will of course be objected that the whole approach I have developed so far in this chapter would force many people to move home and even to move to a different region of England. But this is exactly what has been forced on many people for decades now by a market controlled economy. The basic change in policy, like every other significant change of policy, requires a basic change in the attitude of people. It would also involve the taming of market forces and of the relatively free hand given to developers.

Finally, I briefly discuss one idea that has previously been proposed, which, if taken up, would be just a small move in the right direction. I refer to the taxation of second (holiday) homes.

In some rural areas there are many holiday homes that are vacant for most of the year while local people are unable to find a home. Affluent outsiders buy property, and property prices rise, making it impossible for locals to buy houses. By 1998 this had become a serious matter in South Lakeland, where almost three-fifths of the area lies in either the Lake District National Park or the Yorkshire Dales National Park. A little over half the population live in the five main towns, but most of the rest of the population is spread sparsely over 74 rural parishes. The percentage of homes that are second homes varies greatly within the area, but can be as high as 35% in more rural settlements. The high house prices were forcing young families on low incomes out of the area. As a result, most of the large hotels were recruiting many of their staff from the cities for lack of the local workforce that would otherwise be available. Local schools had come under threat as their recruitment populations fall. Local shops were losing business because second home owners tend to come for short stays only and bring their supplies with them from home. The situation is made much worse by the fact that second home owners get a 50% Council Tax discount on their second homes. Lakeland Councillors wanted the Council Tax discount abolishing. They also wanted discretionary powers to apply a flat-rate tax on second homes. Finally, they wanted the proceeds to be ring-fenced for investment (primarily by purchase) in affordable housing. So far, the Government has not agreed to these proposals, but there is hope that the forthcoming Rural White Paper might have some concessions on these matters (The Times, May 19th 1998, and information kindly supplied to me by Cllr David Vatcher).

Now second homes are not confined to South Lakeland. We saw in Chapter 7 that there are many of them in the Peak District National Park, and they are a common feature of many other rural areas. The problems encountered in the Lake District are found in many other places. So you would think that the Council For the Protection of Rural England (CPRE) would have campaigned vigorously along the lines of Councillors in South Lakeland. So I telephoned CPRE to find out what their position is on this matter. The CPRE told me that they had released a Press Release on Second Homes at the time of the Labour Party Conference in 1999 in relation to a speech by Michael Meacher at a fringe meeting organised by CPRE, and they sent me the Press Release, which ends:

> "CPRE's position on second homes
>
> 6. CPRE agrees that Michael Meacher was right to raise the important issue of affordable housing. The shortage of affordable homes in rural areas has been of major concern to CPRE for many years. We believe that these problems stem from both a lack of resources for the provision of affordable housing and the limited influence the planning system has over the type of housing being built in rural areas. In some areas, affordable housing shortages can be exacerbated by the extra pressures placed on local housing markets by second home owners.
>
> 7. There is a need to increase the supply of affordable housing through adjustments to both housing and planning policy. Affordable housing targets should be included in development plans and a higher proportion of affordable homes provided when new development is permitted in rural areas. The anomaly of second homes only being liable for 50% council tax should also be addressed."

This is not exactly a strong statement on second home taxation, so I wrote to CPRE asking for further clarification. I asked if the CPRE was in favour of second home owners paying full council tax on the second home. I also asked in relation to the possibility of imposing a tax on second homes:

"Am I correct that CPRE has not campaigned for this because it does not agree this should be done?"

The reply I received from a CPRE policy officer noted that the impact of second homes varies depending on local circumstances, but can place additional pressures on the local housing market is some areas such as the south west of England. The letter went on:

> " We do not oppose second homes per se. We recognise that the impact of second homes varies depending upon local circumstances. We have pressed, however, the Government to remove the current anomaly in relation to Council Tax by requiring all second homes to pay full Council Tax. We have also suggested that the Government consider what other measures may be appropriate locally to manage the demand for and impact of second homes. We are hopeful that the forthcoming Rural White Paper will take forward our ideas – this is expected in the next couple of weeks".

The letter concluded with a brief statement on the wider issue of affordable homes.

So the CPRE is in favour of full tax being paid on second homes. But note that my second direct question – on the possibility of imposing a tax on second homes, is not directly answered. Instead we have "what other measures may be appropriate".

Now there is one other thing in this letter that I think is very significant. "We do not oppose second homes per se".

Now why don't they? A central thrust of CPRE policy is minimising green land loss to housing. Second homes are a very inefficient use of land because they are only occupied for a small amount of time each year. While in a few localities second homes might account for over 20% of homes, more usually they probably account for far less – often only 2%. But even 2% over the whole of rural England is an enormous number of dwellings. And then there are moral issues. Is it right for a person to have two homes when they only need one and there are some people with no home at all? Is it right that a person can appropriate a piece of green land simply by virtue of their wealth, whilst the majority of people cannot afford it? The position of CPRE here is I think indefensible.

Why do they adopt this position? I believe it is because they know that many of their own supporters, on whom they depend, are second home owners. Probably underlying their approach are also conservative values (conservative with a small c) in relation to land and home ownership and a sharing of the Englishman's liking for the privately owned dwelling. My criticism of CPRE on the second home issue needs to be linked up with the criticism of CPRE I made in Chapter 10 Section G.

(ii) Agricultural employment for recreating rural communities

Before the Second World War, rural communities centred on agriculture, and agriculture was the major source of employment. More recently, however, average farm size has increased, many 'small farmers' have left the land, specialization and mechanisation has led to a reduced need for the traditional farm labourer, and much work is now done by part-time workers who might spend the rest of their working lives doing non-agricultural jobs, often in towns. The traditional rural community, whatever its defects, was composed of people who both lived close to nature, and were dependent upon it for their livelihood. However much they may at times have abused the countryside, they had the knowledge and understanding to manage the countryside in a sustainable way. The re-creation of the traditional rural community would be a vital component of an effective countryside environmental policy.

Fundamental to any attempt to recreate the rural community would be a strategy to increase employment in farming. This would not only increase the proportion of persons who are involved with management of the environment in the broad sense, but in depopulated communities, help to bring the population back to a level where population density makes it a viable proposition to have a local post office, doctors surgery, etc.

We can think of this strategy to increase employment as having two inter-linked components:
>   (i) finding ways to increase small farm viability and enable newcomers to establish themselves as 'small farmers';
>   (ii) changing agricultural practice to make it more labour intensive.

We will deal with these components in turn.

The whole thrust of farming policy in recent decades has discriminated against the small farmer. There has been a consistent drive to increase the international competitiveness of British Agriculture (Harvey, 1997). To achieve this, unit costs must be reduced. Now the bigger the area farmed, the greater the chance to reduce unit costs, hence the expansion of some farms at the expense of small farming units. The subsidy system, and now, its partial replacement, the area and headage payments systems favour the large producer. The more food produced, and the bigger the hectarage of land farmed, the bigger the profit.

For the farmer, the requirements of the CAP and MAFF policy create a great administrative burden. There seem to be endless forms to fill in, all of which have financial implications.
There is a basic Integrated Administration and Control System (IACS) form, which provides the basis for calculating expenditure and detecting fraud. Its complexity and size rivals any tax return document! It involves among other things estimating the size of all fields in hectares to two places of decimals! On the arable side, for example, it involves giving details of what crops are grown and when, frequency of harvest, and yield, etc. Then each production scheme such as Arable payments, Suckler Cow Premium, Sheep Annual Premium, etc. has its own form to be completed. On top of that there is the possibility of joining an agri-environment scheme, or choosing which scheme to join, involving lots of research, and if the farmer decides to join, more paper work. All this reading and paperwork takes time. But the amount of paper work is not directly proportional to the size of the farm. As farm size increases, there is a far smaller growth of paper work. The financial benefit of joining an agri-environment scheme is greater the bigger the area entered. A small farmer is likely to consider it not worth his while to spend so much time on a scheme for such a small reward. Indeed there is evidence that uptake of the ESA scheme is less amongst small farmers than bigger farmers, and that this is not due to small farmers being less interested in such schemes than big farmers, but rather the administrative and financial disadvantages to small farmers just discussed (Ross and Turner, 1995 based on work by M. Morris and others). A small

farmer is unlikely to be able to have an accountant or financial adviser or farm manager on the payroll, the large farmer will be able to afford this administrative assistance.

Taxation policy in the UK is such that profits made in farming are most effectively re-invested by land and quota purchase (quota was discussed in Chapter 6 Section B). The large profits of 'large farmers' so invested, caused land and quota prices to soar, so that prices are beyond many aspiring new entrants to farming (Ross and Turner, ibid).

As far as dairy farming is concerned, milk quotas were introduced in the European Union in 1984 as a means of limiting total output of milk. Every farmer was given a production quota, the size of which depended on the yield in 1981 which was called the 'base year'. So a budding farmer who wishes to establish a dairy herd on a farm must first of all buy or lease adequate quota, and prices are high. Harvey (ibid) illustrated the financial problem by the example of one couple who established a herd on a fairly small farm (50 acres). They had to spend roughly £14,000 a year on buying and leasing quota - twice as much as the rent they had to pay for the farm! Many dairy farmers have apparently given up dairy farming and simply live on the rental of their quotas. Farmers of retirement age can use quota as a tax-free retirement fund. In contrast to the UK, In Eire there are three milk quota transfer schemes in place to ensure that quota is available for young entrants and small scale producers (Farmers Weekly, 5th May 1995). The 1992 reforms of the CAP introduced quota on the beef and sheep side of the agricultural industry. National Quota Reserves were set up in the UK in relation to the support schemes Sheep Annual Premium (SAP) and Suckler Cow Premium (SCP). Young new entrants to farming can in principle obtain, free, quota from these reserves. These reserves are created by a 'siphon' system: When quota is transferred between farmers without the land being transferred, 15% of the quota transferred is siphoned off into the National Reserves, as mentioned in section (iii) above.

However, these reserves do not only or even primarily provide quota to new entrants, but to other farmers as well. The National Reserve is classified into Categories. Such reserve as has accumulated is first used to satisfy Category One farmers, only then category Two farmers. If any quota is still unused, Category Three requests can be considered, and so on to the last category, Six (b). Now young entrants would come under Category 3b (individual producers who are newcomers to farming and are aged under 40). The other thing to note about the National Reserves is that they are, in MAFF terminology, 'ring-fenced' - the country is divided up into regions, and in general, quota cannot be transferred from one region to another. Now in 1998 I wrote about the situation up to that point as follows: "As far as SCP is concerned, there has always been enough quota to cover all Category 3b requests. The situation has been different for SAP. Here there has always been enough for lowland farms, but with the upland farms of the 'Least Favoured Areas' the situation has been quite different. In 1993 there was enough quota to meet 87.5% of Category Three requests. Since then, Categories One and Two have completely exhausted the National Reserve, and there has been no quota available for category Three (data supplied by MAFF, Nottingham). So no help has been available for new entrants from the quota system. It would be useful for the UK government to apply to change the quota categories of the siphon to give more assistance to new entrants to farming"

In June of this year (2000) I enquired from MAFF whether things had changed since 1998. From conversations and written responses that I received, it appears that the situation with SAP remains unchanged, but the situation with SCP is that no quota could be allocated to the national reserve. In relation to the Agenda 2000 reforms, and the aim to reduce market support, the total SCP quota for England has been reduced - i.e. there is a lower ceiling. To meet this lower ceiling, no quota was put into the National Reserve because this quota was the quota removed to ensure meeting the lower ceiling. The reductions only apply to SCP, and my informant wrote that at the time of writing he was unaware of any proposal to reduce SAP national reserve. There should be enough reserve for lowland farms, but in upland areas it is expected that, as before, higher priority categories will exhaust the limited reserve available. In other words, the situation is unlikely to improve for young farmers.

When it comes to leasing land, the small farmers are often at a disadvantage. Chris Higgins of Broomfield Agricultural College provided the writer with a hypothetical situation, which illustrates the competitive disability of new entrants (unless they have much capital). Farmer A is currently in mixed farming. He would like to maximise his profits by converting the whole of his present farm to arable production, because the arable area payments are so massive. Nearby is a farmer B who has a small area of grass fields he is prepared to lease. On converting to arable, farmer A would like to put his cattle on these fields. Meanwhile, a new entrant to farming, Mr. C, would like to establish a small dairy business and lease the B fields for that purpose. Now farmer B is in no hurry to lease the fields, he can afford to wait and get a good price for his lease. Farmer A can also afford to wait since even if the lease price of the B fields rises appreciably, it will still be worthwhile for him to take the lease. But Mr. C, who has little capital, will not be able to afford the lease if the price rises. The present quota system then, makes things difficult for newcomers to farming to establish themselves.

All these considerations lead to the conclusion that if new entrants and small farmers are to be encouraged, there needs to be a fundamental change of agricultural policy. Now if the government were to buy up agricultural land, as suggested earlier, it would be able to ensure that land could be leased at a reasonable price, and take steps to reduce average farm size. By making it possible for more people to rent small farms the government could do more than simply increase the size of the farming community. In some areas of Britain there are very large farms owned by city-based firms who regard farms simply as financial ventures, and to whom environmental considerations are of no consequence. To divide these farms into smaller units for young farmers would facilitate the development of a more environmentally responsible attitude to farming. For it would put in place people who are living in close proximity to the farming environment and would then be more susceptible to appeals on behalf of that environment. Just as it seems incredible to an outsider that government should not control population size, it equally seems incredible that government does not control the distribution of allocation of the nations land.

Another helpful policy change would be to make more use of the idea of modulation (section (ii) above). While the introduction of any sort of massive and comprehensive modulatory system would require modification of the CAP, it is disappointing that the UK Government does not propose to make the maximum use of the limited options within existing CAP policy. Modulation could for example be effectively employed to increase small farmer uptake of agricultural schemes (if such schemes were to be retained), by tapering payments according to size of area entered.

New entrants and existing small farmers could help themselves by forming co-operatives. For while the co-operative approach is not intrinsically employment generating, it seems to have the potential to sustain small-scale enterprises. Unfortunately the co-operative tradition is not well developed in UK farming (Hird, 1997, reporting on work by S. Craig and J. Sumberg). Co-operatives need not however be confined to farmers alone. They can also involve retailers and consumers, manufacturers of organic produce based foods, and people involved in conservation activities. Such collaborative ventures can be employment generating, and Hird (ibid) gives various examples. One of these is the Birmingham Organic Roundabout, which connects together local organic farmers and regular customers in Birmingham and has generated employment. Such ventures, through increasing contact between the customers, between the farmers, and between customer and farmer, have the potential for community building and for increasing the city folks' awareness of farming processes and the countryside.

Finally, we may note here that encouraging an increase in small farms would do more than increase agricultural employment. Small farms seem to be both environmentally and socially advantageous compared with large farms. In the first place, one might expect that there is likely to be more social cohesion with small farmers - greater density of farmers means more casual contacts between neighbours. And it has been argued that small operators are more likely to buy from local suppliers (Hird, ibid). Smaller farmers may be more protective of the environment than large farmers. This might sometimes be simply because, lacking the capital to change to the more intensive production of large farms, they have not engaged in environmentally damaging operations! (Ross and Turner, ibid, partly based on work by C. Potter and M. Lobley).

We turn now to making agriculture more labour intensive. The increase in specialist arable and livestock farming enterprises in recent decades has been one cause of the decrease in the farm labour force, since generally speaking mixed farming requires more people than specialist farming and gives a more even labour use during the year. Making a deliberate move back to mixed farming would therefore make it easier to get more people into agricultural employment. Organic farming normally operates on a mixed farming basis. A major change to organic farming in the UK would give a significant increase in employment, not only in organic farming in the narrow sense of that term, but in the processing and marketing of organic produce (FoE, 1995). These conclusions are supported by further evidence supplied by Hird (ibid).

There has been a growing pressure from animal welfare activists to modify current intensive farming practice so that livestock can live and be marketed in healthier and less stressful conditions. This is opposed by many farmers who fear loss of income should they revert to less intensive practice. However, such changes, if implemented would not only benefit the animals, it would also lead to increased employment.

One of the areas where welfare concern has been focused is in egg production. Here the issue is whether production should be based on free-range systems, or intensive regimes of which the most extreme is the battery unit system. Supporters of intensive systems have argued that to return to free-range production would considerably increase production costs, and as these costs must at least in part be passed onto the consumer, the result would be prices that many would be unwilling to pay. According to Hird (ibid), recent studies have shown that profitability would not be seriously affected, and people would be willing to pay the small increase in egg costs. The important thing for the present discussion on employment is that a return to free range production would increase employment. Expressing employment in terms of hours employment per 1000 birds, one study found battery intensive systems having 241 hours/1000 birds, free range having 516 hours/1000 birds.

A widely canvassed modulation system that could be used to increase employment as well as improving small farm viability is to incorporate a labour based system of support into the subsidy system. Basically there would be a sliding scale of payments that would give greater payments the more people were employed. If such schemes are to assist small farms, the scheme has to include not only paid labour but unpaid also; because many such farms only have unpaid workers - the owner, the wife, and other members of the family. Such a scheme could be combined in an overall subsidy system, which would retain as another essential element the existing area based payment system (Hird, ibid).

At the present, many voluntary organisations are involved in one way or another with environmental improvement in the countryside. This involvement could be more fully integrated into overall farm management policies (as could local council employment schemes, and the Governments welfare to work programme). From this population of involved persons, a new generation of farm workers could be recruited, including young persons who wish to set themselves up as farmers. By making use of a population of people who have already shown an interest in conservation, we would greatly improve the chances of successfully bringing in a radical new, environmentally friendly, farming practice. Such a deliberate process of recruitment would be greatly facilitated if MAFF extended its educational remit to on-farm training of personnel.

Finally, any attempt to increase employment in the agricultural sector must be integrated into the development of overall employment policy, which in turn must be integrated with the development of the whole sustainable development strategy.

Now the Government's Rural Development Plan aims to revive rural communities, although the basic approach is different to the one outlined above. As pointed out at the end of Section A of the present Chapter, the Plan develops a strategy, which it thinks will help to revive agricultural activity. And the Rural Enterprise Scheme has the objective... ".. providing targeted assistance to support the development of more sustainable, diversified, enterprising rural economies and communities...". However, as noted in Chapter 6,the large variety of schemes available under the RDP has the potential to cause confusion and I think it could be argued that this will not help individual farmers, especially small farmers, to develop a reasonable strategy for their farms.

I have already mentioned that one of the main trends in agriculture during recent decades has been the increase in farm size and the reduction in the number of 'small' farmers. Surely, all efforts should be made to reverse this trend. Yet under the Rural Enterprise scheme we have one of the topics listed which can be helped by the scheme as 'reparcelling' of land. Of this topic the Plan says " In general, the structure of agricultural holdings in England is good: the average size is well above the EU average, with holdings of over 100 hectares representing 64.3% of the total farmed area and those farms below 20 hectares amounting to only 5.3% of the area. Market forces continue to be the main determinant of farm structure. Against this background, this measure is of very low national priority". So the Government seems to approve of large farms, and seems to accept as inevitable the ruling sway of market forces! This approach is inconsistent with any attempt to increase the number of farmers by bringing back the small farmer. The fact that this measure is not a national priority does not distract much from the above criticism.

Only time will show the extent that the Government's strategy will revive rural communities.

C. Custodians of the land

Landowners and other farmers have traditionally been thought of as the custodians of the countryside. But we have seen in Part One of this book that, by and large, they have not lived up to this expectation. We need to assert that the countryside belongs to all the people, and therefore agricultural policy should be re-designed to ensure that farmers do look after the countryside properly on behalf of the people.

While we all contribute to countryside management through our taxes, most of the land of England is actually owned by a minority. In 1982, one percent of the population of Britain owned half the land; two percent owned three-quarters of it. Britain's farm land was owned by two percent of the total population, but half the food grown in Britain was produced by a mere ten percent of all farms (Norton-Taylor, 1982). Some individual owners have massive estates - 24,000 acres, 100,000 acres, up to the largest: 288,000 acres. Some landowners have beautifully maintained parks which provide good habitats for wildlife, but they often exists within much larger areas owned by the same landlord, where environment-destroying conventional modern agriculture is practised (Monbiot, 1995). It should also be noted that this concentration of land ownership in a few hands is different to the situation in continental Europe, where the earlier aristocracy and landowning classes largely failed to hold onto their large estates (Norton-Taylor, ibid). To an outsider, it is incredible that people tolerate most of the land being entrusted to a few people, especially when they see what a mess they have made of it - perhaps they are just not aware of the facts about ownership!

Fundamental to consideration of custodianship are rights associated with ownership of land and buildings, that is property rights (Chapter 6 Section A). Should for example, farmers have the right to environmentally damage the area they farm? At present, such a right exists, albeit curtailed to varied extent. For example, within ESA eligible areas, if farmers do not agree to join the ESA scheme, they are free to continue with aspects of conventional farming which are clearly detrimental to the environment. Even when farmers take up the scheme, they may choose only to take it up at the level of Tier 1a, which only mildly ameliorates environmental damage, and comparatively few farmers may take up the scheme at Tier 2, which brings the maximum reduction of environmental damage.

If we survey the whole gamut of environmental policies which can bring environmental benefit, we see that fundamental to them is the concept of the Management Agreement, as mentioned in Chapter 6 Section A. Farmers and land-owners forego certain rights, and may or may not be compensated for this (Whitby, 1996a). For example, farmers may relinquish the right to cultivate land in a particular way. Such agreements are still the main type of arrangement operating within SSSIs. And they form the contractual basis across the spectrum of agri-environmental schemes. The essence of such agreements is a transfer of rights between the farmer/owner and the body controlling the scheme. There is a great variety of management agreements. The extent that rights are affected varies both in terms of the magnitude of the changes involved (e.g. different tiers in ESA), and the period of time for which they are guaranteed (e.g. in ESA a farmer may revert to damaging practice at the end of the five year agreement period), which vary as we saw in our examination of protected areas and agri-environment schemes in Chapter 6. Generally such agreements are voluntary, and this can mean that vast areas of agricultural land are not covered by them. Leaving that aside, we return to the point made earlier - should farmers have any rights at all not to farm in an environmentally friendly by virtue of the fact that they own the land?

In subsequent sections of this chapter, various ways will be discussed by which the countryside environment could be improved - better financing and design of agri-environment schemes, cross-compliance and regulation, and modifying the CAP to facilitate these and other changes. All such approaches have their problems. One thing that could (not necessarily would) greatly improve the chances of success is the drastic procedure whereby Government, through compulsory purchase, takes over the ownership of all agricultural land. Custodianship would then pass more completely to the Government, and hence, in theory at least, by the democratic process, to the people. Land would subsequently be leased to appropriate parties, the lease agreements insisting on proper environmental management. Long, perhaps sometimes even indefinite period tenancies could be agreed, and in this way people could be encouraged to put their roots down and put every effort into good management, because their descendants will have the opportunity to continue to work the same land despite the fact that it is now owned by the state. It is ironic that in recent times the area of land in public ownership has actually decreased. Local authorities, water authorities, rail and coal authorities and the Forestry Commission have all sold land to the private sector (Shoard, 1997 update at end of Shoard, 1987).

The idea of State ownership of the land is of course not a new one. For example, Akerman (1979) argues for this policy in Sweden. He was writing at a time when the total number of people employed in agriculture was declining, there was increasing absentee ownership, and farm prices had risen so much that it was virtually impossible for a young couple to acquire a farm of their own. Akerman was also concerned with the overuse of chemicals in farming. So there were marked similarities to our situation in the UK. He considered that only drastic measures could solve the problems. As far as farm prices were concerned, the whole concept of ownership must be addressed. He suggested that the State should use a small proportion of the vast pension funds to buy all usable land in the country - perhaps using as little as 25 million Sw.kr. out of a total fund of 120,000million Sw.kr. Then the state would lease the land in lots where prices would change with the interest rate or possibly a little more than the rate of inflation. In this way the rise in value of land would belong to society. We will return to this vision later. For present purposes it is sufficient to say that Ackerman's proposal was never implemented and farms in Sweden are mainly owned privately (personal communication from the UK Swedish Embassy). As far as the UK is concerned, taking land into public ownership would not be something entirely new. In the 1930s some County Councils bought up large estates and divided them up to make new small farms available to new entrants to farming.

Whitby (ibid) has an interesting comment on the public purchase of land in relation to the costs of payments to farmers in the Habitat agri-environment scheme: "The payments offered in this scheme are remarkable in that the highest rates would capitalize, even at 5% real interest, to two or three times the likely market price of the land. Such levels of compensation underline the comparative cost-effectiveness of public purchase of the land". And Baldock and Mitchell (1995) express the same idea in discussing the acquisition of agricultural land for conservation purposes, commenting that although land purchase involves expensive capital investment, in the long term this may be cheaper than indefinitely continuing incentive payments to landowners.

The present writer therefore makes the proposal that the government should take over the ownership of all countryside land. The problems associated with such a move would of course be gigantic. Opposition from landowners is guaranteed; the economic consequences would be far reaching. For example, large tracts of land are held as investment by pension fund and insurance companies.

Shoard (ibid) discusses the pros and cons of the nationalisation of agricultural land. If this took place, would not farm efficiency decline? For tenant farmers might be less motivated to farm efficiently than landowners. Land nationalisation would put present day freehold owners in a similar position to tenant farmers. However she makes use of two surveys on farm productivity to refute this notion. These studies showed that under then existing conditions, there was no clear relationship between farm productivity and form of tenure. More specifically, there was no evidence that people farmed better on land they owned than on land they rented.

However, Shoard does not think that state ownership of land is the way forward for four reasons:

(i) To improve the countryside, there would have to be conditions in the tenancy agreements - a system of 'restrictive covenants'. To ensure that the system worked, there would have to be a whole army of officials not just to draw up the covenants but also to monitor their implementation.

(ii) In theory, state ownership would be totally democratic. In practice Shoard believes that it would be very difficult for the people to influence those who were managing the land. And she does not see why the change of ownership should reduce 'relentless agricultural expansion'.

(iii) The costs of nationalisation to the taxpayer would be enormous, and if the taxpayer were to get a reasonable return on his investment, farm rents would have to rise steeply.

(iv) The idea is a political non-starter anyway. The British tradition of land ownership is too deeply embedded in our society; the right to own land is still seen as an important freedom.

However, answer can be made to these arguments:

Reason number one.
As part of a suite of measures that Shoard considers could contribute to restoring the countryside, she includes extending the existing planning system in urban areas to the countryside. One way would be to legislate to require any land owners or occupiers to seek planning permission from the local planning authority for any activities that would have a significant impact on the rural environment. While she does not think such a measure by itself would solve all our problems, it would be a great step forwards. Yet does not such a system run into exactly the same difficulty as mentioned in reason number one - the beaurocracy involved in setting up and monitoring? More useful in Shoard's view would be to have a rural land tax system. Every hectare of land would be taxed. This would be what is sometimes described as a tax system incorporating negative income tax. Landowners would pay tax creating a tax fund. But landowners who manage the land in a way that was judged to be in 'the national interest' would be rewarded by payments from the tax fund. Landowners would negotiate a land plan for their holdings with the local authorities. Local authorities, instead of devoting time to 'rural development control' would negotiate the contents of land plans with owners. Of course, monitoring of subsequent developments would still be required. So once again, why should this be less beaurocratic and require less personnel than setting up and monitoring a land lease system from nationalised land?

Of course, to develop a land control policy based on State ownership of the land would involve a lot of work, and a lot of people. But surely the very basic point here is that however we wish to change the English countryside, a great deal of time and effort will have to continue to be put into assessing the present state of land, developing methods of control, and monitoring change. One basic problem is that up to now, far too little money has been available for environmental protection, and far too little effort has been made to place environmental considerations at the heart of policy making!

Reason number two.
This actually has two components. Her point about it not been clear that it would check relentless agricultural expansion, is briefly made and vague. We won't therefore consider this further. The rest of the reason is however, important, namely that it would remain difficult for people to make the democratic process effective. However, Shoard, in discussing the implementation of the land tax idea that she favours, talks of local opinion making itself felt through a consultation process which would be an extension of the structure plan consultations already in existence. Citizens who felt that the local council was making things too easy for landowners could appeal to the government against council decisions. So we have the democratic process in action. But why should the democratic process stand a better chance of working with this system than with a State ownership of land - tenancy system? The democratic process will only work if people are interested enough to make it work. But government can build in mechanisms that facilitate democratic control of any process, if they wish to.

Reason number three.
Yes, it would be extremely costly. It would moreover demand a complete revision of basic planning policy, economic policy, and monetary policy! But let us face the facts. Everyone seems to be clamouring for 'Sustainable Development'. Most environmental organisations see Strategic Environmental Assessment, and all that this implies as being vital, if we are to save the environment. But what are the financial costs and implications for the whole economy of such a change of direction? Part of the answer is of course that we will eventually reap the benefit of savings like reducing the costs

of clearing up pollution. But surely, we will never be able to effectively take the environment more seriously unless we put more money and time into it. Shoard claims that farm rents would have to rise steeply. Is this really a necessary consequence of a policy based on land nationalisation? In the first place, why should the State pay full, then existing, land value when it takes over the land? Why should the amount paid not be linked to the size of the holding; why should it not be linked to the environmental record of the owner? Why should not general income tax be modified, even increased, to help pay for the takeover? Ways could surely be found to limit farm rents, indeed to gear the whole farm rent system in such a way that it would assist newcomers to farming who are going to farm small areas, to get established, and in such a way that existing 'small' farmers would be assisted, two desirable changes (see section six of the present chapter).

Reason number four.
This is the real 'heart of the matter', but it has two components - a general one and a specific one. The general component (although it is not stated, only implied) is in effect that any proposal which challenges tradition in any radical way is not feasible. It is basically the same point of view as that expressed by the Town and Country Planning Association in relation to town planning, as discussed in the previous chapter.
This is the central dilemma we face. Environmentalists clamour for radical change. But they nearly always hold back from concrete suggestions for really radical change because they consider them political non-starters. Environmental organisations and individual activists are united in the belief that if we are to save the environment, we have to get public support, and therefore there must be a fundamental change of public attitude. Yet at the same time, most organisations and individuals obviously do not believe this is possible, and consequently their campaigns are fundamentally defective because they assume that policies which would require such a fundamental change of attitude should not even be considered.

The more specific component of the reason is that we could never persuade people to give up their freedom to own land. But as far as the countryside is concerned, we should remember that most of the land is owned by a tiny minority of the population, as we saw earlier. This right to own farmland is potentially, the right of all of us. In practice, it is the right of only a few, and primarily depends on wealth. So it is a freedom based on wealth, and as such is socially divisive. The writer is well aware that there is a vast literature on this subject area and it leads into basic discussions about socialism, which cannot be dealt with in a book of this size. However, the problem of human freedoms will be taken up again in Chapter 13. It is the present writers contention that unless we change the whole basis of land ownership both in town and country, we will not solve the environmental problem. But is must be admitted that reason number four will remain for many people a valid reason for doubting if State ownership of the land could ever become a reality.

Mention was made above of a rural land tax system as an alternative to state land ownership (Shoard, ibid). Such a system would provide a way to ensure environmental improvement, both by penalising harmful practice and rewarding positive improvement. Shoard gives the history of the land tax idea, including a discussion of the tax ideas of Henry George that I described in Chapter 1 Section D and Chapter 11 Section A. A relatively simple graduated land tax was recently briefly described by Seymour (1996). Here the severity of the tax paid would be positively correlated with the size of the land owned, with perhaps owners with as little as ten acres paying nothing. The tax on large land areas would be so punitive that the owner would have to put some of the land on the market. Seymour argues land prices would plummet, so that less affluent people could buy land; one result would be that land ownership would become more evenly spread through the population. And this tax system would clearly be helpful to young people of limited means who wished to take up farming (see section (v) below). To the present writer, however, a land tax system is inferior to state ownership. It is the writer's conviction that land is not something that should be bought and sold by individual people. Mankind is custodian of the world, and therefore of the land and all the wild life on it. Portions of it should not 'belong' to individual people. Land should not be treated as a commodity.

There are various possibilities of action, which fall short of full-scale nationalisation of land. Shoard mentions a system operating in France: this requires that locally based statutory agencies monitor farm sales. If they think a potential buyer is unlikely to manage the farm in a suitable way, they have the power to purchase the land themselves. Norton-Taylor (1982) would abolish the automatic right to inherit estates. This would open up the possibility of estates being handed over to trusts or cooperatives.

D. Re-organisation of farming

(i) The CAP – constraints and possibilities

As we saw in Chapter 6, the CAP has been instrumental in causing environmental degradation in the countryside, and further reform is needed. While Government should make maximum use of such freedom as it has within existing CAP policy to maximise environmental improvement, the constraints imposed on the Government by the CAP are considerable.

As well as constraints arising from the CAP itself, there are also general European Community (EC) restraints. Fundamental to the organisation of the EEC is the single internal market with free movement of goods within the Community (Articles 9 to 37 of the EEC Treaty). And this free movement of goods is specifically referred to in Council Regulation 2092/91, which governs organic farming. Under the heading "Free movement within the Community" Article 12 states:

"Member States may not, on grounds relating to the method of production, to labelling or to the presentation of that method, prohibit or restrict the marketing of products as specified in Article 1 that meet the requirements of this Regulation".

The Community is concerned to maintain a "level playing field" for competition within the community, and the relevant Articles in the Treaty which established the community are Articles 92, 93 and 94. The first paragraph of Article 92 summarises the position:

"Save as otherwise provided in this Treaty, any aid granted by a Member State or through State resources in any form whatsoever which distorts or threatens to distort competition by favouring certain undertakings or the production of certain goods shall, in so far as it affects trade between Member States, be incompatible with the common market".
The limiting effect of Articles 92 – 94 is explicitly acknowledged by the Agri-environment Regulation 2078/92 of the 1992 CAP reform.

These then are general EC constraints under which any policy development is placed.

The constraints arising from the CAP itself are laws of two types - directives and regulations. The former sets out targets which must be achieved, but leaves member states to decide how to achieve them; the latter, however, are laws which become directly applicable in member states under the European Communities Act of 1972 (Abbott, 1990). Even here, the Commission may determine the overall framework for action but member states decide the details of application (the subsidiarity principle).

Despite this welter of constraint, there was Member State flexibility, even before the recent Agenda 2000 reforms. If we consider the agri-environment schemes, we may note that the Regulation 2078/92 gives appreciable Member State flexibility. Article 2 of the Regulation lists the sorts of activity that are eligible for the aid scheme. Article 3 says that Member States shall implement the aid scheme by means of zonal programmes that should "reflect the diversity of environmental situations, natural conditions and agricultural structures and the main types of farming practised...." And the same article speaks of 'derogation' to member states in establishing a general regulatory framework for implementation of the Regulation.

Finally, while Regulation 2078/92 noted the restriction imposed by Articles 92 – 94, it also gives flexibility to Member States in permitting them to adopt additional aid measures. Thus paragraph 10 of the Regulation states:

"This Regulation shall not preclude Member States from implementing, except in the field of application of Article 5(2), additional aid measures for which the conditions of granting aid differ from those laid down herein or the amounts of which exceed the limits stipulated herein, provided that the said measures comply with the objectives of this Regulation and with Articles 92, 93 and 94 of the Treaty" (Article 5(2) concerns only areas subject to the Community set-aside scheme which are being used for the production of non-food products).

The flexibility provided in the Regulation resulted in considerable between-state variation in the way it was implemented by Member States (Scheele, 1996). For example, some member states elected to concentrate their aid under the regulation on a comparatively small part of the total agricultural area, France on a larger part.

We look now at flexibility with just one scheme – Organic Aid. Most governments made the scheme available a) to farmers converting land to organic production, and b), also to farmers for assistance on land already farmed organically, but the UK and a few other governments excluded the latter. Even the rates of payment varied widely between countries. Payments are co-financed by the EU and member governments. The main EU determined constraint is that the maximum rate of Community part-financing was 50%. The UK could have raised its own contribution if it wished to do so, and promote organic farming much more actively -...."..the constraint at present is the attitude of MAFF, which has failed to fully utilise the opportunities presented by EU policies" (N.H. Lampkin, Welsh Institute of Rural Studies, personal communication). In view of the environmental advantages of organic farming over other types of farming, this is highly regrettable. And as Hird (1997) commented: "At a national level, the UK is in the shameful position of having to import 70% of the organic food consumed as it has only 0.3% of land in organic and the slowest rate of conversion in Europe". And over recent years there have been several occasions when the money allocated by the UK government in a given year to the Organic Aid Scheme, and now for its successor, the Organic Farming Scheme, has run out.

The flexibility allowed by EC legislation prior to Agenda 2000 could be seen also by the variation of response of member states to a range of directives and regulations which affect pollution by fertilisers and livestock wastes, including the nitrate directive 91/676/EEC. While it is true that the UK had a nation-wide, but non-compulsory Code of Good Practice for the Protection of Water, and various measures in agri-environment schemes gave some localised control over pollution, its nitrate vulnerable zones scheme, where certain pollution reducing practices are mandatory, only covers a small part of total agricultural area. In contrast Denmark has more comprehensive legislation governing the storage of manure and the spreading of fertiliser in fields. The most stringent controls in Denmark are on application levels. On livestock farms, farmers must match herd size to the land available for manure spreading at specified maximum amount; and farms above a certain size, or with an excess of manure, are required to have fertiliser and crop rotation plans. The Netherlands has limits on the level of phosphate application to agricultural land. There is a levy on 'surplus' manure based on the amount of phosphate produced by livestock; Norwegian farmers pay a fertiliser tax on nitrogen and phosphorus, and so on (Baldock and Mitchell, ibid).

Clearly, the UK government could have done more to limit fertiliser use and reduce pollution. This was recognized by Baldock et al (1996), who listed a series of ways that could reduce farming's adverse impacts in the UK without significant changes in the CAP. They list the following:

(i) using less inorganic fertiliser, and using it more discriminatingly;

(ii) improving the management of farm wastes, including slurry and silage liquor;

(iii) reducing the impact of pesticides by reducing overall use, further withdrawal from the market of the more harmful pesticides, and greater effort to develop less environmentally damaging chemical pesticides. Reducing overall use would be accomplished by a) determining the minimum necessary dose in each case; b) instead of applying pesticides perhaps two or more times a year, determining the best time to apply to produce maximum effect; instead of applying pesticides rather indiscriminately, making maximum use of information about the nature and timing of pest population build up in designing spray programmes;

(iv) protecting water resources (N.B. as mentioned above, there is in Britain a voluntary Code of Good Agricultural Practice for the Protection of Water);

(v) achieving appropriate stocking and grazing patterns;

(vi) protection and management of on-farm habitats and landscape features (the ESA and Countryside Stewardship schemes do not cover the whole country).

Looking at this list, one is struck by the fact that practically all these suggestions are advocated within the Integrated Crop Management system, and are either features of organic farming, or steps along the road to organic farming.

As we saw in Chapter 6, the recent Agenda 2000 reforms of the CAP if anything increased Member State discretion. So while there is little flexibility in the basic agricultural support system, this is tempered with flexibility in terms of modulation of payments, and the possibility of introducing / maintaining measures for environmental improvement through regulation and cross-compliance. For example, as we saw in Section B (viii) of Chapter 6, cross-compliance could be used through Farm Plans, to considerably ameliorate the environmental situation on farms. It is then rather disturbing that the Government proposes only limited regulation and modulation, and has not yet decided on the use to which cross-compliance may be put.

(ii) Farming methods to maximise environmental improvement

It is generally agreed that farming must become less intensive, and should rely much more on natural ecological processes such as predator control of pests, rather than on heavy inputs of fertiliser and pesticides. In this way, farming will become more 'environmentally friendly'. Organic farming (briefly described in Section A of Chapter 6) is the farming method which best conforms to this view of future agricultural practice. And we saw in Section D of Chapter 5 that in terms of the two major divisions of agricultural production - arable and livestock - mixed farming has important advantages. As a general goal then, we could suggest the adoption of mixed farming by the organic method. However, the farming system must take into account the variations of climate and soils over the country, and for this reason we would expect regional variations in the importance of arable and livestock farming. For example, in some hilly areas grazing systems may continue to predominate, but at much reduced stocking rates.

Integrated Crop Management (ICM) (also described in Section D of Chapter 5) shares some of the philosophy, and much of farming practice of organic farming, although it does make use of pesticides. It could therefore sometimes be used as a stepping-stone towards organic farming. This might ease the transition to organic farming and be especially valuable where you have farmers who are not as yet well motivated towards organic conversion. However, it would not speed up the eventual conversion of a farm because during conversion, time must elapse for pesticide residues to disappear before a farm can be declared organic (present EC regulations makes the minimum period two years).

The Government should have the target of totally changing over to the Organic method in all agricultural sectors as soon as possible. While it campaigns for necessary changes in the CAP to allow this to happen, it should be doing all it can to encourage farmers to convert to organic farming, using the Organic Farming agri-environment scheme and assisting existing organic farmers by encouraging farmers cooperatives and farmers markets, and encouraging our supermarkets to make more use of UK organic products. This whole process should be linked with a determined effort to promote own food production in town using organic methods. I previously reported on calculations that suggested that it would be possible for the cities of England, to virtually grow all the vegetables they need (Barker, 1998, Chapter 12). And in Section A of Chapter 3 of the present book I noted other advantages to the community of own food production.

We can think of farming systems are having a dual function - the provision of food and non-food products, and the provision of landscape and of wild life habitats. Now if total conversion to organic farming were achieved, would this bring in its train, all the necessary improvements in landscape and habitat? The answer would appear to be no. Thus Lampkin (1996) considers that simply changing to organic farming would not be able to ensure specific environmental benefits like heather regeneration, recreation of chalk grasslands and maintenance of broad-leaved woodlands. Now although some organic farmers might, because they do regard themselves as custodians of the countryside, work to secure these other benefits, other probably would not. This means that there remains a need for additional measures to secure environmental improvement. There are three approaches to achieve this improvement - agri-environment schemes, cross-compliance and regulation. All three are currently being used, but which of these approaches is best?

Now agri-environment schemes are voluntary, and so it is impossible to be sure of securing sufficient uptake to achieve a wide coverage of farmland. Also, as we saw in Section A of Chapter 6, compensatory payments under agri-environment schemes sometimes offend against the 'polluter pays' principle – why should farmers be paid to reduce pollution rather than paying for pollution and being forced to reduce it. I would go further. We have the right to insist that farmers are the custodians of our countryside. Why should they be paid anything not only for avoiding damaging activities, but also even for restoring the environment they have damaged? On that basis, the whole agri-environment scheme idea is faulty. However, it must be noted that getting rid of compensatory payments would be difficult under the existing CAP, where the idea of compensatory payments is firmly entrenched. Thus Regulation 2078/92 governing the agri-environment schemes specifically states that the measures adopted under the regulation... "..must compensate farmers for any income losses caused by reductions in output and/or increases in costs and for the part they play in improving the environment...." (preamble to the Regulation). And in the new Regulation 1257/1999 on rural development Article 24 speaks of support for agri-environment action for income foregone, additional costs from the commitment given, and the need to provide an incentive.

Cross-compliance is in a sense also voluntary, because farmers need not comply if they do not claim support payments. But at least in its 'red ticket' or 'orange ticket' forms (Box in Section B (iv) of Chapter 6), farmers would not get support payments without accepting cross-compliance. And since the majority of farmers would need the support payments, most would become involved with cross-compliance. If the cross-compliance measures considered by the IEEP study (Dwyer et al 2000), mentioned in Section B (ix) of Chapter 6 were applied, one could ensure that all necessary environmental benefits are produced.

Regulation could be used to achieve the same results as cross-compliance and could work through the same measures as used under cross-compliance. It would in the writers view be better to use regulation rather than cross-compliance for the following reasons. First, although cross-compliance would produce the desired environmental effects for the majority of farms, there might be some farmers who did not claim support payments, so they would be absolved from providing the environmental goods; and as mentioned in Chapter 6, if support payments were greatly decreased, as will probably happen, farmers would have less incentive to apply for such payments since these are linked to the cross-compliance cost and effort of ensuring environmental improvement. Second, it would surely be better to make it perfectly plain to farmers that they are the custodians of the countryside and should be looking after the environment anyway, so enforcement of environmental measures should be completely separated from any payments of any type.

Whether then by cross-compliance or regulation, the Government should ensure that measures are fully adequate to the task of restoring out countryside. All measures should be 'whole farm', not as with some existing agri-environment schemes only covering part of the farm. The whole farm maps that would be needed could be based on the maps currently used in the Integrated Administration and Control System (IACS), and the farm audit system launched by the Linking Environment and Farming organisation (LEAF, 1997). Selection and balance of the environmental measures would vary to some extent between regions and sub-regions so as to take into account the regional variation of environmental problems. If the government adopted the policy of nationalisation of agricultural land, the required environmental measures would form part of the lease arrangements.

Earlier in this section I wrote about reversing trends. I now look at three examples of the sort of reversal of trends that should be aimed for as part of an overall policy maximising environmental improvement.

Consider field size and hedgerows. Hedges are important to wild life, including natural predators of agricultural pests, and in many areas a traditional and much loved aspect of the landscape. Hedgerows would continue to be replanted, walls and hedge banks rebuilt (I say "continue" as such measures are already part of some current schemes). Hedgerows have been removed, partly to enlarge fields to make it possible to use bigger machines and use them more efficiently. They have also been allowed to deteriorate and sometimes removed because maintaining them properly is labour intensive. The eventual aim would be to restore the vast majority of hedges and banks removed since the beginning of the Second World War. Now according to Soper and Carter (1991) the minimum field size in arable agriculture for efficient use of present day large machines, is 20 hectares, which is quite large. So field size reduction and hedgerow restoration in arable farming areas should go hand in hand with a gradual replacement of the large machines with smaller ones, making small fields a viable proposition in farming. Also, the emphasis would have changed away from maximum production, making the large machines unnecessary.

While we are on the subject of field boundaries, we may note that there are some very simple things that could be secured by more regulation without causing any big economic upset. Consider just two wide spread features of our countryside at the moment – a decrease in isolated field side trees, and the habit of mechanically trimming hedges very low and sometimes narrow. It surely would be possible to ensure that (i) all farmers must replace any isolated tree that dies with another, -better, lets say with two or three others (planting protected baby saplings); (ii) minimum hedge height is two metres; minimum width one metre (recall how hedges are often mechanically cut very low, as we saw in Chapter 7). There would be great gains for landscape and wildlife.

The second example concerns the general reversal towards mixed farming, and comes from the dairy industry. The increase of dairy herd size and the change from mixed farming to pure or almost pure dairy farming, where it has occurred, has led to problems of liquid manure handling. The traditional method of dealing with manure was to use straw from the farm as bedding for the cows. With that method the slurry was absorbed into the straw and converted on the spot into farmyard manure, which was then spread out on the land in spring. Increase in herd size and the change over to full dairy farming meant that straw was not available on the farm and the cost of buying it outside and transporting it to the farm was too great, so provision had to be developed on the farm for storing the slurry - pits, towers, etc. The increase of herd size and change in cow housing and milking methods has led to increase in concreted areas - e.g. for penning the cows before milking, and consequent loss of greenland. Sometimes new structures were unsightly, even if this effect was minimized by careful placing of the structures and sometimes planting a screen of trees (Soper and Carter, ibid). As mixed farming gradually spread once more, these trends in practice would be reversed. This would be coordinated with a planned decrease in the total UK herd in relation to changes in dietary practice described in a later section.

My third example does not concern farming method, but distribution of farm produce. There has been much discussion about 'food miles' – the distance farm produce travels, sometimes being processed on the way, between source (the farms) and the consumer. We have all heard stories of produce being transported half the length of the country to some depot and then half way back again to supermarkets. Such a distribution system, which has evolved comparatively recently, has contributed to the increase of truck traffic on the roads, with consequent increase in fuel consumption and noise and harmful vehicle emissions. Clearly it would be a good thing to reverse this trend and thus decrease the harmful effects just mentioned. There could be other benefits of this reversal. It would make possible the development of food supply strategies for cities based on local food production. Such strategies would involve encouraging farmers to form links with consumers with the benefits mentioned in Section B above.

Lastly, two comments on current Government policy in relation to the goal of improving the countryside environment. First, one of the Governments priorities in The Rural Development Plan is ensuring that the countryside environment is properly protected (Chapter 6, section 6.1.2). Policy includes encouraging an agriculture that amongst other things is...
"...environmentally responsible, given its major influence over the countryside, seeking to achieve sustainable land management and contribute to biodiversity, cultural and landscape targets...". It specifically supports organic agriculture through the Organic Farming Scheme, and intends to increase expenditure on this and other agri-environment schemes (see the RDP Chart no. 1). However, it does not see the Organic Farming Scheme as having a priority over other agri-environment schemes; so, within the constraints of present CAP policy, it does not seem to be moving towards a general transformation of agriculture to the organic way. We also saw earlier how the Government does not seem to be keen to attempt to make regulation a major tool for environmental change.

Second, as was noted in Chapter 6, a large variety of schemes are available under the RDP, with overlapping objectives. To some extent this is no doubt inevitable given the nature of present CAP regulations, especially the Rural Development Regulation. However, could not the Government have achieved a somewhat closer integration of the schemes, which would have made it easier to develop a coherent strategy?

E. The allocation of land for various functions

The amount of land required for food production has decreased in recent times through the introduction of improved strains and advances in agricultural technology, and continues to decrease. In 1994 18.5 million ha were in agricultural use in the UK; it was predicted 1-1.5 million ha might become redundant by AD 2,000, 5.5 million ha by AD 2,010 (ETSU, 1994, based on work of Department of Land Economy at Cambridge University). However, if there were to be a massive extensification of agriculture, this could drastically alter the situation. A rather extreme example concerns changing egg production from battery cage systems to free range systems. The 27 million battery hens in the UK could in principle be housed on 135 hectares. Changing entirely to free-range farming would require about 2.7 million hectares (Baldock et al, 1996).

Nevertheless, it seems likely that the trend of reduction of land needed for food production will continue. So the question arises – to what use should redundant agricultural land be put? It is generally agreed that the continued availability of redundant agricultural land will reduce the pressure to contain urban expansion. However, in the previous chapter the suggestion was made that no more land should be made available for such expansion. So we need not here consider this possibility further.

We can begin to work out a land allocation strategy by classifying activities in terms of how they affect the amount of land to be taken out of agricultural production. We have two categories of activity:

(i) those practices which will reduce the extent that land is taken out of agricultural production;
(ii) those practices which require land to be taken out of agricultural production.

Under (i) we have:
a) extensification of agriculture;
b) an increasing use of land for non-food crop production.

Under (ii) we have:
a) the restoration of major wildlife habitat/ landscape areas, such as marshes and ancient woodland, through the SSSI and Nature Reserve systems;
b) the creation of new habitat / landscape areas such as new woodlands.

In the writer's view, much as it is important to restore and create major wildlife habitat areas, priority should go to activities under (i). The reasons are as follows:

1) Agricultural production will remain the main land use in the countryside. It is from this land especially that we get ground and water pollution, and the production of atmospheric pollutants, contributing to global warming. And intensive farming has almost destroyed wildlife on agricultural land. So we can have the greatest positive environmental impact in the countryside by getting rid of intensive farming practice rather than restoring or creating major wildlife habitat areas.

2) Existing SSSIs often contain agricultural land. Further, they are usually surrounded by agricultural land, and we have seen that the health of SSSIs very much depends on the health of surrounding lands. So improving agricultural practice will have a very positive effect on the value of existing wildlife habitat in SSSIs.

3) The restoration of the countryside cannot be divorced from other issues like the need to conserve non-renewable resources by substituting renewable resources and the need to find less polluting sources of energy. Now fuel crops such as willow or poplar from coppice plantations, or certain grasses like *Miscanthus*, are renewable resources, and we will need increasing amounts of land to grow these non-food crops – see Box.
An example of a project to produce electricity using wood chips from willow coppice and 'waste' materials from forestry plantations is the Arbre project by the M62 SW of Leeds. This will produce enough electricity for 18,000 people (Arbre Energy Limited, undated).

4) It has been pointed out that we should keep a reserve of agricultural land so that we can quickly increase food production should any future emergency demand it. One possible group of emergencies arise through global warming. An early result of the global warming process seems to be an increased incidence of severe environmental events, which could affect agriculture as much as urban life. Crops in some areas may be destroyed, requiring production to be made up elsewhere. We still do not know enough about how global warming may eventually alter the feasibility of growing any given crop in any given area. Considerable adjustments may be necessary. We need to keep a freedom of movement of production of each crop type from one area to another, so we need to have land available for such changes. However, one

Fuel crops

Fuel crops produce less harmful emissions than conventional fuels. As far as CO_2 is concerned, wood fuels are 'carbon dioxide neutral' – the carbon dioxide released when the fuel is used is equal in amount to the carbon dioxide taken up during growth. And burning of fuel crops produces a residue (the ash), which is rich in phosphates and potash, which can be returned to the land.

Some people are concerned that growing fuel crops would alter countryside character, even be an eyesore. However, these crops can be grown in a way that blends in with the surrounding landscape, and they can be grown within the traditional field system. Since harvesting would be carried out in winter, there would be no disturbance of breeding birds and other creatures during the spring and summer. And as far as coppice is concerned, fuel crop production can bring other benefits to wild life:

(i) Arable coppice can promote biodiversity within the cropped area, especially since coppicing will only occur once in three to five years; further, cropping will be in rotation, so the whole field will not be cleared, in contrast to food crops. Consequently there will be less disturbance of habitat within the planted area than with normal food production.

(ii) The need for mechanical harvesting requires a broad open area around the crop area, and corridors through the crop area. These areas will provide useful wildlife habitat - it is possible that 10% of the total field area may be taken up by these margins (ETSU, 1994).

The Government is now promoting the development of energy crops through the Rural Development Plan (Section 6, sub-section 14 and Chapter 9, Forestry sub-section). Its chief stated reason for this promotion is reducing greenhouse gas emissions. But other advantages of fuel crop production are recognized –providing new commercial activity for farmers, and hence helping the employment situation, the potential benefits for biodiversity and their value as part of integrated pest management strategies. It is also noted that energy crops have a low requirement of chemical inputs. So that altogether, the Plan concludes, energy crops are a good example of sustainable agriculture.

Mention must be briefly made here of other types of non-food production, which are perhaps going to require an increasing amount of land: crops grown for the pharmaceutical industry and crops grown for the building industry (soya bean as a source of fibre as a component of buildings materials).

cannot simply set aside land for future use and put it under wraps. It needs to be actively maintained. One way to do this would be to extensify agricultural production even more than would otherwise be thought necessary.

In this respect, is using redundant agricultural land for fuel crop production a good thing? If the fuel crop is an annual plant, it would be easy to change back to food production. But what about coppice or perennial C4 grasses? It is true that with coppice reversion would require tree stump or root removal. However, this is apparently much easier than in conventional forestry, and the land could be returned to food cropping in one season (ETSU, ibid).

Another reason for keeping a reserve of agricultural land is usually given, which depends on the forecast that the developing world might increasingly be unable to feed itself. This creates improved opportunities for exports of food from the EU, and therefore we should keep a reserve of land so we can respond to these opportunities. This reasoning is sometimes either underpinned by humanitarian considerations, or alternatively given a humanitarian gloss, concerning our responsibility to help the needy of the world.

In the writer's view, the agricultural situation worldwide is likely to get worse, this being exacerbated by continued human population growth. It is doubtful if the developed world would be able to supply all the extra food that may in future be needed by the developing world. Further, the more food aid given, or food sold by, the developed world countries to developing world countries, the less will the latter countries feel the urgency to solve their food problems. It would be better to concentrate on helping developing world countries to increase their own food production rather than trying to relieve the food deficit in these countries. And one could argue that the best way that we can help the global situation is to put our own house in order, to ensure that in at least one part of the globe, an environmentally friendly countryside management policy is in place, making both a direct contribution to the amelioration of global environmental decline, and providing an example for others to emulate. We should be aiming eventually to replace a large part of current agricultural land with wild life habitat. To start gearing ourselves to meet global needs is likely to tie us down in perpetuity to maximizing the food production area in the UK. Unfortunately, the whole tendency in present EU policy seems to be towards trying to maximize the competitiveness of European agriculture and to make maximum use of future possibilities to export food. This is one central thrust of the proposed further reforms of the Common Agricultural Policy (European Commission, 1997). This whole subject of support to the developing world through food exports and food aid and the correct approach to dealing with world hunger, has of course been much discussed over the years, for example Bennett and George (1987); Cathie, (1982); Hardin, (1974); Lappe and Collins (1986); Marshall and Miller (1995).

5) If, inspired by the long term vision, the policy of massive population reduction is implemented (Chapter 9), much existing urban land will no longer be required for housing and other urban uses. This redundant urban land would be given back to the countryside after the removal of all buildings and other urban structures. Much of this land could be used for the re-creation of major wildlife habitat areas. So rather than making restoration/creation of major wildlife habitat areas a priority now, it would be better to leave this until a future date.

F. Improving wild life habitats

While the priority at the present time should be to extensify food production and develop fuel crop production, attention must also be given to restoring/creating wildlife habitat. The system of Natura 2000 sites together with other SSSIs and other existing wildlife reserves provides a good basis for the future development of a network of wildlife habitats. Eventually, the total area of reserves should be greatly extended. But what should be the priorities at present, for managing and enlarging the reserve area? These are, in the writer's view, three in number:

(i) to improve safeguards against deterioration of existing sites;
(ii) to enlarge the smallest sites, and secure a managed zone around sites, to reduce 'edge effects';
(iii) to connect together existing sites.

We saw in Chapter 5 that existing sites are inadequately protected, and in consequence, many have been severely damaged. Part of the fault, in the view of most conservationists, is that English Nature does not take a firm enough line in protecting sites. The ineffectiveness of English Nature was described in WWF (1997). However, even if English Nature were to pursue its conservation duties with the utmost rigour, it would be unable to provide adequate protection because inadequate legal provision has been made. There will have to be changes in the law. According to WCL (1997):

(i) existing legislation gives no clear stated purpose for wildlife conservation. This has caused real problems for implementation. New legislation should state clearly the goal of protecting and enhancing wildlife;

(ii) as far as Government is concerned, wildlife is not just the concern of MAFF and the DETR. All government departments and government agencies carry out activities that to a greater or lesser extent affect wildlife. The same applies to the activities of local authorities. Most government departments pay little heed to conservation issues. And at present, it is possible for a local authority to be in conflict with English Nature over what activities may be allowed in some SSSIs. So a duty to protect wildlife needs to be made mandatory throughout authority - central government, government agencies and local government;

(iii) voluntary agreements sometimes break down; persuasion and incentives fail. In such cases higher penalties, power to enforce restoration orders and the power to impose 'management orders' must be given to the controlling authorities. To monitor and control activities on sites, conservation officers must be given full access powers.

Now the Government's Countryside and Rights of Way Bill, if it gets through parliament, will go some way to address these matters as the analysis in Chapter 5 Section F shows. In particular, the Nature Conservancy Council will be able to serve a management notice requiring the owner/occupier to carry out certain works. And Council officials will have a right of entry, which will make monitoring more effective.

Any reserve, no matter how well managed, is open to damage from surrounding areas. The extent of this damage will in general tend to be greater, the smaller the area: if we simplify things and consider areas as circular, the ratio of circumference / area gets larger, the smaller the area; so the smaller the area, the greater the risk of damage spreading from out side. Small areas then can generally benefit by being enlarged. But all areas, no matter what their size, are likely to suffer damage at their peripheries. It is therefore important to establish buffer zones round sites in which stricter controls are in operation than in the surrounding countryside.

It is generally accepted that man-induced climate change is taking place. It is therefore likely that there will be major regional shifts and other alterations in the UK climate, during the next couple of centuries. In general, plants and animals can best survive only within a particular climatic regime, and if, in a given place, the climate changes greatly, conditions may make it difficult or impossible for a given species to survive. Migration then provides a way out of the climatic impasse. How successful migration will be will partly depend on the speed at which it takes place in relation to the speed of climatic change. Barriers may prevent dispersal, and a landscape feature that is no barrier to one species, may be a barrier to another species. Thus birds, being highly mobile, may readily pass from one isolated conservation site to another, whereas many plants, dependent upon less rapid and secure dispersal mechanisms, may be less able or unable to cross the barrier between one site and another. As a general principle then, conservation sites should form a continuous network. In so far that redundant agricultural land is used for establishing habitat reserves, it would be best to concentrate entirely or almost entirely on securing connections between existing reserves together with limited enlargement of the smallest reserves. This in practice means that the location of all such possible connections needs to be taken into account in deciding where agricultural land should become redundant, instead of waiting until bits of agricultural land become redundant and then deciding which of these could possibly be used to make connections.

G. Changing human diets

While major wildlife habitat creation is not a priority under existing circumstances, it certainly would be a good thing if such creation got under way as soon as possible. And this would be possible if some way could be found which allowed the area of land given over to food production to be drastically reduced without foregoing the advantages of a) full-scale extensification of farming practice, and b) allowing considerable expansion of the area of land given over to fuel crop production. And there is a way.

So far we have been thinking of agricultural production as geared to current dietary preferences. If dietary preferences changed towards eating more vegetable products and less animal products, this could have a big effect on the amount of land which must be retained for agricultural production. This is because it takes about ten times as much land to feed a person on animal products as it does to feed a person on vegetable products
(Britton, 1990; Potter et al, 1991). The reason for this lies in the loss of energy through the food chain - the fate of energy as it passes from plant food into the bodies of livestock and then into the livestock products that we consume. In the first place not all the energy in the plant food actually becomes incorporated in the bodies of
livestock since not all the plant food is totally digested and absorbed - the animal produces faeces which retain a portion of the energy. Secondly, animals carry out the process of respiration, which releases heat energy, so energy is lost from the body during the whole life of the livestock animal.

Since the greater part of agricultural land is used for producing animal feed, whether as grazing land, or producing crops to feed to cattle (76% of total UK agricultural area in 1987 Britton, ibid), it is clear that a major change in dietary preference towards a more vegetarian diet would release a large area of land from agricultural production. There would be no need for a complete adoption of vegetarianism. All that is required is a major shift in the proportion vegetable: animal products in the diet.

There would be other advantages to such a dietary change:

> (i) There is evidence that eating more red meat than an average daily level of about 90 grams, increases the risk of colonic cancer developing; many people are eating meat in excess of this level. For this and other reasons, many nutritionists consider that reducing meat consumption would improve the health of the nation.

> (ii) Globally we are in the situation where some experts are doubtful whether or not we will be able produce enough food to feed the growing world population. The overall food situation is exacerbated by the tendency to eat more meat in developing countries where the standard of living has begun to rise. Thus in China, more and more people are increasing their meat consumption; cereals are already being imported, and as more meat is consumed, this will increase the need to import grain to feed livestock. And some doubt if the world can produce enough grain surpluses to continue to meet China's need. Rise in meat consumption in the Far East is not however confined to China. For example, according to Harvey (1997) meat consumption has almost trebled during the last fifteen years in South Korea.

At the present, most people in the developing world outside fishing communities, cannot afford to eat as much meat as we in the west eat on average, but they would like to eat more. This is one aspect of a general desire in the developing world to have the benefits of a developed economy. At the same time, as we saw in discussing the I=PAT equation in Chapter 1 Section F, there is a need for developed world countries to contribute towards sustainable development by reducing their levels of affluence. So change in diet in the UK by reducing meat consumption would have useful symbolical significance for the relationship between our country and the developing world. It could be developed for the purpose of, and presented to the world as, creating a system that that is more consistent with a programme for world-wide sustainable development.

While there is already a small tendency to eat less meat in the UK, any major change in dietary preference in the short or medium term could not be brought about by the present system which leaves so much of the planning process at the mercy of market forces. There would need to be some change in government regulation of production. Clearly also, there would need to be a very determined education campaign mounted by the Government, in the teeth of considerable opposition from the livestock lobby. The question of education will be dealt with in Chapter 13. For the moment, the writer makes the proposal that the government should engage in social engineering to change dietary preference.

The present chapter and the previous chapter have dealt with the countryside and urban areas respectively. This does not imply that strategies for these two divisions of our country can be developed separately, indeed we have seen, especially in the present chapter, the interdependence of the two divisions of our country. Now there are various measures that could be applied to the whole country rather than one of the two divisions, and I end this chapter by considering one of these.

H. National Service

We hear a great deal about the lack of physical fitness of our young people – the reduction in time spent on physical education in schools and excessive consumption of trash foods leading to obesity; we see how our young people are frittering away more and more of their time and money on entertainment, with a big increase in weekend Clubbing with concomitant high levels of not only alcohol consumption but also of drug use. Self-discipline seems to have gone out of the window. Young people leaving school often find difficulty in obtaining a job, and employers often find that young people do not have a very responsible attitude to their work and are ill equipped for the rigour and discipline required in the work situation. At the same time, the need for workers to tackle environmental problems, whether this be to improve city parks, or restore hedgerows in the countryside, and to increase urban food production, is more and more urgent.

I suggest that the time has come to re-introduce National Service. But it would be National Service with a difference. Both men and women would have to take part. Besides providing the discipline of a military training, a pool of Nation Service personnel would be created which would provide an environmental task force for dealing with all the jobs that are currently neglected, and especially for taking forward environmental policy in fields like urban food production, monitoring environmental trends and building sea defences (in relation to projected rise in sea levels). There is an ever-increasing need for direct support for the old and infirm; the National Service pool of people could be used to provide this support.

Curricular in schools should be drastically altered to educate young people about the environmental situation, but meanwhile, each year, many young people are leaving school without this education. National Service would enable the Government to make its total education programme more effective by targeting this yearly produced group of people during the period of service.

Military training would however, remain an essential and major part of the National Service programme. I believe there is a very real possibility that conditions world wide, especially in the developing world, may become much worse and we could see widespread total break down of society. Under those circumstances Britain will need a strong defence military capability, if only to repel infiltration through the beaches.

Chapter 13

Human freedoms, and education

When I started to write the present book, I thought that this chapter would consist of the chapter of the same title in my previous book (Barker 1998) with minor revisions. However, events in the last two years have gradually made me realise that there are two areas which I did not deal with before, but which I must deal with now. As far as freedoms are concerned, the neglected area was freedom of expression about immigration. As far as education was concerned, the neglected area is what seems to me to be a widespread ignorance about the facts of population growth in England. Also, at the time I wrote my earlier book, I had been unaware of the writings of Jack Parsons, who has a lot to say on human freedoms in relation to population problems; so I will be referring to his work in this chapter. Nevertheless, I am retaining the general form of my earlier publication, and the arguments that I developed there.

In each of chapters ten to twelve, we have seen that implementing proposals would mean curtailing human freedoms. In Chapter ten, reproductive freedom; in Chapters eleven and twelve the freedom of where to live, set up business, property rights, land and car ownership, food production. What is certain is that in a democratic society, it would be impossible to ensure such curtailment without a fundamental change in the attitude of the people. Such a change of attitude could only come about through a massive education campaign.

A. Human freedoms

(i) Freedoms in general

It is worth remembering that civilisation is impossible without restriction of human freedom. For example, people cannot be allowed to settle their personal vendettas on the street. There is even a limitation on reproductive freedom, which has been a widespread feature of societies past and present - the prohibition of incest (Darlington, 1969). At the same time it is worth noting that restrictions on human freedom may change during the life of a civilisation. New prohibitions may arise, which may at least sometimes be accepted by the majority of the population. Thus the writer can remember the days when one expected to find a smoke filled atmosphere on public transport or in many cafes; more recently we have accepted restrictions on the smoking habit - a major restriction for many people!

G.Hardin in his important paper "The Tragedy of the Commons" (Hardin, 1968) discusses the whole question of human freedom in relation to sustainable development, with special reference to the population problem (although he did not use the term 'sustainable development'). He starts from the situation at the time of early man when all people regarded the whole world as 'common' for all functions (common in the sense for example, of common grazing rights on commons in England). The history of man has partly been the history of the restriction of rights over this commons. For example, early man could deposit his waste products anywhere. Later it became necessary to develop sewage systems which limited disposal to specific sites. Morality, a codification of good conduct, changes over time. He referred here to a paper by J.Fletcher who argued that the morality of an act is a function of the state of a system at the time it is performed. However, morality is conservative, and Hardin goes on to assert that the laws of society really follow ancient ethics that are often poorly suited to the governing of the modern world.

Every restriction on commons rights ('enclosure of the commons') involves the infringement of somebody's personal liberty. But infringements made in the distant past are accepted today almost without comment. The underlying problem is that if we continue to insist on all present-day freedoms we will bring universal ruin. Hardin develops his argument in relation to the growth of the human population, in a way that is very relevant to the sustainable development concept. The world has finite space, consequently population growth must eventually equal zero. When that happens, has the population reached its optimum for mankind, in the sense of 'the greatest good for the greatest number'? Hardin answers -no.

He adduces two arguments.

First, a theoretical point. We are concerned with two variables - population size and human good. We are enquiring if it is possible to maximise the latter when the former is maximised (i.e. at the size where population growth is forced to be zero by the finite state of the earth). Hardin asserts that it has been demonstrated mathematically that it is not possible to maximise for two (or more) variables at the same time. Second, an argument rooted in biological facts. To live, an organism must have a source of energy. This is needed for two purposes. The first is maintenance of the organism, energy to merely stay alive - "maintenance calories". The second (which he terms "work") is for work in common speech, together with all forms of enjoyment, from swimming to automobile racing, to writing poetry or playing music – "work calories". To maximise population size we must ensure that work calories per person approach as close to zero as possible. We can attain the maximum population but only at the cost of severe restrictions.

Hardin concludes that the optimum population, from the point of view of human good, is less than the maximum sized population. To maintain the common good into the future requires a deliberate limitation of population size. This in turn requires coercive action, which overrides personal liberty.

Parsons (1971) also takes up the idea that one can only maximise one variable, and he mentions three – number of people (population size), standard of living and individual liberty, arguing that the last mentioned one is the one we should try to maximise. Individual freedom is a 'macro freedom', which is made up of many individual 'micro freedoms'.

As population size and density increase, some micro freedoms will be enhanced, but, more importantly, others will be diminished. An example of enhancement is the ability to gain anonymity and freedom from control in a large city. For example, pregnant unmarried women from the provinces very frequently lose themselves in London to avoid moral censure.

An example of a diminishing freedom is freedom from beaurocracy. He adduces evidence that as population size increases so does beaurocratic control. And he discusses freedom from crime, citing evidence of a positive correlation between crime incidence and city size in the USA (which I referred to in Chapter 10 Section B). Freedom from social conflict in his view diminishes with increased population density following on increase in population size (discussed in Chapter 1 section F). The more people there are on earth or on a given part of it, within a particular nation for example, the more people must interact with each other and the more they must co-operate " to keep out of each others hair". And he notes that the animal behaviourist Niko Tinbergen comments that we now live at a far higher density than that in which genetic evolution has moulded our species. This together with long distance communication leads to more frequent, in fact continuous, inter-group contact and so to continuous external provocation.

Parsons goes on to argue that as population grows, there comes a point when the most important micro freedoms are diminishing. If that be so, we must decide what is/are the most important micro freedom(s). He argues the most important micro freedom – one we are in danger of losing – is freedom of movement in physical space. Hence in maximising individual freedom, we would put maximising mans movement in physical space as the most essential micro freedom.

Parsons concludes that population growth itself is probably the greatest single threat to individual liberty.

One may argue that in the developed world, we actually live in an age of increasing freedom. Education beyond the three R's has been thrown open to everyone, so that people can more fully explore and develop their potentialities; strictures on marital relations have been relaxed; people have more leisure for entertainment, and the variety of entertainment available has vastly increased; women have increasingly come to have similar freedoms to men - they can vote, and with less difficulty than in former times join a large variety of professions, and so on. Many would argue however, that an improvement in the quality of life has somehow evaded us. Numerous authors, for example E.F.Schumacher and Laurens van der Post assert that people have lost their spiritual roots and so become spiritually impoverished.

The great religions speak of an inner spiritual freedom; for example, for Christians, the essence of the way of life is summed up: "O God...whose service is perfect freedom" (Anglican Morning Service, Second Collect). And many people, Jew, Mohammedan, Gentile, have in the past, and can in the present, testify that they have experienced this freedom even under terribly restricting circumstances like concentration camps. In comparison with such freedom, peoples concern for many material freedoms seems trivial.

No one would deny that the world environment is very different now to what it has ever been before, and that the rate of change of various important variables - human population size, loss of green land to development, total quantity of polluting emissions, depletion of ocean and sea fish stocks, etc. has increased dramatically over all previous centuries. Surely then it is time to re-evaluate human freedoms. We need as Hardin argued, to re-examine freedoms to see which ones are defensible. So now we turn to consider some specific freedoms, to assess the significance of curtailment and any possible mitigation.

(ii) Specific freedoms to curtail

a) Reproductive freedom

While people in Britain might respond to various constraints (income, job permanency, available accommodation, etc.) by attempting to regulate their reproduction, they are not and have not been constrained by law to do so. The principle that individuals have the fundamental human right to determine the number and spacing of their children, as affirmed at the 1994 United Nations Cairo conference on Population and Development, is accepted. This principle stems from the Universal Declaration of Human Rights of 1967. That declaration asserts that the natural and fundamental unit of society is the family. Consequently, decisions about family size must rest with the family itself, and cannot be made by anybody else. This principle seems to have grown out of the situation that was world wide before the modern upswing in population growth but is still widespread in the developing world today, namely, high infant mortality (now however ameliorated) coupled with the need to have children not just to secure the line of inheritance, but to help with food production and to succour the aged. So people often need to produce numerous offspring; therefore attempts from outside to restrict breeding should be opposed. The principle has been supported by the beliefs of some widespread religious groups.

But conditions in the developed world are very different. Mortality rate is very low. Most adults are not farmers, so they do not need children to help them on the land; for those that do farm, farming is not labour intensive. Even if farming does become more labour intensive, it is unlikely to reach the intensive levels of parts of the developing world. Pensions and old age care, however defective the provision system may be, reduce the need to have children for the purpose of looking after aged relatives. In Britain, the vast majority of people could not care less about religion. These considerations lessen the significance of a restriction to freedom of reproduction. Further, a proposal to limit the number of children a woman may bear would still allow the experience of child bearing and rearing, so an essential part of reproductive freedom would remain. And for women who only wanted the number of children aimed at in the policy, there would in effect be no limitation to freedom. So if the aim were one child per woman, any woman who wanted only on child or none at all would not experience any loss of freedom.

Finally there might be room for very limited mitigation of freedom restriction in the following way. Suppose the aim was a reproductive rate corresponding to one child per woman. Consider women who want no children. They would nevertheless have the right to produce one child. They could sell this right to women who wanted to have two children. There would not be a single fixed fee. The fee would be on a sliding scale system depending on the total wealth of each party. The same method could of course apply if the target was two children per woman rather than one child.

b) Landownership, the choice of where to live, car ownership and use

We need to look at possible curtailments of freedom and ask two questions in relation to the population of England:

(i) Is this freedom essential for man's well being? If not, its abolition or curtailment should not be regarded in a serious light.

(ii) Is this freedom available to the majority of people? If it is not, it can hardly be claimed to be a basic human freedom.

Land ownership is clearly not essential to man's well being. Many do not own land but there seems no obvious difference in happiness or any other quality between such people and those who do own land. We saw in Chapter 12 Section C that as far as big landowners are concerned, Britain differs from the rest of Europe in the concentration of land in a few hands. This does not seem to be correlated with any particular difference between states in well-being. And as far as the small landowner is concerned -those who buy a residential plot, we have also seen (in Chapter 11 Section B) that in countries like France a far smaller proportion of the population are house owners. This does not seem to have disadvantaged the French in any way.

Freedom of where to live is in fact already strongly limited for the majority of the population.
People are constrained here by where employment is offered. And if a business with numerous branches closes down in one town, employees are often willing to move to another branch in another town and change residence to achieve this. If we densified the typical suburb, this would require people to give up the 'semi-detached', and move into apartments. But the semi-detached is not the dominant dwelling mode in all European Countries. Apartments are more the norm in some. So the semi-detached can hardly be essential for mans well being. If we focus again for a moment on the need to prevent urban expansion into the countryside, we note that the freedom to buy a house or plot in the affluent low-density outer suburbs, village or countryside, is very much limited to a small minority of the population (the comparatively wealthy). Most people cannot afford to buy the 'desirable residence' of the glossy brochures. Freedom to live where you want in terms of the urban-rural continuum is not then a basic human freedom.

When the present writer was a young person, the vast majority of people neither owned a car nor felt seriously deprived by not having one. And in previous centuries there were no cars. Even today there are many who do not own a car. So owning a car cannot be thought of as a basic human freedom. If cities and transport provision were re-organised as discussed in Chapters 3 and 11, the need for a private car would disappear for the majority of the population. Curtailment of car related freedoms then cannot be said to impinge on mans basic well-being.

c) Food production

Increasing food production in cities (Chapter 3), would require people to use garden space and roof top areas for food production. It would also require people to spend a lot of time on food production.

So food production in towns would mean a loss of freedom for town dwellers. In terms of the time involved in food production, this could be mitigated, in the sort of co--operative society found in the ideal urban village (Chapter 3). A portion of each householder's individually owned or shared land may be required for food production. But this does not necessarily mean that every household must take part in that production. It would be possible to arrange all sorts of exchanges between members of the community. One household might agree to farm the land of a neighbouring household in exchange say for a share in the profits from sale of produce, or in exchange for some service rendered (e.g. baby sitting). Such a system would mitigate the loss of freedom. We should also remember that before the industrial revolution, the majority of people in England were engaged in food production; and many societies in the world at large remain as they have been for centuries - largely composed of people who have to produce food as a major activity in their daily lives. Freedom from food production then, is not some universal human freedom.

d) Conclusions

We can conclude then that the curtailments of freedoms associated with the proposals made, are not as serious as they might seem to be at first sight. Either the freedoms are not essential for mans well-being, or they are not universal, or curtailment can be mitigated. Nevertheless there would be curtailments, and people would never accept them unless they could be convinced they were necessary. And they would not be convinced without a real understanding of the seriousness of the environmental situation. Hence the need for environmental education, which we deal with later in this chapter.

(iii) Freedoms to maintain

I have felt for a long time that there is a general reluctance to discuss population issues, more particularly the implications of population growth and possible population competition. And during the last two years I have come across scientists who have had papers which drew attention to population growth and competition, as causative factors of world problems, rejected by journals or newspapers. For example, the distinguished scientist William I. Stanton MBE notes that an article he wrote on the Malthus Cutoff level (see chapter 1) was rejected by the popular science magazine "New Scientist", although it had accepted his articles on other subjects, and he claims that this magazine regularly attacks the 'demographic doom-mongers', without letting them present their case (Stanton, Esperance, Nov. 1966).

The idea that there was reluctance to discuss/ unwillingness to accept the implications of population growth, surfaced last year in a series of articles and editorials in the British Medical Journal (9th October).

Two of the articles referred to the UN Conference on Population and Development held at Cairo in 1994. Now this conference prepared a Programme of Action, which in the words of the UN Executive Director of the United Nations Population Fund, ...".. focuses on meeting the needs of individual women and men, rather than on achieving demographic targets." Now M. Potts in his article noted that some of the loudest voices at the conference created what was a false and damaging dichotomy, portraying any quantitative concern for population as intrinsically coercive. And M. King in his article referred to an article by McIntosh and Finkle which noted that the three most organised participants at the conference were the United States, the Holy See, and the women's rights movement (predominantly from the United States). King argued that the USA wishes to keep the population debate closed - if the USA was to support population reduction in the developing world, it would be asked in turn to control its own resource consumption, which it was unwilling to do. And of course the women's rights movement is not keen on policies to limit women's family size. And everyone knows the Vatican's opposition to artificial birth control. King himself believes that underlying many attitudes is what has become known as the Hardinian taboo (named after the American ecologist G. Hardin) – a psychological failing, supposedly inherent in our psyche, that makes us unable to control our population numbers.

So it was with interest that I read Parsons recent book (Parsons, 1998), which gives numerous examples of governments, NGOs, and individuals which/who seem to deliberately play down the importance of population factors in discussing a variety of problems, sometimes distorting the facts. For example, on p.590 in talking about the British media he says:

"In leading articles, special supplements, major radio and TV documentaries on world poverty and development – especially on the recurring African famines – there is rarely any mention of population factors except the size of the impending catastrophe or the numbers already starving".

Parsons went on to give the example of a BBC TV 'Assignment' programme on the Sudanese famine:

"However, in 90 minutes of vigorous allegations and counter-allegations, there was not a syllable on any population factor other than the constantly reiterated forecast that 7 to 9 million were in danger of starving to death. Population size, growth rate, pressure, possible over-population, family planning or population control proper, as well as wider ecological issues of carrying–capacity and environmental degradation, were all totally excluded".

Now we like to think that we have freedom of speech in our country. After all, we do not have laws preventing it, and our Government does not imprison and execute people who speak out. However, freedom of speech does not necessarily exist in the absence of legal restrictions and persecution. In modern society, opposition to things can be very 'polite'. If newspapers, radio and television refuse to give a voice to parties with which their controllers or spokespersons disagree, this seriously limits free speech. And the point of view that we need to control population growth and reduce population size is not given anything like a fair hearing either in England or the world at large, I believe. This is a freedom we need to defend. A case in point is the letters to the Guardian newspaper on immigration that I discuss in the following section on education. Which leads me now to   consider immigration.

Immigration is central to one principle concern of the present book – the loss of size of the countryside through the need to construct more housing. People just do not seem to realise the connection between immigration and greenland loss. We will return to this matter in the final two sections of this Chapter. Here I want to continue to explore freedom of speech in connection with immigration.

During the last year, I have listened to the BBC daily, especially the Today programme of Radio 4. Very frequently the subject of immigration has come up: reports that a Government or political party spokesperson, or someone else, has expressed concern at the flow of asylum seekers and other immigrants. The next thing that such a report has usually said is that refugee and allied organisations have criticised what the speaker has said - the language was inflammatory, or the statement promotes racism, or the speaker had misrepresented the situation. The implication is usually that anybody who expresses any concern about the pressure of immigration is a 'racist', which of course is nonsense -recall the discussion of the term 'racism' in Chapter 10 Section F. This is a dangerous manipulation of our language – my language!

It is of interest also, that people speaking out for minority groups and immigrants so roundly condemn the language of those who express concern about immigration, and the growth of ethnic groups, and yet other people who support minority groups and immigrants can say and write things which are for many English people grossly insulting and racially provocative. After I had completed writing this book, the Runnymede Trust published its report on multi-ethnic Britain, complete with its provocative statement about the racial overtones of the words British and English. And then on October 17th the Telegraph newspaper reports that the vice chairperson of the Trust criticises our Royal family ... "They're a symbol of our unmeritocratic tendency and, of course, they're all white. It is part of a very unattractive hierarchy.....". Just imagine if some English person had made disparaging comments about leaders of some ethnic minority – it would create a storm of protest. Apparently she also said, speaking of the report; "we're not at all worried about all the fuss we've caused". Exactly! English people who express concern on immigration or growth of immigrant groups should be very careful what they say, but we can say what the devil we like. Perhaps in re-designing the Law (Barker, 1998) we should re-visit the Law of High Treason so such people can be indicted and at the same time re-introduce the death penalty so we can deal with them once and for all.

A catalyst for comment on these issues came from criticism of the Governments race relations record by the black leader of the Transport and General Workers Union, Bill Morris who had apparently written that government policies were giving life to racists and that government's actions towards asylum seekers were utterly insane, and ministers were fostering a climate of fear and loathing on asylum and immigration issues. The BBC web site 24-4-00, reported the reaction of people to what he had said. As one might expect, some supported Morris, some disagreed with him. A few expressed concern on capacity grounds - the small size of our country and the large population we already have here. Here are comments criticising Morris's use of the race issue:

"Why whenever questions of race and immigration arise do people like Bill Morris just talk about the language being used. This is a complete red herring......instead of discussing the issue rationally they resort to quibbles over semantics and cry 'racist'. It is not a substitute for a real debate".

"There are far too many people in Britain. Something must be done to stop the masses of bogus asylum seekers flocking over here......It's not racist to speak out about immigrants, the media have twisted the word racist to include anyone concerned about immigration. That means my comments are racist......".

" Bill Morris appears not to appreciate the genuine fears of ethnic Britons who see their homeland being made to take increasing number of foreigners and without, apparently, having any power to reverse the situation. To call their fears 'racism' is a travesty of the truth and is effect playing the race card but in reverse"

" As an Englishman by birth, I happen to be white, I can't wait for the day when being English is defined by the country where you were born and not the colour of your skin. The majority of the public want to see asylum seekers treated fairly but not preferentially. By bringing colour into the argument, Bill Morris is playing the race card in reverse. It's a very feeble argument and will not wash with the majority of sound thinking people".

" Is Bill Morris actually claiming that anyone who thinks that British people should be given priority – in Britain – is a racist? That would make most people in this country (and the world) racist.....".

" ....It is not a racist view to say that there should be a limit on immigration, as it happens to be a logical and sensible view....".

" You cannot call people racists for wishing to safeguard the interests of their nationals first....."

" Why is everything 'racist' if a European country does not allow in every individual seeking refuge in their country?...."

" Bill Morris is 'playing the race card', by describing new asylum laws as promoting racism. The asylum laws say nothing about the colour of the asylum-seekers skin. This is not a racial issue, so please stop trying to make it one".

Now one might argue, surely all these quotations prove the point that people are willing to speak out – we do have freedom of speech! I think however, that it is not as simple as that. In the first place, people who phone, write, fax or e-mail the BBC are not a random sample of the population. I think all this labelling of comments as 'racist' does in fact deter many people from speaking out openly -they are too scared or 'prudent' to do so. I suggest that if you can gain the confidence of ordinary English people and ascertain their opinions, you will find that the majority are very much against allowing immigrants in. But they are not going to join in a BBC discussion; they are not going to write to a newspaper; they are not going to stage a protest. And if in years to come we have widespread outbreaks of racial violence, all the do-gooders will raise their hands in horrified mystification -"why are people behaving like this?"

The effect of all this orchestrated criticism of people who do speak out is not, however, confined to deterring people from doing so. It acts like any efficient advertising campaign. That is, it convinces many people of the rightness of the view being advocated, rather than encouraging them to think rationally and way up the pros and cons of the argument. So it shifts the goal posts of discussion. Church leaders and other 'liberals' aid this process, when they speak of the contribution that immigrants can make to society, when in fact the vast majority of these immigrants are not in the slightest bit concerned about British society and its values (what's left of such values). All most of them are concerned about is having a better lifestyle and being able to belong to their own ethnic community, and for some of them, being able to live in safety. So they flock to the inner city, especially London, where they live in effect in enclaves. Parsons (1998) deals at length with this 'takeover' of areas in Chapter 12 of his book.

Jack Parsons (ibid) takes up the issue of immigrant campaigning in his section "principled considerations on immigration control" (pp.592-593). He discusses the morality of self-interested behaviour. He asserts that few would dispute the idea that immigrants are mainly motivated by self-interest. It is also understandable that immigrant pressure groups should avoid contrary evidence, "using illogical and *ad hominem* arguments and generally creating a moral uproar. Within reason, this is functional for their cause; the more they can silence or bamboozle or demoralise their opponents and the general public, then the better their cause will be served, at least in the short run. They can continue with a rapid build up of their numbers and make it more and more difficult for the natives to halt the process, let alone reverse it". To silence, bamboozle or demoralise the public, is inhibition of freedom of speech.

Parsons argues that the question must be asked: " 'What is the self-interest of the native majority?', plus the corollary, 'Are its members equally justified in pursuing their self-interest through the usual democratic channels?' It is hard to find a rationale that legitimates the pursuit of self-interest by aliens while ruling it out for the natives".

And he concludes: "However, it behoves anyone interested in a long-term, more rational, and possibly more ethical understanding – or even in an equally selfish short-term pursuit of his own group's self-interest – to scrutinise both evidence and arguments with care and decide accordingly".

The question of the interests of the native majority was also raised by D. Coleman, a demographer from Oxford University, in the BBC current affairs programme on immigration 16-12-99. He pointed out that one reason why people in England are concerned about immigration is that this process replaces people with whom they are familiar, with people they are not familiar with. He notes how this fear is often derided as being xenophobic or racist; however, he concludes, it needs to be carefully considered. For a Government's first responsibility in a democratic should be to its own electorate rather than the rest of the world.

Now I would question the right of people who are not of English descent to take an active part in determining how we deal with the immigration and asylum seekers questions. English people who descend from a long line of ancestors who have worked and often fought for their country, they have a right to play a part in determining our future. But, at the other extreme, a recently arrived immigrant, I would argue, has no right at all. I would assert that morally speaking, people do not have equal rights. More particularly, in terms of taking part in any debate on the future of the country, and therefore on issues like the control of immigration, we should have a scale of rights. At one end would be English people with a long history of English descent, people whose families have contributed to the state of Britain. They would have full rights. At the other extreme would be recently arrived immigrants, who would have no right at all. Voting right would be included on this scale. There would be a point on the scale dividing those who could vote from those who could not. For example, those people who are the offspring of black West Indians who came here in the fifties and made a genuine contribution to out society would probably have full voting rights.

I think then that we need to be very careful that English people do not lose the freedom to determine their own future by default. Meanwhile, we should ask the question -who are the people in these immigrant and refugee organisations? To what extent are they English people of English descent (or perhaps we should widen it to UK people of UK descent). They should curb their activities. If not, the Government should take steps to do just that. The Government has the responsibility to protect the rights of the majority first and foremost, and ensure that the free speech of that majority is not inhibited. Which leads to my final point in this section.

It appears that there are lawyers in Britain who are assisting illegal immigrants, and asylum seekers who either have not been given permission to remain or have not yet has their cases determined, to fiddle the system and secure residence rights. Thus was the subject of a report in The Independent newspaper on 13th Jan 2000. The report noted that in September Malik Law Associates was awarded the biggest legal aid franchise in London, valued as being worth up to £3m a year. The idea was to eliminate legal aid abuses that had been rampant among immigration solicitors in recent years. During the summer, The Independent sent a reporter to see a legal assistant at the firm, having been tipped off that the firm was offering visitors to Britain bogus identities as refugees from various African countries. The Independent's reporter posed as a Kenyan who had had her application to remain in Britain refused. The legal assistant was secretly videotaped telling her to forget she was Kenyan and think of herself from then on as Rwandan. The reporter was then passed on to a colleague of the legal assistant who said that she would be given a new Rwandan name, coached in a cooked up story about how she became a refugee, and the answers she should give to Home Office Staff!

Then on March 19th 2000 The Sunday Times had a report on the same subject. This time the investigator was a Yugoslav undercover reporter who visited law firms where she stated that she had not suffered any political repression and was not in danger (adding that she had used a fake Italian passport to enter Britain), but would like to stay here. Only one firm would not help her. Others made suggestions to help her such as getting a job despite laws forbidding asylum seekers to work while waiting for their claims to be decided. At one firm, Kothala and Co. a legal adviser, charging £75 for the interview, discussed ways to help her. Noting that she was clearly an economic migrant, he suggested she told him what she wanted to do and then he would see how they could help her. He made various suggestions such as marrying an Englishman, getting a good job 'under the ground', telling a story about ethnic tensions in the Balkans and noting that the photo in the passport was her face and after some time she could change her name to her 'real name'! The report goes on to describe what happened at another solicitors where she was given advice, which would have helped her evade the system.

In connection with reports like these it is interesting to note something that the National Criminal Intelligence Service (NCIS) reported on organised immigration crime (internet link to NCIS from BBC News 2nd Aug 2000). While not specifying that it was talking about crime committed inside Britain, the report said that one of the major problems the NCIS encountered concerned abuse of the asylum system. False asylum claims were increasingly organised, with orchestrated use of false documentation. In other cases, fraudulent claimants for asylum were using a false nationality to enhance their chances of obtaining refugee status.

To return to such lawyers or legal assistants (who we may note seem not to be of English descent) and the question of human freedoms. It is quite clear that their freedom to operate in the ways described should be removed!

One last point about the asylum seeker issue. One of the themes of BBC news during the last three years or so has been protests over asylum seekers crowding into or being crowded into certain areas, especially in the South East Region. LAs said they were being overwhelmed by the number of people seeking asylum, raising the fear that Council taxes could have to rise to provide the money to support these asylum seekers The Conservative MP for Ashford noted that the issue of asylum seekers is a very big one in MPs postbags and surgeries and their is a lot of indignation (BBC news 17-Mar 2000). There have been some outbreaks of violence, between residents and asylum seekers, between different groups of asylum seekers, and between pro-and anti-immigration groups (for example, BBC news 15 Nov 97, 4 and 14 Aug 1999, and 14 Aug 2000). I see these events in the context of the concept of population competition that I explored in Chapters 1 and 10. There is a very real chance that things will get worse, plunging our country into expanding cycles of violence. This breakdown of law and order would very much reduce citizen freedoms.

B. Are radical programmes possible?

You might well say, it is all very well for you to propose radical programmes including limitations on human freedoms, but the proposals are politically impossible to achieve. It is therefore a waste of time to even consider them. An answer, obviously very imperfect, can be developed along the following lines.

First, we must surely take up the position of affirming that we have no right to exercise any freedoms which will deprive future generations of all the freedoms existing today or in recent times. This is after all, a basic aspect of Sustainable Development, which our Government has officially embraced. I argue that unless very radical changes are made, sustainable development cannot be achieved. Therefore the Government must attempt the impossible and go all out to bring about the required radical changes.

Second. "Impossible"? We should remember a lesson from recent history- in the early days of the Second World War it seemed almost impossible that Britain could survive the onslaught of Hitler, but it did do so. The whole field of history at times of major societal change provides other examples of the impossible becoming possible. Imagine then that we were able to go back in time to dates shortly before these changes took place, but retaining our knowledge of what did actually happen. We then interview educated people of the time and put to them the question, do you think so and so is possible within the next X years (mentioning what we know did actually happen). It is the writers contention that the reply would sometimes have been –"highly improbable" or even "impossible"! Take just one example: Rome at the time of the Caesars while Christianity was a minor and much despised and persecuted religion. Suppose we had asked - what do you think the chances are that within fifty years Christianity will not only have spread throughout the Roman Empire, but will have become the official state religion? We would have provoked incredulity (and probably ended up being thrown into prison for our pains).

Third, we must insist on Government really leading the nation; only this will make it politically possible to implement radical proposals. Clearly both government and the people must be persuaded of the necessity for the changes proposed, including the limitations to human freedom that they imply. And we have been caught here for a long time in a vicious circle. The general public either does not realise the seriousness of the situation (on some issues such as population pressures or global warming) or does not notice adverse changes and so is not concerned about them (gradual deterioration of the environment). At the same time it jealously guards all its freedoms even when they are manifestly unsustainable. So the public does not exert a credible pressure on Government to implement a radical strategy. The Government for its part seems unwilling to do anything until it knows it has the approval of the mass of the electorate; it fears it will lose power if it advocates radical measures. The long continued issue of the reform of the transport system and peoples uses of cars is a good example of this paradigm. Whether the Government itself if fully aware of the situation is a moot point. It certainly has been given the facts, often by its own Agencies, also by major environmental NGOs, which have bombarded the Government with fact sheets, analyses and polemics. The only area where I think they may not have been briefed adequately is on the demographic facts. But to be aware of the facts and analyses and really take on their implications are two different things.

Surely we, the public, are entitled to leadership from the Government. But we are not getting it. Most people have very little respect for, and are very cynical about, all politicians. One reason for this is that they have heard so much about corruption, scandal and the going back on promises by people in high places. But I think there is another, less often mentioned reason for the public attitude. That is the sense that Government lacks the moral fibre to take tough decisions. If the Government really began to devise and implement a truly radical strategy, they may well be surprised – people might actually respect and support the Government!

Since I thought I had finished writing this book, a new development really highlights the problem. As I write now (13-9-00), we have a major crisis – high fuel prices have led to blockading of fuel terminals and the consequent disruption of public services and business and private car travel. But interviews with the public on the BBC show that the public either still does not understand the imperative to reduce carbon dioxide emissions, or that people are driven purely by short term selfish motives which put their own individual needs above the national and global need to drastically reduce these emissions. Further more, Government spokespersons, in defending the high fuel taxes, do so almost entirely in terms of the need for these taxes to fund desirable improvements in health and education; they are missing the opportunity to defend the high taxes on fuel on environmental grounds, and thus failing to use the crisis to educate the people.

Now as I pointed out in Chapter 8, the transport problem has not just come upon us in the last few years. It has been with us for several decades. And if we think only of recent times, if Government had made a determined effort to promote public transport, aided by massive injection of funds gained from fuel taxation (hypothecation), and had introduced congestion charging and other measures recommended by environmentalists, and at the same time had launched a massive education programme, this present crisis would never have arisen. We are not getting the leadership from Government that we have the right to expect.

Fourth. As far as a deliberate attempt by Government to get the peoples backing for radical reform is concerned, we need a full-blooded and totally uncompromising propaganda campaign by government. The mere mention of a 'propaganda campaign' is likely to raise the hackles of many or most intelligent people. For they know that propaganda is usually associated with a deliberate distortion of the truth. Even in the British Propaganda at the time of the Second World War, vital information was sometimes omitted, and claims of success exaggerated. Yet the definition of propaganda does not make such distortion a pre-requisite. It is usualy defined along the lines of any programme for, or definite attept at, the propagation of a particular theory or practice.

With the present environmental situation, we don't need any distortion of the truth; the truth, simple and unadorned, is just too terrible to need any distortion of omission or commission to emphasise its seriousness. Government should prepare an education campaign, embracing and integrating all aspects of the environment. It should insist on all television and radio channels taking part in this campaign, and that all newspapers are required to carry a daily or weekly (as appropriate) programme of environmental education. We now look at the education programme.

C. Education

In formal education, it is sometimes argued that to educate students adequately about the environment, we need to develop cross-curricular links between the existing relevant but discrete subjects. A well-educated adult, who already understands the basic principles within each subject area, may find it easy to link these ideas together into a conceptual whole. It is quite a different matter for the average student who has difficulty understanding the basic principles within subjects without having in addition to try to bring these subjects together into a conceptual whole.

Rather then than developing cross-curricular links, we need to create a single subject that integrates all aspects of the environmental problem, and possibly abolish existing subjects as distinct teaching areas in the process. We need then to make this subject the compulsory core of all teaching from pre-school onwards. The subject could be called 'Natural History' because in the wide sense of that term, this is exactly what we are talking about. Alternatively it could be called 'Gaia', after the Greek earth goddess and James Lovelock's hypothesis of a whole planet evolutionary homeostasis. It would be built primarily from the disciplines of mathematics, physics, chemistry, geology, climatology, cosmology, biology. Such a subject would also form the basis for developing education programmes for the general adult public on radio and television.

Such an education programme has the potential to lead people to a changed attitude to the world in which they live. The more one understands about the complexity of natural processes, the more one understands about the beautiful intricacies of structure and function of living organisms, the more one is likely to feel that sense of wonder, of awe, of respect for the natural world. Then people can come to the position where they accept, first, that all other organisms have a right to live, and second, that they have a responsibility to the world around them. They then cease to think of the world primarily from the point of view of what they can get out of it, now, and in the future. In the writers view, only such a fundamental change of attitude will enable us to achieve truly sustainable development.

To develop the idea of other species having the right to live would involve going into what is now a large area of philosophical enquiry at the heart of which is something called 'deep ecology' - a vision of nature and human life as part of one inter-dependent community in which each species has intrinsic worth. The various papers in Gottlieb (1997) give leads into this field of enquiry. One extension of this vision is developed by Wenz (1997) in that volume, who, following other authors, argues that one consequence of valuing nonhuman life for itself is that it leads to man avoiding oppression within human society. He argues that much of this oppression arises out of the prevailing attitude that man has the right to dominate all other forms of life. He points out that in some 'indigenous societies' (what some lay people would call 'primitive' societies) people treat each other better than we do, and he notes the connection in such societies between respect for nature and respect for fellow human beings. In so far that we will never achieve sustainable development unless we bring social justice to the world, these ideas are worth careful attention.

For some interesting discussion of education programmes see Martin (1993), WWF (1994) and UKBSG (1995). A single subject approach is not however advocated.

What I have written so far in this section follows the basic approach I developed in my 1998 book. I did not attempt to spell out in detail the elements of the 'natural history' or 'Gaia' subject. In particular, I did not stress the need to place emphasis on the demographic facts. I cannot leave matters like that now, however. The reason is that, as I now realise, the significance of population growth and immigration is not adequately recognised by environmentalists and others who would draw up the education programme, and there is widespread ignorance about the population of England/UK amongst the public. Perhaps most important for the central concern of this book – the size and quality of the countryside - is the fact that most people fail to realise the significance of population growth for increasing the amount of land that will be lost to new housing, and that immigration is a major cause of this population growth (I raised the question of whether the CPRE held a misconception about demographic facts in this context in Chapter 10).

As far as the public is concerned, there seem to be several related misconceptions about population matters, which, singly or in various combinations, are widely held by people. These are:

(a) the population is not growing but getting smaller;

b) the population is stationary or slightly increasing, but natural increase is no longer taking place;

c) although the population is still increasing, migration is only a minor component of this increase;

d) there continues to be an increase in the number of households, but this is caused primarily through the trend to smaller household sizes, not by population increase;

e) there is no net immigration.

Now this ignorance on population matters has unfortunate consequences:

(i) few people are concerned about population growth and its consequences;

(ii) although people are concerned about illegal immigrants and asylum seekers, they do not realise the full extent of the problem;

(iii) they see any advocacy of population reduction as not only imposing unacceptable curtailment of freedom, but as being positively perverse since the population is getting smaller anyway - misconception (a).

Two letters to the Guardian newspaper illustrate both ignorance about population growth and my fear that freedom of speech is curtailed by the media, and I deal with these letters in the next section.

To return to the education programme – Natural History or Gaia. I believe that a study of the ecology of all living organisms, and especially a study of population growth and carrying capacity, would be central to the programme; this would provide the context for a study of human populations, which in turn would make it possible to deal adequately with the growth of the human population in the UK and the problems associated with this growth.

As far as the media is concerned, there are of course already many programmes and articles about environmental matters. If we just think of BBC programmes, some do get down to grappling with problems within the context of specific UK environments – good examples of this are "The Food Programme" and "Open Country". So many others however miss the opportunity to really educate people about environmental matters, and pander to the widespread desire of people to prettify their own home environments – all these programmes about creating a garden which will give people a nice bit of lawn here, a nice paved stone area there, some pretty flowers arranged in a 'tasteful way', and missing the opportunity to concentrate on things that really matter – working with nature (the organic way) in food production and creating wild life areas. All these programmes about 'do it yourself' in the house, where all sorts of trivial design solutions are advertised, but the idea of producing an environmentally friendly life style is virtually ignored (design for energy efficiency, etc). And there are very few programmes on real population issues (the recent Reith Lectures were very disappointing in this respect).

Finally, to return to the problem of human freedoms. Should not the whole question of freedoms be much more openly and directly explored with the public? We here a lot about 'incentives' to reform the behaviour of people, for example make car fuel more expensive to discourage car use. No doubt these incentives have their place. But it would be much better to concentrate on being completely open with the public and coming to a straight discussion in terms of freedom, pointing out that unless people accept some very real restrictions on their freedom, we are all going to land ourselves in a terrible mess.

D. Some interesting correspondence

In January of this year, at the height of the Asylum seekers controversy, I wrote to the Guardian newspaper:

"Dear Sir/Madam,

The Guardian yesterday (26th) reported 'Asylum seekers up 55% as backlog grows' (Alan Travis, front page). Derek Brown commentating on asylum seekers on the Guardian on-line website, criticized those who would turn these people away, on the grounds that if given entry, they could make a positive contribution to society.

However, we need 'joined-up thinking' on this issue. Todays immigrants are tomorrows householders. Increase in the number of households nationally increases the pressure to release green land for housing, which damages our countryside. This negative effect of immigration needs to be balanced against the positive contribution immigrants might make to our country.

Yours faithfully.

NB. In deciding whether or not to publish the letter, you might like to consider the following two points:
1) From Office for National Statistics. Monitor population and health. PP2 98/1. 10th March 1998: "Total population. The overall population for the UK is projected to rise gradually between 1996 and 2021 from 58.8 million to 62.2 million..." (on page 1)
2) From Champion,T. et al 1998 "The determinants of migration flows in England: A review of existing data and evidence. A report prepared for the DETR" (universities of Newcastle and Leeds):
"At national level, migration was adding more to population in the mid 1990s than was natural change, though its contribution had been running at about one-third of national population growth over the previous decade" (page vi)".

My letter was not published. At least, I carefully checked the Guardian for a few days and my letter did not appear, and a lady in the letters section of the Guardian recently kindly also checked the letters columns and confirmed that my letter had not appeared.

However, about the same time, two other people did write to the Guardian and their letter was published – on 1st February:

"Our parents, to escape from Nazi Germany, were given political asylum in New Zealand. The Holocaust memorial Day (Report, January 27) will be meaningless if the doors of the EU remain closed to all but a small number of those fleeing from oppression. No room? That is a myth. Our existing population is decreasing. Immigrants are not a threat but enrichment

Dr. Barbara Einhorn
Brighton
Revd Dr. Paul Oestreicher
Coventry".

Now the first curious thing about this letter is the second sentence ("The Holocaust.....from oppression"). Why is it made meaningless? No explanation is given. In parenthesis, I feel uneasy about the repeated reference by Jews to the Holocaust when one notes that they usually don't even mention other massive extermination campaigns (Pol Pot Regime, Rwanda). The Jewish emphasis on their own holocaust seems to me best seen in the light of the concept of population competition, rather than as it is usually presented, that is as a moral crusade.

More important however, is the sentence "Our existing population is decreasing". This assertion is false. Note how it is the whole underpinning for the statement that it is a myth that we have no room.

Note also how the Guardian did not print my letter, factually correct, despite my references by which they could have checked the essence of what I said, yet printed a letter that was based on a complete misunderstanding of the actual situation in the UK. There are two possibilities why they published the Oestreicher letter. Either the Guardian people are unaware that population is increasing, not decreasing - In which case, as a national newspaper, on such an important topic, they should know, or, they are aware of the facts, but choose, because of their own 'liberal' line on asylum seekers, to ignore it.

Eventually I got round to writing to Dr. Oestreicher as follows:

> "Dear Dr. Oestreicher,
>
> I have been meaning to write to you for a long time, but have been too busy with more urgent tasks. The issue: your letter to the Guardian of February the 1st".

I then copied his letter and continued:

> "**You are wrong on population**. Our population in England is still slowly increasing and is projected to go on doing so for the next three decades".

After giving him statistics (and references to statistics) showing that our population is projected to increase, that natural increase will continue despite fertility rate being below replacement level, and the extent that immigration is expected to contribute to population growth, I continued:

> "You are quite a well known and respected person. Many people will regard what you write almost as gospel. Your letter will have confirmed for readers what they believed already — population is not growing, so that ground for being concerned about immigrants falls to the ground.
>
> What are you going to do about it? I believe, if you have any concern for the truth, that you should write to the Guardian and ask them to publish a correction. Are you prepared to do this?
>
> I would appreciate it if you would let me know, and also send me a copy of your letter, should you write it and it is accepted.
>
> I do not think that your approach will in the long run help reduce racism and anti-semitism; quite the reverse. When ordinary people find out that you assert a totally misleading claim, they are unlikely to think that you just made a mistake, and they are more likely to become, or become more, anti-semitic.
>
> A final word about the church - I am myself an Anglican. I have tried in my own church to raise population as a matter of concern, only to be badly knocked on the head. There seems to me to be a reluctance to discuss population issues — what has been called the Hardinian taboo, after the American ecologist, G. Hardin. It is to me ironic, that the church, so concerned to get at the facts about the bible — did this or that really happen, all the talk about pre-resurrection and post- resurrection Jesus, etc., seems not to care overmuch about facts outside the religious domain, swallowing all the rhetoric of the do-gooders, giving the impression that the main objective is to demonstrate that members of the church are no different from anyone else. I thought the gospel was about truth, about being willing to face the uncomfortable issues even if that makes one unpopular — or worse!
>
> Yours sincerely,"

Eventually I got a reply – on a postcard dated 17th May. It was handwritten, so I now type it out.

> "Thanks for taking the trouble to write so fully ... was working from a different set of statistics .....future projections are of necessity conjectural. My main argument remains unaffected by which statistic is the more accurate. Europe, including the UK, needs immigration both for social and economic reasons. Immigrants (of course not all immigrants) are not a problem, let alone a curse, but a blessing. I came from New Zealand in 1958 .... but more Brits left than came.
>
>   My best wishes"

(The first line of dots is mine- the postal franking obscures what is written but it is almost certainly "I". The other lines of dots are in the original).

It appears that statistics do not matter. And the letter suggests that even if people were educated about the basic demographic facts, many would probably not change their attitudes.

Conclusions

This book focuses on the countryside, how it has deteriorated and what needs to be done to restore it. However, one cannot deal with the countryside in isolation from the city: whatever happens in the one will, directly or indirectly, affect what happens in the other. So the book also considers the deterioration and restoration of our cities. This connection between town and country is so important that for a while I considered making the title of the book "are we prepared to save our (country)side?" rather than "are we prepared to save our countryside?"

In considering the long-term future of our country, the single most important parameter is the human population, its size, growth and distribution. Contrary to what many people think, our population is projected to continue to increase for quite a long time. The larger the population, the greater the stress that is put on the environment by human activities. The denser the population, the greater the chances of conflict; and the projected increase in the ethnic minority proportion of the population, could lead to increasing racial tensions. The population of England already exceeds carrying capacity, making it very difficult to achieve sustainable development.

The more the population grows, the greater the need for housing, which as far as the countryside is concerned, means the greater the loss of greenfield land to new dwellings. This loss is aggravated by the continuation of counter-urbanisation, motivated principally by a very widespread desire of people to move out of cities to the countryside or at least to the urban fringe. Not only does this lead to more greenland being lost to housing, but also it serves to accentuate the divide between the rich and the poor, a divide which fundamentally saps the well being of our society. On top of this, our formerly distinctive rural communities have lost their cohesion, partly by the inflow of wealthy people, most of who are not employed in rural industries, partly through the outflow of young people seeking employment in the cities.

The main cause of the deterioration of the remaining countryside is the intensification of farming practice since the Second World War. This was caused at least partly by the need to increase food production to feed the growing population. It has been facilitated and maintained by the Common Agricultural Policy (CAP) of the European Union. Intensive farming has led to a lower demand for agricultural labour, which combined with counter-urbanisation has led to the breakdown of traditional agriculture based rural communities. Intensive farming has also caused deterioration of the natural environment, loss of landscape features and a massive decline in wildlife. At the same time, farmers have largely failed to act as custodians of what is after all the peoples' land.

On the basis of this analysis of the situation, a strategy for the future is developed.

Measures should be introduced as soon as possible not only to halt future population growth, but also to bring about a massive reduction of population. Now continued population growth has two almost equally important components – natural increase and net immigration. So to stabilise and reduce the population we should maintain fertility below replacement level, and prevent further net immigration. Such policies would infringe human rights as currently understood. But the cardinal principle here should surely be that we should not insist on protecting a given human right if in doing so we make it impossible to secure other equally or more important human rights.

It is widely accepted that we must radically re-organise our cities so that they become attractive places in which to live, thus reducing counter-urbanisation and the consequent loss of greenland to development. It is also widely agreed that to reduce such greenland loss, we must increase the extent that new building occurs in urban areas in contrast to rural areas by maximising the use of brownfield sites and by a moderate densification of housing in new developments where there is adequate public transport provision. In this book it is argued that to really stem the counter-urbanisation flow it will be necessary in addition to develop a system of 'sticks and carrots', even coercive measures, to bring about population re-distribution between town and country. Further, there needs to be a fundamental re-organisation of existing suburbia both to achieve significant densification of housing and thus minimise greenland loss to housing, and also to make it possible for genuine communities to evolve in our cities. This re-organisation would transform cities dominated by semi-detached housing estates to cities predominantly consisting of urban villages where middle–rise buildings are the dominant building type.

In the countryside, there must be a deliberate return to less extensive farming methods. The long-term aim should be to return to mixed farming and adopt organic methods throughout the farming industry. Fuel crop production should be expanded to help reduce the dependency on non-renewable energy sources. While it is desirable to improve and extend wildlife areas, the top priority in the countryside must be to make agricultural production more environmentally friendly, because agriculture occupies the greatest part of the rural area. While the Government strives to bring about reform of the Common Agricultural Policy, it should meanwhile make maximum use of the considerable latitude allowed

245

under CAP law to make farming more environmentally friendly. Much more use must be made in this connection of two mechanisms known as Cross-compliance and Regulation. Nationalising the land would enable Government through a system of covenants to ensure that farming was carried out in an environmentally responsible manner.

It is argued that if we are to save our (country)side, we have to take a long term view, and develop a vision (goal) of what the country could be like two or three centuries hence. This vision would encompass all aspects of our society and of the environment, and at its centre, would be a given (much reduced) population size. For an intermediate point in time, we need to develop a detailed goal package, which firms up the characteristics of a state intermediate between the present and the long-term goal society.

All this means we need to adopt radical strategies. Many will argue this is politically impossible. If we do not however do this, we will not succeed in saving our (country)side, and at the global level, we face the possibility of totally degrading humanity or bringing about the extinction of the human species. The Government could make the impossible possible in England by launching a massive environmental education campaign.

Two case studies on the Sheffield Region are reported in this book. The first concerns the City of Sheffield. Decline of heavy industry and other factors has left Sheffield in a run-down condition. The economy of South Yorkshire, which includes Sheffield, is under-performing against every economic indicator, so much so that the Region has recently been able to secure EU Objective One funding status. Sheffield illustrates national urban features and trends, such as run down housing estates, and the ability of wealthy people to segregate themselves in low-density housing enclaves in peripheral areas. The activity of a small number of dedicated environmental activists, assisted by some NGOs and with limited assistance from the City Council, has led to the transformation of some former industrial areas into havens for wildlife. However, as far as overall city form and function is concerned, a study of official documents and other evidence leads to the conclusion that the City Council together with the coterie of senior planners, and senior business people, has not developed any convincing vision for the future of the city, placing reliance rather on worn out rhetorical formulae. It is too early to say if the recent change of political leadership of the Council will make an appreciable difference to the situation.

The second case study concerns the Peak District National Park. This concludes that National Park designation, apart perhaps from limiting house building, has done little to prevent further deterioration of the environment. Such limited environmental improvement that has been secured in the Park area has been largely the responsibility of national bodies, not the Park authorities. Unless the National Park Authority was given much greater powers, it would be better to abolish it, and the money so saved used to help the national bodies that operate in the Peak District area.

The policies of some well-known campaigning environmental organisations are discussed. It is concluded that some policies are defective; and it is suggested that one reason for this is probably that these organisations do not wish to offend a major part of their support constituencies.

Personal note

I think it is unlikely that radical programmes will be adopted in England or the world at large, and consequently I think it probable that within five or at the most ten years, England and the whole world will be set on a pathway of TOTAL IRREVERSIBLE environmental and social decline.

References

Organisations as authors are listed by abbreviation as given at the beginning of this book

Abbott, M. (1990). Combinable crops and the European Community. BSP Professional Books.

ADAS. (1993). Environmental evaluation of the beef and sheep pilot extensification schemes. ADAS.

ADAS. (1997a). Environmental monitoring in the South West Peak ESA 1993-1996. ADAS.

ADAS. (1997b). Monitoring of breeding birds in the North Peak ESA 1994-1996. ADAS.

ADAS. (1997c). Environmental monitoring in the North Peak ESA 1988-1996. ADAS.

ADAS. (1997d). Landscape monitoring in the North Peak ESA 1988-1996. ADAS.

ADAS. (1997e). Biological monitoring of moorland in the North Peak ESA 1988-1996. ADAS.

Agra Europe. (1999). UK unveils "modulation" boost for rural economy. Agra Europe December 10, 1999.

Agra Europe. (2000). CAP monitor. Agra Europe, London

Akerman, N. (1979). Can Sweden be shrunk? Development Dialogue 1979,2: 71-114.

Andelson, R. V. (1991). Commons without tragedy: the congruence of Garrett Hardin and Henry George. In Andelson, R.V. (ed). Commons without tragedy. Shepheard-Walwyn, London.

Anderson, P. et al. (1997). Restoring moorland. Peak District moorland management project. Phase III report. PDNPA.

Ansell, D.J. & Tranter, R.B. (1992). Set-aside in theory and in practice. Reading University.

Arbre Energy Ltd. (undated). The growing energy business. Arbre Energy Ltd, Leeds.

Ashmead, D. (1997). Standing room only. Our overcrowded planet. Robert Hale, London.

Baker Associates et al. (1998). Yorkshire and the Humber Regional settlement potential and development options study. Baker Associates.

Baldock, D. et al. (1996). Growing Greener. CPRE.

Baldock, D. & Lowe, P. (1996). The development of European agri-environment policy, in Whitby, M. (ed) The European Environment and CAP reform. CAB International.

Baldock, D. & Mitchell, K. (1995). Cross-compliance within the Common Agricultural Policy. IEEP.

Barker, J.F. (1998). England AD 2,200. How would you like it to be? Gaia Watch, Sheffield.

Barton, H. et al. (1995). Sustainable settlements. A guide for planners, designers and developers. University of the West of England and Government Management Board.

Bate, R. et al. (2000). On the move. The housing consequences of migration. JRF

Bennett, J. & George, S. (1987). The hunger machine. The politics of food. Polity Press.

Bengtsson,T. (1992). Lessons from the past: the demographic transition revisited. Ambio 21: 24-25.

Bengtsson,T. ed (1994). Population, economy, and welfare in Sweden. Springer-Verlag.

Bengtsson,T. & Ohlsson, R. (1994).The demographic transition revised. In Bengtsson,T. ed (see above).

Bibby, P. & Shepherd, J. (1997). Projecting rates of urbanisation in England, 1991-2016: methods, policy application and results. Town Planning Review 68,1: 93-124.

Binfield, C. et al eds. (1993). The history of the city of Sheffield 1843-1943. Sheffield Academic Press.

Birdlife International. (1997). A future for Europe's rural environment. Reforming the Common Agricultural Policy. Birdlife International, Brussels.

BLI. (1997). A future for Europe's rural environment. Reforming the Common Agricultural Policy. BLI.

Blowers, A. (1993). The time for change. In Blowers, A. (ed) Planning for a sustainable environment. TCPA.

Bongaarts, J. (1994). Population policy options in the developing world. Science 263: 771-776.

Bramley, G. (1996). Housing with Hindsight. CPRE.

Brass, W. (1989). Is Britain facing the twilight of parenthood?. In Joshi,H. (ed) The changing population of Britain. Blackwell

Brassley, P.W. (1995). The Common Agricultural Policy of the European Union. In Soffe, R.T. (ed) The agricultural notebook. Blackwell

Breheny, M. (1997). Local authorities and residential densities - an attitude problem? Town and Country Planning 66,3: 84-87.

Breheny, M. & Rookwood, R. (1993). Planning the sustainable city region. In Blowers, A. (ed) Planning for a sustainable environment. Earthscan.

Britton, D. ed. (1990). Agriculture in Britain: changing pressures and policies. CAB International.

Broberg, P. (1981). Spräng inte betonglimporna de kan bli framtidens bästa bostäder. Hem frittid. 11: 110-111 & 122.

Brouwer, F. & Lowe, P. (2000). CAP regimes and the European Countryside. CABI Publishing, Wallingford.

Brown, A. F. & Shepherd, K. B. (1991). Breeding birds of the south Pennine moors. JNCC Report no. 7.

Brown, L.R. (1990). Feeding the world in the nineties. In NAVF. Sustainable development, science and policy. The conference report. NAVF.

Brown, L.R. (1994). State of the world 1994. Earthscan.

Brown, L.R. (1995). State of the world 1995. Earthscan.

Brown, L.R. (1996). State of the world 1996. Earthscan.

Brown, L.R. (1997). State of the world 1997. Earthscan.

Brown, L.R. et al. (1994). Vital signs. The trends that are shaping our future 1994-1995. Earthscan

Brown, L.R. et al. (1998). State of the world 1998. Worldwatch Institute.

Brown, L.R. et al. (1999). State of the world 1999. Worldwatch Institute.

Brown, L. R. et al. (1999). Vital Signs. Worldwatch Institute.

BTCV. (1996). People working for the environment. BTCV.

Buckingham, H. et al. (1999a). Hidden heaths. A portrait of limestone heaths in the Peak District national Park. PDNPA.

Buckingham, H. et al. (1999b). Meadows beyond the millenium. The future of hay meadows in the Peak District National Park. PDNPA.

Butterfly conservation. (1997). West midlands regional action plan. Butterfly conservation.

CA. (2000). The state of the countryside. CA.

Campbell, L.H. & Cooke, A.S. eds (1997). The indirect effects of pesticides on birds. JNCC.

Canfield, C. (1990). Ecocity Conference 1990. Urban Ecology, California and Cerro Gordo Town Forum, Oregon.

Cannell, M.G.R. et al. (1999). Indicators of climate change in the UK. DETR and Centre for ecology and hydrology.

Cathie, J. (1982). The political economy of food aid. Gower Publishing Company.

Champion, T. (1997). The facts about the urban exodus. Town and Country Planning 66,3: 77-79.

Champion, T. (2000). Flight from the cities? In Bate, R. et al. On the move. The housing consequences of migration. JRF.

Champion, T. et al. (1998). The determinants of migration flows in England: a review of existing data and evidence. University of Newcastle upon Tyne.

Clout, H. (1984). A rural policy for the EEC? Methuen.

Cobb, D. et al. (1999). Integrating the environmental and economic consequences of converting to organic agriculture: evidence from a case study. Land use policy 16: 207-221.

Coleman, D.A. (1992). Does Europe need immigrants? Population and work force projections. International Migration Review. 26, 2: 413-461.

Coleman, D. A. (2000a). Immigration and the countryside. Country Life. May 11th 2000.

Coleman, D. A. (2000b). Uses and abuses of immigration. Toronto National Post 31st March 2000.

Coleman, D. A. (2000c). Letter to The Times, 22nd June 2000.

Coleman, D. and Salt, J. (1992). The British population. Patterns, trends and processes. Oxford University Press.

Concepcion, M.B. (1994). Population policies in south east Asia. In Lutz, W. ed The future population of the world. What we can assume today. Earthscan.

Cordy, T. (1997). Why I wouldn't sign. Town and Country Planning 66,3: 66

Cousins, C. (1997). The houses - where can they be dumped? Town and Country Planning 66,3: 74-75.

Coward, R. (1999). The CAP doesn't fit. The Ecologist 29, 5: 293-295.

CPRE. (1992a). Where motorcar is master. CPRE.

CPRE. (1992b). Wheeling out of control. CPRE.

CPRE. (1993). Preparing for the future. CPRE's submission to the government during its preparation of the UK strategy for sustainable development. CPRE.

CPRE. (1995a). Losing landscape.A review of recent research on environmental change in the countryside. CPRE.

CPRE. (1995b). Parking mad. The loss of land to roads and parking. CPRE.

CPRE. (1995c). The great transport debate. CPRE.

CPRE. (1996a). CPRE's traffic trauma map. CPRE.

CPRE. (1996b). Lost lanes. CPRE.

CPRE. (1996c). Dry stone walls. CPRE.

CPRE. (1998). Hungry Housing. CPRE.

CPRE. (1999a). Regional Chambers: their role and relevance to the campaigning work of CPRE. CPRE.

CPRE. (1999b). Regionalism. CPRE's new frontier. CPRE, Sheffield, Peak District and South Yorkshire Branch. Newsletter no.78.

Darley, G. et al. (1991). Tomorrow's new communities. JRF.

Darlington, C.D. (1969). The evolution of man and society. George Allen and Unwin.

Day, L.H. (1992). The future of low-birthrate populations. Routledge.

DETR. (1996). Greening the city. A good practice guide. DETR.

DETR. (1998a). Planning research programme. The use of density in urban planning. DETR.

DETR. (1998b). Planning for the communities of the future. DETR

DETR. (1998c). Planning for sustainable development: towards better practice. DETR.

DETR. (1998d). Strategic environmental appraisal. Report of the International Seminar, Lincoln, 27-29 May 1998. DETR.

DETR. (1999a). Projections of households in England to 2021. DETR.

DETR. (1999b). Sustainable development. A better quality of life. A Strategy for sustainable development for the UK. SO.

DETR. (1999c). Review of the National air quality strategy. A consultation document. DETR.

DETR and DoE (various dates) Planning policy guidance. HMSO.
        PPG1. General policy and principles (1997).
        PPG2. Green Belts (1995).
        PPG3. Housing (2000).
        PPG6. Town centres and retail development (1993).
        PPG7. The countryside - environmental quality and economic and social development 1997.
        PPG9. Nature conservation (1994).
        PPG11. Regional Planning (2000).
        PPG12. Development plans and regional planning guidance (2000).
        PPG13. Transport (1994).
        PPG13. A guide to better practice (1997).

DoE. (1992a). Circular 1/92. Planning controls over Sites of Special Scientific Interest. DoE and Welsh Office.

DoE. (1993). Environmental appraisal of development plans. HMSO.

DoE. (1992b). The UK environment. HMSO.

DoE. (1996a). Indicators of sustainable development for the United Kingdom. HMSO.

DoE. (1996b). Rural England. A nation committed to a living countryside. HMSO.

DoE. (1996c). Digest of environmental statistics no. 18. HMSO.

Downton, P. (1997). Ecological community development. Town and country planning 66,1: 27-29.

Dwelly, T. ed. (1996). Living in the future. 24 sustainable development ideas from the UK. The UK National Council for Habitat.

Dwyer, J. et al. (2000). Cross-compliance under the Common Agricultural Policy. A report to the Department of the Environment, Transport and the Regions (DETR).IEEP, London.

EC. (1995). The agricultural situation in the European Union. The 1994 report. EC.

EC. (1995b). Strategic environmental assessment legislation and procedures in the community. Office for official publications of the European Communities.

EC. (1996). The Common Agricultural Policy in transition. EC.

EC. (1997). Agenda 2000: for a stronger and wider union. EC

EC Energy Directorate (undated). Lancashire and Yorkshire renewable energy planning study final report. Contract no. XVII/4. 1030/Z/95-004. Terence O'Rourke plc

Ehrlich, P. & Ehrlich, A. (1990). The population explosion. Hutchinson, New York.

Elkin, T., McLaren, D.& Hillman, M. (1991). Reviving the city. Towards sustainable urban development. FoE.

EN. (1996a). English Nature.The first five years. EN.

EN. (1996b). English Nature 5th Annual Report 1 April 1994 - 31 March 1995. EN.

EN. (2000). Annual Report. 1 April 1999 – 31 March 2000. EN

ETSU. (1994). An assessment of renewable energy for the UK. HMSO.

Ferguson, A. (1998a). The carrying capacity and ecological footprints of nations. OPT, Manchester.

Ferguson, A. (1998b). Spreadsheet. The carrying capacity and ecological footprints of nations. OPT, Manchester.

Flavin, C. (1999). Global temperature goes off the chart. In Brown, L. (1999b)

FoE. (1991). Off the treadmill. A way forward for farmers and the countryside. FoE.

FoE. (1994). Planning for the planet. Sustainable development policies for local and strategic plans. FoE.

FoE. (1995). Working future? Jobs and the environment. FoE.

GAD. (2000). Information and assumptions for the 1998 based population projections. GAD. GAD web site: www.gad.gov.uk

Gardner, B. (1996). European agriculture, policies, production and trade. Routledge.

Garnett, T. (1996). Growing food in cities. A report to highlight and promote the benefits of urban agriculture in the UK. SAFE.

Gordon, D. (1990). Green cities. Ecologically sound approaches to urban space. Black Rose books, New York.

Gorz, A. (1985). Paths to paradise. On the liberation from work. Pluto Press.

Gottlieb, R.S.ed (1997). The ecological community. Environmental challenges for philosophy, politics, and morality. Routledge

Gwilliam, M. et al. (1998). Sustainable renewal of suburban areas. York Publishing Services Ltd, York.

Handley, C. & Rotherham, I.D. (2000). Woodhouse washlands – a major urban nature reserve. In South Yorkshire biodiversity conference: action for sustainable countryside in urban and rural South Yorkshire. South

Yorkshire Biodiversity Research Group.

Handley, J.F. (1996). The post industrial landscape – a resource for the community, a resource for the nation? Manchester University.

Hanley, N. (1999). Assessing the success of agri-environmental policy in the UK. Land use policy 16: 67-80.

Hardin, G. (1968). The tragedy of the commons. Science 162: 1243-1248.

Hardin, G. (1974). Lifeboat ethics - the case against helping the poor. Psychology today 8,4: 38-43,& 123-126.

Harris, S. et al. (1995). A review of British mammals. JNCC.

Harrison, F. (1991). The crisis of transition from the commons: population explosions, their cause and cure. In Andelson, R.V. (ed). Commons without tragedy. Shepheard-Walwyn, London.

Haskey, J.C. (1992). Demographic characteristics of the ethnic minority populations of Great Britain. In Bittles, A.H. & Roberts, D.F. (eds) Minority populations. Genetics, demography and health. Macmillan, London.

Haughton, G & Hunter, C. (1994). Sustainable cities. Jessica Kingsley, London

HO. (1999). Control of immigration: statistics United Kingdom 1998. SO.

HoL. (1999). A reformed CAP? The outcome of Agenda 2000. Select Committee on the European Communities, House of Lords. SO.

Harvey, G. (1997). The killing of the countryside. Jonathan Cape.

Hird, V. (1995). Europe's agriculture and environment: UK environmental land management policy. SAFE.

Hird, V. (1997). Double Yield. Jobs and sustainable food production. SAFE.

Hobcraft, J. (1996). Fertility in England and Wales: a fifty-year perspective. Population Studies 50: 485-524.

Holdgate, M.W. (1995). Environmental and agricultural policies. In Priorities for a new century - agriculture, food and rural policies in the European Union. Paper 31 Reading. CAS.

Holman, C. (1996). Control of pollutant emissions from road traffic. In Harrison, R.M. ed Pollution.Causes,effects and control. RSC.

HMSO. (1996). Britain 1997. An official handbook. HMSO.

Huckle, J. (1988). Global environment Education Programme. Brazil. What we consume. Richmond Publishing Company.

IIED. (1995). Citizen action to lighten Britain's ecological footprints. IIED.

Irvine, S. & Ponton, A. (19880. A green manifesto. Policies for a green future. Macdonald Optima, London.

Jackson, K & Chilton, T. (1999). Control of immigration: statistics United Kingdom, first half 1999. Home Office Statistical Bulletin. 20/99.

Jacobs, M. (1993). Sense and sustainability. Land use planning and environmentally sustainable development. CPRE.

Jones, P.J., Rehman, T., Harvey, D.R., Tranter, R.B., Marsh, J.S., Bunce, R.G.H., & Howard, D.C. (1995). Developing LUAM (Land Use Allocation Model) and modelling CAP reforms. CAS.

JRF. (1994a). Enquiry into planning for housing. JRF.

Keyfitz, N. (1981). The limits of population forecasting. Population and development review 7: 579-593.

Keyfitz, N. (1996). Population growth, development and the environment. Population studies 50: 335-359.

King, M. (1999). Commentary; Bread for the world – another view. British Medical Journal 319: 988.

Lampkin, N. (1996). Impact of EC Regulation 2078/92 on the development of organic farming in the European Union. CEPFAR/IFOAM seminar, Vignola, Italy, June 1996.

Lappé, F.M. & Collins, J. (1986). World hunger: 12 myths. Grove Press, USA.

LEAF. (1995). Guidelines for integrated crop management. LEAF.

LEAF. (1997). The LEAF audit. Farming into the millenium. LEAF.

Lee, R.D. (1987). Population dynamics of humans and other animals. Demography 24: 443-465.

Leonard, D. (1993). The Economist guide to the European Community. The original and definitive guide to all aspects of the EC. Century.

Llewelyn-Davies. (1994). Providing more homes in urban areas. SAUS.

Llewelyn-Davies. (1997). Sustainable residential quality: new approaches to urban living. DETR.

Llewelyn-Davies. (2000). Sustainable residential quality. Exploring the housing potential of large sites. London Planning Advisory Committee.

Lowe. P.,& Murdoch, J. (1993). Rural sustainable development. RDC.

Lowry, I.S. (1991). World urbanisation in perspective. In Davis,K. & Bernstam,M.S. ed Resources, environment and population. Present knowledge and future options. OUP.

Lutz, W. ed (1994). The future population of the world. What can we assume today? Earthscan.

Lutz, W. (1994). Future reproductive behaviour in industrialized countries. In Lutz, W. ed (see above).

Lutz, W. ed. (1996). The future population of the world. What can we assume today? Revised and updated edition. IIASA. Earthscan.

Lutz. W. & Scherbov, S. (1999). First probabilistic population projections for the European Union. In Compendium of family studies in Austria 1999. Schriftenreihe des ÖIF 7: 123-139.

MAFF. (1992). Code of good agricultural practice for the protection of air. MAFF.

MAFF. (1993). Code of good agricultural practice for the protection of soil. MAFF.

MAFF. (1996). Agriculture in the United Kingdom 1996. MAFF.

MAFF. (1997). Farm incomes in 1996. News release 35/97.

MAFF. (1999a). Agenda 2000 CAP reform. A new direction for agriculture. An economic note. MAFF.

MAFF. (1999b). Agriculture in the United Kingdom 1999. MAFF.

MAFF. (2000). England Rural Development Plan 2000-2006. MAFF.

Mansfield, T.A., & Lucas, P.W. (1996). Effects of gaseous pollutants on crops and trees. In Harrison, R.M. ed Pollution. Causes, effects and control. RSC.

Marshall, B.J. & Miller, F.A. eds. (1995). Priorities for a new Century – agriculture, food and rural policies in the European Union. CASR.

Martin, P. (1993). Past imperfect to future perfect: education, the environment and sustainable development. WWF.

McKnight, A.J. et al. (1996). Breeding birds of the North Staffordshire Moors. EN & RSPB.

McLaren, D. et al. (1997). Tomorrow's world. FoE.

McMichael, A.J. & Powles, J.W. (1999). Human numbers, environment, sustainability and health. British Medical Journal 319: 977-980.

Meadows, Dennis and Donella et al. (1972). The limits to growth. Earth Island Ltd, London.

Milne, A. (1988). Our drowning world. Prism Press.

Monbiot, G. (1995). Whose land? The Guardian, 22nd February,1995.

Monbiot, G. (1997). Land reform in Britain (Schumacher Lecture). Resurgence 181: 5-8.

Moss, C. E. (1913). Vegetation of the Peak District. Cambridge University Press.

Myers, N. (1993a). Ultimate security. The environmental basis of political stability. W.W. Norton London.

Myers, N. (1993b). The big squeeze. Earthwatch. November/December 1993: 25-30.

Myers, N. (1994). Population and biodiversity. In Graham-Smith, F.ed (1994). Population - the complex reality. RS.

NFU. (1999). The human cost of the farming crisis. Audit for action. Public affairs September 99. NFU.

Nix, J. (1996). Farm management pocket book. Wye College, London University.

Norton-Taylor, R. (1982). Whose land is it anyway? Turnstone Press.

Oberg, S. (1994). Spatial and economic factors in future south-north migration. In Lutz, W.ed. The future population of the world. What can we assume today? Earthscan.

Ockenden, J., & Franklin, M. (1995). European agriculture. Making the CAP fit the future. RIIA / Pinter.

ONS (1999a). International Migration. Migrants entering and leaving the United Kingdom and England and Wales, 1997. ONS Series MN No.24. SO

ONS (1999b). 1996-based National Population Projections. ONS Series pp2 No. 21. SO

ONS (2000). Population trends 99. Spring 2000. National Statistics. SO.

Oswald, A.J. (1999). The housing market and Europe's unemployment: a non-technical paper. Warwick University.

Owen, D. (1996). Size, structure and growth of the ethnic minority populations. In Coleman, D & and Salt, J (ed) Demographic characteristics of the ethnic minority populations. HMSO.

Parsons, J. (1971). Population versus liberty. Pemberton Books, London.

Parsons, J. (1998). Human population competition. A study of the pursuit of power through numbers. Edwin Mellen Press, Lampeter, Wales.

PDNPA. (1996). Census of population 1991: special workplace statistics, Peak District National Park. PDNPA.

PDNPA. (1997). Survey of employers in the Peak District. PDNPA.

PDNPA. (1999a). Farm and Countryside Service: Annual review (A562/JJL). PDNPA.

PDNPA. (1999b). Annual review 1998-1999. PDNPA

PDNPA. (2000). 1999-2000 yearbook. PDNPA.

Philips, J. et al. (1981). Peak District moorland erosion study: Phase 1 report. PDNPA.

Potter, C., Burnham, P., Edwards, A., Gasson, R.,& Green, B. (1991). The diversion of land. Conservation in a period of farming contraction. Routledge.

PPJPB. (1994). Peak National Park Structure Plan. Adopted replacement Final Edition 1994. PPJPB.

Preston, S.H. (1994). Population and the environment: the scientific evidence. In Graham-Smith, F.ed (1994). Population - the complex reality. RS.

Price, F. & Greig, S. eds. (1998). Our city – our future. Towards sustainability in Sheffield. SCC.

Raleigh, V.S. (1999). World population and health transition. British Medical Journal 319: 981-984.

Raven, P.H. (1999). Plants in peril: What shall we do? Address at the XVI International Botanical Congress.

RAYH. (1999). Advancing together. Towards a spatial strategy. Draft Regional Planning Guidance. RAYH

RCEP. (1994). 18th Report. Transport and the environment. HMSO.

RCEP. (1996). 19th Report. Sustainable use of soil. HMSO.

RCEP. (1997). 20th Report. Transport and the environment - developments since 1994. HMSO.

RDC. (1993a). The rural housing problem. RDC.

RDC. (1993b). The future of the rural development programme process. RDC.

RDC. (1994). Rural development strategy for the 1990's. RDC.

RDC. (1995). Rural economic activity. RDC.

RDC. (1996). Rural transport - the vital link. RDC.

Reid, C. (1994). Nature conservation law. W.Green.

Rogers, A. (1993). English rural communities: an assessment and prospect for the 1990's. RDC.

Ross, T.C., & Turner, S. (1995). Farming foundations: Policies to support a diverse UK farming system. SAFE.

Rotherham, I.D. (1995). A short guide to Sheffield's wildlife on the brink. I.D. Rotherham, Sheffield Hallam University, unpublished.

RS. & NAS. (1992). Population Growth, resource consumption, and a sustainable world. RS & NAS.

RSPB. (1992). Our countryside, our future. RSPB.

RSPB. (1994). Review of agri-environment schemes. RSPB.

RSPB. (1996). Countryside Stewardship Scheme. RSPB.

RSPB. (1999). The state of the UK's birds in 1999. RSPB.

Salt, J. (1996). Immigration and ethnic groups. In Coleman, D & Salt, J. Eds. Ethnicity in the 1991 census.Vol.1. HMSO.

SCC. (1987). Population and housing. Policy background paper no.1. Population and household projections. SCC.

SCC. (1998). Sheffield a city for people. Sheffield Unitary Development Plan. SCC.

SCC. (1999a). The Sheffield housing land survey 1999. SCC.

SCC. (1999b). Sheffield's countryside strategy. SCC.

SCC. (2000a). Sheffield City Council area action initiative. Draft south west area plan. SCC.

SCC. (2000b).Sheffield unitary development plan. A city for people. First monitoring report. SCC.

Scheele, M. (1996). The agri-environment measures in the context of the CAP reform. In Whitby, M. ed The European environment and CAP reform. Policies and prospects for conservation. CAB International.

Schumacher, E.F. (1973). Small is beautiful. A study of economics as if people mattered. Vintage.

Seymour, J. (1996). Beating back the bandits. In TLIO Land Essays 2. TLIO.

Shaw, C. (1994). Accuracy and uncertainty of the national population projections for the United Kingdom. Population Trends 77. National Statistics. HMSO.

Shaw, C. (1998). 1996-based National Population Projections. Population Trends 91. Spring 1998. National Statistics. SO.

Sheffield First Partnership. (1999). Putting Sheffield first – achieving excellence. A strategy for Sheffield. SCC.

Sherlock, H. (1991). Cities are good for us. Paladin, London.

Shoard, M. (1997). This land is our land. Gaia Books.

Sinclair, G. (1992). The lost land. Land use change in England 1945-90. CPRE.

Smith, M. et al. (1998). Greening the built environment. Earthscan.

Solly, L.D. et al. (1999). National sample survey of SSSI woodland. EN

Soper, M.H.R. & Carter, E.S. (1991). Farming and the countryside. Farming press.

South Yorkshire Forum. (2000). South Yorkshire Objective 1 Programme 2000-2006. Single programme document. South Yorkshire Forum.

South Yorkshire Local Authorities (SYLA). (2000). Provisional joint local transport plan South Yorkshire. SYLA.

Sporton, D. (1993). Fertility: the lowest level in the world. In Noin, D. & Woods, R. eds. The changing population of Europe. Blackwell.

SSE. (1996). Household growth: where shall we live. SO.

Stanton, W.I. (1996). The Malthus Cutoff Level: Carrying capacity adapted to a competitive world. Esperance. November 1996.

Stanton, W.I. (1999). Letter to David Heathcoat – Amory MP.

Stevens, V. (1999). Tomorrow's world. A critique. ECO website http://www.gn.apc.org/eco/pubs/tomworld.html.

SWGMT. (1963). Traffic in towns. HMSO.

Tallis, J. (1997). Peat erosion in the Pennines: the bad lands of Britain. Biologist 44 (1): 277-279.

Tarling, R., Rhodes, J., North, J. & Broom, G. (1993). The economy and rural England. RDC.

TCPA. (1997b). Response by the TCPA to the DoE discussion paper Household growth: where shall we live? TCPA.

Therivel, R., & Thompson, S. (1996). Strategic environmental assessment and nature conservation. EN.

Tolkien, J.R.R. (1954). The lord of the rings. Allen and Unwin.

UKBSG. (1995). Biodiversity: The UK Steering Group Report. HMSO.

UKG. (1998). Regional Development Agencies Act. UKG.

UKG. (2000). Countryside and rights of way bill. Bill 78, House of Commons. HMSO.

UKRTSD. (1996a). First Annual Report. DoE.

UKRTSD. (1997a). Housing and urban capacity. UKRTSD.

UKRTSD. (2000). Delivering sustainable development in the English regions. UKRTSD.

UN. (1992a). Long-range world population projections. UN.

UN. (1992b). Patterns in low-fertility settings. UN.

UN. (1995b). World urbanisation prospects. UN.

UN. (2000). Long-range world population projections: based on the 1998 revision. UN population Division, New York

UNEP. (1999). Global environmental outlook. Earthscan, London.

UNPD. (2000). Replacement migration: is it a solution to declining and ageing population? UNPD.

Urban Task Force. (1999). Towards an Urban renaissance. Taylor and Francis Group plc. London.

Van Steenis, D. (1999a). Opencasting of coal and its effects on health. Unpublished, Dr. D Van Steenis.

Van Steenis, D. (1999b). Incineration, co-incineration and health. Unpublished , Dr. D. Van Steenis.

Wackernagel, M. & Rees, W. (1996). Our ecological footprint. Reducing human impact on the earth. New Society Publishers, Canada.

Wade, S. et al. (1999). Rising to the challenge. Impacts of climate change in the South East in the 21st century. Technical report. WS Atkins, Epsom.

WCL. (1997). Wildlife law.Time for reform. WCL.

Wenz, P.S. (1997). Environmentalism and human oppression. In Gottlieb, R.S. ed. The ecological community. Environmental challenges for philosophy, politics and morality. Routledge.

Whitby, M. ed (1996). The European environment and CAP reform. Policies and prospects for conservation. CAB International.

Whitby, M. (1996a). The United Kingdom. In Whitby, M. ed (see above).

Whitby, M. (1996b). The prospects for agri-environment policies within a reformed CAP. In Whitby, M. ed (see above).

Whitby,M. & Adger, N. (1993). UK land use and the global commons. In Harper, S. ed. The greening of rural policy. International perspectives. Belhaven Press.

Wilkinson, D. et al. (1994). Strategic environmental assessment: implications for the English countryside. Final report for the Countryside Commission. IEEP.

Willey, D. (1996). Optimum population for Europe. Paper presented at the International Workshop on Population and Environment, Rome, October 28th and 29th, 1996.

Willey, D. (1997). Overpopulation and genocide in Central Africa. OPT Newsletter.January 1997:8-9.

Willey, D. (1999a). Oil production. OPT Newsletter January 1999: 8-9

Willey, D. (1999b). Will opinion-formers take any notice of our papers? OPT Newsletter: July 1999: 3-4.

Willey, D. (1999c). Sustainable population for Europe. OPT briefing sheet 99/3.

Winter, M. et al. (1998). The effects of the 1992 reform of the Common Agricultural Policy on the countryside of Great Britain, CC.

Woods, A., Taylor, J.P. & Harley, D.C. (1988). The reform of the Common Agricultural Policy: new opportunities for wildlife and the environment. RSPB.

Worcester, B. (1993). Address at The Green Alliance Annual Meeting. GA.

WWF. (1994). Changing directions: towards a green Britain. WWF.

WWF. (1997). A muzzled watchdog? Is English Nature protecting wildlife? WWF.

WWF. (2000). Living planet report. WWF.

WWF. & various other NGO's. (1996). Green gauge '96. Indicators for the UK environment. WWF et al.

WWF. et al. (1996). Green Gauge '96 indicators for the UK environment. WWW et al.

Zlotnik, H. (1994). Migration to and from developing regions: A review of past trends. In Lutz, W. ed. The future population of the world. What can we assume today? Earthscan.

Postscript

The floods that swept our land in late October and November illustrate very well the fundamental role of population growth in environmental deterioration. What caused these floods? Two things. Fist, global warming. This, as predicted, is leading to more severe climate effects. Second, the despoliation of our land – I use the word here for physical land, not as a name for our country. We have removed vegetation round our rivers, reclaimed our swamps, damaged our soil by intensive agriculture so that it cannot absorb and hold the water, and so we removed the "sponge". Two immediate causes. But behind both the same fundamental cause – the growth of the human population.

We can sermonise till the cows come home about the fact that the Americans and the rest of us in the Developed World cause far more environmental damage than the citizens of the Third World and therefore we should mend our ways. Nevertheless, the basic problem remains. The more people there are, the more consumption, the more cars, the more factories, the greater the emissions of carbon dioxide and other pollutants, so the greater the damage to the atmosphere. Total carbon dioxide emissions are first and foremost a function of the size of the global human population.

Why have we damaged our habitats in England? Fundamentally because we have intensified our agriculture. Why have we intensified our agriculture? Well, farmers have intensified production for financial reasons. But, they would not have done this if there were an insufficient population to buy their increased quantities of food. Farming has been intensified because the human population has grown. To summarise - the cause of the floods is the growth of the human population; we have greatly exceeded England's carrying capacity. And in the next few years, we will have more disastrous floods, and land losses because of rising sea levels because of global warming because of human population growth.

The Government's Urban and Rural White papers, financially pre-figured by the Chancellor's pre-budget report, came out too late (16th and 28th November respectively) to be considered in the body of this book.

The Urban White Paper (UWP) adopts many of the recommendations of the Lord Roger's report, sometimes with modification. Two examples. 1) The report said making public funding and planning permissions for area regeneration schemes should be conditional on production of an integrated Spatial Masterplan. The UWP says the Government will encourage all significant area regeneration schemes to use Master Plans and will encourage Master Plans being given formal status in Supplementary Planning Guidance. 2) In relation to the objective of making maximum use of existing buildings, the Report had recommended that VAT rates on refurbishment and conversion be harmonised at a zero rate. The UWP says the Government will cut the VAT rate to 5% for residential conversions and will make an adjustment to zero rate of VAT to provide relief for the sale of renovated houses which have been empty for 10 years or more.

Although the UWP does refer readers to PPG3, there is no stress in it on the need to densify development. Indeed the gloss given is that Government plans do not mean cramming people closer together, rather development should be at reasonable densities.

The Countryside White Paper contains many measures to ensure the provision of affordable homes in the countryside. Amongst these is the proposal to give LAs discretion to charge full Council Tax on second homes. However, there is no radical policy against second homes, indeed the Paper says that some authorities may wish to encourage second home owners who can bring a useful input to the local economy. LAs should make greater use of policy tools, and there is no reason why small villages should not match every new market house with an affordable home. Altogether, we are likely to see a proliferation of housing in rural areas.

The paper notes that within the Rural Development Plan Government is more that doubling the amount to be spent on agri-enviromnment schemes. Yet its target for increasing the amount of land farmed organically is extremely modest: 430,000 ha converted or converting to organic farming by 2007.

The murder of Damilola Taylor on 27th November serves to remind us that in high-density populations in deprived areas of large cities, tribal, racial, social status, even within-race/tribe between-neighbourhood differences, can spark off conflict, and this reminds us that continued immigration will exacerbate the whole situation.

The BBC's Money Programme on the 29th of November, called "The people smugglers", provided evidence that there is indeed a continuous stream of people entering England illegally; and it also pointed out that once inside, many of them become asylum seekers. And then I remember that in the spring of this year politicians who said that we were being flooded by bogus asylum seekers were immediately jumped on for exaggerating the situation and provoking racism. The evidence clearly points to a steady and not inconsiderable stream of people gaining entry to England illegally. Today PO Stena Line started its lorry inspections at Calais. By midday 22 stowaways had been detected (BBC web-site)!

The Countryside and Rights of Way Bill became the Countryside and Rights of Way Act 2000, receiving Royal Assent at the beginning of December.

Through recent poor attendance, SWCG has discontinued.

6th December AD 2,000.

FACT SHEET ON POPULATION TRENDS

1) The Population of England continues to increase. It is projected to increase by roughly 5 million between 2000 and 2036.

2) The increase has two components, natural increase (excess of births over deaths) and net immigration.

3) Despite the fact that fertility rate is below replacement level, natural increase continues, because of the historic age composition of the population and population ageing.

4) During the next few decades, net immigration is projected to contribute more to population growth than natural increase.

5) It is projected that already by mid-century, the ethnic minority proportion of the population will have changed from 5.6% (mid-1990s) to 15%.

6) Succeeding projections in recent times have consistently underestimated national population growth. The two causes of this were underestimating immigration, and underestimating life expectancy.

7) Considering recent projections (1994-based, 1996-based and 1998- based) the immigration component of population growth in the immediate future has been successively increased. For the UK as a whole, in the 1994 projections, as in previous projections, it had been assumed that there would be a net inflow in the immediate following years of 50,000 persons a year. The 1996-based projections raised this to 65,000 per year. And the 1998-based projections raised the level to 95,000 per year.

8) There was a change in assumptions between the 1994 and earlier projections on the one hand, and the later projections. In the former, it was assumed that after about 20 years, net immigration would gradually decrease to zero. With the two later projections, this assumption is abandoned – the projected net inflow (65,000 and 95,000 respectively) is maintained for the whole projection period.

9) The contribution of asylum seekers to net immigration has fluctuated considerably during the last two decades. But in very recent years applications have increased considerably.

10) Population projections are based on assumptions about fertility, mortality and migration trends. Demographers seem to be largely agreed that more uncertainty is attached to migration than to fertility and mortality. Also, data on immigration is very incomplete. There are various reasons for this – inadequacy of survey methods as far as immigration is concerned, unwillingness of some people to give information at the census, and lack of adequate information on illegal immigration.

11) Although data on illegal immigration is very incomplete, it seems likely that it is not inconsiderable. This was highlighted during last year by the discovery of illegal immigrants in the backs of lorries coming in from Europe, and by BBC reports on people smugglers. And there is evidence that there are law firms in London assisting illegal immigrants to become successful asylum seekers. Then last year, PO Stena Line, a major user of lorries, finding it was paying large fines for illegal immigrants discovered in lorries, decided to try to cut its expenses by having its own inspectors at Calais. They started on 6th December. By mid-day, 22 stowaways had been detected.

12) Population growth leads to household growth leads to more house building, leads to loss of green countryside land for housing. Changes in household structure (the formation of single person households etc) is projected to be a smaller component of household growth than the growth of the adult population.